Empire in the New Testament

 McMaster Divinity College Press
McMaster New Testament Studies Series

Patterns of Discipleship in the New Testament (1996)

The Road from Damascus: The Impact of Paul's Conversion on His Life, Thought, and Ministry (1997)

Life in the Face of Death: The Resurrection Message of the New Testament (1998)

The Challenge of Jesus' Parables (2000)

Into God's Presence: Prayer in the New Testament (2001)

Reading the Gospels Today (2004)

Contours of Christology in the New Testament (2005)

Hearing the Old Testament in the New Testament (2006)

The Messiah in the Old and New Testaments (2007)

Translating the New Testament: Text, Translation, Theology (2009)

Christian Mission: Old Testament Foundations and New Testament Developments (2010)

Empire in the New Testament

edited by
STANLEY E. PORTER
and
CYNTHIA LONG WESTFALL

☙PICKWICK *Publications* · Eugene, Oregon

EMPIRE IN THE NEW TESTAMENT

McMaster Divinity College Press New Testament Study Series 10

Copyright © 2011 Wipf and Stock Publishers. All rights reserved. Except for brief quotations in critical publications or reviews, no part of this book may be reproduced in any manner without prior written permission from the publisher. Write: Permissions, Wipf and Stock Publishers, 199 W. 8th Ave., Suite 3, Eugene, OR 97401.

McMaster Divinity College Press
1280 Main Street West
Hamilton, Ontario, Canada
L8S 4K1

Pickwick Publications
An Imprint of Wipf and Stock Publishers
199 W. 8th Av.e, Suite 3
Eugene, OR 97401

www.wipfandstock.com

ISBN 13: 978-1-60899-599-8

Cataloging-in-Publication data:

Empire in the New Testament / edited by Stanley E. Porter and Cynthia Long Westfall

xii + 306 p. ; 23 cm. — Includes bibliographical references and indexes.

McMaster Divinity College Press New Testament Study Series 10

ISBN 13: 978-1-60899-599-8

1. Church history — Primitive and early church, ca. 30–600. 2. Religion and politics — Rome — History. 3. David, King of Israel. 4. Bible. O.T. Isaiah — Criticism, interpretation, etc. 5. Bible. N.T. Matthew — Criticism, interpretation, etc. 6. Bible. N.T. Luke and Acts — Criticism, interpretation, etc. 7. Bible. N.T. John — Criticism, interpretation, etc. 8. Bible. N.T. Epistles of Paul — Criticism, interpretation, etc. 9. Fathers of the Church. I. Porter, Stanley E., 1956–. II. Westfall, Cynthia Long. III. Title. IV. Series.

BS2545 E5 2011

Manufactured in the U.S.A.

Contents

Preface | vii

Abbreviations | ix

Contributors | xiii

Introduction: Empire, the New Testament, and Beyond
—*Stanley E. Porter and Cynthia Long Westfall* | 1

1. The Old Testament Context of David's Costly Flirtation with Empire-Building—*Douglas K. Stuart* | 17

2. Walking in the Light of Yahweh: Zion and the Empires in the Book of Isaiah—*Mark J. Boda* | 54

3. Matthew and Empire—*Warren Carter* | 90

4. King Jesus and His Ambassadors: Empire and Luke–Acts —*Craig A. Evans* | 120

5. "I Have Conquered the World": The Death of Jesus and the End of Empire in the Gospel of John—*Tom Thatcher* | 140

6. Paul Confronts Caesar with the Good News —*Stanley E. Porter* | 164

7. "This was Not an Ordinary Death": Empire and Atonement in the Minor Pauline Epistles—*Matthew Forrest Lowe* | 197

8   Running the Gamut: The Varied Responses to Empire in Jewish Christianity—*Cynthia Long Westfall* / 230

9   The Church Fathers and the Roman Empire
   —*Gordon L. Heath* / 259

Modern Authors Index / 283

Ancient Sources Index / 289

Preface

THE 2007 H. H. Bingham Colloquium on the New Testament at McMaster Divinity College in Hamilton, Ontario, Canada was entitled "Empire in the New Testament." The Colloquium was the thirteenth in a continuing series. At the Colloquium, scholars from all over North America took the opportunity to exchange important perspectives on this current and controversial New Testament theme, perspectives that demonstrated a variety of approaches in discovering the relationships among the New Testament, early Christianity, and the Roman Empire. An interested public attended, heard the papers, and responded with insightful questions and comments. There was some spirited interest between the participants as well. We hope that this volume will be of interest to general readers and serve as a useful textbook or supplemental source for the study of the context of, content of, and interpretive approaches to the New Testament. We also trust that it makes a cogent contribution to the ongoing discussion of this important topic.

The Bingham Colloquium is named after Dr. Herbert Henry Bingham, who was a noted Baptist leader in Ontario, Canada. His leadership abilities were recognized by Baptists across Canada and around the world. His qualities included his genuine friendship, dedicated leadership, unswerving Christian faith, tireless devotion to duty, insightful service as a preacher and pastor, and visionary direction for congregation and denomination alike. These qualities endeared him both to his own church members and to believers in other denominations. The Colloquium has been endowed by his daughter as an act of appreciation for her father. We are pleased to be able to continue this tradition.

Other Colloquia published in this series include the following: *Patterns of Discipleship in the New Testament* (1996), *The Road from Damascus: The Impact of Paul's Conversion on His Life, Thought and Ministry* (1997), *Life in the Face of Death: The Resurrection Message of the New Testament* (1998), *The Challenge of Jesus' Parables* (2000), *Into God's*

Presence: Prayer in the New Testament (2001), *Reading the Gospels Today* (2004), *Contours of Christology in the New Testament* (2005), *Hearing the Old Testament in the New Testament* (2006), *The Messiah in the Old and New Testaments* (2007), *Translating the New Testament: Text, Translation, Theology* (2009), and *Christian Mission: Old Testament Foundations and New Testament Developments* (2010).

Finally, we would like to thank a number of people for their particular contributions. First, we would like to thank the individual contributors for accepting the assignments, for all their efforts in the preparation and presentation of papers that make a significant contribution of benefit to biblical scholars, students of the Bible, and believers concerned about the historic context of the New Testament, hermeneutics, and the Christian's relationship to governing authorities, all of whom should be engaged with this timely topic. We would also like to thank the staff and student helpers and volunteers at McMaster Divinity College, all of whom were integral in creating a pleasant environment and a supportive atmosphere. Thanks particularly go to Matthew Lowe for suggesting the topic for the colloquium, and to Beth Stovell who worked with the manuscript. Both of us were co-chairs of the conference and edited this volume with the hopes that it will further the important discussion on the relationship between the New Testament and the Roman Empire.

Stanley E. Porter
Cynthia Long Westfall
McMaster Divinity College
Hamilton, Ontario, Canada

Abbreviations

AB	Anchor Bible Commentary
ABD	David Noel Freedman, editor. *The Anchor Bible Dictionary*
ACCS	Ancient Christian Commentary Series
AGJU	Arbeiten zur Geschichte des antiken Judentums und des Urchristentums
AnBib	Analecta biblica
ANEP	James B. Pritchard, editor. *The Ancient Near East in Pictures Relating to the Old Testament*. Princeton: Princeton University Press, 1954.
ANET	James B. Pritchard, editor. *Ancient Near Eastern Texts Relating to the Old Testament*. 3rd ed. Princeton: Princeton University Press, 1969.
Ath. Mitt.	Mitteilungen des deutschen archäologischen Instituts, Athenische Abteilung.
BAR	*Biblical Archaeology Review*
BASOR	*Bulletin of the American Schools of Oriental Research*
BECNT	Baker Exegetical Commentary on the New Testament
BETL	Bibliotheca ephemeridum theologicarum lovaniensium
Bib	*Biblica*
Bull. Corr. Hell.	*Bulletin de correspondence hellénique*
BZAW	Beihefte zur Zeitschrift für die alttestamentliche Wissenschaft
BZNW	Beihefte zur Zeitschrift für die neutestamentliche Wissenschaft
CBQ	*Catholic Biblical Quarterly*
CIA	*Corpus Inscriptionum Atticarum*, after 1903 known as *IG* I
CIG	*Corpus Inscriptionum Graecarum*
CIL	*Corpus Inscriptionum Latinarum*

COS	William W. Hallo and K. Lawson Younger, editors. *The Context of Scripture.*	
ESV	English Standard Version	
ET	English Translation	
fl.	flourished	
FN	*Filología neotestamentaria*	
IBM	Inscriptions of the British Museum	
ICC	International Critical Commentary	
IG	*Inscriptiones Graecae consilio et auctoritate. Academiae litterarum reglae borussicae editae. Editio Minor.* Berlin, 1924–	
IGR	*Inscriptiones Graecae ad res Romanas pertinentes* 1, 3, 4. Paris: Leroux, 1906–1927.	
Int	*Interpretation*	
JBL	*Journal of Biblical Literature*	
JGRChJ	*Journal of Greco-Roman Christianity and Judaism*	
JNES	*Journal of Near Eastern Studies*	
JRA	*Journal of Roman Archaeology*	
JRH	*Journal of Religious History*	
JQR	*Jewish Quarterly Review*	
JSNT	*Journal for the Study of the New Testament*	
JSNTSup	*Journal for the Study of the New Testament* Supplement Series	
JSOT	*Journal for the Study of the Old Testament*	
JSOTSup	*Journal for the Study of the Old Testament* Supplement Series	
LCC	Library of Christian Classics	
LCL	Loeb Classical Library	
LNTS	Library of New Testament Studies	
LSJ	H. G. Liddell, Robert Scott, and H. Stuart Jones. *Greek-English Lexicon*	
MAMA	*Monumenta Asiae Minoris antique* 1–8	
MNTS	McMaster New Testament Studies	
NAC	New American Commentary	
NASB	New American Standard Version	
NewDocs	G. R. Horsley and S. R. Llewelyn, editors. *New Documents Illustrating Early Christianity*	
NICNT	New International Commentary on the New Testament	

NICOT	New International Commentary on the Old Testament
NIGTC	New International Greek Testament Commentary
NovT	*Novum Testamentum*
NovTSup	Supplements to Novum Testamentum
NRSV	New Revised Standard Version
NTL	New Testament Library
NTS	*New Testament Studies*
OBT	Overtures to Biblical Theology
OGIS	W. Dittenberger. *Orientis Graeci inscriptiones selectae*
OTG	Old Testament Guides
OTL	Old Testament Library
RSV	Revised Standard Version
RevExp	*Review and Expositor*
SB	*Sammelbuch griechischer Urkunden aus Aegypten.* Edited by F. Preisigke et al. 1915–
SBLDS	Society of Biblical Literature Dissertation Series
SBLMS	Society of Biblical Literature Monograph Series
SBLSP	Society of Biblical Literature Seminar Papers
SBLSS	Society of Biblical Literature Semeia Studies
SBLSymS	Society of Biblical Literature Symposium Series
SCO	*Studi classici e orientali*
SEG	*Supplementum Epigraphicum Graecum*
SIG	W. Dittenberger. *Sylloge Inscriptionum graecarum*
SH	Scripture and Hermeneutics Series
SJT	*Scottish Journal of Theology*
SNTSMS	Society for New Testament Studies Monograph Series
SWJT	*Southwestern Journal of Theology*
TDGR	Translated Documents of Greece and Rome
TDNT	Gerhard Kittel and Gerhard Friedrich, editors. *Theological Dictionary of the New Testament.* Trans. Geoffrey W. Bromiley. 10 vols. Grand Rapids: Eerdmans, 1964–1977
TLNT	*Theological Lexicon of the New Testament.* 3 vols. Peabody, MA: Hendrickson, 1994
TNIV	Today's New International Version
TUGAL	Texte und Untersuchungen zur Geschichte der altchristlichen Literatur
TynBul	*Tyndale Bulletin*

UBSGNT	United Bible Societies' *Greek New Testament*
VT	*Vetus Testamentum*
WBC	Word Biblical Commentary
WUNT	Wissenschaftliche Untersuchungen zum Neuen Testament
ZAW	*Zeitschrift für die alttestamentliche Wissenschaft*

Contributors

Mark J. Boda, Professor of Old Testament, McMaster Divinity College, Hamilton, ON, Canada

Warren Carter, Professor of New Testament, Brite Divinity School at TCU, Fort Worth, TX, USA

Craig A. Evans, Payzant Distinguished Professor of New Testament, Acadia Divinity College, Wolfville, NS, Canada

Gordon L. Heath, Associate Professor of Christian History, McMaster Divinity College, Hamilton, ON, Canada

Matthew Forrest Lowe, PhD candidate, McMaster Divinity College, Hamilton, ON, Canada

Stanley E. Porter, President, Dean, and Professor of New Testament, McMaster Divinity College, Hamilton, ON, Canada

Douglas K. Stuart, Professor of Old Testament, Gordon-Conwell Theological Seminary, South Hamilton, MA, USA

Tom Thatcher, Professor of New Testament, Cincinnati Christian University, Cincinnati, OH, USA

Cynthia Long Westfall, Assistant Professor of New Testament, McMaster Divinity College, Hamilton, ON, Canada

Introduction

Empire, the New Testament, and Beyond

Stanley E. Porter and Cynthia Long Westfall

The relationships among the New Testament, early Christianity, and the Roman Empire have been a topic of growing interest in New Testament studies. Some discussion of this is unfortunately a fad fostered by those who are constantly seeking after something new or an approach that will distinguish their work from that of others. However, there are substantive reasons for examination of this topic that have led us to publish the papers presented in this volume. The development of social-scientific methodologies and the discussion of the importance of the layers of context in the meaning of a text have offered tools and approaches that raise legitimate new questions regarding the voice of those subordinated to others and the embeddedness of their discourse within specific contexts. Other sets of questions have been raised due to dramatic recent historic trends and events such as the Holocaust and the breakup of Western empires. Consequently, there has been increased attention to the relationships among the Roman Empire, the New Testament, and early Christianity—as a subject in its own right and as one that may speak to our present situation. There has also been a related focus on the relationship between Judaism and the succession of empires that pressured and controlled it, arriving finally at one of the most continuously and widely discussed ancient regimes, the Roman Empire, which often serves as an emblem for modern conceptions of empire. In addition, postcolonial interpretation has drawn parallels between the experiences of modern colonialism and those of the diverse subjugated individuals and people groups in the Roman Empire, and liberation theologies of various types have challenged the use of the New Testament for supporting repressive regimes or empires.

The Bingham Colloquium of 2007 brought scholars from across North America to present substantive papers on empire in the New Testament in order to answer the poignant question, "How does a Christian render unto Caesar what is Caesar's, and unto God what is God's?" The scholars examined various understandings of empire in the ancient world as the context into which Christianity was born and to which it responded. Papers were given on the Old Testament concept of empire as it relates to the New Testament. Then the various authors of the New Testament were examined, with a view to their response to the notion of empire, both human and divine.[1]

The first paper, by Douglas K. Stuart on David's empire, looks at the mentality of empire in the ancient Near East and the Old Testament's resistance to this mentality. Stuart then examines David's plans for an empire in the light of 2 Samuel 24 and 1 Chronicles 21, which record King David's attempt to establish an army large enough to conquer foreign nations and establish an empire. The mentality of empire in the ancient Near East assumes that certain nations have the right to establish empire at the expense of other nations. The imperialistic establishment and continuing control and subjugation of foreign lands is a mark of greatness of the ruler, the "home" nation, and their national god. This mentality therefore justifies the financial bleeding of conquered/subjugated lands through tributes, taxes, and tolls; the use of propaganda techniques to influence the subjugated people to accept their fate; religious imperialism to acknowledge the greatness and superiority of the empire's god; the right to rearrange populations via deportations to maintain control and establish peace; and expectation that conquered kings would bring their nation's practices and values into conformity with the values of the controlling empire.[2]

The Old Testament displays a general resistance to the Near East mentality of empire by portraying all human empires in a negative light. However, it is not wrong to speak of the domains of Saul, David, or Solomon as empires, if one means a reign over a "continuous" empire

---

1. We wish to thank the individual contributors who provided abstracts of their papers, which we have drawn on in the summaries that follow.

2. This is a summary of Stuart's thirteen ingredients of the mentality of empire in the ancient Near East.

formed of a grouping of contiguous territories. Furthermore, empires are created by warfare, and there was a concept of Holy War, codified in Deut 20:1–20 and exemplified and supplemented throughout the Old Testament. The nature of the Holy War is that it was a religious undertaking where Yahweh did the real fighting, the goal was total annihilation of an evil culture, and it was characterized by decisive rapid victory. The concept included qualifications, such as that there could be no standing army, no pay for soldiers, no personal plunder, and no land conquered or defended other than the Promised Land. There were specific limitations as well, including that war could only be launched at Yahweh's call, the divine call could only come through a prophet, and it would be undertaken with various forms of religious self-denial such as fasting and abstinence from sex. Those who violated the rules were enemies of God and Israel, though some exceptions and mutations were possible.[3]

Stuart maintains that David understood war and what it could accomplish in terms of both Holy War and the Near Eastern mentality of conquest. The census that David took in 2 Samuel 24//1 Chronicles 21 appears to have taken place after he had subdued the traditional boundaries of Israel. It was an attempt to build a standing army to extend and augment the Israelite "core" through conquest, probably to gain additional revenue to finance his temple construction campaign. So it seems that David violated the rules of Holy War, departing from the traditional Israelite/Old Testament hostility towards empire, and embracing the pagan Near Eastern mentality of empire, which produced disaster but was turned around by God for a spiritual end.

Stuart's focus on David's empire in the contexts of the ancient Near East and the Old Testament theology of Holy War is directly related to the Davidic royal tradition, which is an important point of reference for New Testament motifs such as Second Temple messianic expectations, the person of Jesus, and the nature of the kingdom of God. However, Stuart's paper addresses David's failings more than his function as a model in any of these areas. In so doing, Stuart provides some foundational elements for understanding empire in the New Testament. First, his helpful summary of the ancient Near Eastern concept of empire is descriptive of concepts underlying the Roman Empire on every point. Second, an Old Testament theology of Holy War that stands in contrast to the pagan Near Eastern mentality could conceivably inform the

3. This is a summary of Stuart's twelve propositions that summarize Holy War.

encounters with and criticisms of the Roman Empire by Second Temple Judaism and early Christianity. Third, he provides an excellent example from the Old Testament where the context of the concept of empire in the ancient Near East is a key to interpreting two parallel passages that, apart from this context, provide a classic puzzle.

The second paper is by Mark J. Boda on the treatment of empire within the book of Isaiah. The book of Isaiah is one of the few texts in the Old Testament designed to shape the response of the people of God throughout the time when a succession of ancient Near Eastern empires shaped its destiny: the Assyrian (Isaiah 7–39), Babylonian (Isaiah 40–55), and Persian (Isaiah 56–66) periods. The prophetic book opens with a presentation of the prophet's vision of Zion, a Hebrew tradition closely linked with Israel's own imperial tradition. It is Zion that is the most common designation for the people of God throughout the book, first as Jerusalem seeks to live an existence independent of surrounding empires (chs. 7–39), then as an exilic community among the empires (chs. 40–55), and finally as a restored community living as a colony among the empires (chs. 56–66).

The Zion tradition represents the imperial tradition that is the ideal threatened in Isaiah's day. The Holy One of Israel rules the world from Zion, but the city does not reflect the character of its emperor—according to both the Old Testament and pagan contexts, the city's inhabitants were obligated to bring themselves into conformity with the emperor's values.

The Assyrian threat in Isaiah 6–39 is connected to a concern over the nations and God's clear message, from both historical and cosmic points of view, that he will defeat Assyria and the other great imperial powers of Isaiah's time. Isaiah's message to Judah's kings (Ahaz and Hezekiah) was that they must not be intimidated by empire, nor be tempted to trust other anti-imperial political forces, so foreign empire is viewed very skeptically. The call to trust Yahweh as having the authority and power to rule the nations demanded that the two kings discharge their claims to kingship in Judah and entrust themselves and their kingdom into the hands of Yahweh to ensure that Judah would survive and thrive. Both kings ultimately failed the test, which resulted in the ruin of Judah by Assyria and Babylon.

The audience in Isaiah 40–55 is the community in the Babylonian period, which experienced the discipline resulting from the failure of kings Ahaz and Hezekiah in chs. 6–39. The trust of the two kings in rising Mesopotamian forces led to the exile of Judah to the heart of the Mesopotamian empire. This section includes three strategies for dealing with the challenge to faith of the atrocities and pain that the community experiences: a theological appeal of redemption and creation by the Holy One of Israel throughout the section; the revelation of the "arm of the Lord" in chs. 41–48 that will bring salvation and deliverance to Israel initially through Cyrus; and the Servant of the Lord, or Jacob-Israel, as the exilic community who brings justice and functions as a "light" for the Gentiles and "a covenant for the people," but ultimately ends in suffering and death that will bring atonement for sin and salvation from exile. In chs. 49–55, the cry of daughter Zion at the outset (49:14) has been answered through the revelation of the arm of the Lord expressed through the Servant Jacob-Israel. Isaiah 40–55 continues to evaluate empire negatively. Even though the Persian Cyrus is raised up for Yahweh's purposes, there is a reluctance to collapse the hope of Israel into the politics of the Persian Empire—the establishment of the empire of Yahweh and the loss of power of the pagan empire really occurs ironically through the suffering of the Servant at the hands of the nations.

Isaiah 55–66 targets a restoration community during the Persian period that did not live up to the expectations created in chs. 40–55, but prophesies hope for the future with a universal vision in which the nations enter into a relationship with Yahweh and worship him. Only the people who respond to Isaiah's message will experience full restoration of a temple, a city, and a community, and they will see the ultimate purpose of Yahweh fulfilled in regard to the Gentiles. The Persian Empire is virtually ignored as irrelevant in this section—Zion is God's imperial capital on earth. Ultimately, the people are called to believe God's imperial vision or presentation of reality rather than that of the nations. They are not to trust political alliances or military preparation, and they are not to accept the empire's view of their status as victims. But neither are they to trust the might of Israel or the Davidic line. Prerogatives are shifted from the Davidic line to others (such as Cyrus), the community, and to Yahweh as king. Jerusalem remains the seat of the divine emperor and the political and religious center of the world, but this location appears to be distanced from a physical Jerusalem.

Boda's focus on Isaiah provides an appropriate complementary view of empire in the Old Testament, because Isaiah offers some of the earliest theological reflection on Judah's identity in a world dominated by near eastern empires. Judah experienced increasing and enduring imperial domination in three phases, in each of which there was a distinct response to empire. Boda also makes a connection in his conclusion between Isaiah's treatment of empire and Jesus' announcement of the realization of Isaiah's vision of Zion and the kingdom of God in Luke 4:14–19. Therefore, Boda demonstrates a very significant example of the use of the Old Testament in the New Testament, showing how both an Old Testament text that concerns empire and Israel's concepts of empire and interaction with empire provide an identifiable context for the interpretation of a central passage in the New Testament.

The third paper is by Warren Carter on Matthew's negotiation of the Roman Empire. His thesis is that the Roman Empire comprises the foreground of the New Testament rather than the background. His comments are divided into two sections, the first dealing with method, and the second with content, specifically Matthew's plot, Christology, eschatology, and ecclesiology. After identifying five methods or approaches to interpretation that have interfered with the detection of the book's interaction with the Roman Empire, he outlines a multi-layered or interdisciplinary approach that he labels "cultural intertextuality." His fivefold approach is comprised of historical studies, classical and archaeological studies, social-science models of empire, cultural anthropology, and postcolonial studies, to which he adds some forms of narrative criticism.

Carter's detection of the negotiation of the Roman Empire begins with the historical analysis of likely daily conditions within the empire experienced by the early Christians who were the recipients of Matthew's Gospel. Carter suggests Antioch-on-the-Orontes, the provincial capital of Syria, as a possible milieu, and uncovers some of the realities of the Roman imperial presence in that context through classical sources and archaeological discoveries, while also recognizing the partial nature of the material or artifactual remains. He therefore draws upon social-science models of agrarian-aristocratic empires to provide a holistic framework of the imperial structure, which allows the various pieces to be joined into a bigger picture. Carter also draws upon a social-science model of empire, noting eight arenas in which the Roman Empire exercised political, economic, social, military, and religious power and maintained its hierarchical world. Another social-science model involves the dynamics of power in contexts where there are massive differentials of power, such as peasant economies where resistance is usually disguised in self-protective and calculated ways and open revolt is relatively infrequent. Finally, the discipline of post-colonial studies is particularly utilized to unmask the dynamics of imperial power.

Carter argues that Matthew's Gospel is a work of imperial negotiation through focusing on its plot, Christology, eschatology, and discipleship/ecclesiology. The plot tells the story of Jesus crucified by the empire because he challenges its power. He is a crucified provincial whom Rome cannot keep dead—the story denies Rome's claims to power, exposes it as bringing death, and celebrates God's life-giving power through Jesus' words, works, and resurrection. This story is meant to shape and form the identity and alternative societal existence of early Christians so that they live accordingly. The Christology of Matthew, revealed in the presentation of Jesus as the agent of God who is chosen to manifest their sovereignty, will, and wellbeing among human beings, contests imperial claims and interacts with the central claims of Roman theology. The eschatology of Matthew, revealed in the resurrection, portrays Rome's limited power. The ecclesiology, revealed in the manifestation of God's rule/empire, creates a counter-cultural community committed to God and Jesus with an alternative worldview and set of societal practices. In summary, according to Carter, the Gospel negotiates Rome's power through a self-protective yet contestive approach that offers a (largely) alternative, though in part also imitative, worldview and social experience lived out in the practices of a community of Jesus' followers.

Carter's work is representative of post-colonial interpretation as well as of the application of models from social science, as he employs his multidisciplinary approach in connection with recognition of his own experience of growing up in a colony of the former British Empire. As such, he offers an invaluable contribution to the discussion with the application of his interpretive methods, and presents new perspectives for consideration in hermeneutics, the Gospel of Matthew and its synoptic relations, and biblical theology.

The fourth paper by Craig A. Evans is on political imagery in Luke–Acts. In the New Testament Gospels, Jesus is acknowledged as king by both his followers and his enemies alike. In Luke, Jesus is compared to the "benefactors" of his time, thus criticizing and at the same time adopting an important political epithet. This interesting political dimension is furthered in the book of Acts, where Paul the ambassador is presented as an ambassador of King Jesus. Evans's essay is composed of three parts: Jesus as king in the Gospels and early Christian literature; Jesus as benefactor; and the apostles as Jesus' ambassadors.

Evans shows that Jesus was perceived as a king and rival to Caesar himself in all four Gospels and in the first two or three generations of early Christianity. In the Gospels, he is shown as king primarily in his interrogation and execution, though there are proclamations of Jesus' kingship earlier in Matthew and John. Evans also highlights affirmations of Jesus' kingship in Paul, Revelation, and the *Martyrdom of Polycarp*, and suggests that the nature of the charges and accusations brought against Jesus and the early Christians indicate that Jesus was Caesar's rival.

Evans further suggests that Luke presents a distinctive interpretation of Jesus' kingly status as benefactor. He shows that, in Luke 22:25, Luke's variation from Mark 10:42 and Matt 20:25 adds the word "benefactors": "The kings of the Gentiles exercise lordship over them; and those in authority over them are called 'benefactors.'" After surveying literature and inscriptions from late antiquity, as well as Jewish literature, Evans concludes that Luke's readers would readily interpret the reference to "benefactors" in the context of the rulers and the mighty. However, Evans suggests that Jesus did not forbid his disciples to be benefactors and conveyors of benefaction, but to avoid the examples of the "kings of the Gentiles" in how they exercise authority.

In Acts, the ministry of Jesus is also described in terms of benefaction. King Jesus has a redemptive ministry of seeking and saving, for which he sends his apostles who are true emissaries of a king and function as ambassadors. First, Evans discusses how Paul refers to himself as an ambassador in his letters (2 Cor 5:20; Eph 6:18–20; Phlm 8–10), then he discusses the language and imagery of "ambassador" and "envoy" in ancient Israel and its literature, and finally he shows how the language of the ambassador functions in Paul's second telling of his Damascus road conversion to King Agrippa II in Acts 26:11–18. The result is the proclamation of Jesus as king, who has sent his apostles and ambassadors with the mission to proclaim good news and reconcile the world to God.

Evans's paper contributes to the discussion on empire in terms of both methodology and exploration of the context of benefaction and ambassadorship in ancient inscriptions and literature. He utilizes redaction criticism in comparing Luke with Matthew and Mark to suggest that Luke may have had more of an interest in presenting Jesus as a benefactor than the other two Evangelists. His survey of literature in regards to benefaction is impressive and may also contribute to a wider understanding of the patron–client relationship in the culture of the Roman Empire. Finally, Evans makes a contribution to the understanding of the distinctive theology of Luke–Acts as it relates to empire.

The fifth paper, by Tom Thatcher, focuses on how the story of Jesus' death in the Gospel of John is a response to empire. Thatcher maintains that the cross reflects the mythical substructure of Roman rule, and John's response is a complete reversal of everything that crucifixion represents, so that Jesus is shown to be greater than Caesar in every way. Thatcher first highlights the challenges that the Gospel of John presents to a study on empire in the New Testament, then he outlines a reading strategy that exposes the social values of Roman crucifixion and John's reversal of those values.

At first glance, John does not appear to be interested in the Roman Empire. He seems more interested in theology than politics—he says nothing about certain topics that are included in the Synoptics that might reveal a posture towards Rome, such as attitudes to tax-collectors and soldiers, paying taxes, the pejorative nature of Gentile authority, the portrayal of Jesus as a "king," or development of the theme of the kingdom of God. These omissions combine with overt theological interests in Christology that are often treated as spiritual and esoteric. However, an inspection of key events from Jesus' career in the Gospel of John reveals that John's concept of the "Son of God" was deeply influenced by the cultural realities of Roman rule.

Thatcher suggests that John's crucifixion story can be read at two levels. John both develops Christology and radically reverses the premises of Rome's power—the interplay of Christology with the premises of Rome's power defines the christological value, showing that Christ is superior to Caesar in every way. Drawing on Yael Zerubavel's work on twentieth-century Zionists and Michael Foucault's model of "countermemory," Thatcher suggests that crucifixion was one of Rome's public rituals that was undergirded by "commemorative narratives" that rationalized and maintained the imperial status quo. Crucifixion was not only an act of extreme violence but also a dramatic reenactment of Rome's conquest of the world with pointed propaganda objectives—the message was that Rome was capable of suppressing every threat to its sovereignty. John admits the public events of the cross but denies their normal commemorative value by offering a counter-memory of Jesus' death. He arranges the pieces of the historical puzzle to create new and often subversive images of what occurred. He completely subverts Rome's values by reinterpreting the public events of Calvary to demonstrate Jesus' absolute control over everyone involved in the situation.

While John achieves this effect through several literary devices, Thatcher highlights his appropriation of the theme "fulfilled prophecy" as a means of denying the Roman claims surrounding crucifixion. On the surface, every scene in the Fourth Gospel's crucifixion account seems to follow the logic of Roman domination: John paints a plausible portrait of Rome's physical and psychological power exercised in the crucifixion through six distinct scenes. However, John adds a second layer of meaning to the events by treating Scripture as a causal force that compels the soldiers to do what they do. In addition to the theme of prophetic fulfillment, John presents Jesus' last words as proclaiming victory, rather than saying "what he ought to say" in such a situation. In the process, the reader is shown that Caesar's agents ultimately serve Christ's purposes, and that the cross was actually the moment when Jesus conquered the world.

Thatcher utilizes an interdisciplinary model that professedly touches on interests ranging from historical, sociological, anthropological, political, and literary to areas of communication theory and folklore. However, his method can probably be best characterized as a narrative approach, where story is primary in making meaning. This allows John to tell the story in terms of his own story world— but Thatcher also interfaces it with historical data to demonstrate that John is telling a story plausible to the first-century reader. Narrative criticism of the Gospels is a growing field and Thatcher demonstrates how it can yield insights for Gospel studies. Therefore, the three papers on the Gospels offer an interesting variety of approaches and methodologies to the discussion of empire and the New Testament.

The sixth paper, by Stanley E. Porter, is on Paul and empire, specifically about the relationship of Romans and 1 and 2 Corinthians to Roman imperialism manifested in the emperor cult. One of the most important recent transformations in the study of Paul has been from seeing Paul as the Jewish religious teacher into recognizing Paul the world-citizen within the Roman Empire. This paper draws upon the conceptual background reflected by a number of inscriptions that show the growing Roman emperor cult. In particular, Porter draws on the bi-lingual calendar inscription from 9 BCE to shed light on the three Pauline letters.

Porter draws into discussion a number of public inscriptions from around the Roman Empire that venerate the various emperors. He maintains that, at the time he wrote Romans, Paul was very familiar with the widespread use of terms that divinized the Caesars—he only had to have his eyes open as he traveled throughout Asia Minor. Porter suggests that, in Romans, Paul styles himself as the erector of a new inscription to the true Lord, Jesus Christ, when he expands the introduction of the portion of the opening that specifies the sender. In the prescription, Paul seems to have captured the power differential between the great proconsul Paulus Fabius, who erected the calendrical inscription, and Paul the slave of God. While the calendrical inscription proclaimed the birthday of the divine Caesar, Paul proclaimed the good news of the coming of Jesus Christ. The calendrical inscription states that good favor has fallen on all humanity because of the divine Augustus on account of the good things that he has done. Paul in turn lays out a number of factors that appropriate the language used for deified Caesars to identify Jesus Christ as the ruler who trumps Caesar. The calendrical inscription notes the benefits that come about through divine beneficence, but Paul sees the divine benefit in terms of what we receive through the Lord Jesus Christ: status in the spiritual and material spheres. The inscription ends with words of worship and obedience, but Paul transforms the kind of obedience that is expected into the response of faith in all the nations.

By noting this, Porter focuses upon one particular aspect of the relationship of Paul's letters to the Roman Empire—how Paul creates a competing narrative of empire to displace the one concerning Caesar with one concerning the Lord Jesus Christ. The implications are seen for interpretation of another key passage, Rom 13:1–7. Paul has already shown himself to be an opponent of the Roman regime in the epistle's opening. In Romans 13, the authorities are called to account to be just authorities, and, because Christians are under the Lordship of Christ, they are called to obey just authorities—unjust authorities fall outside the parameters that Paul defines.

The implications of such a Christ-focused hierarchy are also seen in 1 and 2 Corinthians. Paul argues for a replacement of one hierarchy of the Greco-Roman patronage system, which was the basis of abuse in the Corinthian church, with a divine hierarchy that incidentally overthrows distinctions based on status, power, and wealth. Paul is not replacing authority with no authority or hierarchy with no hierarchy, but he is replacing a false "son of god" with the true "son of God." In 1 Corinthians 7, God is seen as the ultimate authority, Jesus Christ is the mediator between God and humanity, and Paul is his trustworthy communicative servant to the Corinthian church. Similarly, in the passage about the collection that Paul was taking up for the Jerusalem church in 2 Corinthians 8, there is a clear hierarchy of beneficence that begins with the Lord Jesus Christ and passes through Paul to the believers in Corinth and then to the believers in Jerusalem. Paul replaces the position of Caesar with that of the Lord Jesus Christ, with a resulting moral accountability to God. There is no divide between serving God and the state. One can only serve the state by following the Lord Jesus Christ.

Porter demonstrates how layers of context constrain and interpret texts on empire. In light of the calendrical inscription, Paul's letter opening is a displacement of the empire narrative with the competing narrative of the Lord Jesus Christ. Porter uses this understanding to explicate and constrain Rom 13:1–7, a problem passage in the relationship of early Christianity and empire, where he similarly sees the authorities relativized by the Lordship of Christ so that only just authorities are to be obeyed. He finds this approach consistent with the concept of hierarchy and authority in 1 and 2 Corinthians, a larger circle of literary context in the Pauline corpus.

The seventh paper, by Matthew Forrest Lowe, is on atonement and empire in the Minor Pauline Epistles. Notwithstanding the authorship disputes concerning this corpus, Lowe adopts a presupposition of basic unity, both of canon and thought, among the books. This paper shows that, in his minor (shorter) epistles, Paul sought out ways of *contextualizing* and *circumscribing* Rome's power, largely through his appropriation of language and imagery from two very different frameworks: the traditions of his Scriptures on the one hand, and the ideologies of Rome on the other. The resulting dialectic helped Paul to construct a counter-imperial theology of the atonement: crucified and resurrected life in the face of imperial death.

In Ephesians, the language of Christ's supremacy over the "powers" and the appropriation of divine-warfare myths from the Old Testament are placed in imperial contexts. Earthly political forces would be considered among the pantheon of powers in Eph 6:12. With the citation of Ps 68:18 and its application in Eph 4:8–16, Paul depicts Christ at his resurrection leading his captives in an imperial triumph that evokes demonstrations of power in Roman military practice—a "victorious siege" and a triumph over his opponents.

Written while Paul was in imperial imprisonment, Philippians uses the prison context to focus upon citizenship, peace, and the crucifixion as the focal point of the Christ-hymn in Philippians 2. The reference to citizenship in heaven in Phil 3:20 indicates a degree of expatriated discontent with Roman citizenship. The peace of God in Phil 1:2 is inimical to the Roman peace. The Christ hymn in Phil 2:6–11 combines Jesus' obedience to Rome's power over life and death at the death of the cross (a clear stamp of empire) with his ascent and exaltation, reminiscent of the exaltation of a Roman emperor in the description of the ascension.

Similarly, there is empire and triumph imagery in Col 1:15–20 and 2:14–15. Christ is the image of the invisible God that counters the logos of Rome and its sustaining myth of *pax Romana*. Christ is supreme over all power and authority, including Rome's. The state execution of Christ by Rome is the means of reconciliation. Then Christ disarms the powers and authorities at his moment of greatest weakness and triumphs over them.

In 1 and 2 Thessalonians, while references to idol worship and kingdom/dominion are directed at empire, the strongest locus of imperial content is located in 1 Thess 4:13–18 and 5:3, where the Lord's *parousia* contains loaded imperial content, and the empire's offer of peace and security is nullified. Paul renders the *parousia* as a clear imitation of the imperial event of a royal visitation, where the tombs and mausoleums of the dead are encountered first and a greeting committee meets him and escorts him back. The timing of his coming will disrupt the imperial program of peace and security.

Paul also co-opts imperial terms, slogans, and titles in Titus and 1 and 2 Timothy. These terms include savior, king, and despot, and represent language normally reserved for human masters and rulers. Lowe maintains that there is serious risk in this kind of counter-rhetoric—it is only effective when it remains distinctive from both its sources and opposition.

Finally, Paul interacts with the Roman ideology of captivity and mastery in Philemon. Paul himself is in captivity enforced by Rome and argues for a broader "ethic of liberation" informed by Christ's death on a cross, which disrupts empire's societal structure by disrupting the "proper" channels of power.

As it corresponds in many points to Thatcher's paper concerning the challenge to empire of the Gospel of John's story of the crucifixion, Lowe's paper makes a significant contribution in giving direction to a New Testament biblical theology of the cross in the face of empire. His emphasis upon finding consistent theological themes that counter empire in all of the minor Pauline letters adds to the strength of his analysis.

The eighth paper is by Cynthia Long Westfall on the varied responses to empire in early Jewish Christianity. Westfall maintains that the early literature of Jewish Christianity in the General Epistles, Hebrews, and Revelation may provide the clearest and most overt examples of resistance to the Roman Empire in the New Testament. Her analysis draws directly from the traditions of Judaism and the relationship of Judaism with past empires including Egypt, Assyria, Babylon, Persia, and Greece. Jewish Christianity occupied an increasingly difficult position as hostility built between the Roman Empire and Christianity, and between the Roman Empire and Judaism, and alienation increased between Jewish Christians and Jews. The resulting economic, social, and even legal losses, as well as threats to life and property, in the Jewish Christian communities provided harsh realities that required a response and various strategies.

Each one of the texts of early Jewish Christianity in the non-Pauline epistles and homilies has a tendency to negotiate one aspect of empire more distinctively than others, so that Westfall chooses a different lens through which each epistle is viewed. James is analyzed with an economic model, and addresses economic issues including exploitation, materialism, and poverty. 1 Peter is analyzed with a social patronal model, in terms of secured honor and dignity for the powerless. In 2 Peter, Jude, and the Johannine Epistles, the relationship of Christian values to the culture of the empire is examined, because they each stress the ethics and values that set God's kingdom apart. Hebrews is analyzed with a religious/political model because it challenged the Roman view of reality and kingdom. Finally, Revelation is viewed as running the gamut of the concerns that Jewish Christianity faced as it negotiated a perilous path among the Roman Empire, Judaism, and Gentile Christianity.

The spectrum of issues in the other books is sharpened by persecution and martyrdom. John holds the Roman Empire responsible for idolatry, blasphemy, sexual immorality, persecution, exploitation, and materialism. The Roman Empire is described as being in competition with God's sovereignty and is doomed to destruction. The believer's response to an oppressive empire begins with personal repentance that disassociates from the patterns of abuse and includes non-violent active resistance. Positively, believers find their position, value, and reality in the kingdom of God.

Similar to Lowe, Westfall surveys empire themes in an identifiable corpus, but she suggests that the corpus of Hebrews, the General Epistles, and Revelation shares the common context of Jewish Christianity that creates an identifiably different response than that found in the Pauline letters to the Gentile churches. The nature and purpose of the texts is quite different from that of the Gospels, so that the relationship of these texts to imperial issues is comparatively more overt and identifiable than in Matthew and John (arguably Jewish Christian literature). The Jewish Christian communities occupied a far more vulnerable position as they fought for their existence on two fronts. The direct interaction with this shared context produced sharper, less veiled responses to empire on the same trajectory as the historic response of Israel to its other oppressors, so that Westfall's paper is directly related to Stuart's argument that the Jewish literature displays a general resistance to the pagan mentality of empire.

The final paper is a response to and interaction with the previous papers by Gordon Heath. However, this paper is cast in the nature of giving "the rest of the story." Heath begins his interaction with the presentations with an overview of some of the issues that have shaped post-Holocaust New Testament studies. After a brief summary, Heath provides an examination of the earliest church fathers' view of empire as a foil to the arguments in the papers. Heath contends that the early church fathers were critical of Rome, but that criticism did not include an outright rejection of the benefits of Roman rule—the early church "did not follow the book of Revelation in identifying Rome with Antichrist."[4] Elements that indicated support of the empire included the use of military metaphors, Tertullian's use of the Old Testament that was not explicitly hostile, and positive actions and statements that con-

---

4. As quoted from Bainton, *Historical Survey*, 75.

cerned Christians serving in the Roman military. Even Tertullian urged Christians to pray for their rulers because the empire was holding back disaster. The criticisms of it prophesied its demise, judged it for its sins, prohibited service in the military and as a magistrate, and chose martyrdom rather than to submit to emperor worship or other idolatrous demands. However, Heath claims that the critical issue was idolatry, not resistance to imperial power.

Therefore, Heath concludes that the refusal to say "Caesar is Lord" is not to be confused with an anti-imperial attitude; there was a high degree of sympathy for the empire, the church fathers help us deal with contentious passages such as Romans 13, and finally, we need to see that a progression to Constantine and a Christian empire was not a radical departure from the early years of Christianity under Rome. In Heath's view, the early church fathers navigated the context of the Roman Empire with the tension of dual citizenship.

Heath's paper cautions against buying every critical theory within the postmodern world, suggesting that in some theories the intention of the author becomes at best a secondary concern. While he grants that Revelation is directed at the Roman Empire, he questions whether this was the intention of the other New Testament writers.

After each paper was presented in its oral form, questions were invited from the other presenters and those in attendance. At the end of the day, we had a panel discussion that allowed further interaction among the individual contributors and between the contributors and the general audience. A number of different questions were raised and insights were gleaned that became a platform for further work on the topic for some of the contributors. What is most apparent in review is that, individually, the resulting chapters offer a diverse representation of different methods and positions in regard to understanding the relationship of empire and the New Testament. Together, however, the papers offer a representative and thorough sample of the current state of study of the notion of empire and the New Testament.

BIBLIOGRAPHY

Bainton, Roland. *A Historical Survey and Critical Re-evaluation*. Nashville: Abingdon, 1988.

1

The Old Testament Context of David's Costly Flirtation with Empire-Building

Douglas K. Stuart

THIS PAPER IS AN admittedly ambitious attempt to do three things: first, via a brief but hopefully representative survey, to seek a basic understanding of the nature of the "mentality" of empire in the ancient Near East; second, by another brief but hopefully representative survey to identify the "mentality" toward empire of the Old Testament; and, with these contexts as background, to analyze an attempt made by King David to begin to establish an empire of his own.

THE MENTALITY OF EMPIRE IN THE ANCIENT NEAR EAST[1]

Consider an initial example of the ancient Near Eastern mentality of empire: In the following excerpt of a relatively short Egyptian histori-

1. The characterization of the mentality (outlook/attitude/mode of thought) of empire in the ancient Near East that I propose here (in this case, from "scratch") is, to my judgment, not inconsistent with the theory of empire advanced by Motyl, *Imperial Ends*. My summary of the ancient imperialistic mentality is obviously in part conjectural as well as admittedly inductive and synthetic. It represents an assessment of common factors in the *Weltanschauung* of ancient Near Eastern empires, even though it can hardly be doubted that various cultures and kings would have had somewhat different ways of looking at and rationalizing their imperialism. We have no single document from the ancient world in which an empire-minded monarch tells us systematically all the reasons that went into his decision to try to build an empire. But we do have a considerable number of documents in which kings speak or are spoken about in connection with one or more of the reasons why they set about to increase their territories by annexing or in some way controlling the territories of others. Putting these statements together

cal record,[2] Pharaoh Ka-mose states his case for re-establishment of the Egyptian empire (Upper and Lower Egypt and, presumably, the traditional buffer territories adjoining them north and south) in a speech to his advisors, ca. 1575 BCE:[3]

> His majesty spoke in his palace to the council of nobles who were in his retinue: "Let me understand what this strength of mine is for. (One) prince is in Avaris,[4] another is in Nubia, (and) here I sit associated with an Asiatic and a Nubian! Each man has his slice of this Egypt, dividing up the land with me ... No man can settle down, being despoiled by the taxes imposed[5] by the Asiatics. I will grapple with him, that I may cut open his belly! My wish is to save Egypt and to smite the Asiatics!"

His advisors suggest doing nothing except being ready defensively, since there have already been decades of fighting against the Hyksos[6] and they do not want more war:

> The great men of his council spoke: "Behold it is Asiatic *water as far as Cusae*[7] . . . [and] *we are at ease in our (part of) Egypt. Elephantine is strong, and the middle (of the land)* is with us as

---

and analyzing them, subjective as that process may be, permits at least a general picture of the ancient Near Eastern mentality of empire to emerge. The picture here set forth derives inductively from a variety of sources—annals, chronicles, law codes, treaties, proclamations, etc. —and yet, even though it is a composite from such sources, I believe it may be considered an approximate portrayal of the actual attitudes that prevailed widely in the ancient world.

2. In all probability, a propagandistic one designed in part to provide an *apologia* for the pharaoh's accomplishments during his reign.

3. The translation is mostly verbatim from Wilson's rendering of "The War against the Hyksos" in *ANET* 232–33, with minor modifications (for example, what he translates as "Negro" I have translated as "Nubian," and what he translates as "impost" I have translated as "taxes imposed," etc.).

4. Probably Tell El-Dab'a, a Nile delta city occupied by the Hyksos and made their capital in Egypt. It has sometimes been identified with biblical Zoan/Tanis, but this identification is now generally disputed as unlikely.

5. I.e., imposed on native Egyptians in the enemy-held regions previously held by Egypt.

6. Hyksos were Asiatic imperialists who had conquered Egypt and ruled it (though not always the entirety of its territory) from about 1725 to 1550 BCE. The term *Hyksos* is a hellenization of the original Egyptian ḥk3w ḫ3swt, lit., "rulers of mountainous places," i.e., "foreign rulers."

7. Egyptian *Qis*, modern *el-Qusiya*. It was the capital of the fourteenth nome of Upper Egypt.

far as Cusae ... He [the enemy] holds the land of the Asiatics; we hold Egypt.[8] Should someone come *and act [against us]*, then we shall act against him!"

Pharaoh Ka-mose was having none of this stay-safe-at-home, limited-territory advice:

> Then they were hurtful to the heart of his majesty: "As for this plan of yours, ... he who divides the land with me will not respect me. [*Shall I res*]*pect* these Asiatics ... ? I shall sail north to reach Lower Egypt. If I fight with the Asiatics, success will come ... Ka-mose, the protector of Egypt!"

Having rejected the advice of his counselors as inferior to that of his divine counselor, the god Amon, the pharaoh went on the attack and succeeded in restoring much of lower Egypt to Egyptian sovereignty, paving the way for the further conquests of the upcoming Eighteenth Dynasty:

> I went north because I was strong enough to attack the Asiatics through the command of Amon, the just of counsels. My valiant army was in front of me like a blast of fire. ... I attacked him. I broke down his walls, I killed his people ...

A second example involves Sargon of Akkad (ca. 2371–2316 BCE), usually thought of as the greatest of the early Mesopotamian emperors. In the following excerpt of what is typically called either the "Legend of Sargon" or the "Birth Legend of Sargon," he is quoted speaking of his own far-ranging imperialistic exploits, but also tellingly of his expectation that the kings who follow him in governing his empire should do the same if they are truly worthy of the office:[9]

> The black-headed [people][10] I ruled, I gov[erned];
> Mighty [moun]tains with chip-axes of bronze I conquered,
> The upper ranges I scaled,
> The lower ranges I [trav]ersed,
> The sea *[lan]ds* three times I circled.

---

8. In fact, they held only half of Egypt and were putting the best face on a bad situation in order to avoid war with the Hyksos Asiatics.

9. Taken from Speiser, "The Legend of Sargon," *ANET* 119; also in Hallo and Younger, eds., *Context of Scripture* [hereafter *COS*]), 1.133.

10. This was a standard designation in Akkadian for Sumerians as well as Semites in general.

> Dilmun[11] my [hand] cap[tured],
> [To] the great Der[12] I [went up] ...
> [K]azallu[13] I destroyed and ...
> Whatever king may come up after me, ...
> Let him r[ule, let him govern] the black-headed [peo]ple,
> [Let him conquer] mighty [mountains] with chip axe[s of bronze],
> [Let] him scale the upper ranges,
> Let him traverse the lower ranges,
> Let him circle the sea *[lan]ds* three times!
> [Dilmun let his hand capture],
> Let him go up [to] the great Der and ... [14]

Clearly, conquering distant lands was a mark of greatness in Sargon's view, and he challenges his successors to do the same—not necessarily as a way of boasting of his uniqueness ("Just try to do what I've done if you think you can!") but more likely as an example of what proper successor emperors should likewise do ("If I've done it, you should, too!").[15]

---

11. Dilmun was an idealized land referred to in many Mesopotamian myths, something of a cross between an earthly Eden and a heavenly paradise. Some scholars have identified what Sargon claims to have captured with Bahrain, for which there is some later inscriptional support, but this may be the result of later naming the impressively-situated island of Bahrain after the earlier-heralded ethereal location first imagined by the Sumerians in myths (cf. the way that a number of places in Britain, Canada, and the U.S. are named "Eden"). In other words, Sargon may be saying something like, "I conquered to the very edge of heaven!"

12. Modern Tel-Aqar, a powerful ancient Mesopotamian city, whose impressive great temple dates to 2500 BCE.

13. Kazallu was the capital of a small, independent Amorite empire ruled by dynasty in the nineteenth and eighteenth centuries BCE. When Sargon conquered it, it was probably, likewise, the center of some sort of modest empire.

14. Although it might appear from the heavy use of brackets and italics that Speiser has taken liberties in his restoration of the text, in fact he was working with two neo-Assyrian copies and one neo-Babylonian fragment, from the collation of which (and from the internal repetitions) he could make confident reconstructions, as King had also earlier done for the same document (King, *Chronicles*, 87–96).

15. Sargon's "legend" may have been embellished as regards his origins (prominent in the legend was the claim that he had been born secretly and set adrift in an ark of bulrushes on the waters of the Euphrates, not unlike Moses, and that he was rescued and brought up by a farmer). But the point of this was clearly to highlight the fact that it was his drive for greatness via empire that made him a success as an emperor, rather than that he simply inherited an empire from someone else by reason of royal birth. In his adult life, he served first as a "cupbearer" (i.e., a court administrator, not merely a household worker) to a king of Kish, but as soon as he himself won kingship, he set out enthusiastically for foreign conquests, initiated by invading the empire of King Lugal-

As a third example, we cite portions of the prologue to the famous law code of Hammurabi the Great (ca. 1728–1686 BCE), in which Hammurabi makes certain claims about his right to rule a great empire and to impose upon it his will, including his will in the form of legal practices to be standardized and extrapolated from[16] throughout his empire:

> When lofty Anum, king of the Annunaki,
> (and) Enlil, lord of heaven and earth,
> the determiner of the destinies of the land,
> determined for Marduk, the first-born of Enki,
> the Enlil functions over all mankind,
> made him great among the Igigi,
> called Babylon by its exalted name,
> made it supreme in the world,
> established for him in its midst an enduring kingship,
> whose foundations are as firm as heaven and earth—
> at that time Anum and Enlil named me
> to promote the welfare of the people,
> me, Hammurabi, the devout, god-fearing prince,
> to cause justice to prevail in the land,
> that the strong might not oppress the weak,
> to rise like the sun over the black-headed (people),
> and to light up the land.
>
> [I am] the one who strides through the four quarters of the world;
> who makes the name of Babylon great;
> who rejoices the heart of Marduk, his lord; . . .

Zage-Si and adding it to Akkad. He invaded Syria and Canaan four separate times, and devoted three full years to the conquest of the countries of "the west" (he even speaks of getting copper in "Magan" [Oman]) in order to annex them to Mesopotamia, thus forming, as he boasted, "a single empire." He subdued northern Mesopotamia, including Gutium and the Elamite empire, which he annexed to his own. His armies placed statues of Sargon at several sites on the Mediterranean in honor of his victories. He built and rebuilt both cities and palaces in central and southern Mesopotamia, financed by the spoils of the conquered lands. Sargon's sons were weak, but his grandson Naram-Sin carried on his imperialistic enterprises and conquered such places as Oman (taking its king prisoner), Ebla (the headquarters of an empire of its own) and a place called "Armani" that is arguably to be identified with Armenia. Naram-Sin regularly referred to himself in official documents as "King of the Four Quarters [of the world]," and also enjoyed the title "god of Akkad."

16. As in Pentateuchal law, the individual prescriptions were intended to serve not only as determinative in their own right but as examples to be extrapolated from in deciding related cases.

> god among kings, acquainted with wisdom . . .
> the one who seizes the foe . . .
> who pacifies the heart of Adad, the warrior . . .
> the chief of kings, a fighter without peer . . .
> who made his kingdom great;
> the first of kings;
> the subduer of the settlements along the Euphrates with the help of Dagan, his creator . . .
> the king who has made the four quarters of the world subservient . . .[17]

Hammurabi connected his influence throughout his empire to a greatness given him by the gods, a greatness he exercised by right, from his point of view, appropriately imposed by force upon other people groups and their territories for the good of all concerned.

A fourth example comes from the beginning of the "Decree of Cyrus" in Ezra 1:2:

> This is what Cyrus king of Persia says: "The Lord, the God of heaven, has given me all the kingdoms of the earth . . ."

Here Cyrus attributes his right to rule and the actual accomplishment of his empire, in typical Persian syncretistic fashion, to Yahweh, who as "the God of heaven" had decided that Persia should rule the known world starting in the middle of the sixth century BCE.

From many texts of which these are but examples, very disparate though such texts are in provenance, we can learn something of what I believe may be posited as the common "mentality of empire" in the ancient Near East. The ingredients of that mentality of empire may be summarized as follows.

1. Certain kings, selected and favored by the gods, and the nations they rule, have both the divine right and a divinely-assigned duty to subdue, annex, or subjugate others, thus creating an empire. It is their destiny to do this, just as it is the destiny of other nations to be subdued and made subservient to an empire.[18]

---

17. *ANET* 163–80; *COS* 2.131.

18. As an example, an excerpt from the Egyptian version of a treaty of Ramses II with the Hittites, reproduced on the walls of the Amon temple at Karnak, shows the sense of the pharaoh that his imperialism was the will of the gods: ". . . his majesty was . . . doing the pleasure of his father, Amon-Re, Har-Akhti, Atum, Lord of the Two Lands, the Heliopolitan, Amon of Ramses Meri-Amon, and [Seth], the Great of Strength, the Son of Nut, according as they give him an eternity of jubilees and an infinity of years

2. As various gods contend with one another for power in the heavenly realm,[19] those gods (usually national gods) who emerge supreme in the pantheon naturally will cause their client nations to emerge supreme on the earthly scene. Thus the fortunes of the nations are tied to the fortunes of the gods.[20]

3. Empires exist for the benefit primarily of the controlling monarchy and the "home" nation, rather than as commonwealths. Thus the financial bleeding of conquered or subjugated lands via tribute, tax, and toll[21] is permissible and expected. It is the right of some nations to enrich themselves via empire and the required role of other nations to provide the riches.[22]

---

of peace, while all lands and all foreign countries are prostrate under his soles forever . . ." *ANET* 200. And from a historical prism of the Assyrian emperor Tiglath-Pileser I (1114–1076 BCE): "With the help of Ashur (and) Shamash, the great gods, my lords, I, Tukultiapilesarra, King of Assyria . . . am a conqueror (of the regions) from the Great Sea which is in the country of Amurru as far as the Great Sea which is in the Nairi country." From the "throne inscription" and bronze gate inscription of Shalmaneser III (858–824 BCE): "(I am) Shalmaneser, the legitimate king, the king of the world, the king without rival, the 'Great Dragon,' the (only) power within the (four) rims (of the earth), overlord of all the princes, who has smashed all his enemies as if (they were) earthenware, the strong man, unsparing, who shows no mercy in battle . . . a conqueror from the Upper Sea to the Lower Sea . . . At that time [Ashur, the great lord . . . gave me scepter, staff] . . . necessary (to rule) the people . . ." *ANET* 276–77; cf. *COS* 2.113A.

19. See, e.g., the series of Hittite myths such as "The Moon that Fell from Heaven," the Kumarbis myth published as "Kingship in Heaven," "The Song of Ullikummis," "The Myth of Illuyankis," and "The Telepinus Myth" (tr. A. Goetze), *ANET* 120–28; cf. *COS* 1.57. All these myths involve rivalries and battles among the gods, and were important to the ancients not because of mere story interest, but because they explained how the fortunes of earthly peoples' gods related to earthly peoples' fortunes.

20. In one sense, *mutatis mutandis*, this concept that what happens on earth reflects what happens in heaven is biblical. Deborah, following the concepts of Holy War (see below), describes how "the stars fought from the heavens/the stars fought with Sisera" (Judg 5:20) as a poetic way of indicating heavenly leadership in the battle for control of northern Canaan. Psalm 18:14 depicts God's lightning bolts as the equivalent of heavenly artillery dispersing Israel's enemies. Pagan notions of the gods' warfare as influencing that on earth can be understood as degenerated, polytheistic reflections of a valid theology.

21. E.g., Ezra 4:13, 20; 7:24.

22. Ah-mose, a boat captain in the military of Thut-mose I (1570–1545 BCE) tells of seven different times when he was awarded gold by the pharaoh as part of the sharing of the spoils of war, as well as slaves (captured prisoners) and other plunder. In speaking of the emperor's attitude, he adds: "[Thut-mose] went forth to Retenu [Syria-Palestine] to assuage his heart throughout the foreign countries . . . His Majesty made a great

4. It is predictable that conquered or subjugated lands will attempt to rebel so as to throw off the yoke of empire. Therefore a mark of a great emperor is his ability to keep foreign lands subjugated and obedient within the empire.[23] Propagandistic techniques of various sorts may be required to help subjugated nations realize and accept their role and to help the imperialistic "core" nation put forth the necessary effort to maintain its empire.[24]

5. One indication of the greatness of a national god and, likewise, of the king that he[25] sponsors in empire-creation is the extent of the empire in size and wealth.[26] Another is the speed with which the emperor conquers other territories.[27]

6. Another indication of the greatness of a god and his emperor is the duration of the empire—including both the ability of kings to pass on their empires to their heirs (with the help of the sponsoring god) and their ability (and their heirs' ability)[28] to protect it from rebellion by subjugated peoples or takeover by other empires, because, in spite of

---

slaughter among them. There was no number to the living prisoners that His Majesty carried off by his victory." (*ANET* 233–34; *COS* 2.1).

23. Perhaps the parade example of this is Darius I's defeat of nine kings in nineteen different major battles in a single year, 522–521 BCE, in the process of re-establishing the Persian empire that had begun to slip away after the death of Cyrus, and—in spite of Cambyses' successes in Egypt and elsewhere—especially quickly after the death of Cambyses. Sustaining an empire was often very hard work.

24. "Thus the target of Assyrian royal propaganda was not only the people of the Assyrian Empire but also those in the heavens and those in the future" (Sparks, *Ancient Texts*, 355).

25. Or, theoretically, "she," but there appear to be few examples of an empire sponsored specifically by a female national god in the ancient Near East.

26. Even though the notion that Alexander "wept that he had no more worlds to conquer" is modern and apocryphal, Virgil did say in the Aeneid that Caesar, out of noble envy, wept at the victories of Alexander, as also did Plutarch, who quotes Caesar as saying after considering Alexander's achievements, "'Do you think,' said he, 'I have not just cause to weep, when I consider that Alexander at my age had conquered so many nations, and I have all this time done nothing that is memorable?'" See Clough, trans., *Plutarch's Lives*, 299.

27. See Stuart, "The Sovereign's Day of Conquest."

28. Illustrative of this is a demand of Esarhaddon (681–669 BCE) to various vassal kings requiring them to be loyal to his son and successor Asshurbanipal: "You will love Asshurbanipal as yourselves" (49 col. iv, cited in Wiseman, "Vassal-Treaties," 266–68). See also the collation of similar expressions in Moran, "Background," 77–87.

propaganda to the contrary, there was a sense that no empire could last forever.[29]

7. Thus, when one empire can take over another in its entirety, it is a mark of real greatness, something to be coveted for one's press reports, as it were.[30] If an empire can take over another and then continue to extend its empire even further, it is indeed a mark of true greatness.[31]

8. An empire's worth or legitimacy was a matter of subjective perspective—the decision being essentially chauvinistic and self-centered. If your territory were conquered, you tended to hate the empire and reject its validity; if you conquered another nation in the process of establishing your empire, you tended to have no doubt as to the divine right of your conquest. Thus, in spite of many examples of pragmatic willingness to cooperate with empires out of a motive of self-preservation (such as is exemplified by the Judean kings during the days of the neo-Assyrian empire in the eighth and seventh centuries BCE), generally, subjugated

---

29. Even though empire-minded kings and their supporters surely wanted it so and may have employed wishful thinking to try to make it seem so. The remarkably careless attitude of Belshazzar described in Daniel 5 (feasting with the empire's leadership as the enemy Persian armies were at the gates of Babylon) is sometimes thought to reflect a resignation to the inevitable and therefore the desire for one last fling before destruction, but it could equally have been an evidence of denial by one who saw himself the latest in a long line of great and powerful monarchs of an empire that could hardly be imagined as ever coming to an end.

30. The Esarhaddon Chronicle, a Babylonian chronicle from a time when the Babylonians recognized the Assyrian king Esarhaddon as their king, conveniently leaves out negative or embarrassing events during the reign of the neo-Assyrian king Esarhaddon (681–669 BCE), presenting Esarhaddon always in a good light, and omitting any mention of the major defeat in his sixth year, i.e., the capture and plundering of the city of Sippar by the Elamites, something Esarhaddon was apparently unable to prevent. Thus the chronicle keeps alive via pretense of the empire mentality that Esarhaddon had preserved the Assyrian empire in its entirety.

31. So the desire of the neo-Babylonians, especially via the conquests of Nebuchadnezzar, to outdo what the neo-Assyrians had done, and the Persians under Cyrus the Great to extend their empire even beyond (but certainly including) what the Babylonians had captured, etc. In a certain sense, this "ever bigger, ever better" mentality forms part of the context for Daniel's revelation of the "kingdom of the saints of the Most High" (Dan 7:18, 22, 25, 27) as the stopping point for all this succession of progressively greater empires, since once the saints inherit "the kingdom" they keep it—nobody else is allowed to come along and threaten their possession, because the very nature of the kingdom has changed to one that is no longer merely a matter of human, earthly conquest and control.

peoples were hostile to the empires that subjugated them and eager for freedom from the bondage of being forced into an empire.[32]

9. Empires had a right to be religiously imperialistic.[33]

10. Empires bring peace and tranquility to a series of lands. It is the right and responsibility of an emperor to dominate his own people and subjugate other peoples in order to establish this peace.[34]

11. The will of the gods and the will of the emperor were coordinated, if not one and the same.[35]

There was an alliance between the religious and the political in the mentality of empire. Political decisions to attack and conquer and/or threaten and subjugate other nations were made by a king and his advisors politically, but these were seen at the same time as decisions made in heaven by gods, most especially the national god of the imperialistic nation, whose will the human king and his nation were carrying out. Kings rarely omit reference to their divinely-directed mission at the same time

---

32. Thus even a puppet king like Zedekiah, who owed his throne to appointment by an emperor (2 Kgs 24:15–17) eventually was willing to risk everything for the sake of freedom from under the boot of the empire (2 Kgs 24:20—25:7). In fact, he never stood a chance, but he was willing, somewhat naively, to try.

33. For the Egyptians, this came naturally from the theology that their king was a god. The pharaoh was frequently referred to as "the good god" (Gardiner, *Egyptian Grammar*, 75), a beneficent spreader of influence through conquest, one who could put subdued territories on a right course.

34. Even if that peace is established in the manner of a *pax romana*. As Gardiner comments, the Egyptian pharaohs were considered rightfully the rulers of the world, and this was indicated even via the use of the cartouche to encircle their names: "... the idea was to represent the king as ruler of all 'that which is encircled by the sun,' a frequently expressed notion" (Gardiner, *Egyptian Grammar*, 74).

35. Consider this evidence of imperialistic divine-human symbiosis, in which Amon-Re, the sun god and god of Thebes, speaks to the eighteenth-dynasty pharaoh Thutmosis III (1479–1425 BCE): "My son, my avenger, Menkheperre [Thutmosis' prenomen] may he live eternally. I shine forth through your love. Endue my hands— your body—with the protection of life. How sweet is your pleasure against my breast! I establish you in my sanctuary. I marvel at you. I place your might and the fear of you in all lands, dread of you to the limits of the four supports of heaven" (Gardiner, *Egyptian Grammar*, 90, translation slightly modified). Assyrian Annals had "bombastic and superlative descriptions of the king as well as . . . self-aggrandizing descriptions of building projects, military feats, and booty lists" (Sparks, *Ancient Texts*, 370).

that they speak frankly of their political-military agendas and accomplishments.[36] Not to seek empire was a sign of failure and weakness.[37]

12. The right to control other countries extended even to the right to rearrange their populations via deportations (exiles)—something used both as a threat and actually conducted regularly throughout the second and first millennia BCE as a means of securing the stability of an empire.[38]

13. Conquered kings were expected to bring their nations' practices and attitudes into conformity with the values of the empire into which they had been placed. Indeed, their right to remain as (vassal) kings depended on their conformity with the empire, especially in the provision of tribute, tax, and toll,[39] but also in supplying slaves, soldiers, ships, and

---

36. So in his exploits the Ugaritic King Keret is depicted as a dependent client of El, tenderly watched over by the top god: "And in his dream El descends / In his vision the Father of Mankind / And he approaches asking Keret / 'What is wrong with Keret that he weeps? / the beloved child of El that he cries? / Is it a kingship like Bull, his father's he desires? / Or authority like the Father of Mankind?'" (Keret epic, A 34–43; *ANET* 143; cf. *COS* 1.102). So, also, for example, from the Hammurabi prologue: "[Anum and Enlil] called Babylon by its exalted name, made it supreme in the world..." (lines 18–19); "the king who made the four quarters of the world subservient, the favorite of [the goddess] Inanna am I" (lines 10–12); "When Marduk [patron god of Babylon] commissioned me to guide the people..." (lines 15–16); and from the epilogue: "I, Hammurabi, the perfect king, was not careless or neglectful of the black-headed people, whom Enlil had presented to me..." (lines 11–15); "With the mighty weapon that Zababa and Inanna entrusted to me, with the insight that Enki [god of wisdom] allotted to me, with the ability that Marduk gave me, I rooted out the enemy above and below..." (lines 26–30).

37. A document usually referred to as "The Sins of Nabû-šuma-iškun" "depicts the eighth-century reign of Nabû-šuma-iškun of Babylon as a series of increasingly unwise and impious acts against the state and the gods." Most notably: "*he stopped going to war ...*" (Sparks, *Ancient Texts*, 373).

38. Note that already in Hammurabi's day (late eighteenth century BCE) the threat of exile was used effectively against an emperor's foes (Hammurabi Code epilogue, reverse xxvi:75 threatens against any king who tries to subvert Hammurabi's law "the dispersion of his people" and reverse xxviii:22–23 says "may they carry him away to lands hostile to him").

39. Giving of tribute to an emperor is portrayed as a great privilege in, for example, an inscription describing the Egyptian vizier Rekhmere's reception of tribute from leaders in Crete on behalf of Thutmosis III, accompanying the scene in which it is depicted, on a wall painting in Thebes: "Coming in peace by the chieftains of Crete and the islands in the midst of the sea, bowing down, bending the head, because of the might of His Majesty, King of Upper and Lower Egypt, Menkheferre [prenomen of Thutmosis], granted life eternally, because they hear of his victories over all countries; their trib-

various other goods and services to the empire, and emulation of the empire's practices.[40]

THE MENTALITY OF EMPIRE IN THE OLD TESTAMENT

In light of the uniqueness of outlook of the Old Testament in so many areas of life as compared to its surrounding cultures,[41] it should not prove surprising if we were to find that the Old Testament does not reflect the same sort of mentality about empire that is so widely manifest elsewhere in the ancient Near East.[42] In fact, a negative attitude toward empires seems to be the case: the Old Testament does not endorse either empires or imperialism, and actually has a considerable amount to say against them.

Is it therefore wrong to speak of the "Empire of Saul" or the "Empire of David" or the "Empire of Solomon" as is commonly done? Not necessarily. If one defines "empire" in a modern way, using, for example, Motyl's categories,[43] these three kings (and other Israelite or Judean kings, to a lesser degree) could be understood to have reigned over a small "continuous" empire, that is, a grouping of contiguous territories that might

---

ute on their backs, in quest of being given the breath of life, through desire of being loyal subjects of His Majesty, so that his might may protect them" (Gardiner, *Egyptian Grammar*, 233, translation modified).

40. When Antiochus IV put a statue of Zeus in the Holy of Holies in the Jerusalem temple, he was doing what he thought was his right and duty and the right and duty of the Jews to accept. Ahaz's building of an Assyrian-style altar at Jerusalem as a replacement for the Solomonic altar is given in the Old Testament as evidence of his monumental corruption religiously, but from his empire-cultivating point of view it was presumably an improvement modeled on the latest and best that had been imported to Damascus by the Assyrian emperor Tiglath-Pileser (2 Kgs 16:10–18). Zephaniah's mention of the "princes and the king's sons and all those clad in foreign attire" (Zeph 1:8) reflects the easy acceptance of empire fashion by those who should have been resisting it.

41. See, e.g., Wright, *Old Testament against Its Environment*.

42. The perspective of this paper is that there is a consistent, univocal Old Testament theology and that therefore various Old Testament passages from various genres and loci, if handled carefully and responsibly, can be adduced in support of a systematic analysis of an Old Testament theme such as empire. Those who take the position that the Old Testament contains a variety of different and conflicting theologies might approach the problem of deciding what the Old Testament says about empire in quite a different way, of course.

43. These are: *continuous* (all territories contiguous on land), *discontinuous* (ruled territories not adjacent to the core nation, whether overseas or just elsewhere on land), and *hybrid* (a combination of these two).

have otherwise wanted to be independent of one another (as Israel and Judah became after Solomon's death)—areas united by force of conquest (via Saul's partially successful attempts and David's remarkably successful campaigns) and ruled from a central capital (eventually Jerusalem, captured for just such a purpose by David).

This is not the same thing as a typical ancient Near Eastern empire, however. One difference may be seen in how the Old Testament views the territory that David conquered as opposed to how an empire's territory was usually viewed in the non-Israelite ancient Near East. The Old Testament does not see the kingdom of Israel at its height under David as territory made up (again in Motyl's terms) of a core and a periphery (a core nation whose king initiates the conquest of an empire, and the periphery, various lands and their monarchs that he defeats and subjugates to create the empire), but rather as the *inherited* territory of a *single* people that was specially chosen many centuries in advance to inhabit it. Additionally, the Old Testament sees the united kingdom of Israel as located in a place that has precisely defined boundaries, established not by trial and error in wars of conquest or by either divine or human ambition, but by a divine plan revealed very early on in the process, and brought to fruition by the *importation* of a population that had not been there before—essentially the exact opposite of the *deportations* that were usually employed by emperors to help establish control over conquered territories in typical empire-building.

Part of the challenge of deciding whether or not the Old Testament views the concept of "empire" in any particular way is the fact that the Old Testament does not have a vocabulary dedicated to designating "empire."[44] Most modern English translations of the Old Testament employ the word "empire" sparingly, if at all, and do so, in fact, somewhat subjectively. Even if we bring in the LXX and its terms βασιλεία and κυριεία (as close as the LXX gets to rendering "empire" by a single word) we are still no further ahead: "empire" is found to be rendered by circumlocutions at best, and it can be argued that there is no term, individual or compound, in either the Hebrew or Aramaic vocabulary of the Old

---

44. Words rendered as "empire" in sample versions: Esth 1:20 מַלְכוּת KJV/NKJV; Esth 4:11 מְדִינוֹת הַמֶּלֶךְ [LXX B: βασιλεία] Esth 10:1 הָאָרֶץ NIV/TNIV; Jer 34:1 מַמְלְכוֹת אֶרֶץ NIV/TNIV; Dan 11:2 הַכֹּל NASB; Dan 11:3 מִמְשָׁל [LXX B: κυριεία]; Dan 11:4 מַלְכוּת (twice) NIV/TNIV; ESV, none; Young's Literal, none; RSV/NRSV, none.

Testament that *requires* translation into English as "empire." Certainly, we cannot take the approach that a word is the same thing as a concept, and it is certainly the *concept* of empire in the Old Testament that we are seeking to analyze. But the mere paucity of vocabulary is at least a clue to the Old Testament's own unwillingness to "dignify" the concept with unequivocal, dedicated vocabulary.[45]

The general Old Testament perspective on empires may be summarized as follows: Since God wants to save, and since God alone *can* save, he will always and unalterably oppose human inventions that cannot save, from idols to empires. No single verse of the Old Testament says as much, of course, but what the Old Testament does say on the matter, via the sorts of passages adduced in the following brief survey, adds up to such a conclusion.[46]

A starting point for our survey might be Deut 32:8: "When the Most High gave the nations their inheritance, when he divided all mankind, he set up boundaries for the peoples according to the number of the children of Israel." The context of this statement is an early (Mosaic) poetic covenant lawsuit (*rîb*) in which Israel is warned not to disobey God's creation and covenant standards, and the nations of the earth are also warned that they must not do so, especially in connection with trying to subjugate Israel, Yahweh's special inheritance. The point of the verse is that God from the beginning established national boundaries as a firm divine inheritance in such a way that no nation could properly get so big in territory that it could justify conquering Israel out of some sort of notion of "manifest destiny" (right of empire). Deuteronomy 32:8 is, in

---

45. I am not here endorsing anything like a Whorfian hypothesis about vocabulary (the idea of the late Benjamin Whorf that vocabulary specificity signals perceptual specificity, so that if a language lacks a separate, dedicated word for something, speakers of that language are probably not clearly aware of that thing). Nor do I think that the lack of individual words for "empire" in the Hebrew or Aramaic of the Old Testament stems *automatically* from the "negative" view of the Old Testament toward empire: it may be noted that a very large number of negative concepts (sin, murder, treachery, etc.) do have specific vocabulary words that attach to them in the Old Testament. Our point is simply that any writer or group of writers can refuse to "dignify" a concept by referring to it with one or more "harmless" or "neutral" vocabulary words as a *conscious* and *intentional* way of reminding the reader that the concept is foreign to the outlook of the writer(s).

46. These sample passages are from after David's time as well as before David's time, and it might be argued that only passages from before his time should be adduced. Such a requirement would be appropriate if it could be proved that the view of empire in the Old Testament evolves over time, but I see no evidence of that.

other words, a parade example of the Old Testament anti-imperialistic outlook.

A further insight into the Old Testament's view on empire comes from Isa 10:5–14 (the full context is actually even broader), which reads:

> "Woe to the Assyrian, the rod of my anger, in whose hand is the club of my wrath! I send him against a godless nation [Israel, deserving to be punished], I dispatch him against a people who anger me, to seize loot and snatch plunder, and to trample them down like mud in the streets. But this is not what he intends, this is not what he has in mind; his purpose is to destroy, to put an end to many nations. 'Are not my commanders all kings?' he says . . . 'As my hand seized the kingdoms of the idols, kingdoms whose images excelled those of Jerusalem and Samaria—shall I not deal with Jerusalem and her images as I dealt with Samaria and her idols?'" When the Lord has finished all his work against Mount Zion and Jerusalem, he will say, "I will punish the king of Assyria for the willful pride of his heart and the haughty look in his eyes. For he says: 'By the strength of my hand I have done this, and by my wisdom, because I have understanding. I removed the boundaries of nations, I plundered their treasures; like a mighty one I subdued their kings. As one reaches into a nest, so my hand reached for the wealth of the nations; as men gather abandoned eggs, so I gathered all the countries . . .'"

Assyria is here portrayed as displaying the mentality of empire, and God is clearly not impressed or amused, and certainly not in agreement. He will destroy them, once he has used them to do his will against his morally wayward people.[47]

From the Old Testament perspective, the success of any empire can be only temporary. Pagan imperialism may serve God's purposes by teaching a lesson to disobedient nations, but God allows no nation's empire to endure for long, since it is the kingdom of his own people that he ultimately will shepherd into eternal triumph. Meanwhile, an empire may think itself to have achieved greatness, even though its achievements are nothing more than the outcome of divine manipulation. For example, Jer 28:14:

---

47. Abandoning Israel to a foreign conqueror is a standard Mosaic Covenant curse. Cf. Lev 26:17, "Those who hate you will rule over you"; Deut 28:33, ". . . nothing but cruel oppression all your days . . ."; 28:48, "You will serve the enemies Yahweh sends against you; he will put an iron yoke on your neck."

> This is what the LORD Almighty, the God of Israel, says: "I will put an iron yoke on the necks of all these nations to make them serve Nebuchadnezzar king of Babylon, and they will serve him. I will even give him control over the wild animals."

This might seem virtually akin to Marduk's purported sponsorship of Babylon in neo-Babylonian theology, but it is not. It is merely Yahweh's use of Babylon as a convenient tool, after which Babylon's "seventy years" (Jer 25:12; 29:10) will conclude and that nation will perish from the world scene, as Jeremiah was also inspired to announce:

> Announce and proclaim among the nations . . . "Babylon will be captured; Bel will be put to shame, Marduk filled with terror . . . A nation from the north will attack her and lay waste her land. No one will live in it . . . For I will stir up and bring against Babylon an alliance of great nations from the land of the north. They will take up their positions against her, and from the north she will be captured. . . . So Babylonia will be plundered; all who plunder her will have their fill," declares the LORD. . . . She will be the least of the nations—a wilderness, a dry land, a desert. Because of the LORD's anger she will not be inhabited but will be completely desolate. All who pass Babylon will be horrified and scoff because of all her wounds . . . Therefore this is what the LORD Almighty, the God of Israel, says: "I will punish the king of Babylon and his land as I punished the king of Assyria." (Jer 50:2—51:18)

Zechariah's vision of the four horns (Zech 1:18–21) is a cheerful, simple vision of God's control over empires that had threatened Judah historically (Egypt, Assyria, Babylon, Persia). The prophet, in a typical unfolding (progressive) vision, first sees four horns, and then gradually understands that these are atop some cattle that farm hands (NIV incorrectly, "craftsmen") can easily shoo back (NIV incorrectly, "terrify . . . throw down") to their paddocks.[48]

> Then I looked up—and there before me were four horns! I asked the angel who was speaking to me, "What are these?" He answered me, "These are the horns that scattered Judah, Israel and Jerusalem." Then the LORD showed me four craftsmen. I asked, "What are these coming to do?" He answered, "These are the horns that scattered Judah so that no one could raise his head, but the craftsmen have come to terrify them and throw down

---

48. On the translation, see my forthcoming *Micah–Malachi*.

these horns of the nations who lifted up their horns against the land of Judah to scatter its people."

The point is that no matter how much empires may seem at one point or another in time to have unstoppable control over various nations under their domination, in God's plan they are as simple to get rid of as cows that have broken through a fence and need to be herded back home. Empires are like that from the Old Testament point of view: nations grown too big for their britches, powerful beasts to those whom they terrify, but merely big, stupid, out-of-bounds animals to God, who can put them in their place as and when he chooses.

Daniel 7 records the vision of four beasts symbolizing four coming kingdoms,[49] the fourth of which will be the ultimate in imperialism. The following excerpt is generally summational of the message of that great vision.

> He gave me this explanation: "The fourth beast is a fourth kingdom that will appear on earth. It will be different from all the other kingdoms and will devour the whole earth, trampling it down and crushing it. The ten horns are ten kings who will come from this kingdom. After them another king will arise, different from the earlier ones; he will subdue three kings. He will speak against the Most High and oppress his saints and try to change the set times and the laws. The saints will be handed over to him for a time, times and half a time. But the court will sit, and his power will be taken away and completely destroyed forever. Then the sovereignty, power and greatness of the kingdoms under the whole heaven will be handed over to the saints, the people of the Most High. His kingdom will be an everlasting kingdom, and all rulers will worship and obey him." (Dan 7:23–27)

Here the death knell of earthly empires is sounded. Only the kingdom of the Most High can be allowed to last forever. Every other kingdom, no matter how extensive, powerful, and impressive, must ultimately give way to God's. Every other ruler, no matter how feared or admired, must ultimately bow the knee to the only eternal King.[50]

---

49. Daniel's vision took place at the end of the Babylonian Empire. Although it is far outside the scope of this paper, I would contend (against a fairly widespread scholarly consensus) that a convincing case may be made for the identification of these kingdoms as, respectively, Persia, Greece, and Rome, rather than Persia, Greece, and the Seleucids.

50. Warnings against reliance on other empires implies that there is something

Part of the Old Testament's outlook in hostility to empires and imperialism is found in the concept of the "Day of the Lord." Somewhat ironically, this concept actually owes its idiomatic familiarity to the fact of empire in the ancient Near East. The origin of the concept may be found in the ancient idea that a truly great sovereign could vanquish his enemies in a single day. Such a great king would win not just *battles* in a day, but entire *wars* of conquest "in a day." Building on this well-documented notion from the ancient world,[51] the Old Testament prophets were inspired to assert that Yahweh, sovereign over all earthly sovereigns, could obviously dispatch not just any given foe, but all foes at once in a single day. Therefore the Day of Yahweh would be a day in which his special intervention on the human scene would set right all wrongs and bring to judgment all nations. As Joel, for example, puts it, Yahweh can gather all nations at once in the "Valley of Decision" and deal with them all at once as if they were simply a group of defendants in some sort of crime, being herded to court and judged openly for their crimes, their conviction easily obtained.[52]

On this analogy, a variety of other Old Testament prophets describe the "Day of the Lord" as any day of special divine intervention on a grand scale, including the conquest of Judah by the Babylonians (part, of course, of a massive empire conquest of many nations), and also of the first coming of Christ as a Day of Yahweh. Appropriately, the New Testament describes the second coming of Christ as a Day of the Lord as well, since it fits the criteria: a time of decisive divine intervention in human history to correct human error and establish the will of God widely.[53] The size and scope of the biblical concept of the Day of Yahweh, then, tends to crowd out any human reliance upon or awe at human empires. They are nothing before Yahweh, because his day of conquest is so much greater than and so opposed to and destructive of any human sovereign's puny-by-comparison day of conquest.

---

inherently wrong if God's people welcome the legitimacy of those empires. Cf. Isa 30:1–5; 31:1–9; Jer 46:25; 2 Kgs 18:21; 2 Chr 16:8; et al.

51. See Stuart, "The Sovereign's Day of Conquest," and the examples therein of the "victory in a single day" idea. Von Rad also argues that the "Day of the Lord" had its origin in the concept of Holy War, in Yahweh's subjugation of his foes on behalf of his people (von Rad, *Old Testament Theology*, 1:17 etc.).

52. Joel 3:9–14.

53. 1 Thess 5:2–9; cf. 2 Pet 3:10; 1 Cor 5:5; et al.

Another way to say this is to point out that the Old Testament envisions that all earthly empires of any sort will eventually be destroyed by divine fiat so that the age of the new creation can be characterized by a democratized access to Yahweh and his blessing via conversion to the faith once housed provisionally only in Israel:[54]

> In that day Israel will be the third, along with Egypt and Assyria, a blessing on the earth. The Lord Almighty will bless them, saying, "Blessed be Egypt my people, Assyria my handiwork, and Israel my inheritance." (Isa 19:24–25)

In this happy scenario, would-be emperors need not apply. They will have no chance to exercise their lust for dominance over others and others' territory. Empires will be gone forever, supplanted by a whole new order that obviates both their motives and methods.

Empires are created by warfare, and from a human point of view, the greater a king's ability to lead a people in war successfully, the greater his likelihood of producing an empire. David was, of course, a great king in terms of his ability to lead people in war. But not all wars—or all types of warfare—are alike. When David had his successes in war, it was not because he was a skilled military tactician or strategist in the manner of any skilled military leader in the ancient Near East. David succeeded because he consciously fought Holy War, a rather special type of warfare with a very special purpose.

The Israelite encounter with the Amalekites at Rephidim represents an early example of Old Testament Holy War, an instance that anticipates the fuller delineation of the concept in later texts. The principles of Holy War are codified in Deut 20:1–20, but important examples and supplemental aspects of the concept are found in many locations. Holy War may be summarized by twelve propositions:[55]

1. No standing army was allowed. This meant that the battles were fought by amateurs—volunteers—who had to depend on God for their success, and could not boast in their own accomplishments or claim special military prowess. A potential soldier was allowed—indeed invited—to give

---

54. As implied, e.g., in Isa 2:4; 14:1–2, 18; 29:7–8; 52:10; Jer 3:17; 25:31; et al.

55. The summary of Holy War given here follows closely a summary that I have published recently in Stuart, *Exodus*, 395–97.

virtually any excuse for not serving in a battle,[56] because God wanted only those who desired to be used by him as his warriors.[57]

2. No pay for soldiers was permitted. The entirely volunteer army could not seek personal reward by means of financial compensation for their efforts. Instead, they were to understand themselves as responding to God's call and not to any other incentives. They were going to war as his agents of justice, not as people seeking their own advantage.

3. No personal spoil/plunder could be taken. It was the standard practice in the ancient world for warriors to be attracted by the promise of spoil/plunder upon successfully conquering an enemy. The rule outside Israel was that a soldier could keep anything he could take from the enemy (or the enemy city or land) and carry off.[58]

4. Holy War could be fought only for the conquest or defense of the promised land. Israel had no right to any other land, or to warfare for any other purpose. Thus, as we shall discuss in more detail below, when David tried to build an empire and take a census in preparation for the wars that would be required to extend that empire beyond the boundaries of the promised land, he and Israel (the people had for the most part willingly participated) were severely punished (2 Sam 24:1–17).[59]

---

56. Accordingly, Deut 20:5–8 requires that the military leaders must openly invite those who may not have wanted to assert an excuse on their own behalf to go home and not participate in the battle, on the basis of almost any sort of prior commitment, samples of which are announced to the assembled troops.

57. David's Philistine mercenaries were, of course, an exception to the Holy War provisions and thus, unfortunately, a violation of the principles of Holy War. David's most egregious violation of the Holy War rules took place as described in 2 Sam 24 (see below on point 4).

58. See, e.g., the foiled expectation described in Deborah's Song, Judg 5:28–30, or the description of joy attending the division of spoils in Isa 9:3.

59. One might then ask how the battle at Rephidim, which was outside of the confines of the promised land of Canaan, could be considered properly an instance of Holy War. The answer is that just as despoiling the Egyptians (3:21–22; 12:36) represented a first step in making it possible for the Israelites to get to the promised land, and the defeat of Pharaoh's army at the Red Sea represented a second step in the same progression, defeating the Amalekites was simply a third step in the process of getting to Canaan. Had Israel not been able to prevail against Amalek, the conquest and defense of the promised land would have been mooted.

5. Only at Yahweh's call could Holy War be launched. There was no opportunity to hold a national referendum or for a king or any other person, including the High Priest, to declare Holy War. God alone was the arbiter of when such a war would be undertaken, if at all, and a true Holy War was thus fought strictly and only at his call.[60]

6. Solely through a prophet could that divine call come. Prophets were spokespersons for God, who did not make up their messages but said what God had placed in their minds to say. Neither priest nor king nor nobles nor tribal leaders nor any other authorities except a prophet were in a position to declare a Holy War. Moses was, of course, at all times a prophet.[61]

7. Yahweh does the real fighting in Holy War, because the war is always his. On the cosmic scale, Holy War is a war to defeat Satan and his angels, whose influence over earthly matters is invariably harmful. Israel was simply his human, earthly delegate to represent Yahweh's will, but he did the real fighting, with the Israelite people more or less conscious that they were "going through the motions."[62]

8. Holy War was a religious undertaking, involving fasting, abstinence from sex, and/or other forms of self-denial.[63] It was an act of obedience to God and not of national pride or military strategy.

9. A goal of Holy War was the total annihilation of an evil culture (the enemy, the Canaanites). This is based on Gen 15:12–16, in which God

---

60. When the Israelites first decided to try to fight the Canaanites on their own, they lost miserably, because the battle had not been called by Yahweh, but was, rather, fought against his will (Num 14:41–45).

61. Indeed, Moses is the paradigm prophet (Deut 18:15–22) whose ministry sets the standards for all subsequent prophets.

62. This is reflected, for example, in Judg 5:20 ("from the heavens the stars fought") and in Paul's summation of our proper focus in our part of the ongoing Holy War (Eph 6:12, "For our struggle is not against flesh and blood, but against the rulers, against the authorities, against the powers of this dark world and against the spiritual forces of evil in the heavenly realms"). The parade example of Israel's going through the motions of war in cognizance of the fact that the Lord actually does the fighting for them is found in Joshua 6, where Jericho falls after symbolic, rather than actual, warfare.

63. On fasting in Holy War, see 1 Sam 21:1–6, where David and his men are engaged in Holy War and therefore are very hungry from their repeated fasting; or 1 Sam 14:24–45, a lengthy story resulting from Saul's oath requiring fasting during a campaign against the Philistines. On abstinence from sex, see 1 Sam 21:4–5 and 2 Sam 11:11–13.

reveals to Abraham the plan of conquest as a means of eliminating the "Amorites" (Canaanites) once their progressively evil culture had become so corrupt that God could do nothing other than to exterminate it. The total annihilation of the enemy and all that might have been taken as plunder followed logically from this commitment.[64]

10. The violator of the rules of Holy War becomes an enemy. Those who violate the rules, such as by not practicing the required self denial or the required disdain for spoils or the like, must normally be punished with death, just as death is the due of the enemy being fought against.[65]

11. Exceptions and mutations were possible, especially in the case of combat with those who were not original inhabitants of the promised land, and therefore who were not automatically to be exterminated.[66] Accordingly, the Amalekites as non-inhabitants of the promised land, are added to the list of those who must be wiped out by special divine decree in Exod 17:14, because otherwise the Israelites might not have been certain as to whether to spare Amalekite lives or not.

12. Decisive, rapid victory characterized faithful Holy War. It was the expectation that if God was behind a war, that war would essentially be concluded in a day, the "Day of Yahweh" or "Day of the Lord." In the ancient world, there is a somewhat fuzzy distinction between a "battle" and a "war," because each military encounter with each new ethnic group or city state could be considered *either* a separate war or a separate battle within a protracted war of conquest. Nevertheless, God was regarded as capable of vanquishing all his foes in a single day.[67] That Moses should anticipate a battle against the Amalekites in a single day is consistent with this understanding of Holy War.

---

64. For an example, see Josh 6:17–19, 21.

65. On death for the person who breaks the fast, see 1 Sam 14:43–44; on death for the person taking plunder/spoil, see Josh 7:24–26.

66. See Deut 20:10–15; Josh 8:2, 27.

67. See Stuart, "The Sovereign's Day of Conquest," which argues that the origin of the phrase "the Day of the Lord" is to be found in the ancient Near Eastern notion that a truly great sovereign could win a war in a day, vanquishing all his foes and establishing full justice and order throughout his realm. Yahweh is the paramount great sovereign. His day of intervention, when it would come, would represent a decisive divine intervention in human history—joyously welcome to his allies and horrendously deadly for his foes.

As we have already noted, there is a basic and necessary relationship between empire and war: empires are gained mainly by warfare. Even where a given nation or group of nations may agree "voluntarily" to submit to the domination of an empire, this happens not because of their desire for some sort of commonwealth or mutually-beneficial relationship with the empire to which they submit, but because of the threat of destruction of all that they hold dear via warfare if they do not submit. Without war and its threat of devastation, empires in the ancient Near East could not have been built.

David understood war and what it could accomplish. He was an expert at it. The implications of that expertise for David's actions as described in 2 Samuel 24/1 Chronicles 21 are many, and it is to these implications and David's actions that we now turn.

DAVID'S COSTLY FLIRTATION WITH EMPIRE-BUILDING

Second Samuel 24 and its parallel in 1 Chronicles 21 tell the story[68] of David's instigating an extensive census of the fighting men throughout Israel. There are challenges to understanding exactly at what point in his career David undertook to demand this census,[69] but it would appear that it was some time after[70] he had subdued all that could be considered

---

68. It may be regarded, indeed, as a single story, easily and responsibly harmonized, with most wording shared verbatim and those portions that differ being explained occasionally by textual analysis and often by the different demands of the two different writers' literary programs for the benefit of their audiences. I do not here offer an analysis of the way I think the harmonization can be accomplished, because it has little effect on my discussion of David's purposes and actions. The differences are generally well explained in Pratt, *Chronicles*, 167–76; and Gordon, *Samuel*, 316–22.

69. The placement of 2 Sam 24 within the structure of the "appendix" of 2 Samuel is part of a chiastic arrangement in which several documents relevant to David's reign are collected and arranged symmetrically, but not necessarily chronologically, and not necessarily reflective of the end of his reign. Most of the commentaries discuss the structure well, and point out that the integrity of the account in 2 Sam 24 is not threatened by its inclusion in the appendix.

70. According to 2 Sam 8:1–13//1 Chr 18:1–13, David had in fact dominated by warfare all the areas that fell within the boundaries of the promised land by a point relatively early in his reign, as well as neighboring states whose boundaries either encroached on the promised land or whose past behavior had demonstrated that they eyed territory within the promised land as desirable. The fact that Solomon was able to tell Hiram of Tyre, "The Lord my God has now given me rest all around; there is no enemy or crisis" (1 Kgs 5:4) suggests that David so well finalized his conquest that it lasted well into the next generation.

the "traditional" boundaries of the promised land.[71] In instigating this census, it would appear that David took leave of the traditional Israelite/Old Testament hostility toward empire and embraced, for his own ends and via his own evolving values, the pagan Near Eastern mentality of empire (2 Sam 24 in normal type, 1 Chr 21 in italics below):

> [1] Again the anger of the LORD burned against Israel, and he incited David against them, saying, "Go and take a census of Israel and Judah." *[1] Satan rose up against Israel and incited David to take a census of Israel.*
>
> [2] So the king said to Joab and the army commanders with him, "Go throughout the tribes of Israel from Dan to Beersheba and enroll the fighting men, so that I may know how many there are." *[2] So David said to Joab and the commanders of the troops, "Go and count the Israelites from Beersheba to Dan. Then report back to me so that I may know how many there are."*
>
> [3] But Joab replied to the king, "May the LORD your God multiply the troops a hundred times over, and may the eyes of my lord the king see it. But why does my lord the king want to do such a thing?" *[3] But Joab replied, "May the LORD multiply his troops a hundred times over. My lord the king, are they not all my lord's subjects? Why does my lord want to do this? Why should he bring guilt on Israel?"*
>
> [4] The king's word, however, overruled Joab and the army commanders; so they left the presence of the king to enroll the fighting men of Israel. *[4] The king's word, however, overruled Joab; so Joab left and went throughout Israel and then came back to Jerusalem.*
>
> [5] After crossing the Jordan, they camped near Aroer, south of the town in the gorge, and then went through Gad and on to Jazer. [6] They went to Gilead and the region of Tahtim Hodshi, and on to Dan Jaan and around toward Sidon. [7] Then they went toward the fortress of Tyre and all the towns of the Hivites and Canaanites. Finally, they went on to Beersheba in the Negev of Judah. *[6] But Joab did not include Levi and Benjamin in the numbering, because the king's command was repulsive to him. [7] This command was also evil in the sight of God; so he punished Israel.*

---

71. The outer extent of the promised land was defined for the Israelites by referring to such passages as Gen 15:18; Num 13:21; 34:1–12; Deut 2–3, esp. 3:12–17; Josh 13:2–5 and Josh 13–22. It clearly includes lands thereafter (and also before) occupied against the will of Yahweh by Philistines, Arameans, Ammonites, Moabites, Edomites, etc.

⁸ After they had gone through the entire land, they came back to Jerusalem at the end of nine months and twenty days.

⁹ Joab reported the number of the fighting men to the king: In Israel there were eight hundred thousand able-bodied men who could handle a sword, and in Judah five hundred thousand.

⁵ Joab reported the number of the fighting men to David: In all Israel there were one million one hundred thousand men who could handle a sword, including four hundred and seventy thousand in Judah.

¹⁰ David was conscience-stricken after he had counted the fighting men, and he said to the LORD, "I have sinned greatly in what I have done. Now, O LORD, I beg you, take away the guilt of your servant. I have done a very foolish thing." *⁸ Then David said to God, "I have sinned greatly by doing this. Now, I beg you, take away the guilt of your servant. I have done a very foolish thing."*

¹¹ Before David got up the next morning, the word of the LORD had come to Gad the prophet, David's seer: *⁹ The LORD said to Gad, David's seer,*

¹² "Go and tell David, 'This is what the LORD says: I am giving you three options. Choose one of them for me to carry out against you.'" *¹⁰ "Go and tell David, 'This is what the LORD says: I am giving you three options. Choose one of them for me to carry out against you.'"*

¹³ So Gad went to David and said to him, "Shall there come upon you three years of famine in your land? Or three months of fleeing from your enemies while they pursue you? Or three days of plague in your land? Now then, think it over and decide how I should answer the one who sent me." *¹¹ So Gad went to David and said to him, "This is what the LORD says: 'Take your choice: ¹² three years of famine, three months of being swept away before your enemies, with their swords overtaking you, or three days of the sword of the LORD—days of plague in the land, with the angel of the LORD ravaging every part of Israel.' Now then, decide how I should answer the one who sent me."*

¹⁴ David said to Gad, "I am in deep distress. Let us fall into the hands of the LORD, for his mercy is great; but do not let me fall into the hands of men." *¹³ David said to Gad, "I am in deep distress. Let me fall into the hands of the LORD, for his mercy is very great; but do not let me fall into the hands of men."*

15 So the Lord sent a plague on Israel from that morning until the end of the time designated, and seventy thousand of the people from Dan to Beersheba died. 14 So the Lord sent a plague on Israel, and seventy thousand men of Israel fell dead.

16 When the angel stretched out his hand to destroy Jerusalem, the Lord was grieved because of the calamity and said to the angel who was afflicting the people, "Enough! Withdraw your hand." The angel of the Lord was then at the threshing floor of Araunah the Jebusite. 15 And God sent an angel to destroy Jerusalem. But as the angel was doing so, the Lord saw it and was grieved because of the calamity and said to the angel who was destroying the people, "Enough! Withdraw your hand." The angel of the Lord was then standing at the threshing floor of Araunah the Jebusite.

16 David looked up and saw the angel of the Lord standing between heaven and earth, with a drawn sword in his hand extended over Jerusalem. Then David and the elders, clothed in sackcloth, fell facedown.

17 When David saw the angel who was striking down the people, he said to the Lord, "I am the one who has sinned and done wrong. 17 David said to God, "Was it not I who ordered the fighting men to be counted? I am the one who has sinned and done wrong.

This story, in two slightly different accounts (as certainly might be expected in light of the Chronicler's well-known special emphases and different audience) may be considered to raise several questions that deserve to be addressed.

1. Did David Understand the "Rules" of Holy War, Rules That Included Authorization Only for the Taking and Holding of the Promised Land?

Indications are that he did. In the past, as a military chieftain working closely with Saul and Jonathan, David had fought under Holy War standards. For example, on the occasion described in 1 Samuel 14, when Jonathan ran afoul of Holy War fasting regulations because he was "out of the loop" and unaware that Saul had proclaimed a Holy War, Jonathan ate honey against his father's decree and incurred the wrath of Israel for so doing.[72] If Saul was practicing Holy War, it surely cannot have been lost on his chief general, David.

---

72. 1 Sam 14:24–30.

David also shows awareness of Holy War in his encounter with Ahimelech, the priest at Nob.[73] In that story, David acknowledges that he and his men "as usual" practiced Holy War, as indicated by his affirmation that they did not engage in the pleasures of the flesh (indicated via synecdoche by the clause "women have been kept from us") while at war. This allows the high priest to give him and his men the showbread to eat.

Not only so, but David showed a regular attitude that he knew that he and Israel with him were fighting under the leadership of Yahweh and acted according to revealed standards of engagement whenever they fought. Even in his encounter with Shimei, he knew that he could not select opponents for slaughter but must go into battle only against those persons or people whom God designated via a prophet.[74] At the very end of his life, David reneged again on this firm commitment to a strict Holy War attitude by assigning over to Solomon the goal of taking care of those who had made themselves David's enemies,[75] since during his lifetime David did not feel authorized to do it.

It might be argued that David broke the rules of Holy War by having Philistine (Kerethite, Pelethite and Gittite) mercenaries in his employ as professional soldiers.[76] However much this may have represented a "stretching" of the rules, these were his personal bodyguard, not the army of Israel.[77] Otherwise David seems to have understood and, usually, practiced systematically the Holy War principle of having an all-volunteer, non-standing army.

It also would seem that the Old Testament refers to David's reaching a point when, although he had not gone abroad to try to build an empire, he had instead achieved the status of control over all potential foes.[78] In other words he had consciously stopped wars of conquest because he had reached the limits of the promised land. Thus he, as of that time at

---

73. 1 Sam 21:1–6.

74. 2 Sam 16:5–14.

75. 1 Kgs 2:5–9. This is one of several moral low points in David's career.

76. See 2 Sam 15:18 and 2 Sam 8:18; 15:18; 20:7, 22; 1 Kgs 1:38, 44. This would not imply that he did not *know* the rules of Holy War, in any case.

77. This was somewhat in the same manner as the Swiss Guards protect the Pope to this day, a guard force of foreigners whose disinterest in the internal affairs of Israel would help them keep their loyalty to the king regardless of his policies as these might rile or affect the attitudes of native Israelites.

78. 2 Sam 8:1–13//1 Chr 18:1–13.

least, had probably observed consistently the provision that Holy War was permissible only for the taking and holding of the promised land.

2. Did David Understand the Implications of a Census?

The story of 2 Samuel 24//1 Chronicles 21 is the story of a census and its aftermath. While on rare occasions in the ancient world there may have been a purpose for taking a census that fell outside of either taxation or preparation for war, these two purposes seem to be the only two that are actually found in the Old Testament.[79]

As Mendenhall has argued, the only purpose for a census described as counting "fighting men" ("those who draw the sword"), as already in Numbers 1 and 26, is for war; Israel is overtly mentioned in a number of contexts related to the exodus and conquest of Canaan as being specifically organized for war.[80] What was the purpose of the war for which the censuses of Numbers 1 and 26 were taken? It was, indeed, conquest, taking somebody else's territory away from them. This is why the Israelites were counted tribe by tribe, and why they are described as being organized as an army.[81] Israel's assignment was to enter territory where they had not before set foot[82] and destroy a native population.[83]

Warfare was necessary to accomplish this, but not just *any* warfare: this was Holy War, in which the Israelites fought symbolically as agents of Yahweh's long-demanded justice.[84] It is hard to imagine that David would have been unaware of the nature of the conquest and of the nature, including the dangers, of the censuses that initiated the gathering of the troops in the days of Moses for that conquest.

---

79. On census lists as virtually invariably for the purpose of taxation or war (and these two purposes only), see Sparks, *Ancient Texts*, 377–78, who mentions the existence of seventeen extant Assyrian census lists, and several others from Ugarit, Babylon, Egypt, and Mari.

80. Mendenhall, "Census Lists."

81. E.g., the Israelites marched out of Egypt "by their divisions" Exod 6:26; see also 7:4; 12:17, 41; Num 1:3, 52; 2:3 and other passages.

82. Deut 1:18, 21; see also Gen 15:7; 28:4; Exod 23:30; Josh 1:3; et al.

83. Note how different this is from the usual idea of imperialism, which is to subdue people and put them to work for the empire. About the only people the Israelites were able, at least at first, to subdue from the native population of Canaan were the Gibeonites, who fooled the Israelites into allowing them to live as servants by pretending to be outsiders to Canaan (Joshua 9).

84. Gen 15:14, 16.

The potential for abuse in a census (namely, using a census to establish a standing army) carried with it a special penalty, as enumerated in Exodus. The payment of the ransom money was a means of forestalling such a penalty.[85] What was the penalty? It was a plague—the danger of which Joab surely knew from his words in 2 Samuel 24//1 Chronicles 21, and which David likewise surely knew.[86]

3. Would David Have Had Any Reason to Desire to Establish an Empire?

Money may have been part of the motivation, as it usually was in ancient imperialism. For some time, David had obviously been eager to begin a significant temple construction campaign, which he proposed to God in 2 Samuel 8.[87] But how would he finance such a project? One generation later, when Solomon undertook to complete what his father had initiated, he found the costs so crushing that he ended up not only having to establish a forced-labor system to provide enough manpower,[88] but also having to cede land to the general contractor in order to try to cover the debt incurred.[89]

The account in 2 Samuel 24//1 Chronicles 21 of David's flirtation with empire-building might also be seen to raise, implicitly at least, the question of whether or not David thought that he had yet achieved an empire in the course of his subduing the promised land. I would argue that he did not—that he would have understood his accomplishments prior to that point as simply gaining the promised land, and nothing more. Interestingly, there is no evidence that in his prior accomplish-

---

85. Exod 30:11–16. See Stuart, *Exodus*, 635–39.

86. Indeed, it can hardly be doubted that if David had been in any way fuzzy on the concept of the risk of taking a census, he was clear on it by the time Joab had finished explaining it to him in the conversation of which that account is surely a précis.

87. He had committed himself at that point, at least, to building a temple (which meant, in fact, a large temple complex where the united tribes of Israel could gather for worship of Yahweh).

88. 1 Kgs 4:6; 5:14; 9:15–22; 11:28 (?); 12:4. His entire labor system was so burdensome that it was a central point in the rebellion of the northern tribes upon Solomon's death. The text nowhere specifically links the forced labor system to temple construction, but it is hard to imagine that such a great project would avoid utilizing such an available labor force.

89. Solomon's giving twenty towns to Hiram of Tyre, and Hiram's dissatisfaction with the payment (emphasizing all the more the huge cost of the temple) is described in 1 Kgs 9:10–14.

ments he needed to take a census; everything points to the fact that he had relied on a volunteer army in classic Holy War fashion (aside from the Philistine personal retinue mentioned above). But to go *beyond* the borders of the promised land? That apparently suggested to him quite vividly the need to put together as large an army as he could, with which he could begin to expand beyond Israel's assigned and traditional borders.

Does this mean that there is something wrong with a large kingdom, and that only small kingdoms are good? Here we find no evidence in the Old Testament for such an outlook. As far as can be discerned, the Old Testament says nothing either way about the desirability of small kingdoms as opposed to large kingdoms. But a mere kingdom (a single nation within a single recognized territory of a people who see themselves as united) is not the same thing as an empire (amalgamated from a variety of peripheral foreign nations subdued under the control of and for the benefit of a core nation).

4. Is the Story of the Census in 2 Samuel 24//1 Chronicles 21 Purposely Told in Such a Way That the Reader Is Intended to Understand That David Wanted to Establish an Empire—and Is the Reader Expected to Understand That Such a Lust for Empire Was a Major Sin?

I think that the answer to each part of this question is yes, and offer the following considerations from the details of the story in support.

First, consider the timing in David's career. The events take place at a point after David had in fact conquered the entire promised land and placed under his hegemony even surrounding nations in one form of oversight or another. The nation is unified, the necessity for new and large-scale warfare to gain yet more ground from enemy occupiers is no longer present, the army commanders such as Joab are freer than they would otherwise have been to undertake the planning for a war of empire, including the taking of a nationwide census, etc. All these point rather tellingly to a time when David was free from prior military commitments and could consider "going further." [90] The census itself was, as it were, ready and waiting—if empire was the goal.

---

[90]. A necessary caution comes in the fact that chs. 21–24 of 2 Samuel constitute a special appendix, which, as we have already commented, appears to be structured chiastically and thematically rather than chronologically, and to contain materials from various times in the king's career.

Second, there is the fact that David insisted on using Joab and senior military commanders to take the census. It is reasonable to assume that he wanted them to do the job not merely because they would be better at it than subordinates, but for two other reasons: First, because their confidence in the results was necessary if the substantial commitment required for such a war of conquest of empire was going to take place; and second, because their "clout" would be needed to convince the people being counted to cooperate. What David was doing was much bigger than a routine count to establish or continue "preparedness" for the holding of the promised land.

The strenuous objection of Joab[91] is certainly a major consideration in the way that the story is told. Joab, David's nephew, had served as his military commander/chief of staff for a very long time, and had engineered the stunning comeback against the far more numerous forces of Absalom in the battle of the Ephraimite woods.[92] His prior loyalty to David had been, as far as we can tell, absolute and unwavering.[93] For him now to object, and strongly, to what David has in mind suggests that there is something unprecedented in David's plan. It is not more of the same, but represents a plan to go beyond what Joab, and presumably anyone else, had "signed on for."

The narrator also brings to our attention a tell-tale wording that Joab uses in his as-diplomatic-as-possible speech of resistance to the king's desire for the count of the people: "May the Lord multiply the troops a hundred times over."[94] By using such a wording, Joab obviously indicates that he understands that what David wants is nothing short of a huge increase in the people under his rule. Joab indicates that he would be very happy to see a geometric increase in the population of Israel—but that is obviously not what David wants, or there would be no disagreement, no resistance on Joab's part to David's plan. What David wants is a huge increase, but not of the Israelite population by natural means during his lifetime. Far more likely, he seeks a conquest of non-

---

91. 2 Sam 24:3//1 Chr 21:3.

92. 2 Sam 18:1–17.

93. This included his willingness to assist David in dealing with Uriah as described in 2 Sam 11:14–25, in which there can be no doubt that Joab was a fully-informed and deliberate accomplice of David.

94. 2 Sam 24:3//1 Chr 21:3.

Israelite territories for the purpose of establishing an empire that will extend and augment the Israelite "core."

There is also a second significant wording that Joab uses: "will bring guilt on Israel." This wording, selected by the narrator to include in the account, leaves no doubt that Joab finds the order of the king flatly immoral. If the "guilt" was only a potential guilt for not taking the census correctly, the use of the prescribed ransom payment system would easily have put to rest that anxiety. This is apparently something altogether different. Joab fears that the nation will be in trouble with its God if the plan of the king is carried through. Imperialism requires not merely the will of a king but the compliance of a nation, whose people must be willing to (in the case of Israel) adopt a war footing beyond that required for the preservation of their own promised land inheritance and a willingness to send large armies massed against resistant foreign nations in order to subdue those nations decisively. This would indeed be a thing producing "guilt" and Joab is portrayed as not wanting to start the process for fear of the severe consequences.

A third tell-tale sign is found in Joab's refusal to count Levi and Benjamin in the census as described in the account found in 1 Chronicles 21, "because the king's command was repulsive to him."[95] Joab did indeed eventually bow to the king's insistent pressure, but not without dragging his feet on part of the count, so that two tribes were omitted in the figures, and their numbers presumably merely extrapolated from the counts otherwise found out by actual survey.[96] Our understanding of this refusal is that Joab (and presumably the military officials assisting him in the census) calculated that these two tribes represented the two places where they would be most likely to encounter hostility: one theological, the other political. He surely knew that the Levites, guardians of the doctrines of the Mosaic covenant, would oppose the census in light of its imperialistic purpose, because of their shared knowledge of the teachings of Moses.[97] He also surely knew that the tribe that had longest and more ardently opposed David's rule, the Benjaminites, would likely put

---

95. 1 Chr 21:6.

96. In other words, what Joab did to get around the especially delicate issue of counting the Levites and the Benjaminites was to guess intelligently at their numbers based on the other counts he had made and report them to the king, if at all, separately (as a harmonization of 1 Chr 21 with 2 Sam 24 would indicate).

97. As, e.g., in both in Exod 30:11–16 and Deut 20.

up resistance to his taking a census within their territory—something the kings they favored[98] would presumably never have done. Accordingly, Joab and his officers astutely avoided going into Benjaminite territory and simply presented the figures for that tribe as they did for the Levites: via extrapolation from the counts they were coming up with from other tribes who did allow them access to the people.

The elaborate geography of the census as described in 2 Samuel 24//1 Chronicles 21[99] is also surely intended to tell us that it was extraordinary, and perhaps even to make sure we get the point that it was taken against opposition. In general, the taking of narrative space to present details in Scripture is usually an indication of some sort of message being conveyed by such a taking of space.[100] In this instance, a census that takes the better part of a year and that was pressed in every village and town, every region and area (where cooperation was thought possible), is a census that seeks a certain kind of result: the enrollment of every possible soldier in light of the massive military task ahead that establishing an empire would represent.

The manner of the respective narrators in introducing the census story in 2 Samuel 24 and 1 Chronicles 21 is also significant. In the 2 Samuel account, the narrator begins by saying, "Again, the anger of the LORD burned against Israel and he incited David against them . . ." The Chronicler says essentially the same thing, but in what may be considered an even more dramatic fashion,[101] "Satan rose up against Israel and

---

98. I.e., Saul and his sons, as summed up in the brief history of Saul versus David told from a Benjaminite's point of view by Shimei in 2 Sam 16, esp. v. 8.

99. Most of the place names are omitted in the 1 Chr 21 account in a manner consistent with the Chronicler's avoidance of virtually anything northern, as he writes for the southern audience just returning from the exile in 530 BCE. See Cross, "Reconstruction."

100. A parade example of this is the detail expended in Judges 19 about the hospitality shown the Levite by his father-in-law as contrasted to the lack of hospitality shown him by the people of Gibeah, in whose city he had sought refuge precisely to receive Israelite hospitality as opposed to Jebusite hostility. Another example would be the detail given in Josh 7 about the use of the Urim and Thummim to determine who had taken spoils during the conquest of Jericho in the opening phase of the invasion of Canaan. Such detail makes clear that there was no doubt of divine disclosure in the use of the Urim and Thummim. In other words, Achan and his family were not put to death on the basis of somebody's casual detective work, but on the basis of a divinely-guided hand through multiple repetitions of the process of elimination, as elaborately recorded in the text.

101. The question may be raised: Is it more ominous to mention Satan as the proximate agent of inciting such a sinful act, or to mention that God himself was angry

incited David . . ." In the case of the Chronicler's wording, it is noteworthy that Satan is described as "standing" to incite.[102] This is the posture of the accuser in a court setting, as also found in Zech 3:1–2, Ps 109:6, and somewhat less overtly in Job 1–2.[103]

Editorial evaluations of immorality are so rare in the Old Testament as to be noteworthy whenever they surface. Thus, for the Chronicler to say in v. 7 of his account, "This command was also evil in the sight of God" is the equivalent of placing high in bright neon for the reader the reality that the king's plan was of great moral consequence, and therefore of horrendous scope.[104]

Further, the narrator in each account makes sure that the reader hears David's own full and frank admission of the greatness of his own guilt in seeking to establish a standing army for imperialistic purposes in 2 Sam 24:10//1 Chr 21:8, "David was conscience-stricken after he had counted the fighting men, and he said to the LORD, 'I have sinned greatly in what I have done . . . I have done a very foolish thing.'"[105]

Yet another consideration of the narrative's clues to us that the king's plan was far more than anything modest in scope is the intervention of a prophet at God's behest and as God's spokesperson.[106] Since under the rules of Holy War only a prophet can announce war (because no one else can be trusted to speak God's word directly and verbatim

---

enough to incite the action that he knew would result in punishment? The Chronicler's wording could in fact be considered gentler, because it does not as overtly say that the census was itself a punishment brought about by the wrath of God.

102. Heb. וַיַּעֲמֹד שָׂטָן עַל־יִשְׂרָאֵל, lit., "and Satan stood up against Israel."

103. In the Job prologue, Satan and the other principalities and powers present themselves before Yahweh in his heavenly court, and are therefore surely standing, but not specifically as prosecutors against a defendant (accusers of a saint or of the saints), as is Satan in the other Old Testament contexts where he is named. The present passage is one of only four contexts in the Old Testament where Satan is mentioned by name (i.e., places where Heb. שָׂטָן, śāṭān, functions as a proper noun/title in the Old Testament rather than as a common noun, "opponent/adversary"), the others being the prologue to Job (Job 1 and 2); Zech 3; and Ps 109.

104. The writer of 2 Samuel had already said essentially the same thing in v. 1 of his account. For another rare instance in the Former Prophets, see 2 Sam 11:27, "But the thing David had done displeased the LORD" (referring to David's "great sin," the adultery with Bathsheba and the murder of Uriah).

105. Paralleled to some extent in the open confession of David as to his guilt in 2 Sam 12:13.

106. Again parallel to 2 Sam 12:1–15 where the prophet Nathan is sent by God to announce to David the consequence of his sin.

in such an important situation) it is fitting that the prophet Gad arrives to underscore the divine disapproval and to offer the divine options for punishment. In other words, it is not David or anyone else in his retinue that comes up with the idea of the punishments as a penance, but rather it is God himself who insists that major punishment must be meted out for so major a sin.

The appearance of the Angel of Yahweh to handle the punishment is yet another indicator of the severity of what David has set in motion, particularly since here alone in the Old Testament the Angel of Yahweh plays the role of a dispenser of punishment against Israel. In all other places he is a protector and benefactor of God's people and one who leads them into blessing.[107]

Additionally, comparable to the way that the threat via punishment is huge (three three-time period options, administered in the event directly by the Angel of Yahweh, etc.) the removal of the threat is huge—David's being able to see the Angel of Yahweh, his buying the threshing floor of Araunah and there building an altar in parallel to the altar stories of Abraham, Jacob, and Moses; and most especially God's sending down "fire from heaven"[108] to accept his sacrifice, an event of great supernatural portent parallel to the indication of approval by fire in the story of Elijah's prayer contest with the prophets of Baal in 1 Kings 18.

To sum up: it is hard to imagine that the Bible writer in either 2 Samuel 24 or 1 Chronicles 21 would or could likely say more by way of condemnation of David's plan. What else would have effectively added to the many, varied, overt indications of what a serious violation of God's covenant this was? If the writer had added anything else, he or she might well have risked offending the sensibilities of the audience. It already borders on excess to say so much by way of condemnation of this census and its implicit purpose. And therefore, by implication, were we *not* to go so far as to identify David's actions as indicating a plan for an empire we might be reasonably accused of exercising more caution than the remarkably special nature of this account warrants. In light of the unprecedented nature of the condemnatory elements worked into the narrative by its respective writers, it would seem that we are expected

---

107. E.g., Gen 16:7–14; 22:11–18; Exod 3:2–12; et al. The Angel of the Lord opposes Balaam (Num 22:21–27) but that is for the benefit of the Israelites.

108. 1 Chr 21:25, more briefly rendered in 2 Sam 24:25 via the simple statement, "then the LORD answered prayer . . ."

to see David's goal as unprecedented as well: an expansion of Israel that would be nothing short of the creation of an empire.

Finally, notice that the story concludes in such a way as to suggest an alternative to empire building—a goal different from empire that is in fact the "more excellent way" that God intends for his people and therefore for David to pursue as their leader. David's attempt at empire was divinely truncated because of the way that imperialism represented a defiance of God's purposes for his covenant people. In effect, God graciously diverted David's energies toward an altogether appropriate covenantally-approved direction, that of establishing finally the centrality of worship in Jerusalem in fulfillment of the promises and predictions of the central sanctuary in Deuteronomy 12.[109] It is in this direction that the story ends, with David chastened, the people shocked into obedience, no more thought of empire, and a grateful king and people focused on worship of the true God rather than violation of one of his basic conditions of their existence in the promised land.

Summary

David knew both the mentality of the ancient Near East that was positive toward empire, and the "mentality" the Old Testament—God's mentality—that was hostile toward empire. After operating within the Old Testament mentality in his early years of completing the conquest of the promised land, he became infatuated with the Near Eastern mentality of empire and decided to give it a try. This produced disaster, but a pre-emptive one, in which God prevented David from taking to fruition his intent, an intent shown in his taking of a census in preparation for a war or wars of imperialistic conquest. God graciously turned the entire fiasco around, though not before exacting a heavy toll on David and his people by way of punishment and warning, and provided instead a spiritual focus as a substitute for what had been potentially a disastrous military-political one.

---

109. This is, of course, what David had wanted to do in the first place (1 Sam 8, at a time in his life when his goals were more properly focused), and should have been happy to settle for, however much he would rather have built the temple himself than allowing Solomon that honor.

BIBLIOGRAPHY

Clough, A. A., trans. *Plutarch's Lives*. Vol. 2. Hazleton, PA: Penn State Electronic Classics Series, 2003.
Cross, F. M., Jr. "A Reconstruction of the Judean Restoration." *JBL* 94 (1975) 4–18.
Gardiner, Alan. *Egyptian Grammar*. 3rd ed. London: Oxford University Press, 1966.
Gordon, Robert. *1 and 2 Samuel*. Grand Rapids: Regency/Zondervan, 1998.
Hallo, William W., and K. Lawson Younger, editors. *The Context of Scripture*. 3 vols. Leiden: Brill, 1997–2002.
King, L. W. *Chronicles concerning Early Babylonian Kings*. Vol. 2. London: Luzac, 1907. Reprint, Ann Arbor: University Reprints, 2005.
Mendenhall, George. "The Census Lists of Numbers 1 and 26." *JBL* 77 (1958) 52–66.
Moran, W. L. "The Ancient Near Eastern Background of the Love of God in Deuteronomy." *CBQ* 77 (1963) 77–87.
Motyl, Alexander J. *Imperial Ends: The Decay, Collapse, and Revival of Empires*. New York: Columbia University Press, 2001.
Pratt, Richard. *1 and 2 Chronicles*. Fearn, U.K.: Mentor, 1998.
Sparks, Kenton L. *Ancient Texts for the Study of the Hebrew Bible*. Peabody, MA: Hendrickson, 2005.
Speiser, E. A. "The Legend of Sargon." *ANET* 119.
Stuart, Douglas. *Exodus*. NAC. Nashville: Broadman & Holman, 2006
———. *Micah–Malachi*. WBC. Nashville: Thomas Nelson, forthcoming.
———. "The Sovereign's Day of Conquest." *BASOR* 221 (1976) 159–64.
Von Rad, Gerhard. *Old Testament Theology*. 2 vols. New York: Harper, 1962.
Wilson, John A., translator. "The War against the Hyksos." *ANET* 232–33.
Wiseman, D. J. "The Vassal-Treaties of Esarhaddon." *Iraq* 20 (1958) 266–68.
Wright, G. Ernest. *The Old Testament against Its Environment*. London: SCM, 1950.

2

Walking in the Light of Yahweh
Zion and the Empires in the Book of Isaiah

MARK J. BODA

INTRODUCTION

IN THE EARLY EIGHTH century BCE, two kings rose to power in Israel and Judah whose long reigns witness to the independence of their kingdoms from external influence. Under Uzziah (Judah) and Jeroboam II (Israel), the combined territory of the two kingdoms would equal that boasted for Solomon. Ironically, Uzziah's reign of 52 years (2 Kgs 15:2) and Jeroboam II's reign of 41 years (2 Kgs 14:23) represented not the beginning, but the end of the period of imperial freedom for the kingdoms. It was in many ways the calm before the storm.

Jeroboam II would be followed by a quick succession of kings (Zechariah, Shallum, Menahem, Pekahiah, Pekah) whose relatively short reigns highlight the political instability of the northern kingdom. Menahem's tribute to Tiglath Pileser III, noted in the Old Testament and ancient Near Eastern inscriptions (2 Kgs 15:19–20; see *ANET* 283; *COS* 2:285 2.117A; 2:287 2.117B), would only slow the rising Assyrian threat. Five years and two monarchs later, the same Assyrian king would depose the Israelite Pekah and install his own puppet Hoshea (2 Kgs 15:29–30; *COS* 2:288 2.117C), signaling the end of Israel's independence. Propped up by the Assyrians, Hoshea would last a decade on the throne, but upon his refusal to pay tribute to Shalmaneser V and his appeal to the Egyptian So for help (2 Kgs 17:3–6), the Assyrians would bring an end to Israel as a vassal kingdom, incorporating its territory as a province into its empire and exiling many of its people to Mesopotamia.[1]

These imperial incursions against the northern kingdom (Israel) were a harbinger of things to come for the even weaker Judean kingdom to the south. Uzziah's death, approximately fourteen years after that of Jeroboam II, would also signal a new era in Judah's relationship with the surrounding empires. The instability of the kingdoms to the north (Israel and Aram-Damascus) meant that the buffer zone between Mesopotamia and Judah was in danger of disappearing. The desperation of these two northern kingdoms also explains their threats against the kings who followed Uzziah, especially Ahaz (Isaiah 7).

It is in this historico-political context that Isaiah appears on the national stage (Isa 6:1). Although Israel and Judah had experienced imperial threats prior to this point, even paying tribute to Mesopotamian powers,[2] the second half of the eighth century would see a transition to a permanent imperial political presence in the Levant, evidenced in the incorporation of Aram-Damascus and Israel as provinces within the growing Assyrian empire.

It is clear from ancient sources that Ahaz and Hezekiah felt Assyrian pressure, the latter experiencing an invasion at the hand of Sennacherib probably designed to incorporate Judah into the Assyrian empire. Although, after Hezekiah, pressure from Assyria was slightly reduced, ancient inscriptions reveal that Assyrian pressure on Judah continued until at least the mid-seventh century BCE, with tribute being delivered to Sennacherib's successors Esarhaddon and Ashurbanipal.[3] The weak-

---

1. In the Assyrian annals, it is Sargon II (Shalmaneser's successor) who would claim to have defeated Samaria and exiled its people: see *ANET* 284–87; *COS* 2.118A; *COS* 2.118D. Some have suggested that Sargon was the general under Shalmaneser or that Shalmaneser died during the siege of Samaria so that Sargon was king by the time the city was defeated. Notice *COS* 3:270–71, a court order from Samaria concerning repayment of a loan for work animals with evidence of a mixed population in Samaria (cf. 2 Kgs 17:24–30).

2. Notice the tribute paid by Jehoash (father of Jeroboam II) to Adad-nirari III in 796; Jehu's tribute to Shalmaneser III in 841 (*ANET* 280–81; *COS* 2.113F); Shalmaneser III's defeat of Ahab and Hadad-ezer of Damascus at Qarqar in 853 BCE (*COS* 2:263–64) and the much earlier invasion of Shishak (Shoshenq I) into the Levant (*ANET* 242–43, 263–64; *ANEP* 349; 1 Kgs 14:25–28).

3. *ANET* 291 shows evidence of Manasseh taking tribute to Esarhaddon (678 BCE) and of Ashurbanipal's defeat of Manasseh along with the kings of Tyre and Edom

ening state of Assyria after Ashurbanipal's death (631 BCE) is probably reflected in the long reign of Josiah (640–609 BCE). This short respite from Mesopotamian pressure would function much like that of Uzziah in an earlier era. However, the death of Josiah at the hand of the Egyptian Pharaoh Neco at Megiddo signaled the end of Judean control over their own political affairs, as first the Egyptians and then the Babylonians would set up their own puppet kings in the "vassal" kingdom.[4] By 587 BCE Nebuchadnezzar's patience with rebellious Judean vassals had come to an end, so the Babylonian emperor reconstituted Judah as a province within his empire with Mizpah as provincial capital, while exiling its elite to the Mesopotamian heartland.[5] The fall of Babylon, however, in 539 BCE at the hands of the Persians would provide no reprieve for the Jews from imperial domination. Although the Persians would facilitate their return to the land and reconstruction of their temple in Jerusalem, Judah (now, Yehud) would remain a tiny province, at first within the satrapy of Babylonia-Abar-Nahara (the former Babylonian empire), and later the even smaller satrapy of Abar-Nahara within the sprawling Persian empire. Persian control would eventually give way to Greek (332 BCE). Judah would not regain kingdom status until the hiatus of the Maccabeans in the second century BCE, brought to an end by the invasion of the Roman Pompeii in 63 BCE.

The book of Isaiah thus offers some of the first theological reflections on Judah's identity in a world dominated by empire and, as the book progresses, it presents audiences living under increasing and enduring imperial domination.[6] In the first phase (chs. 6–39), Judah is presented

---

(*ANET* 294–95). *ANET* 301 shows tribute given to Ashurbanipal by "the inhabitants of Judah" along with tribute from Ammon, Moab, and Edom.

4. Interestingly this perspective is expressed most accurately by the Chronicler. See Boda, "Identity and Empire."

5. See Lipschitz, *Fall and Rise of Jerusalem*.

6. This paper generally avoids discussing the much larger issue of the authorship and redaction of the book of Isaiah. For detailed presentation of the history of scholarship on this see Sweeney, *Isaiah 1–4*, 4–54; Williamson, *Isaiah*. I am treating the book as a canonical unity and offering a reading of the book in light of the shifting audience(s) which can be discerned as the book progresses sequentially. For recent forays in this direction, see especially Childs, *Introduction*, 325–34; Clements, "Unity"; Brueggemann, "Unity and Dynamic"; Davies, "Destiny"; Evans, "Unity and Parallel Structure"; Seitz, "Isaiah 1–66"; Webb, "Zion in Transformation"; Oswalt, "Nations in Isaiah," although cf. Sawyer, *Fifth Gospel*; Carr, "Reaching for Unity"; Carr, "Reading Isaiah"; Coggins, "Do We Still Need Deutero-Isaiah?"

as an independent kingdom facing the threat of an imposing yet external imperial force. In the second phase (chs. 40–55), Judah is depicted as a community exiled to the center of a foreign empire. In the third phase (chs. 56–66), Judah is portrayed as living in its own land as a province within the largest empire the world had ever known. Each of these three phases provides its own unique approach to empire and the purpose of this paper is to highlight the way in which the book of Isaiah shaped Judah's response to empire. Isaiah 1–5, with its focus on Zion, introduces these various phases in the Isaianic witness. It is there that this paper will begin in order to see how it shapes the reading of the book as a whole.

ISAIAH 1–5: THE HOLY ONE AND ZION

It is surprising to many, especially those who have read the books of Jeremiah and Ezekiel, that the call of the prophet Isaiah is not reported until ch. 6. Some have explained this historically, noting that Isa 1:1 refers to Isaiah's ministry during the reign of Uzziah, concluding that Isaiah 1–5 represents the prophet's utterances in the earliest period.[7] Others have challenged this, noting that a ministry that spanned the reigns of Uzziah to Hezekiah is inordinately long. A closer look at the initial chapter of Isaiah suggests that these initial chapters were placed at the beginning of the book of Isaiah for literary rather than historical reasons.

Isaiah 1

The two superscriptions at 1:1 and 2:1 divide Isaiah 1–5 into two sections. The first one (1:1) appears to function as a superscription for at least Isaiah 1–39, in that it identifies the kings who appear in the first and last superscriptions tied to the reign of a king (6:1; 36:1). An investigation of Isaiah 1 confirms the suspicion that it does not reflect the period before the death of Uzziah. Reference is made in this section to a Jerusalem that is in serious trouble, a city under siege and left alone among the fortified cities (1:7–8). Reference is made to survivors who barely escaped from this siege (1:9). The period that appears to be reflected in this opening chapter is that of Sennacherib's siege against the land of Judah during the reign of Hezekiah. There Jerusalem is left as the last holdout after the Assyrians had taken all the Judean fortified cities (36:1) and there

---

7. Thus Isaiah 6 would be a commissioning for a task and not Isaiah's initial call. Cf. Kaplan, "Isaiah 6:1–11"; Milgrom, "Did Isaiah Prophesy"; Williamson, *Isaiah*, 33 n. 7.

is an emphasis on the remnant that survived Assyrian aggression (Isa 37:4, 31–32). This preliminary evidence, therefore, suggests that Isaiah 1 represents the latest phase of Isaiah's prophetic utterances (during the reign of Hezekiah) rather than the earliest phase.

This opening chapter consists of two prophetic pieces: a covenant lawsuit in 1:2–20 followed by an announcement of judgment in 1:21–31. In the covenant lawsuit, the prophet outlines a clear case against the people, ending the speech with an invitation to repent, accompanied by a warning that refusal will lead to destruction. The announcement of judgment in the second half of the chapter reveals that the people ultimately would not turn from their rebellion, but instead would be refined by God's judgment, a process that would transform Zion into a righteous and faithful city.

In this way Isaiah 1 is a fitting introduction not only for chs. 1–39, but also for the entire book.[8] Speaking to a people who are rebellious and stubborn, the prophet will offer them grace, but in the end, when they do not turn, they will be judged. This judgment will not be merely for punishment's sake, but for purging them of their impurities. Additionally, this opening chapter identifies the two major characters of the book of Isaiah: Zion-Jerusalem (1:8, 21, 26, 27) and Yahweh, the Holy One of Israel (1:4).

Isaiah 2–5

Isaiah 2:1, however, comprises a second superscription, one that distinguishes ch. 1 from chs. 2–5 in what appears to be this literary introduction to the book. In these chapters the prophetic messages vacillate back and forth between two visions of Zion-Jerusalem. Isaiah 2:1–5 offers the vision of the great purpose of the book of Isaiah, and many have noted resonances between this section and Isaiah 66 where the book ends.[9] Isaiah 2:1–5 describes the ultimate goal of Jerusalem, that is, that it would become a hub for the nations. Centripetal and centrifugal forces are evident in this Zion, with the nations being drawn to it (vv. 2b–3a, centripetal) and the Torah going out from it (vv. 3b–4, centrifugal).

This will happen because the mountain will become chief among the mountains of the world, an image that shows Zion to be the place

---

8. Cf. Fohrer, "Jesaja 1."

9. See Davies, "Destiny," 93. See also Sweeney, "Isaiah as Prophetic Torah," who shows how the vision of Torah in Isa 2:1–5 is developed throughout the book as a whole.

where the ruler of the universe, Yahweh the king, sits and reigns (compare Psalm 48).[10] But how will such a radical vision ever become a reality, since ch. 1 has described a vastly different city and nation than this? How will Zion become such a place for the nations? The answer is that it must first become the community described in ch. 4. In 4:2–6 the prophet looks to a day when Zion and Jerusalem will be filled with a remnant that is holy (vv. 3–4) and will be protected by Yahweh's presence in its midst (vv. 5–6).

In contrast, the other pericopae in chs. 2–5, which surround these two positive visions, highlight the present reality of Zion. Exemplary is 5:1–7, which employs the image of the vineyard and describes Israel, Judah, and Jerusalem as a vineyard that has not responded to the care of the vinedresser. At the core of chs. 2–5, then, lie two competing visions of Zion, vacillating in this section between the present bad Zion and the future good Zion.

Zion and Empire

The introduction of the book of Isaiah highlights Zion as a key leitmotif for the book.[11] The centripetal and centrifugal vision of Zion's role on earth in ch. 2 resonates with the broader presentation of the Zion tradition in the Old Testament.[12] For instance, Psalm 48 reveals that Zion is the city of the great king, the joy of the whole earth, impregnable to the crafty designs of rebellious kings. Psalm 2 reveals that Zion is the place on earth from which Yahweh rules over the kings and nations of the earth.

The Zion tradition represents the imperial tradition within the Old Testament because the Holy One of Israel is depicted as ruling the world

---

10. This echoes the ultimate purpose of the book of Isaiah, which envisions by the end in Isa 66:18–21 the nations gathering to see Yahweh's glory.

11. As does Seitz, "Isaiah 1–66," 122, suggesting the book could be called: "The Drama of God and Zion." Seitz, *Zion's Final Destiny*, 146, identifies Zion theology as being "responsible for the extension of Isaiah's oracles beyond their original eighth-century setting." Cf. Roberts, "Isaiah in Old Testament Theology," 136; Dumbrell, "Purpose of the Book of Isaiah"; Williamson, *Isaiah*, 241–42; Clements, "Zion"; Hoppe, *Holy City*. Oswalt, "Nations in Isaiah," 42, 51, and Davies, "Destiny," 105, emphasize the relationship between Zion and the nations.

12. For this see especially Porteous, "Jerusalem-Zion"; Weinfeld, "Zion and Jerusalem"; Ollenburger, *Zion*; Clements, "Zion"; Hess and Wenham, eds., *Zion, City of Our God*; Hoppe, *Holy City*; Levenson, *Sinai and Zion*. With thanks to Hyukki Kim and Lois Fuller Dow for rich conversations about Zion. See Dow, *Images of Zion*.

from Zion.[13] And yet it is this ideal that is threatened in Isaiah's day. The city does not reflect the character of its emperor and so either its inhabitants must bring themselves into conformity with his values or the city will be purified by Yahweh's judgment.

Strikingly absent from the Zion tradition at the outset of Isaiah, however, is a connection to the Davidic royal tradition, a connection seen in Psalms 2, 110, and 132.[14] Although Ollenburger has argued cogently that the Zion tradition should be neither subsumed under the Davidic tradition nor inextricably linked to it, the absence of the latter is striking in light of the close association with Davidic figures in the next section of Isaiah (chs. 6–39).[15] The focus in the introduction to the book (chs. 1–5) is exclusively on the imperial rule of the Holy One of Israel from Zion-Jerusalem, his capital. In this capital, holy citizens will enjoy their emperor's presence and protection. To this capital the nations will come to pay homage and from this capital justice will emanate to the nations.

ISAIAH 6–39

Isaiah 6: The Prophet and the Holy One

This image of Zion as imperial seat of the Holy One of Israel informs the presentation of Isaiah's call in ch. 6. In a visionary experience dated to the year of the death of the Davidic king Uzziah, the prophet is granted a vision of Yahweh as divine "king" (v. 5) seated on an exalted throne (v. 1),

---

13. On the imperial ideology and Zion, see Roberts, "Zion in the Theology of the Davidic-Solomonic Empire," 108; Weinfeld, "Zion and Jerusalem," 94–100.

14. Contra von Rad, *Old Testament Theology*, 1:174; Roberts, "Zion in the Theology of the Davidic-Solomonic Empire"; Weinfeld, "Zion and Jerusalem"; Mays, "Isaiah's Royal Theology"; and Roberts, "Isaiah in Old Testament Theology," who import too much Davidic theology into Isaiah's Zion theology. Von Rad suggests this problem when he writes that it is "strange to see how detached and almost unconnected the two traditions are even as late as Isaiah" (*Old Testament Theology*, 1:174). So also Roberts, who admits: "Isaiah very often appears to ignore the human king" ("Isaiah in Old Testament Theology,"138). More accurate on this is Ollenburger, *Zion*, 139–40, who concludes: "While in the Near Eastern texts the language is always employed in the interests of glorifying the king, in the Zion texts of the Old Testament it is always Yahweh who is glorified, never the king." Some of the problem is confusion between the sociological origins and the theological use of the Zion traditions.

15. See Ollenburger, *Zion*, and Levenson, "Zion Traditions," 6:1100, yet compare Roberts, "Davidic Origin of the Zion Tradition"; Roberts, "Zion in the Theology of the Davidic-Solomonic Empire."

surrounded by heavenly attendants (v. 2), identifying him as the "holy, holy, holy" one whose "glory" fills the whole earth (v. 3). The call of the prophet is to proclaim to the people until all that is left is "a holy seed" (v. 13), that is, a community whose character matches their king.

What is envisioned here is a two-stage purification; the first results in a great destruction that will literally decimate the population, leaving only a tenth as a remnant. But even this surviving remnant will be destroyed and the only "memory" left will be the "seed" of a once mighty tree. These two stages foreshadow the reality described in Isaiah 7–39. Ahaz's folly would result in the decimation of the kingdom in Hezekiah's day as Assyria overran the nation. Although Hezekiah would survive as a remnant, his own folly with the Babylonian envoys—reported in ch. 39—would cause the ultimate complete destruction and exile of Judah.

Isaiah 7–12 and 36–39: The Tale of Two Kings

Isaiah 6, thus, introduces the larger literary complex of Isaiah 7–39, a section that is bracketed by the narratives of two Judean kings who were the first to face the growing Mesopotamian imperial threat: Ahaz (7–12) and his son Hezekiah (36–39).[16] These two sections of Isaiah share several elements in common:

- Both contain a mixture of narrative and poetry.
- Both have an assault on Jerusalem by a foreigner (Isa 7:1–6 and 36:1–2).
- Both narratives are set in motion by a meeting "at the aqueduct of the Upper Pool, on the road to the Washerman's Field" (Isa 7:3 and 36:2).
- In both, Isaiah calls on the king to trust in Yahweh, beginning both speeches with the phrase "Do not be afraid" (Isa 7:4 and 37:6).
- In both, a sign accompanies a promise from Yahweh (Isa 7:14 and 38:7–8). The latter is linked to Ahaz by the fact that Hezekiah's sign takes place on Ahaz's stairway.
- Both use the phrase "zeal of the Lord Almighty will accomplish" (Isa 9:7 and 37:32).

16. See Seitz, *Zion's Final Destiny*, 195–96; Conrad, *Reading Isaiah*, 34–51; cf. Oswalt, *Isaiah 1–39*, 55, 629–30.

But while these elements connect the two sections, a series of differences identify Ahaz as a foil, that is, a dark backdrop against which one is to see Hezekiah more brilliantly:

- While Isaiah must go to Ahaz (Isa 7:3), Isaiah is invited by Hezekiah (37:2).
- While Ahaz considers Assyria the answer to his problem, Hezekiah faces Assyria as the problem.
- While Ahaz faces the threat of invasion by two small nations (Isa 7:1), Hezekiah faces an actual invasion by a vast army (36:8–10, 36).
- While Ahaz does not trust God by making alliance with Assyria, Hezekiah ultimately trusts God and sees the defeat of Assyria.

The key theme that drives this comparison is that of faith, introduced first in Isaiah's speech to Ahaz in 7:9: "If you will not believe, you surely shall not last" (NASB). Faced with an invasion by the kingdoms of Israel and Aram-Damascus, Ahaz succumbs to the temptation to appeal to Assyria for help. In the short run this alleviated the pressure from the kingdoms directly to the north, but in the long run it led to the demise of those northern kingdoms and the advance of the Assyrian imperial borders to just north of Jerusalem. It is of this that Isaiah reminds the audience in 8:7–8 when he describes the Assyrian emperor as "the strong and abundant waters of the Euphrates," which will "rise up over all its channels and go over all its banks" and then "it will sweep on into Judah, it will overflow and pass through, it will reach even to the neck; and the spread of its wings will fill the breadth of your land, O Immanuel" (NASB). What Ahaz invites in his own time, because of a lack of trust in Yahweh, will ultimately flood his own land, a prophecy of the military invasion experienced by his son Hezekiah a generation later.

The description of Hezekiah's response to the invasion in his time stands in stark contrast to that of his father Ahaz. He responds to the Assyrian emperor's (Sennacherib's) first intimidating speech by tearing his clothes, entering the temple of Yahweh, and appealing to Yahweh's prophet Isaiah (37:1–7). After Sennacherib's second intimidation through a letter, Hezekiah voices his trust in Yahweh through a prayer in the temple (37:14–20), to which Yahweh responds with a prophetic message through Isaiah (37:21–35).

Isaiah 13–35: The Destiny of the Nations

These two accounts of Judean kings function as a bracket around chs. 7–39 and are designed to influence the reading of the sections that lie between them.[17] What dominates chs. 13–35 is a concern over the nations and God's clear message that he will defeat these nations, including the great imperial powers of Isaiah's time. At the heart of the oracle series in chs. 13–23 are two oracles introduced by the term *hoy* and found in 17:12–14 and 18:1–7. The nation referred to in 18:1–7 is explicitly identified as Cush (18:1), and most commentators agree that the nation in 17:12–14 is Assyria. Thus at the center of this complex of nations are the two nations vying for imperial status in the days of Isaiah. Bracketing this entire section are Babylon (13:1–22) and Tyre (23:1–18), two people groups in the Assyrian period representing key western (Tyre) and eastern (Babylon) groups, powerful naval (Tyre) and land (Babylon) forces, and commercial (Tyre) and cultural (Babylon) forces. Interestingly, at the end of the collection (Isa 23:13), in a section concerning the destruction of Tyre, the prophet calls Tyre to look at the land of the Babylonians whose city has experienced destruction at the hand of the Assyrians.[18] What is clear from all of these oracles against the nations in chs. 13–23 is that the nations will be no match for the divine warrior Yahweh. The message of chs. 13–23 is as follows: do not put your trust in the nations for they will all meet their demise at the hand of Yahweh who rules the world.

---

17. This is not to discount the way in which the account of Hezekiah in chs. 36–39 functions as a transition to the latter half of the book, cf. Ackroyd, "Interpretation of the Babylonian Exile"; Ackroyd, "Isaiah 36–39"; Clements, "Unity," 120–21; Childs, *Isaiah*, 266. It should be noted that the connections to chs. 7–12 are to be found in chs. 36–38. Chapter 39 is the passage that shows the failure of Hezekiah. The same may be said for chs. 34–35, which Clements, "Beyond Tradition-History," 98, says "consciously anticipates and summarizes the major themes of chs. 40–55"; cf. Childs, *Isaiah*, 255–56.

18. Although rooted in the Assyrian crisis, the prophecies against Babylon at the outset of this collection also foreshadow the ultimate imperial role played by Babylon seen in ch. 39. In this way those responsible for the final form of Isaiah are applying principles from the Assyrian period to later communities. See, e.g., Begg, "Babylon in the Book of Isaiah," 123; Williamson, *Isaiah*. Clements applies the development of chs. 13–14 as a model for the development of the book as a whole; see Clements, "Unity."

This international vision is expanded in what is often called the "Little Apocalypse" in Isaiah 24–27, as two cities are contrasted: the earthly city of destruction (24:12) and the divine city of salvation (26:1). Using universal and cosmic imagery, this section sums up the message of chs. 13–23, that is, that God will judge the nations, establishing his rule from Zion and bringing honor to himself. His people, the remnant, will emerge in the end but will need to live through those times by faith.

Having dealt with the nations in a particular historical manner (13–23) and in a universal cosmic manner (24–27), Isaiah 28–33 then focuses on the inappropriate responses of the community of Isaiah's day.[19] At the core of this section are the woe (*hoy*) oracles of 29:1—31:9, which attack the human schemes and alliances (see עֵצָה; 29:15; 30:1) between the people of Jerusalem and the national powers of the day, a vivid example of the lack of trust these people had in their God. The message of this section of Isaiah is for the people to trust in Yahweh rather than in the nations (28:16; 30:15, 18; 31:1). Chapters 34–35 conclude the core of Isaiah 7–39 with its focus on the nations by offering a summary of its main themes, focusing on both God's judgment and his grace and foreshadowing the next literary phase of the book in Isaiah 40–55.

The Kings and the Nations

Isaiah 13–35, with its description of the ultimate destruction of the nations and empires, is designed to shape the reader's evaluation of Ahaz's folly and the reader's experience of Hezekiah's challenge in chs. 36–37. The narrative of chs. 36–37 reveals that when stripped of all his resources, Hezekiah did indeed cast himself and his nation upon the mercy of God, and Yahweh answered his prayer. Ultimately, however, ch. 39 reveals that even as Hezekiah displayed the faith commanded in 7:4–9 and prompted by chs. 13–35, he succumbed to the folly of trusting in the nations by dialoguing with the Babylonian envoys, forging a relationship with the Babylonians that initiated the ultimate demise of Judah. This represents the fulfillment of Isaiah's prophetic vision in ch. 6. The decimated remnant represented by Hezekiah in Zion would be ultimately destroyed, leaving only a memory through the seed of exilic Judah.

---

19. On the role of chs. 28–33 in the book of Isaiah as a whole, see Stansell, "Isaiah 28–33."

Isaiah 6–39 and Empire

As already noted in the historical introduction, the long reigns of Uzziah and his counterpart in the north, Jeroboam II, represented the final period of Israelite independence before the permanent rise of Mesopotamian imperial power.[20] It is thus not surprising that the account of Isaiah 6–39 begins in the year of Uzziah's death and provides a vision of Yahweh as king. As the Judeans are busy rearranging the chairs on their monarchial Titanic, the prophet is given a vision of one who is truly the king of the world. This thrice holy king rules from his palace on Zion, from which his glory permeates the whole earth.

Sent from the presence of this King, the Holy One of Israel, the prophet's message to Judah's royal house enthroned in Jerusalem is that they must not be intimidated by empire, nor tempted to trust in other anti-imperial political forces. Rather they are to trust in Yahweh alone who will protect and sustain them. Faced with political ruin, two kings are called by the prophet to put their faith in Yahweh and not fear the nations and empires of their day. Although the prophet provides pictures of the kind of royal figure demanded by Yahweh (Isa 9:6–7; 11:1–12; 16:4–5; cf. 32:1–2),[21] both of the Davidides in the book ultimately fail the test and their failure results in the ruin of the nation by the successive empires of Assyria and Babylon.[22]

Foreign empire in Isaiah 6–39 is viewed skeptically. Imperial forces are not to be trusted and interactions with them will only lead to disaster. The consistent call is to trust in Yahweh as the Holy One of Israel who has the authority and power to discipline and rule the nations. The Judean royal house is tempted to conceptualize itself in light of the view of empire prevalent in its day. Yahweh challenges this royal house

---

20. Josiah would enjoy a period of independence, but only because the imperial "baton" was being passed from Assyria to Babylon; cf. Boda, *Haggai/Zechariah*.

21. See Boda, *1–2 Chronicles*, 147–64. Although Quinn-Miscall is correct in noticing Isaiah's concerns with the kings in his own era, his attempts to interpret allusions to an ideal royal figure as merely hope for general messianic conditions are inappropriate. See Quinn-Miscall, *Reading Isaiah*, 172.

22. As admitted by Roberts, "Isaiah in Old Testament Theology," 139: "To a great extent Isaiah's description of the ideal future king, as does his description of the future Jerusalem, represents a devaluation or criticism of the present holders of that office; and his disgust with the contemporary house of David may be one reason why the promises to David figure no more prominently in his message than they do. Moreover, as in the case of the Zion hymns, Isaiah was more concerned with glorifying the divine king than with spelling out the role of his human agent."

to adopt a view of human and divine empire shaped by the vision of the Holy One of Israel. Although such a vision would ensure that Judah would not merely survive but thrive within its political environment, this vision demands that the royal house discharge all claims to kingship in Judah and entrust themselves and their kingdom into the hands of Yahweh.

ISAIAH 40–55

The historical context of the audience addressed after Isaiah 39 is not explicitly articulated in the text. Whereas throughout Isaiah 1–39 historical superscriptions link the material to a particular time period (1:1; 2:1; 6:1; 7:1; 14:28; 36:1), from Isaiah 40 onward such superscriptions are absent. The structure of Isaiah 1–39, ending as it does with the prophecy of the exile in 39:5–7, is the first indication that the audience of Isaiah 40 is the community in the Babylonian period.[23] The prophecy itself confirms this with clear evidence that it is directed to a community in need of comfort, which is situated in Babylon and nearing the end of its "hard service."[24] For this community, a Persian king named Cyrus who arose during the Babylonian period is identified as an expected deliverer.

Therefore, Isaiah 40–55 addresses the community that would experience the discipline resulting from the folly of Ahaz and Hezekiah in chs. 6–39. The trust of these two kings in rising Mesopotamian imperial forces (Ahaz in Assyria, Hezekiah in Babylon) is linked in 39:5–7 to the exile of Judah to the heart of the Mesopotamian empire ("in the palace of the king of Babylon"). It is to this community that Isaiah 40–55 is addressed.

---

23. What Clements, "Beyond Tradition-History," 98, calls "an important editorial 'bridge' between the threat to Jerusalem posed by the Assyrians and that which was later posed by the armies of Babylon," cf. Clements, "Unity," 120–21; Begg, "Babylon in the Book of Isaiah," 121–25. Some treat all of chs. 36–39 or even chs. 34–39 in this way, cf. Conrad, *Reading Isaiah*, 50–51; Clements, "Unity," 120–21; Seitz, *Zion's Final Destiny*. I appreciate the distinction Webb makes between chs. 36–37, which are more closely related to what precedes, and chs. 38–39, which look to what follows. See Webb, "Zion in Transformation," 69–70.

24. Contrast Seitz, *Zion's Final Destiny*, 206, who argues against fixation on an exilic context. However, the one responsible for 48:20 ("Leave Babylon, flee from the Babylonians!") appears to point in another direction.

Isaiah 40:1–11

Isaiah 40:1–11 functions for Isaiah 40–55 much as Isaiah 6 functions for Isaiah 6–39, depicting what appears to be a prophetic calling experience.[25] While the tone of Isaiah 6 was clearly negative, not just expecting but ensuring the refusal of Judah to repent, the tone of Isa 40:1–11 is positive, announcing comfort for the exiles. As Isaiah 6 introduced the prophetic calling through a vision of the thrice holy God, Isa 40:1–11 concludes with a vision of Yahweh (40:9c: "Here is your God") as Sovereign and Shepherd Lord. This twofold vision of Yahweh is expressed through two images of the "arm," the one in 40:10 denoting a powerful arm and the one in 40:11 a tender arm. The message is directed to a community, called "my people" and "Zion," which is nearing the end of a period of discipline for past sins (40:1–2). The mention of Zion highlights the role of Isa 40:1–11 within the book of Isaiah as a whole, drawing on the key theme of the earlier part of the book and introducing the new phase of prophetic witness.[26]

Isaiah 40:12–31 and 49:14–26

This prophetic "call" in 40:1–11 is followed by a section that sets the tone for 40:12—49:13. Isaiah 40:12–31 constitutes a disputation series, a form that employs questions to develop an argument (e.g., Job, Malachi). Key to this series is 40:27:

> Why do you complain, Jacob,
> Why do you say, Israel,
> "My way is hidden from Yahweh;
> my cause is disregarded by my God"?

Here the prophet cites the cry of someone named Jacob-Israel, an individual who will be identified as "my servant" in the coming chapters (41:8; 44:1–2, 21; 45:4), and, at least at first, represents "my people" in need of the comfort that is to typify this new era of Judah's history (40:1).

---

25. See the connections between Isaiah 6 and 40 noted by Rendtorff, "Jesaja 6"; Carr, "Reaching for Unity"; Williamson, *Isaiah*, 37–38, esp. n. 21. Cf. Seitz, *Zion's Final Destiny*, 197, and literature cited there, esp. Cross, "Council of Yahweh."

26. So also Seitz, *Zion's Final Destiny*, 199, who writes: "It is above all the focus on Zion-Jerusalem in 40:1–11 that points to an awareness of the Hezekiah-Isaiah narrative portrayal."

The lament of the servant Jacob-Israel in 40:27 is matched by another lament voiced by Zion–Jerusalem in 49:14:

> But Zion said,
> "Yahweh has forsaken me
> The Lord has forgotten me."

Although Zion has been called to proclaim "Here is your God" (40:9) and this God is presented as powerful and good (40:10–11), the problem for the servant and Zion is that this powerful and good God does not appear to regard or remember them.

It is interesting that the identities of those who voice these two laments match the audience addressed within the sections which follow each lament, a fact borne out by the following chart.

	Addressed Directly or Speaks	Referred to
Israel	40:27; 41:8, 14; 43:1, 22; 44:1, 6, 21; 45:4; 46:3; 48:1, 12; 49:3 (by servant)	41:16, 17, 20; 42:24; 43:3, 14, 15, 28; 44:5, 6, 23; 45:3, 11, 15, 17, 25; 46:13; 47:4; 48:2, 17; 49:5, 6, 7; 52:12; 54:5; 55:5 (cf. 56:8; 60:9, 14; 63:7, 16)
Jacob	40:27; 41:8, 14; 43:1, 22; 44:1, 2, 21; 45:19; 46:3; 48:1, 12	41:21; 42:24; 43:28; 44:5; 44:23; 45:4; 48:20; 49:5, 6, 26 (cf. 58:1, 14; 59:20; 60:16; 65:9)
Jerusalem	40:2, 9; 51:17; 52:1, 2, 9; 62:6	41:27; 44:26, 28 (cf. 62:1, 7; 64:10; 65:18, 19; 66:10, 13, 20)
Zion	40:9; 49:14; 51:16; 52:1, 2, 7; 60:14; 62:11	40:9; 41:27; 46:13; 51:3, 11; 52:8 (cf. 59:20; 61:3; 62:1, 11; 64:10; 66:8)

This shows that these two laments function as structural signals in Isaiah 40–55, dividing the section into 40:12—49:13, with its addresses to the Servant Jacob-Israel and 49:14—54:17 with its addresses to Daughter Zion-Jerusalem.[27] As can be seen from the chart, both characters are referred to in each section, a fact that shows their intimate relationship. Both figures represent, at least in some way, the community in exile (e.g., 49:3; 51:16).

---

27. On the key role of the laments, see Westermann, *Isaiah 40–66*; cf. Boda, "Uttering." On differences between the two sections of Isaiah 40–55, see especially Blenkinsopp, "Second Isaiah."

The prophet responds to the first lament (servant Jacob-Israel's) in Isa 40:27 with a litany of questions that address two possible and related reactions to the exile. Exilic Israel might have interpreted the defeat of Judah as an indication that (1) the people and leaders of the empire must be in control, and (2) the gods of the empire must be in control.[28] The remainder of this passage vacillates between these two possible responses with vv. 12–17 and 22–24 addressing the conclusion that the political powers of the empire had won the day and vv. 18–20 and 25–26 addressing the conclusion that the religious powers of the empire had emerged victorious. The answer to these concerns that lay behind Jacob-Israel's cry was theological in character. This is not surprising in light of the fact that the basic message for Zion in 40:9 is "Here is your God." Each of the pericopae in 40:12–26 answers the conclusions of exilic Israel in the same way: God is the Creator and in comparison the nations are but a "drop in the bucket," a "speck of dust on the scales," the rulers are but "grasshoppers" and "meaningless," while the gods are but metal or wood fashioned by an artisan. The section ends with the comforting offer of renewed strength to those who will put their hope in Yahweh (40:29–31). The lament of Servant Jacob-Israel in 40:27 prompts the prophetic messages of Isa 40:12—49:13 with the initial response in ch. 40 pointing the exilic community to Yahweh as Creator who can be trusted.

The second lament, that of Daughter Zion-Jerusalem in Isa 49:14, interestingly follows the call to creation in 49:13 to break into a song of praise. Creation's song introduces vocabulary that will be repeated constantly throughout chs. 49–54:

> For the LORD has comforted (נחם) his people
> And will have compassion (רחם) on his afflicted.

However, this is hardly the expression on the lips of Zion. While the entire creation is called to gleeful praise at the thought of the restoration of his afflicted people, Zion herself is toeing a different line. From the heights of the praise of Isa 49:13 the book plunges to the depths of lament in 49:14, which states: "The LORD has forsaken me, and the Lord has forgotten me." What has caused such lament by Zion? The answer to this question is best answered by observing a key phrase repeated throughout this section: "do not fear":

---

28. See Seitz, *Zion's Final Destiny*, 200, who shows how Isaiah 36–38 prepares the reader for these two emphases.

> 51:7: "do not fear the reproach of humanity"
> 51:12: "who are you that fear mortals"
> 54:4: "do not fear"

Overwhelmed by fear of human power, strength, and glory, Daughter Zion-Jerusalem is stripped of her faith and obedience and led to "forget Yahweh" (Isa 51:13). According to the prophet, it is not Yahweh who has forgotten her (49:14), but rather fear of human power that has made her forget Yahweh. Yahweh's goal is to transform Zion from the depths of this lament in 49:14 to match the song of praise of all creation in 49:13, and the end of this section of Isaiah (52:7–10; 54:1–17) will provide evidence of such praise.

The divine council scene in 40:1–11 and the two introductory laments in 40:27 and 49:14 structure Isaiah 40–55 but also introduce the key motifs and characters that will dominate its content. The challenges to the faith of the exilic Jacob-Israel and Zion-Jerusalem, that is, those religious and political challenges that arise from empire, are answered with a presentation of the Holy One of Israel, the arm of the Lord, the Servant Jacob-Israel, and Daughter Zion-Jerusalem.

Holy One of Israel

First, scattered throughout this section of Isaiah are consistent appeals to God as the "Holy One of Israel." As already noted, Isaiah 6–39 speaks much of this "Holy One," an appellation that finds its source in Isaiah's initial call and mission in ch. 6 (6:3). It dominates the content of his message as the consistent theme on his lips (see 30:8–11), is a repeated phrase of the oracles in chs. 1–39 (1:4; 5:16, 19, 24; 10:17, 20; 12:6; 17:7; 29:19, 23; 30:12, 15; 31:1; 37:23), and represents the goal of Isaiah's mission (to produce a holy seed; 6:13). The reference to "the Holy One" in 40:25 is the last time this term is used on its own in reference to Yahweh. From there on, "Holy One" is always accompanied by another element, identifying Yahweh as "Creator" or "Redeemer" and sometimes both. The Holy One of Israel is the Creator of the world (40:25; 41:20; 43:15; 45:11), but is also the Redeemer of Israel (41:14; 43:3; 43:14; 47:4; 48:17; 49:7ab). In 54:5, for example, these two are intertwined.

The consistent use of this phrase "Holy One of Israel" reveals the intricate link between this initial revelation of God as the Creator in 40:12–31 and the revelation of God as the Savior of Israel from exile. As the prophet speaks to a generation in exile, experiencing great atrocities and pain in their lives, he has the audacity to discuss theology. This is not a theology abstracted above their circumstances, but one that invites an encounter of faith between Israel and Yahweh. He constantly returns to a theology of redemption and of creation as the foundation for their life in the midst of their suffering.

Arm of the Lord

The second strategy for dealing with these challenges to faith is the revelation of the "arm of the Lord." Isaiah 41–48 (esp. chs. 43–48) increasingly reveals the context that lies behind this contest between Yahweh and the idols. Babylon is mentioned in 43:14 where Yahweh promises to make this feared people "fugitives." Isaiah 44:28 and 45:1, 13 mention the figure of Cyrus, who will both subdue nations and restore Jerusalem and its temple. Isaiah 46:1 links the idolatry directly with the Babylonian cult (Bel, Nebo) and chs. 47 and 48 finally depict the destruction of Babylon and the flight of "his servant Jacob" (48:20) from the city.

Isaiah 41–48 looks to the salvation that God will bring to exilic Israel living under the imposing power of the Babylonian religious cult. Although the message is mostly focused on encouragement and salvation, there are warnings of judgment on "rebels" within Israel who have been enticed by Babylonian idolatry (42:18–25; 46:8–12; 48:1–22). The true "citizens of the holy city" who "rely on the God of Israel" (48:2) are those who "Leave Babylon, flee from the Babylonians" (48:20). But for the wicked, "there is no peace" (48:22).

In this context the prophet reveals the "arm of the LORD," a synecdoche for the military power of Yahweh that develops throughout this section of Isaiah. It is introduced from the outset in Isa 40:10 in the message that was to be delivered to the cities of Judah: "with his arm ruling for him." It reappears in 51:1–8 as God promises "my arm will bring justice to the nations" (51:5), and finally at the outset of 51:9—52:6, as the prophet arouses Yahweh to enact salvation for captive Israel: "Awake, awake, O arm of the LORD" (51:9).[29]

When news reaches Zion of God's victory, specific reference is made to the "arm of the LORD" (52:10), functioning as the climax of this long series of references to "arm" in chs. 40–55. The recipient of this arm's

---

29. See the related image of the "hand" in 50:2 in the Disputation series (49:15—50:11) as God reassures exilic Israel, "is my arm too short to save?"

destructive power is identified in chs. 47–48, which claim that Yahweh will carry out his pleasure on Babylon, "his arm against the Chaldeans" (48:14).

It is the "arm of the Lord," then, that leads to the deliverance of God's captive people—for they are immediately commanded in 52:11–12 to "Depart, Depart," a command reminiscent of the flight from Egypt, but with emphasis on the need for ritual purity as they leave unclean Babylon with its evil practices.

This defeat of Babylon and release of Israel from captivity suggests to many the fulfillment of Yahweh's prediction in Isa 44:28 and 45:1–3, 13 concerning Cyrus. Indeed, reference is made in these prophecies to Cyrus's role in defeating mighty kings (45:1–3), freeing captives (45:13), and restoring Zion (44:28; 45:13). It appears, then, that within chs. 41–48, Cyrus is closely associated with the fulfillment of the arm of the Lord against the Babylonians. However, while Cyrus takes the stage in chs. 41–48, in chs. 49–55 the focus shifts to another figure, one called the "servant" who was first introduced in ch. 41, but whose character is progressively revealed throughout chs. 41–55.[30] This servant represents a third strategy in Isaiah 40–55 for dealing with these imperial challenges to faith.

Servant of the Lord

This servant is identified first as Jacob-Israel in Isa 41:8, that is, the exilic community. In 42:1–7 the servant's mission is identified as bringing justice by opening the eyes of the blind, freeing captives from prison, and releasing from the dungeon those in darkness. In addition or possibly connected with these actions of justice, this Jacob-Israel servant is described as a "light" for the Gentiles and "a covenant for the people." Unfortunately, it is unclear in 42:6 what "people" were in view in this covenant. Was this a reference to the Gentiles or to Israelites? If the former, then the Jacob-Israel servant would be a group or an individual reaching out to the Gentiles; if the latter, then this servant must be an individual or smaller group within the exilic community who would do something for the exiles.

While Isaiah 42 is unclear, ch. 49 identifies the servant as one within Israel who will minister to Israel and on Israel's behalf. Isaiah 49:6 declares

---

30. Blenkinsopp, "Second Isaiah," sees a development but attributes this to a shift away from Cyrus who is the servant in chs. 40–48.

that this servant (who is called Israel in 49:3) will "raise up the tribes of Jacob" and "restore the preserved ones of Israel," besides bringing light to the Gentiles. Thus references to the dispensing of justice and freeing people from bondage refer to the function of this servant in releasing exilic Israel from bondage in the land of their captivity.

As mentioned earlier, this hoped-for release appears to be preceded by the victory of God announced in Isa 52:7–10, which calls Zion ("ruins of Jerusalem") to break into song in 52:9 because "the LORD has comforted his people, he has redeemed Jerusalem." Therefore, this looks to the fulfillment of this new phase of prophetic witness introduced by Isa 40:1 ("comfort, comfort") and by creation's praise in 49:13 ("Yahweh comforts his people") and mentioned regularly elsewhere in this section (51:3, 12).

What is envisioned in 52:7–10 is the image of messengers approaching a city with news of a momentous military victory. The messengers emerge from the mountains and are spied first by the watching guards on the city walls, those responsible for allowing the messengers into the city to relay the news of victory. The victory is followed by the return of the victorious king to the cheers of the city (52:8: "When the LORD returns to Zion").

One cannot miss the striking similarity between the vocabulary found here in 52:7–10 and that found at the outset of chs. 40–55 in 40:9–10. In 52:7–10 the messenger *to* Zion (prophet) relays the message that Zion will relay in turn to the cities of Judah.

Prophetic voices now announce the victory as messengers returning from a battle they have observed. As the message comes to Zion, "forsaken" and "forgotten" in 49:14, the message is simply "Your God reigns," transformed from and yet related to the earlier "Here is your God" in 40:9. This declaration is backed up by the description of battle in 52:10: "Yahweh will lay bare his holy arm."

Entering now into 52:13, the initial verse, which introduces the servant as "raised up, lifted up, exalted," is not surprising. The servant has been included all along the way as integral to this redemption and salvation and now his role will be clarified. In 49:1–12 it was the work of Yahweh through his servant that brought forth the praise of all creation in 49:13. This is now equated with the arm of the Lord, which is what brings forth the call to Zion to praise. But what is found in 52:14 and following is shocking. Rather than the picture of triumphant destruction, the prophet is confronted by a portrait of suffering and death.

This is hardly the picture expected as the reader first encounters the servant at the beginning of Isaiah 42. There one finds the presentation of "my servant" (עַבְדִּי הֵן), strikingly reminiscent of the terminology here in 52:13 (הִנֵּה עַבְדִּי). In between these two is heard the testimony of the servant himself in 49:1-6 and 50:4-9, explaining and describing God's commission (see esp. 49:3: עַבְדִּי־אָתָּה).

While it is clear that in every case this servant figure will have an impact on the Gentiles (Isa 42:6; 49:6; 52:15), one can see a development in the revelation of the servant in two ways. First, there is an increasing revelation of a servant figure within the broader context of Israel, from ch. 42 with its unclear distinction between individual and community, to ch. 49 with the servant title and function clearly attached to both community (49:3) and individual (49:6), to ch. 50 with the servant addressing the community (50:10), to chs. 52–53 with the focus on the individual alone. Accompanying this development is an increasing emphasis on the suffering of this servant figure from ch. 42, which mentions no suffering, to ch. 49, which provides a little insight (49:7), to ch. 50 with its mention of beating, hair pulling, mocking, and spitting, to chs. 52–53 with their grotesque depiction.[31]

In Isaiah 52–54 there is a creative dovetailing of the images of the Servant and of the arm of the Lord. Encountering this sight of the suffering servant, the prophet queries: "Who has believed our message and to whom has the arm of Yahweh been revealed?" (53:1). Here the prophet is given a glimpse of the identity of the "arm of Yahweh," that image of the glorious and powerful return of the sovereign LORD who will conquer all through his servant, even though all he sees is the servant figure, suffering beyond description.

The comforting message for the community is that out of the depth of suffering will come atonement for sin and salvation from exile. Within suffering exilic Israel the prophet sees one who suffers on their behalf and through him brings restoration to the nation. Who would believe

---

31. This progression in the revelation of a servant figure who will do something *for* servant Israel and suffer, may be related to the concerns expressed in chs. 41–48. There the prophet reveals the condition of some within the present exilic Servant Israel whose trust in idols (42:17) has proven that they are still deaf and blind (42:18-20; cf. 6:9-10).

such a message? To whom has such an arm ever been revealed? This is the shocking character of this prophetic witness. The arm of the Lord triumphs ironically through the suffering of the servant on behalf of the rest of the community and, according to Isa 52:13–15, even those outside the Jewish community.

Daughter Zion-Jerusalem

While it was the lament of the servant Jacob-Israel that first voiced the pain of Israel in exile in Isa 40:27, it is the voice of Zion-Jerusalem that echoes this pain in 49:14. As noted above, servant Jacob-Israel is the focus of the address in Isa 40:12—49:13, but in 49:14—54:17 addresses shift from Jacob-Israel to Zion-Jerusalem. The presentation of this second figure develops throughout chs. 49–55.[32] She is first encountered in 40:2 as one bereaved and in 49:14 as one barren. She cowers before humanity (51:12), drunk and vulnerable (51:17). But Yahweh calls her to awake and leave her bonds (52:1-2) and rejoice, for her barrenness has been removed (ch. 54).

This development in the presentation of Daughter Zion-Jerusalem throughout this section of Isaiah brings this figure into close association with the figure of Servant Jacob-Israel. This has been described sensitively by Sawyer:

> In the dozen or so passages about Zion there is a clear progression, from abandonment, loneliness and fear to fulfillment and joy; and the same goes for the Servant whose fortunes are traced from a time when he is weak and afraid and feels like a worm (41.14) to heroic suffering and triumph in ch. 53. Neither story is told as a continuous narrative, but the plot and the characters in both cases are referred to sufficiently often and regularly for the progression and continuity to be maintained.[33]

It is in Isaiah 52–54 that the arm of the Lord, Servant Jacob-Israel, and Daughter Zion-Jerusalem are interlinked.[34] In Isaiah 54 Zion is called

---

32. See Biddle, "Lady Zion's Alter Egos," for the way in which the Zion poems in chs. 49–55 play off of the Babylon poem in ch. 47.

33. Sawyer, "Daughter," 99.

34. Wilshire, "Servant-City"; Wilshire, "Jerusalem"; and Seitz, *Zion's Final Destiny*, 203–204, notice the close associations between Zion and the Servant and suggest that this means Zion is to be equated with the Servant figure. Hoppe, *Holy City*, 109, probably overstates his case when he compares Zion and the Servant in Second Isaiah and concludes that "Zion is the more significant figure."

to burst into song and shout for joy, the same response that was commanded of her in 52:7–10 when the arm of the LORD worked salvation.[35] The victory as well as the arm and servant of the LORD of chs. 52–53 is directly related to the restoration of the community to the land (54:2–3, 7) by the redeeming Holy One of Israel, who is at the same time the "God of all the earth" (54:5). The implications for Zion are clear as God promises to rebuild and refortify the once afflicted city and establish righteousness in her midst (54:14).[36] The cry of Zion at the outset of chs. 49–55 (49:14) has been answered through the revelation of the arm of the LORD expressed through the Servant Jacob-Israel.[37]

This section of Isaiah comes to an end in ch. 55 with an invitation to the community to "Seek Yahweh while he may be found, call on him while he is near. Let the wicked forsake their way and the evil their thoughts. Let them turn to Yahweh and he will have mercy on them, and to our God, for he will freely pardon" (55:6–7).[38] The promise of God is salvation from the suffering of exile, but this comes to those who repent and turn to him.

Isaiah 40–55 and Empire

It is thus through the weakness of a suffering figure, a suffering that atones for past transgressions, that Yahweh's empire is established on earth at Zion. While there is a role for the Persian Cyrus to play in the release of Israel suffering in exile, in the restoration of destroyed Zion, and in the establishment of Yahweh's universal reign (Isa 44:24—45:7), it is the figure of the suffering servant who accomplishes all this according to chs. 52–54.

Isaiah 40–55 thus continues to evaluate empire negatively as a threat to the community and to call the community to trust in Yahweh rather than the political and religious potential of the empire. At the

---

35. Although see Quinn-Miscall, *Reading Isaiah*, 201, who leaves the question of the identity of this woman in ch. 54 open. He says it could be Sarah or Hannah as well.

36. For superb reviews of Zion within Isaiah 40–55, see Ollenburger, *Zion*; Spykerboer, "Isaiah 55:1–5"; Webb, "Zion in Transformation"; Seitz, *Zion's Final Destiny*, 203; Clements, "Zion"; Hoppe, *Holy City*. Interesting is Wilshire, "Jerusalem."

37. This emphasis on Zion prompts Seitz to write: "it should be clear that concern over Zion's final destiny stands in the foreground in chs. 49–55" (Seitz, *Zion's Final Destiny*, 205).

38. Wilson, *Nations*, 327–28, and Spykerboer, "Isaiah 55:1–5," argue that the banquet of ch. 55 takes place in Zion.

same time there is, at least initially, a positive evaluation of the figure of the Persian Cyrus who is raised up for Yahweh's purposes to bring an end to the Babylonian empire, restore his imperial city Zion and his people to the land, and bring universal acknowledgment of his name on earth. As empire could be used by Yahweh to bring punishment on an unfaithful Judah (compare Isaiah 6 with Isaiah 39), so empire could be used by Yahweh to bring salvation to a faithful Judah.

While the establishment of Yahweh's imperial rule on earth is closely associated with the victory of Cyrus in Isaiah 41–48, this is not the case in Isaiah 49–55. In these chapters the empire of Yahweh is established through a figure suffering on behalf of the community. This countertestimony suggests at least a reticence to collapse the hope of Israel into the *realpolitik* of the Persian empire, if not an outright rejection of initial Persian imperial realities.[39] The victory of God is somehow connected to exilic suffering, so that, in an ironic twist, it is Israel's suffering at the hands of the nations that ultimately leads to the empire's loss of power. This echoes an important theological principle in Judah's reflection on empire. From the beginning Yahweh's empire was to be established not by a powerful human king, but rather through a community that trusted in Yahweh. Unlike the nations with their mighty kings to lead them into battle, "weak" Israel was to trust Yahweh to win their battles.

ISAIAH 56–66

Isaiah 40–55 looks to a day when the community will be released from exile in Babylon, a day that would be made possible initially through the actions of the triumphant Cyrus. The shift from Cyrus to Servant in the second half of chs. 40–55 may suggest an audience disappointed by the new Persian context. Many have noted, however, that with ch. 56 the reader moves into a new literary as well as historical context. A signal of the distinct character of chs. 56–66 is found at the outset in 56:8:

> The Sovereign LORD declares—he who gathers the exiles of Israel:
> "I will gather still others to them besides those already gathered."

This prophecy, declaring the fulfillment of Moses' instruction in Deut 30:4 that after the exile a penitent community would be gathered

---

39. Blenkinsopp, "Second Isaiah," 195, relates this shift to the disappointment of the exilic community with Cyrus, resulting in a shift of his tasks to the exilic community and its prophets.

from the nations, suggests that the target audience is those who are living in a period when exiles have already been gathered from the nations, but there is an expectation of still others yet to be gathered.[40] The earliest this would be is 539 BCE, at the beginning of the Persian period, as Cyrus (cf. Isa 44:28; 45:1, 13) defeats the Babylonians (cf. Isaiah 47–48). This community would begin the long and arduous process of rebuilding the city of Jerusalem and territory of Judah. What is envisioned here in Isaiah 56–66 is life as the exilic nightmare continues after the first signs of restoration hope. It targets a community for whom the early restoration did not live up to the expectations created by Isaiah 40–55, providing an explanation for the present realities while prophesying hope for the future of the community and Zion.[41]

Isaiah 56:3-8; 66:7-24

Setting the tone for all of Isaiah 56–66 are two sections that function as bookends around the entire collection.[42] Here is expressed a universal vision, one in which the nations enter into relationship with and worship Yahweh. On the one end, Isa 56:3-8 envisions the temple as a house of prayer for foreigners who "bind themselves to Yahweh" in covenant relationship. On the other end lies Isa 66:7-22, which describes how this will happen, as Yahweh invites all the nations to behold his glory and even uses some of the remnant to "proclaim my glory among the nations" (66:19).

Isaiah 61:4-9

This universal vision on both ends of the collection can also be discerned in what is considered by most to be "the nucleus of the collection"[43] in Isaiah 60–62. At the core of this nucleus is the speech

---

40. Westermann, *Isaiah 40–66*, 297.

41. Clements, "Unity," 128, notes how the central concern of chs. 56–66 is with "Jerusalem, instead of the wider political entity of Israel."

42. Although I am skeptical of many chiastic theories, I have found the proposal of Polan (cf. Emmerson) convincing and follow it here with a little modification. Cf. Polan, *Ways of Justice*; Emmerson, *Isaiah 56–66*, 20. See also chiastic proposals by Bonnard, *Le second Isaïe*, 318; Lack, *La symbolique du livre d'Isaïe*, 125–32. See the caution of Oswalt, *Isaiah 40–66*, 461–63 and Boda, "Chiasmus in Ubiquity." For a redactional theory of how this developed around the nucleus of chs. 60–62, see Westermann, *Isaiah 40–66*, 296–308.

43. Blenkinsopp, "Second Isaiah," 198; Westermann, *Isaiah 40–66*, 296. This nucleus

of God in 61:4–9. Although a large portion of ch. 61 is the testimony of a figure anointed by Yahweh (see below), vv. 4–9 appears to be a speech by Yahweh himself ("I, the LORD," v. 8). This central section describes the anticipated blessing that the LORD will bring; that is, in terms of 56:1–2, the salvation that "is close at hand" and the righteousness that "will soon be revealed." This blessing is the restoration of the ruins of exile, the reversal of roles so that the nations will now serve Israel, and the fulfillment of Israel's mission to be "priests of the LORD . . . ministers of our God," a role that suggests special access to God's presence, but also a special role for the nations (Exod 19:5–7). Foundational to this new era is God's promise in Isa 61:8b that he will make "an everlasting covenant" with them. Covenants in Israel's past (Abrahamic, Sinaitic, Davidic, Priestly) consistently promised both the blessing of secure land and abundant progeny, two promises that are echoed here in vv. 7 and 9.

Isaiah 61:1–3, 10–11

Surrounding this central divine speech promising covenantal relationship and blessing to God's people is placed the testimony of an individual speaking of his work for and reward from Yahweh, who is called at the beginning (61:1) and end (61:11), Sovereign Yahweh. The identity of this first person figure is not clearly stated, but the role he plays suggests that he is the servant introduced in Isaiah 40–55.[44] In 61:1–3, the figure identifies his role, which is clearly one of proclamation of salvation to those who are afflicted, broken-hearted, captives, mourning, and fainting. This proclamation will offer comfort and, in this way, continues the role of the comforting prophet of 40:1. In 61:10–11, the servant rejoices in his reward, describing how God has granted him the garment of salvation and robes of victory. It is the picture here of a conqueror returning from triumph.

---

constitutes the continuity of thought with Isaiah 40–55. The fact that ch. 61 is dominated by the voice of the Servant figure who speaks of his "anointing" suggests that ch. 61 functions as the two earlier prophetic "call" pieces in ch. 6 and ch. 40.

44. Although the term servant is not used in this section, this individual is not Yahweh himself (for he speaks about Yahweh/God in vv. 1, 2, 3, 10, 11 and is endued with the Spirit of Lord Yahweh in v. 1) and has the same calling and empowerment as the Servant of Yahweh in Isa 42:1–7 (see esp. v. 1: "I will put my Spirit on him," and v. 7: "to free captives from prison and to release from the dungeon those who sit in darkness").

Isaiah 60:1–22; 62:1–12

Bracketing the testimony of the servant are two announcements of salvation in Isaiah 60 and 62. These represent the comforting proclamation of Yahweh's favor. They both speak to Zion-Jerusalem and envision great splendor for her future with a promise of restoration. Such salvation is focused outward to influence the entire world. This is displayed vividly in the echo between 60:3 and 62:2:

> 60:3 And nations will come to your light,
> And kings to the brightness of your rising.
> 62:2 And the nations will see your righteousness,
> And all kings your glory.

These two passages highlight Zion once again as the focus of Yahweh's salvific purposes in the book of Isaiah. The salvation afforded Yahweh's people through the proclamation of his servant in ch. 61 is intricately related to the restoration of Zion as Yahweh's imperial center on earth.

Isaiah 59:15b–21; 63:1–6

Surrounding this theological core of chs. 56–66 are the two sections 59:15b–21 and 63:1–6. A perusal of the two passages reveals significant links between these two sections, confirmation of their structural relationship (cf. 59:16 with 63:5; 59:17 with 63:3–4).

The servant figure in Isaiah 61 proclaimed the restoration as a sign of covenant renewal with Yahweh. This is the "favorable year of the Lord" as the announcements of salvation in chs. 60 and 62 revealed. But the servant figure also spoke of the "day of vengeance of our God," and such a day is in view in these two sections. It is in 59:15b–21 and 63:1–6 that Yahweh dons the garments of vengeance to bring judgment on his enemies. Yahweh as Divine Warrior is a prominent theme throughout the Old Testament, beginning with his great victory at the Red Sea (Exodus 15), but also celebrated at regular intervals throughout the Old Testament (e.g., Deuteronomy 33; Habakkuk 3).[45] This Divine Warrior battles against the nations (Isa 59:18; 63:6) bringing salvation to Zion (59:20). It is important to note that such Divine Warrior activity is for the sake of those who repent (59:20) and enter into the eternal covenant through the Spirit with Yahweh (59:21).

---

45. See Miller, *Divine Warrior*; Kang, *Divine War*; Longman and Reid, *God is a Warrior*; Sherlock, *God Who Fights*.

Isaiah 56:9—59:15a; 63:7—66:6

The qualification that salvation is afforded those who repent suggests that all is not well with the audience of Isaiah 56–66. To this point, this section of Isaiah has stressed Yahweh's role as Divine Warrior proclaimed by his Servant to restore an eternal covenant with Israel. Furthermore, emphasis has been placed on the ultimate global impact of this renewed community and city. The remaining sections of chs. 56–66, however, reveal that there are serious challenges in the present life of the community that need to be dealt with in order for them to experience the glories of a restoration with cosmic significance. In two prophetic liturgies (Isa 59:1–15a; 63:7—64:12)[46] the frustrated people ask in the midst of the ongoing frustration of exile: "Why, God? Where are you?"[47] And the answer from God in 56:9—58:14 and 65:1—66:6 is that the question is not, "Where is God?" but rather, "Where is his people?" Both of these sections, first of all, emphasize that neither Yahweh nor his worship is limited to the temple. Second, both sections teach that the worship of Yahweh extends into the hearts of the truly humble and contrite, that is, those "who tremble at my word." Those who exemplify or respond to this message will experience the full restoration for which they long, a restored temple, city, and community, and even better, they will see the ultimate purpose of Servant Israel fulfilled, which is the transformation of the nations into communities of worship at Yahweh's throne in Zion.

Isaiah 56–66 and Empire

The core of Isaiah 56–66 announces to the Persian period community that God will renew relationship with his people, restoring both land and progeny to the once exiled and decimated people and giving them the role of bringing light to the Gentiles. This is proclaimed by the Servant as the "favorable year of Yahweh" and the "day of vengeance of our God," a day which will be enacted by Yahweh himself as Divine Warrior. Representative of this renewal of the community will be a restoration of Zion's glory and Zion's role (first introduced in Isa 2:1–5 and 4:2–6) as God's imperial capital on earth.[48]

---

46. Boda, "From Complaint to Contrition," see esp. 192.

47. Much like what was seen in the study of Isaiah 40–55 above, especially in the laments of 40:27 and 49:14.

48. On the significant role of Zion tradition in Isaiah 56–66, see Roberts, "Isaiah in Old Testament Theology," 141. Many have noted connections between Isaiah 1–5

While imperial figures and nations are explicitly mentioned in Isaiah 6–39 and 40–55, chs. 56–66 make no mention of human empire, speaking usually in more generic terms of nations and kings, and referring in passing to smaller political entities (60:6–7; 63:1; 66:10). Although human empire is certainly existent in this period, by ignoring it the prophet implies its irrelevance. Instead, Yahweh declares that since there was no one else at hand to intervene, he himself would achieve salvation for Zion (59:16; 63:5). There is also no mention of a future Davidic royal figure, and at one point Zion seems to assume the position once held by the Davidic line. Isaiah 62:12 declares that any nation (גוי) that does not serve (עבד) Zion will surely perish (אבד), vocabulary strikingly similar to the warning found in Ps 2:11–12 concerning the nations and their submission to Yahweh and the Davidic king.

Although this section does speak in many places of an earthly Jerusalem, there are indications at times that the empire in view is one that will be administered from a heavenly Zion.[49] Playing off the initial vision of Isaiah 6,[50] Isa 57:15 records the word of the "high and exalted one, the one who lives forever, whose name is holy" as: "I dwell on a high and holy place, and with the contrite and lowly of spirit."

Standing in the way of this vision for community and Zion, however, is the enduring rebellion of a people whose patterns of behavior echo those of Zion the bad in Isaiah 1–5.[51] The cry of the prophet reveals that although the restoration is something that only the Divine Warrior Yahweh can enact, such divine action is dependent on a penitential

---

and Isaiah 65–66: see Liebreich, "Isaiah 1" and "Isaiah 2"; Carr, "Reaching for Unity"; Sweeney, *Isaiah 1–4*; Emmerson, *Isaiah 56–66*, 37–39. Tomasino, "Isaiah 1:1—2:4 and 63–66," argues that 63:7—66:24 were created based on 1:1—2:4.

49. Westermann, *Isaiah 40–66*, 298, reflects this tension in this section of Isaiah when he claims that "the salvation which Trito-Isaiah proclaims is conceived in terms of this world . . . still tied to the realm of history," and yet also speaks of "a few passages which do go beyond this, and where the salvation promised has traits incompatible with the realm of history." What Porteous, "Jerusalem-Zion," 248, calls "a transcendental reality"; cf. also 65:17–19 where new heavens and earth are closely associated with new Jerusalem.

50. See Williamson, *Isaiah*, 38–39.

51. In a brilliant essay, Biddle, "Lady Zion's Alter Egos," 124–39, shows how Isaiah 57 reveals that Zion's alter ego has reappeared and that she is then doomed to the same fate as Babylon in Isaiah 48. The only hope is a "New Jerusalem." As Babylon fell, so must the harlot Zion. Jerusalem will not be restored, but replaced: a new heaven, a new earth, a new Jerusalem.

response from the people. The tone of this final section echoes in a thematic way the tone of the initial section of Zion. Undiminished is the hope for Zion to realize its role as Yahweh's imperial capital on earth.

CONCLUSION

Isaiah 1–5 expresses an imperial hope for a Zion to which the nations will stream and from which the law will go forth. From the beginning the reader encounters grave challenges to this vision. In chs. 6–39 one observes the struggles that took place in Zion as Ahaz and Hezekiah were challenged to trust in Yahweh against superior imperial forces. Chapters 40–55 present the struggle of Zion in exile, dwarfed by the empire in which they lived, and learning to trust Yahweh and reject foreign religious and political power. And, finally, chs. 56–66 depict the community in the wake of the Babylonian exile, struggling with a restoration that fell short of earlier ideals while looking for Zion to serve its role among the nations.

Through all of this the prophetic witness calls the people of God to believe Yahweh's imperial vision rather than that of the nations, typified by the invitation to Jacob in Isa 2:5 to "walk in the light of the LORD." In the monarchial age the kings and people were not to adopt the values of human empire with its focus on political alliance and military preparation. Instead they were to trust Yahweh as the emperor who would protect them. But the performance of the Davidic kings was disappointing, and after ch. 39 there is a decisive shift away from this royal line. After ch. 39, not only is the Davidic line ignored, but its prerogatives are shifted to others (Cyrus in 45:1, the community in 55:3–5), and Yahweh is explicitly identified as king (41:21; 43:15; 44:6).[52] Furthermore, the conventional dating of prophetic material according to human kingship is abandoned as the reader enters the imperial Divine Council, which sets the tone for this new phase (Isa 40:1–11; cf. Isaiah 6).[53]

---

52. See Roberts, "Isaiah in Old Testament Theology," 140–41; Williamson, *Variations*, 122–25, and especially Sweeney, "Reconceptualization." Such a shift also can be discerned at the end of Chronicles: see Boda, "Identity and Empire."

53. Contra Childs, *Introduction*, 332, who argues that the lack of superscriptions places the oracles in chs. 40–66 in the historical context of the eighth-century prophet. I find Seitz's description of the divine council as the "theological provenance" of Second Isaiah as helpful; cf. Seitz, *Zion's Final Destiny*, 206.

In the exilic age (Isaiah 40–55), the people were not to accept the empire's definition of their status as victims unable to survive imperial might.[54] Instead they were to trust Yahweh who promised to bring an end to Babylonian imperial abuse. In Isaiah 40–48 Yahweh promises to work through his anointed figure Cyrus, but according to Isaiah 49–55, the victory of Yahweh is to be enacted through the suffering servant. In an ironic twist, it is through suffering that Yahweh brings his victory on earth. Here one can discern a trend similar to Isaiah 6–39. Whereas a key human royal figure initially carries out Yahweh's imperial will (Hezekiah, Cyrus), in the end these efforts prove disappointing.[55] This casts considerable doubt over the ability of human empire to fully accomplish the will of Yahweh.

It is this skepticism that may explain the absence of any hope placed on human empire in the final phase of Isaiah (chs. 56–66). At the core of this collection (chs. 60–62) Jerusalem remains as "the political and religious center of the world, a circle of bright light surrounded by the darkness in which the nations languish."[56] But emphasis is placed in this section on Yahweh's direct intervention to secure his imperial victory and on the role of the humble servant in proclaiming Yahweh's victorious deliverance. The seat of this divine emperor appears to be more distanced from a physical Jerusalem. Echoing the introduction to the book as a whole (Isaiah 1–5), the people are called to obedience in order that Zion may truly reflect the glory of its emperor. Thus the book of Isaiah ends with strong invitations to obedience in order that Zion may truly realize its potential among the nations.

Isaiah represents an extensive testimony to Israel's reflection on empire. The book as a whole struggles over the imperial ideals of Zion as the seat of Yahweh's rule on earth, a picture presented at the outset of the book in chs. 1–5. Fulfillment of this role as imperial capital would mean trust in Yahweh in the face of the great kingdoms of the world, a theme that is consistent throughout the entire book. Ultimately Yahweh's imperial reign is established, not by the might of Israel nor ultimately through the Persian Cyrus, but rather through the suffering of Yahweh's servant, which will prompt Yahweh's direct intervention in history.

---

54. See Brueggemann, "At the Mercy of Babylon."
55. Blenkinsopp, "Second Isaiah."
56. Ibid., 198.

Although commenting on the broader Zion tradition, probably Porteous captured long ago the development of the imperial theme throughout the book of Isaiah when he wrote:

> In Israel there was a unique, though not a complete, break with the compact symbolism of the ancient imperialisms. Israel became aware of the dimension of the transcendent, but had to accommodate itself to life in a world of increasing complication. This is the [eternal] problem of the Church in the world, the problem of the life which has to be lived in unrelaxing tension. We have been watching the process in the Old Testament by which Jerusalem, the chosen city of God, not just the chosen city of David, gradually gave its name as a symbol of the transcendent action of God in creating a people for himself in the world, that is, in bringing in his Kingdom. The Old Testament made a wonderful beginning but it had to be left to the New Testament to complete the story.[57]

This "completion of the story" begins with a man in a synagogue in Nazareth who would read Isaiah 61 (that nucleus of Isaiah 56–66), announcing the inauguration of the realization of this vision of Zion and the kingdom of God. As Servant he would suffer for exilic Israel and in himself realize the function of Israel among the nations. And as Immanuel he would remind a community living under Roman hegemony that Yahweh was their only hope for release from imperial bondage. When Jesus read from the scroll of Isaiah, he stopped halfway through a sentence, laying down the scroll after announcing "the favorable day of the Lord" and before declaring "the day of vengeance of our God" (Luke 4:14–19). In this he was inaugurating his new era of salvation and restoration ("the favorable day of the Lord"), but promised to return one day as Divine Warrior (Revelation 19) to usher in the "day of vengeance of our God." Prompted by the book of Isaiah, during this "favorable day of the Lord" the church is to live purely in both worship and ethics as she takes on the role of the Servant by declaring God's glory among the nations (Acts 13:46–48), even through suffering (1 Pet 2:20–25).

---

57. Porteous, "Jerusalem-Zion," 250.

BIBLIOGRAPHY

Ackroyd, Peter R. "Interpretation of the Babylonian Exile: A Study of 2 Kings 20, Isaiah 38–39." *SJT* 27 (1974) 329–52.

Ackroyd, Peter R. "Isaiah 36–39: Structure and Function." In *"The Place Is Too Small for Us": The Israelite Prophets in Recent Scholarship*, edited by Robert P. Gordon, 478–94. Sources for Biblical and Theological Study. Winona Lake, IN: Eisenbrauns, 1995.

Begg, Christopher T. "Babylon in the Book of Isaiah." In *The Book of Isaiah—Le livre d'Isaïe: Les oracles et leur relectures. Unité et complexité de l'ouvrage*, edited by Jacques Vermeylen, 121–25. Bibliotheca Ephemeridum theologicarum Lovaniensium 81. Leuven: Leuven University Press, 1989.

Biddle, Mark E. "Lady Zion's Alter Egos: Isaiah 47:1–15 and 57:6–13 as Structural Counterparts." In *New Visions of Isaiah*, edited by Roy F. Melugin and Marvin A. Sweeney, 123–39. Sheffield: Sheffield Academic, 1996.

Blenkinsopp, Joseph. "Second Isaiah—Prophet of Universalism." In *The Prophets*, edited by Philip R. Davies, 186–206. Biblical Seminar 42. Sheffield: Sheffield Academic, 1993, reprint from *JSOT* 41 (1988) 83–103.

Boda, Mark J. "Chiasmus in Ubiquity: Symmetrical Mirages in Nehemiah 9." *JSOT* 71 (1996) 55–70.

———. *1–2 Chronicles*. Cornerstone Biblical Commentary 5A. Carol Stream, IL: Tyndale House, 2010.

———. "From Complaint to Contrition: Peering through the Liturgical Window of Jer 14,1—15,4." *ZAW* 113 (2001) 186–97.

———. *Haggai/Zechariah*. Grand Rapids: Zondervan, 2004.

———. "Identity and Empire, Reality and Hope in the Chronicler's Perspective." In *Community Identity in Judean Historiography: Biblical and Comparative Perspectives*, edited by Gary Knoppers and Ken Ristau, 249–72. Winona Lake, IN: Eisenbrauns, 2009.

———. "'Uttering Precious Rather than Worthless Words': Divine Patience and Impatience with Lament in Isaiah and Jeremiah. In *Lament: Israel's Cry to God*, edited by Mark J. Boda, Carol Dempsey, and LeAnn Snow Flesher. Library of Hebrew Bible/Old Testament Studies. London: Continuum, forthcoming.

Bonnard, Pierre E. *Le second Isäie, son disciple et leurs éditeurs: Isäie 40–66*. Études bibliques. Paris: J. Gabalda, 1972.

Brueggemann, Walter. "At the Mercy of Babylon: A Subversive Rereading of the Empire." *JBL* 110 (1991) 3–22.

———. "Unity and Dynamic in the Isaiah Tradition." *JSOT* 29 (1984) 89–107.

Carr, David M. "Reaching for Unity in Isaiah." *JSOT* 57 (1993) 61–80.

———. "Reading Isaiah from Beginning (Isaiah 1) to End (Isaiah 65–66): Multiple Modern Possibilities." In *New Visions of Isaiah*, edited by Roy F. Melugin and Marvin A. Sweeney, 188–218. Sheffield: Sheffield Academic, 1996.

Childs, Brevard S. *Introduction to the Old Testament as Scripture*. Philadelphia: Fortress, 1979.

———. *Isaiah*. OTL. Louisville: Westminster/John Knox, 2001.

Clements, Ronald E. "Beyond Tradition-History: Deutero-Isaianic Development of First Isaiah's Themes." *JSOT* 10 (1985) 95–113, reprinted in *The Prophets*, edited by Philip R. Davies, 128–146. Biblical Seminar 42. Sheffield: Sheffield Academic, 1993.

———. "The Unity of the Book of Isaiah." *Int* 36 (1982) 117–29.

———. "Zion as Symbol and Political Reality: A Central Isaianic Quest." In *Studies in the Book of Isaiah: Festschrift Willem A M Beuken*. Edited by J. T. A. G. M. van Ruiten and Marc Vervenne, 3–17. Leuven: Leuven University Press/Peeters, 1997.

Coggins, Richard J. "Do We Still Need Deutero-Isaiah?" *JSOT* 81 (1998) 77–92.

Conrad, Edgar W. *Reading Isaiah*. OBT 27. Minneapolis: Fortress, 1991.

Cross, Frank M. "The Council of Yahweh in Second Isaiah." *JNES* 12 (1953) 274–77.

Davies, Graham I. "The Destiny of the Nations in the Book of Isaiah." In *The Book of Isaiah—Le livre d'Isäie: Les oracles et leurs relecteurs: Unité et complexité de l'ouvrage*, edited by Jacques Vermeylen, 93–120. Bibliotheca Ephemeridum theologicarum Lovaniensium 81. Leuven: Leuven University Press, 1989.

Dow, Lois Fuller. *Images of Zion: Biblical Antecedents for the New Jerusalem*. New Testament Monographs 26. Sheffield: Sheffield Phoenix, 2010.

Dumbrell, W. J. "The Purpose of the Book of Isaiah." *TynBul* 36 (1985) 111–28.

Emmerson, Grace I. *Isaiah 56–66*. OTG. Sheffield: JSOT Press, 1992.

Evans, Craig A. "On the Unity and Parallel Structure of Isaiah." *VT* 38 (1988) 129–47.

Fohrer, Georg. "Jesaja 1 als Zusammenfassung der Verkündigung Jesajas." *ZAW* 74 (1962) 251–80.

Hess, Richard S., and Gordon J. Wenham, editors. *Zion, City of Our God*. Grand Rapids: Eerdmans, 1999.

Hoppe, Leslie J. *The Holy City: Jerusalem in the Theology of the Old Testament*. Collegeville, MN: Liturgical Press/Michael Glazier, 2000.

Kang, S.-M. *Divine War in the Old Testament and in the Ancient Near East*. BZAW 177. Berlin: de Gruyter, 1989.

Kaplan, Mordecai M. "Isaiah 6:1–11." *JBL* 45 (1926) 251–59.

Lack, Rémi. *La symbolique du livre d'Isäie: Essai sur l'image littéraire comme élément de structuration*. Analecta Biblica 59. Rome: Biblical Institute Press, 1973.

Levenson, Jon D. *Sinai and Zion: An Entry into the Jewish Bible*. New Voices in Biblical Studies. Minneapolis: Winston, 1985.

———. "Zion Traditions." In *ABD* 6:1098–1102.

Liebreich, Leon J. "The Compilation of the Book of Isaiah, 1." *JQR* 46 (1955–1956) 259–77.

———. "The Compilation of the Book of Isaiah, 2." *JQR* 47 (1956–1957) 114–38.

Lipschitz, Oded. *The Fall and Rise of Jerusalem: Judah under Babylonian Rule*. Winona Lake, IN: Eisenbrauns, 2005.

Longman, Tremper, and Daniel G. Reid. *God is a Warrior*. Studies in Old Testament Biblical Theology. Grand Rapids: Zondervan, 1995.

Mays, James Luther. "Isaiah's Royal Theology and the Messiah." In *Reading and Preaching the Book of Isaiah*, edited by Christopher R. Seitz, 39–51. Philadelphia: Fortress, 1988.

Milgrom, Jacob. "Did Isaiah Prophesy during the Reign of Uzziah?" *VT* 14 (1964) 164–82.

Miller, P. D. *The Divine Warrior in Early Israel*. Cambridge, MA: Harvard University Press, 1973.

Ollenburger, Ben C. *Zion, the City of the Great King: A Theological Symbol of the Jerusalem Cult*. JSOTSup 41. Sheffield: JSOT Press, 1987.

Oswalt, John. *The Book of Isaiah, Chapters 1–39*. NICOT. Grand Rapids: Eerdmans, 1986.

———. *The Book of Isaiah: Chapters 40–66*. NICOT. Grand Rapids: Eerdmans, 1997.

———. "The Nations in Isaiah: Friend or Foe; Servant or Partner?" *Bulletin of Biblical Research* 16 (2006) 41–51.

Polan, Gregory J. *In the Ways of Justice toward Salvation: A Rhetorical Analysis of Isaiah 56–59*. American University Studies. Series VII, Theology and Religion 13. New York: Peter Lang, 1986.

Porteous, Norman W. "Jerusalem-Zion: The Growth of a Symbol." In *Verbannung und Heimkehr (Rudolph Festschrift)*, edited by Arnulf Kuschke, 235–52. Tübingen: Mohr Siebeck, 1961.

Quinn-Miscall, Peter D. *Reading Isaiah: Poetry and Vision*. Louisville: Westminster John Knox, 2001.

Rendtorff, Rolf. "Jesaja 6 im Rahmen der Komposition des Jesajabuches." In *The Book of Isaiah—Le livre d'Isäie: Les oracles et leurs relecteurs: Unité et complexité de l'ouvrage*, edited by Jacques Vermeylen, 73–82. Leuven: Leuven University Press, 1989.

Roberts, J. J. M. "Davidic Origin of the Zion Tradition." *JBL* 92 (1973) 329–44.

———. "Isaiah in Old Testament Theology." *Int* 36 (1982) 130–43.

———. "Zion in the Theology of the Davidic-Solomonic Empire." In *Studies in the Period of David and Solomon and other Essays, International Symposium for Biblical Studies, Tokyo, 1979*, edited by Tomoo Ishida, 93–108. Winona Lake, IN: Eisenbrauns, 1982.

Sawyer, John F. A. "Daughter of Zion and Servant of the Lord in Isaiah: A Comparison." *JSOT* 44 (1989) 89–107.

———. *The Fifth Gospel: Isaiah in the History of Christianity*. New York: Cambridge University Press, 1996.

Seitz, Christopher R. "Isaiah 1–66: Making Sense of the Whole." In *Reading and Preaching the Book of Isaiah*, edited by Christopher R. Seitz, 105–26. Philadelphia: Fortress, 1988.

———. *Zion's Final Destiny: The Development of the Book of Isaiah—A Reassessment of Isaiah 36–39*. Minneapolis: Fortress, 1991.

Sherlock, Charles. *The God Who Fights: The War Tradition in the Holy Scripture*. Rutherford Studies in Contemporary Theology 6. Lewiston, NY: Mellen, 1993.

Spykerboer, H. C. "Isaiah 55:1–5: The Climax of Deutero-Isaiah. An Invitation to Come to the New Jerusalem." In *The Book of Isaiah—Le livre d'Isäie: Les oracles et leur relectures. Unité et complexité de l'ouvrage*, edited by Jacques Vermeylen, 357–59. Bibliotheca Ephemeridum theologicarum Lovaniensium 81. Leuven: Leuven University Press, 1989.

Stansell, Gary. "Isaiah 28–33: Blest Be the Tie That Binds (Isaiah Together)." In *New Visions of Isaiah*, edited by Roy F. Melugin and Marvin A. Sweeney, 68–103. Sheffield: Sheffield Academic, 1996.

Sweeney, Marvin A. "The Book of Isaiah as Prophetic Torah." In *New Visions of Isaiah*, edited by Roy F. Melugin and Marvin A. Sweeney, 50–67. Sheffield: Sheffield Academic, 1996.

———. *Isaiah 1–4 and the Post-exilic Understanding of the Isaianic Tradition*. BZAW 171. Berlin/New York: de Gruyter, 1988.

———. "The Reconceptualization of the Davidic Covenant in Isaiah." In *Studies in the Book of Isaiah: Festschrift Willem A M Beuken*, edited by J. T. A. G. M. van Ruiten and Marc Vervenne, 41–61. Leuven: Leuven University Press 1997.

Tomasino, Anthony J. "Isaiah 1:1—2:4 and 63–66, and the Composition of the Isaianic Corpus." *JSOT* (1993) 81–98.

Von Rad, Gerhard. *Old Testament Theology*. Edinburgh: Oliver and Boyd, 1962.
Webb, Barry G. "Zion in Transformation: A Literary Approach to Isaiah." In *The Bible in Three Dimensions*, edited by David J. A. Clines, Stephen Fowl, and Stanley E. Porter, 65–84. JSOTSup 87. Sheffield: JSOT Press, 1990.
Weinfeld, Moshe. "Zion and Jerusalem as Religious and Political Capital: Ideology and Utopia." In *The Poet and the Historian: Essays in Literary and Historical Biblical Criticism*, edited by Richard E. Friedman, 75–115. Chico, CA: Scholars, 1983.
Westermann, Claus. *Isaiah 40–66: A Commentary*. OTL. London: SCM, 1969.
Williamson, H. G. M. *The Book Called Isaiah: Deutero-Isaiah's Role in Composition and Redaction*. Oxford/New York: Clarendon/Oxford University Press, 1994.
———. *Variations on a Theme: King, Messiah and Servant in the Book of Isaiah*. Didsbury Lectures 1997. Carlisle: Paternoster, 1998.
Wilshire, Leland E. "Jerusalem as the 'Servant City' in Isaiah 40–66: Reflections in the Light of Further Study of the Cuneiform Tradition." In *The Bible in the Light of Cuneiform Literature: Scripture in Context III*, edited by William W. Hallo, Bruce W. Jones, and Gerald L. Mattingly, 231–55. Ancient Near Eastern Texts and Studies. Lewiston, NY: Mellen, 1990.
———. "Servant-City: A New Interpretation of the Servant of the Lord in the Servant Songs of Deutero-Isaiah." *JBL* 94 (1975) 356–67.
Wilson, Andrew. *The Nations in Deutero-Isaiah: A Study on Composition and Structure*. Ancient Near Eastern Texts and Studies 1. Queenston, ON: Mellen, 1986.

3

Matthew and Empire

WARREN CARTER

I BEGIN WITH SOME reflections on method, a fundamental issue in exploring how the Gospels of Matthew[1] and Mark[2] negotiate the Roman Empire. I identify five methods that have either rendered this negotiation invisible or significantly mis- or under-represented it. I then outline a multi-layered approach comprising cultural intertextuality that provides access to the Gospels' imperial negotiation. In Part 2 of the paper I employ this multivalent approach to examine four dimensions of Matthew's imperial negotiation.

My argument is that the Roman Empire comprises not the New Testament background but its foreground. Matthew and Mark are works of imperial negotiation. They tell the story of Jesus crucified by the Empire because he challenges its power, yet he is raised by God thereby revealing the limits of Roman power and the sovereign power of God. They negotiate Rome's power through a self-protective yet contestive approach that offers a (largely) alternative (though in part also imitative) worldview and social experience lived out in the practices of the community of Jesus' followers (ecclesiology).

---

1. Carter, *Matthew and the Margins*; Riches and Sim, eds., *Matthew in Imperial Context*; Mowery, "Son of God." Space prevents a rich documentation of many of the issues raised by this paper; readers can find support and elaboration in my previous publications.

2. Horsley, *Hearing the Whole Story*; Liew, *Politics of Parousia*; Myers, *Binding the Strong Man*.

SOME OBSERVATIONS ON METHOD

One of the reasons that imperial matters have come to the fore in recent Gospel studies involves the selection of methods. At least five methods have either rendered the Gospels' imperial negotiation invisible or misrepresented it. So for example, the arguably dominant contemporary hermeneutic comprising interiorized and spiritualized Bible reading focuses on individual needs and personal discipleship. It scarcely has contemporary politics, societal structures, and empires on its radar, let alone ancient ones. Its frequent encouragement of ready compliance or submission does not encourage the systemic analysis and communal focus necessary to engage matters of imperial power.

Second, much historical-critical work has viewed the Gospels as religious texts, in the case of Matthew, constructing and examining "religious" conflicts between the Gospel and another religious group, the synagogue "down the street," and debating whether Matthew should be classified as Christian Judaism or Jewish Christianity.[3] This "religion-only" approach has failed to take account of various factors that because of space can only be named here: Diaspora synagogues were not primarily or exclusively religious communities; they were not insular societal entities;[4] synagogues were involved in negotiating the empire; the Gospel's story of the death of its main character by crucifixion signals a fundamental conflict with the religiously-sanctioned, political-economic-societal entity of Rome's empire; the so-called "religious leaders" in the Gospels were allies, supporters, and beneficiaries of Rome's empire; and the Gospel shapes disciples who are committed to one crucified by the empire yet raised by God. While Matthew has often been viewed as the "Jewish" Gospel, any understanding of that term that omits these factors or understands it to be in some way antithetical to or untouched by imperial matters is simply inadequate.

Third, when Rome's empire has been in view, persecution has sometimes figured prominently in some reconstructions. No evidence, though, supports a view that the empire subjected late first-century followers of Jesus to daily, life-or-death persecution.

Moreover, fourth, the relegation of the empire to "New Testament backgrounds" has failed to recognize the dominant socio-political,

---

3. Carter, "Matthew's Gospel."
4. Barclay, *Jews*.

cultural, and religious force at the foreground of the first-century world, and masked significant interactions between it and Jesus-centered communities.

And fifth, while "church-and-state-in-the-New-Testament" approaches at least recognize that there may be some interaction between "church" and "state,"[5] this language reflects contemporary questions more than first-century imperial realities. And the approach, typically discussing only passages that explicitly refer to governing powers, is patchy, fails to engage the whole Gospel, and does not expose imperial structures and dynamics in which the texts participate.

The inability of these five approaches to adequately engage the complex question of the various relationships between the Gospels and the Empire necessitates other approaches.

A multi-layered or inter-disciplinary approach—perhaps best described as cultural intertextuality—enables access to various dimensions of the interaction between Gospel texts and the imperial world.[6] Julia Kristeva describes cultural intertextuality as locating a text "within (the text of) society and history." This approach involves placing these specific Gospel texts "within the general text (culture) of which [they are] a part and which is in turn part of [them]."[7] To locate these Gospel texts within the text of their society and history requires a six-fold approach comprising historical studies, classical and archeological studies, social-science models, insights from cultural anthropology, post-colonial approaches, and forms of literary criticism (audience-oriented and narrative studies). I employ this multi-disciplinary approach along with my own experience of growing up in a colony of the former British Empire.

One starting point for this interdisciplinary approach involves analysis of likely daily conditions within the empire experienced by Jesus-followers. The provenance of neither Matthew nor Mark is clear. Scholars have suggested Rome and Galilee for Mark's Gospel. I have argued elsewhere that Antioch-on-the-Orontes, the provincial capital of the Roman province of Syria, provides a possible provenance for Matthew, though no certainty is possible.[8]

---

5. For example, Pilgrim, *Uneasy Neighbors*, 37–124.

6. Limits of space mean a focus predominantly on Matthew's Gospel. For broader discussion, see Carter, *Roman Empire*.

7. Kristeva, "Bounded Text," 36–37.

8. Carter, *Matthew and the Margins*, 14–17.

If we assume at least some viability for Antioch as a possible provenance of Matthew's Gospel, we can begin to delineate something of the daily imperial realities in which followers of Jesus lived their discipleship. Roman power was evident in Antioch and surrounding areas in various material and systemic ways: administrative and public buildings, statues and gates, personnel like the emperor-appointed governor and his administration, several legions of soldiers (Josephus, *Ant.* 18.1; *J.W.* 7.58-59), control of land and resources, alliances with local elites, coins, taxes, temples, and civic celebrations of the imperial cult involving sacrifices, prayers, offerings, processions, games, street-parties, and distributions.[9] Antioch was a marshaling area for the troops of the Roman general Vespasian (emperor from 69 to 79 CE) for the Judean war of 66 to 70 CE (Josephus, *J.W.* 3.8, 29). Syria was a source of grain and other necessities levied for his son Titus's army (Josephus, *J.W.* 5.520). *Judea Capta* coins with images of defeated Judeans circulated there after the defeat of 70 CE.

This pervasive Roman presence required negotiation by the city's extensive Jewish population (Josephus, *J.W.* 7.43). During the 66–70 war, hostility toward and divisions among Jews were evident when an elite, highly acculturated Jew named Antiochus accused other Jews of plotting to burn the city. He used Roman troops to compel Jews to join him in offering sacrifices (to city and/or imperial gods?), abolished Sabbath observance, and incited violence against Jews (Josephus, *J.W.* 7.41–62). The victorious Roman general Titus, returning to Rome for the triumph with his father Vespasian and displaying Jewish captives and booty in Syrian cities on the way (Josephus, *J.W.* 7.96), visited Antioch, and resisted demands to expel Jews from the city or to rescind their rights (Josephus, *J.W.* 7.103, 106–11).

But while such investigation begins to uncover some of the realities of Roman imperial presence that followers of Jesus in Antioch negotiated daily, the limited and partial nature of the surviving data, its dependence on written texts with a few artifacts,[10] and its bias toward elites, public political events, and military actions, and bias against non-elites and discreet and self-protective actions cannot provide anything like an adequate picture of the vast range of human and communal experience impacted by the empire. Classical and archaeological studies of

---

9. Carter, *Matthew and Empire*, 37–46.
10. Kondoleon, *Antioch*.

phenomena from other areas (given limited excavations at Antioch), such as cities (Pompeii; Ephesus), imperial cult observances,[11] ethnic and occupational associations,[12] elite imperial negotiation,[13] food supply,[14] entertainments,[15] or anything else, may provide helpful elaboration. Of course it cannot be assumed that what happens in one part of the Empire is true for all areas.

Not only does the partial nature of the material or artifactual remains present one problem, so also does the challenge of relating the various existing pieces to each other. Importantly, material or artifactual remains assume, belong to, and gain significance in the context of a larger, complex, imperial structure of power relations that the archaeological record itself cannot reconstitute. Social-science models of agrarian-aristocratic empires usefully provide a wholistic framework, a heuristic view or map of the imperial structure allowing dots to be joined and the significance of individual pieces or areas to be seen in relation to the whole.

Gerhard Lenski's model of agrarian-aristocratic empires (see Fig. 1[16]), modified by John Kautsky's work, has been helpful for New Testament scholars.[17] Lenski focuses on the exercise of power, posing the question, "Who gets what and why?" In Rome's agrarian empire, a small group of about 1 to 3 percent of the population controlled the power, wealth (land, slave-labor, rents, taxes), and status, consigning the remaining 97 percent or so to relative powerlessness and degrees of poverty. The empire was very hierarchical, with a huge gap between the wealthy and powerful elite and the rest. There was no middle class, and little opportunity (apart from trade or patronage) for economic advancement, which, even if experienced, did not necessarily bring improved social status. For the elite, life was quite comfortable; for most, the poor of varying degrees, it was a desperate struggle for daily existence.[18]

---

11. Price, *Rituals and Power*; for discussion of the imperial cult in relation to 1 Peter's instruction to honor the emperor, see Carter, "Honoring the Emperor," 13–43.

12. Harland, *Associations*.

13. Swain, *Hellenism and Empire*.

14. Garnsey, *Food and Society*; Garnsey, *Famine and Food Supply*.

15. Futrell, *Blood in the Arena*.

16. This diagram, used with permission, comes from Arlandson, *Women, Class, and Society*, 22.

17. Lenski, *Power and Privilege*, 189–296; Kautsky, *Politics*; Duling, "Empire."

18. Whittaker, "The Poor"; Stark, "Antioch."

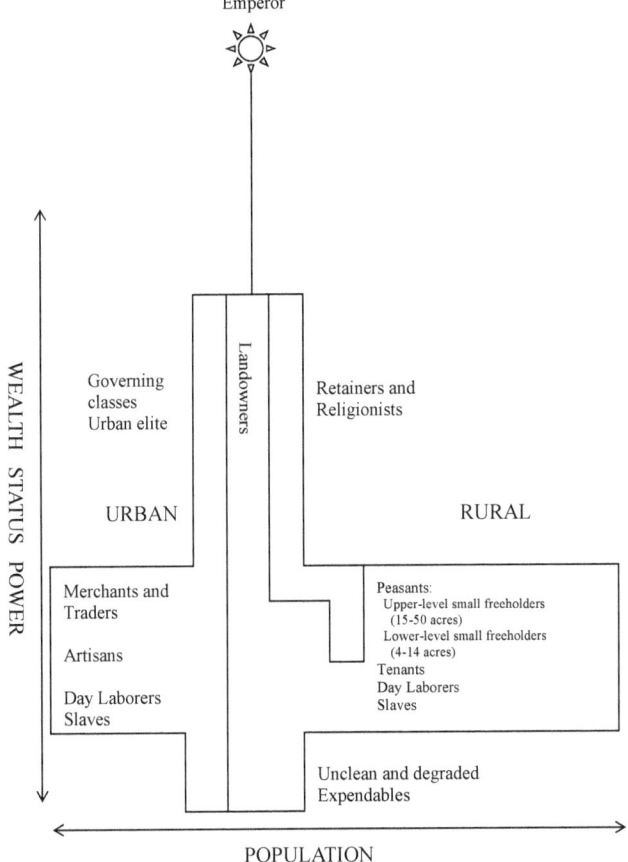

FIGURE 1: Model of Agrarian-Aristocratic Empires

Rome-based and/or allied elites exercised political, economic, social, military, and religious power and maintained their hierarchical world through various means. I will note here eight arenas briefly with little elaboration.

(1) Economic control meant ownership of resources, notably land, labor (slaves, day laborers, tenant farmers, etc.), and production (food supply).

(2) Taxes and tributes, usually collected in kind, transferred wealth from peasant farmers, fishermen, local artisans etc. to various elites spanning local landowners/officials to the emperor. Refusal to pay taxes constituted an act of rebellion.

(3) Roman military power, both actual and legendary, ensured compliance and maintained Roman honor.

(4) War, however, is expensive, as is a large bureaucracy. Rome avoided expensive war and minimized bureaucracy through alliances with provincial elites, with whom they shared power and spoils (taxation; status) and from whom they expected loyalty and the maintenance of the status quo. Such alliances involved cooperation and dependency, compliance and tension, reciprocity and competition for honor, power, and control of resources. Often elites were centered in cities and towns, often in local councils or, as in Jerusalem, in the temple, with (in)vested interests in maintaining the status quo. This observation has enormous implications for understanding the roles of the so-called (but misnamed) "religious" leaders in the Gospels of Matthew and Mark.

(5) Such alliances incorporated participants in networks of patron-client relationships. Patronage from the emperor down ensured interlocking favors and loyalty, privilege and dependency, as well as conflict and competition. Elites valued calculated and self-benefiting displays of wealth, power, and civic euergetism (the sponsorship of a festival, building, group meetings, statue, handout, etc.). They competed against each other for honor. Cities competed with other cities. Euergetistic acts enhanced status through influence and wealth and often provided enough beneficence to non-elites to alleviate some hardship while maintaining the status quo.

(6) Imperial theology, asserted through civic celebrations of victories and rulers as well as by image-bearing coins, statues, buildings, personnel, festivals, poets, writers, etc., claimed that the gods, especially Jupiter, had chosen Rome and its emperor to rule the world and manifest the gods' will and blessings among the nations. The imperial cult, frequently promoted by local elites, provided a means of constructing and interpreting Rome's world and a mostly voluntary means of expressing loyalty through sacrifices to images in temples, and at games, street parties, artisan guild meals, etc.

(7) Rhetoric, notably as the art of persuasive speech, was prominent at civic occasions. Whereas military force employed fear to coerce compliance, spoken and written rhetoric sought consent by persuasion, thereby

securing social control, cooperation, and cohesion. Speeches appropriate to various civic occasions and written texts articulated the power relations of domination that maintained the civic order and privileged role of the elite.

(8) Roman "justice" protected elite members; bringing charges, for example, against a corrupt governor, while possible, was extremely difficult. Yet harsh action was taken against threats to imperial structures. Punishments often fitted not the crime but the offender's social status. Crucifixion, for instance, was reserved for non-citizens and low-status provincials who threatened the state (only citizens guilty of treason were, appropriately, crucified).[19]

This model of the larger structure of Rome's empire, nuanced and elaborated by classical and archaeological studies, allows the function and significance of specific parts to be seen in relation to the whole. The model focuses on power, and so broadens a conventional historical concern with politics, war, religion, or "great men" to the overall structure, to the interrelatedness of parts, to collective movements, and to non-elites so often ignored in historical studies but crucial for the early Christian movement.[20]

Other approaches provide specific insight into the dynamics of power in contexts such as peasant economies where there are massive differentials of power. Cultural anthropologist James Scott , along with others,[21] recognizes that whenever power and control are asserted, opposition and resistance are inevitable. Scott examines multiple forms of domination and diverse expressions of resistance in societies like Rome's empire in which there are massive power inequalities. Scott identifies three means or spheres whereby elites extend domination and exploitation: material (appropriation of grain, taxes etc.), status (acts of humiliation and assaults on dignity), and ideological (justifications for practices: coins, inscriptions, buildings, texts, ceremonies, personnel, speeches etc.).[22] Each sphere of domination does not create grateful and blessed submission throughout the populace, despite the claims of the public

19. Garnsey, *Social Status*.

20. For the use of "People's History" approaches, see Carter, "Matthew's People."

21. Scott, *Domination*; Scott, *Weapons of the Weak*; Barbalet, "Power and Resistance."

22. Scott, *Domination*, 198.

transcripts or "official" versions of reality crafted by elites (coins, rituals, texts, etc.), and dominating action is as much for elite consumption to enhance elite power as for non-elite intimidation.

Rather, these assertions of domination create both compliance and numerous forms of resistance. Open, violent, and direct challenges to power, what Scott calls "forms of publicly declared resistance," are relatively infrequent. When they do occur, public resistance to material domination may comprise, for example, boycotts, non-payment of taxes, attacks on ruling personnel, and seizing property and resources. The Jewish revolt of 66–70 CE was one such form of public resistance. Public responses to status domination or humiliation involve public assertions of worth and dignity in gestures, clothing, speech, or violation of symbols. Public responses to ideological domination comprise counter-ideologies that negate an elite's claims with counter visions and claims.

But much more often in peasant societies, resistance is expressed in more covert, self-protective, and calculated ways, taking the form of "disguised low profile undisclosed resistance or infra-politics." Disguised forms of resistance to material domination may involve pilfering, foot-dragging, poaching, evasion, anonymous threats, cheating on taxes, sabotage, go-slows, etc. Disguised forms of resistance to status domination comprise apparently inadvertent non-expressions of honor (a sneer, no greeting),[23] anger, retaliation in rituals, subversive songs and stories, tales, rumor, development of autonomous space, and disarming acts of seizing initiative from the powerful like carrying a soldier's pack further than the stipulated mile, or handing over one's under garment as well as the outer garment, thereby exposing the harshness of the powerful one's demand (Matt 5:38–42), etc. Disguised forms of resistance to ideological domination involve the development of a dissident subculture such as millennial religions, social banditry, or world-upside-down imagery. Where there is autonomous space away from the always-controlling eyes of the elite, non-elites nurture alternative versions of reality or hidden transcripts. These hidden transcripts of counter-ideology contest and negate the elite's dominant public version, assert the honor and dignity of the powerless, keep alive hopes and visions of different forms of societal interaction, imagine another world, and legitimize self-protective (and occasionally publicly rupturing) forms of dissent.

---

23. Ibid., v, cites an Ethiopian proverb that sums up active, non-violent, self-protective resistance: "When the great lord passes, the wise peasant bows deeply and silently farts."

In relation to Matthew and Mark, Scott's work exposes the inadequacies of the view that since Jesus did not advocate open revolt, the gospel story is "apolitical" or "pre-political" or "politically indifferent" or "spiritual."[24] Scott's work, consistent with classical studies, recognizes the interrelatedness of political, economic, social, and religious spheres and acknowledges religion as an integral part of cultural and political arenas. In Scott's terms, Matthew and Mark's stories of Jesus, crucified by Rome but raised by God to expose the limits of Roman power, is a hidden transcript that contests the public transcript or elite, "official," normalizing view of reality. Jesus articulates and enacts a hidden transcript of the empire of God that condemns imperial domination, repairs its damage in Jesus' healings, exorcisms, and feedings, and anticipates the justice of God. Jesus exemplifies the politics of disguise and anonymity, notably through his proclamation and demonstrations of the rumor of God's imminent removal of Rome's world and establishment of God's empire. Both Gospels, however, recognize that Jesus occasionally ruptures the political order with direct challenges to the ruling powers (the temple attack) who respond by executing him.

To focus on the dynamics of imperial power—both its exercise and its effect—evokes the disputed[25] and diverse discipline of post-colonial studies.[26] Postcolonial studies unmask the complex experiences, dynamics, strategies, impact, and legacy of imperial power—political, economic, societal, cultural, religious, military—on minds, bodies, resources,

---

24. For discussion of Scott's work and the Gospels, see Horsley, ed., *Hidden Transcripts*.

25. Late first-century Antioch is not a *post* colonial situation; Roman power is a present, not past, reality. Nor is Antioch a *colonia*, in the sense of being founded as a settlement of veterans. Nor is Rome's empire, so the argument goes, comparable to recent capitalist empires (what Lenin called "the highest stage of capitalism"). While empires have different forms and motivations, common is the key reality of imperialism, "the practice, the theory, and the attitudes of a dominating metropolitan center ruling a distant territory" (Said, *Culture and Imperialism*, 9). Though Rome was not a nineteenth-century capitalist empire, its elite knew numerous ways of being a "dominating metropolitan center," and of exercising the power discrepancy between the powerful center (Rome) and the provinces.

26. The bibliography is immense. For example, Fanon, *Wretched of the Earth*; Said, *Culture and Imperialism*; Bhabha, *Location of Culture*; Castle, ed., *Postcolonial Discourses*. For biblical studies, Donaldson, ed., *Postcolonialism and Scriptural Reading*; Segovia, *Decolonizing Biblical Studies*; Sugirtharajah, *Postcolonial Bible*; Sugirtharajah, *Postcolonial Criticism*; Sugirtharajah, *Bible as Empire*. For Roman studies, Webster and Cooper, eds., *Roman Imperialism*; Mattingly, ed., *Dialogues in Roman Imperialism*.

societal interactions, cultural expressions, institutions, media, the past and the future, etc. Particularly important is the subjugated's engagement with or negotiation of the power differential between itself and the dominating imperial power. This negotiation is complex because of the diverse means and effects of imperial control. It is effected, as I have noted above, not only through force, intimidation, and spin, but also through complex and disguised means such as alliances, client-kings, interdependence, patronage, calculated benefits, and self-beneficial euergetism. This hybridity of straddling various worlds, of ambivalent and ambiguous interactions between oppressor and oppressed, interweaves benefit with subordination, gift with obligation, opportunity with exploitation, mimicry with opposition, appreciation with resentment, complicity with coercion, enablement with critique, submission with resistance, participation with alternative visions.[27] Local experiences of imperial power include self-benefiting accommodation, cooperation and/or co-optation, self-protective compliance, and mimicry,[28] as well as calculated and disguised forms of resistance, fantasies of revenge and destruction, and open protest (non-violent and violent) that directly confronts the ruling power. This partial "catalogue" is not to suggest that provincials chose one means of interaction, but illustrates a complex range of frequently simultaneous interactions and negotiations among elite and non-elite. Such diverse negotiations of imperial power complicate binaries of domination and subjugation, exploitation and deprivation, power and resistance, oppression and injustice, good and bad—as apt as they often seem to be.

27. For example, Reg, the fictional leader of the People's Front of Judea and staunch opponent of Roman control in the movie *Life of Brian*, expresses the ambiguity of complicity in oppositional practices by conceding (in a list that also reflects his creator's socialization) that the Romans have provided "better sanitation, medicine, education, irrigation, public health, roads, freshwater systems, baths and public order." Contemporary studies have noted the ambiguous roles of African mission schools that were both a means of imperial control (imposing western language/culture and silencing local languages), while simultaneously productive of power in providing educated leaders who articulated dissent, organized protest, and subsequently led independent states.

28. Fanon (*Wretched of the Earth*, 52) illustrates envy and mimicry in the "permanent tension" of the oppressed: "The settler's world is a hostile world, which spurns the native, but at the same time is a world of which he is envious." Envy translates into desire for the power and benefits of the oppressor's world. Mimicry seeks to gain that which is hated and despised. Mimicry means the quest for counter-mastery in various forms. See Bhabha, "Of Mimicry and Man."

Postcolonial approaches offer at least a double focus for Gospel studies, one involving the imperial circumstances of the Gospels' origin and address, and the other involving the imperialism of contemporary Western biblical studies that focus on these Gospels as religious texts and fail to engage imperial contexts, then and now. Sugirtharajah describes postcolonialism as "an interventionist instrument which refuses to take the dominant reading as an uncomplicated representation of the past and introduces an alternative reading."[29] Edward Said has emphasized a "contrapuntal reading" of imperial sources that engages the official discourse as well as resistant discourse and the interactions between the two.[30] Such approaches frame discussions of Matthew's and Mark's Gospels as resistant discourse that contests dominant scholarly views of Rome's empire that for too long have regarded the Empire as irrelevant to the Gospels.

I have briefly identified a fivefold, multilayered approach of cultural intertextuality as a means of engaging the Gospels' imperial negotiation comprising historical studies, classical and archaeological studies, social science models of empire, cultural anthropology, and postcolonial studies—to which I am now going to add a sixth element in the second section, namely some forms of literary criticism (audience-oriented and narrative studies).

FOUR INVESTIGATIONS: MATTHEW'S GOSPEL

I will briefly employ such approaches in elucidating four aspects of Matthew's Gospel's negotiation of the Roman Empire. The focus will be on the Gospel's plot, Christology, eschatology, and discipleship or ecclesiology.

Matthew's Plot [31]

In his work *On the Art of Poetry* (chs. 6–17), the leading literary theorist in the ancient world, Aristotle, argued that plots comprise not just a series of events but an ordered combination of incidents that forms a unity of action, comprising a beginning, middle, and end. The end is a

---

29. Sugirtharajah, *Bible as Empire*, 3.

30. Said, *Culture and Imperialism*, xxv. Compare Scott's public and hidden transcripts.

31. Carter, *Matthew: Storyteller*, 132–53.

"necessary or usual consequence" of the carefully structured sequence of preceding events. Causation and consequence guide this sequence. Events must be probable and/or necessary in relation to the end.

I have argued elsewhere that Matthew's plot unfolds through a six-fold sequence of events.[32] Space permits only a generalized statement:

(1) Matt 1:1—4:16: God initiates the story in the conception and commissioning of Jesus to manifest God's saving presence. Jesus is threatened by Herod, witnessed about by John, sanctioned by God in baptism, tempted by the devil, and validated by Scripture.

(2) Matt 4:17—11:1: Jesus manifests God's saving presence, the kingdom or empire of God, through constituting a community of followers, preaching, healing, and exorcizing.

(3) Matt 11:1—16:20: Jesus' actions and words reveal his identity as God's commissioned agent and the life-giving purposes of God's empire. He draws positive and negative responses. Powerful elites conflict with him over his societal vision and practices.

(4) Matt 16:21—20:34: Jesus teaches his followers that conflict with the elite will result in his crucifixion in Jerusalem and God's resurrection of him from the dead. This event has numerous implications for their lives as followers.

(5) Matt 21:1—27:66: Jesus enters Jerusalem, challenges the center of the elite's power in the temple, conflicts with them over societal leadership, and condemns their world as temporary and facing imminent destruction under God's judgment. The alliance of Jerusalem leaders and the Roman governor crucifies him.

(6) Matt 28:1-20: God's saving purposes overcome the worst that the elite can do and expose the limits of imperial power by raising Jesus. He participates in God's authority over all creation. He commissions his followers to worldwide mission, promising to be with them.

In elaborating this plot as a means of imperial negotiation, I will be guided by Aristotle's focus on the end as the consequence of the sequence of events. The plot ends with the resurrection of the crucified Jesus; its central dynamic comprises conflict between Jesus and the

---

32. Ibid., 140–53; Carter, *Matthew and the Margins*, 555–56.

Rome-allied Jerusalem leaders.[33] Attention to the dynamics of Roman imperial power noted above alerts us to the Judean leadership as Rome's allies and to the vast extent of their power far beyond what we would tamely identify as "religious."

Their societal power is evident in Matthew 2 when Herod, ally of Rome and "king of the Jews" because Rome allowed him the throne, hears the magi's news of the birth of another "king of the Jews"(Josephus, *Ant.* 15.387; 16.311). The announcement challenges the world as Herod and the Jerusalem leadership know it. He summons his allies, "the chief priests and scribes of the people," to inquire about messianic expectations (2:4–6). The interconnectedness of politics and religion is clearly demonstrated; messianic expectations, though neither unitary nor universal, were anti-Roman in envisioning a new world without Rome's societal, elite-benefiting structures. Herod is the face of imperial sin. The chapter reveals standard expressions of tyrannical imperial power—allies (the Jerusalem elite, 2:4–6), lies (false claims of worship, 2:8), spies (2:7–9, 12) and murderous violence (2:16)—that protect its power and maintain its privileged world. Herod is but one of many "kings of the earth" (so Ps 2; Matt 17:14) who resist God's just purposes and whose sin profoundly impacts the vulnerable Rachels (Matt 2:16). From such violent and oppressive sinfulness Jesus is to save the world through his life, words, actions, death, resurrection, and return (Matt 1:21).

Thereafter, through their conflict with Jesus, the Gospel consistently exposes and condemns imperially-allied leaders for shaping a society contrary to God's just and life-giving purposes. Like Mark, Matthew presents these leaders as constituting an alliance of chief priests, scribes, Pharisees, and Sadducees who are primarily Jerusalem-based allies of Rome.[34] Matthew introduces the chief priests and scribes as Herod's allies (Matt 2:4–6). From 12:14 (cf. Mark 3:6), the Pharisees plot Jesus' death and work with the chief priests to arrest Jesus (21:45–46; 26:4, 47). In Jerusalem Jesus verbally conflicts with "chief priests and scribes" (21:15), "chief priests and elders" (21:23), "chief priests and Pharisees" (21:45), "Pharisees" (22:15–22, 34–46), and Sadducees (22:23–33).[35] In ch. 23, he repeatedly curses and condemns "the scribes and Pharisees"

---

33. Kingsbury, "Figure of Jesus."

34. Correctly, Saldarini, *Pharisees, Scribes and Sadducees*, 35–49; Tilborg, *Jewish Leaders*. See also Kingsbury, *Conflict in Mark*.

35. Cf. Mark 11:18, 27; 12:12–13, 18.

(cf. Mark 12:38–40). "Chief priests, scribes, and elders" (Matt 26:3–5, 14, 57–68) work with Pilate to execute Jesus (27:1–2).[36] These rulers with soldiers of the Roman governor formulate a story to counter God's raising of Jesus (28:11–15).

In concentrating power in the hands of the Jerusalem-based leadership, Matthew accurately presents in general terms not only Judean power structures but also Rome's common practice of ruling provinces through alliances with local elites. Josephus declares the chief priests, appointed by the Romans, to be the rulers of Judea as local agents of Roman power (Josephus, *Ant.* 20.249–251). The "most notable Pharisees" allied with "powerful citizens" cooperated with Rome in resisting moves toward war in 66 CE (Josephus, *J.W.* 2.330–332; 2.410–418). Though relationships between Rome and local elites, between dominant and dominated/allies, were often tensive because the rewards and benefits of power were considerable, they had vested interests in preserving the status quo.

Matthew's Jesus questions the legitimacy of these Jerusalem-based, Roman client-rulers. In Matt 9:36 (cf. Mark 6:34), after further healings (4:23–25; chs. 8–9), Jesus "had compassion for [the crowds] for they were harassed and helpless[37] like sheep without a shepherd." In so describing people under Rome's yoke (11:28–30),[38] Matthew employs a common metaphor for rulers and leaders.[39] The image of shepherd refers to important leaders such as Moses (Exod 3:1), Moses and Joshua (Num 27:15–23), and David (2 Sam 5:2), and, in Matt 2:6, Jesus.

In Greek and Roman traditions, the metaphor of "shepherds" frequently refers to kings and emperors. Suetonius has the emperor Tiberius reject a provincial governor's requests for increased taxes by saying, "it was the part of a good shepherd to shear his flock not skin it."[40] Dio Chrysostom says that a king or emperor should be "a shepherd of his people not . . . a caterer and banqueter at their expense."[41] Quoting Homer, he speaks against the excessive use of power in reminding the

---

36. Cf. Mark 14:1–2, 43, 53–65; 15:1.

37. Carter, *Matthew and the Margins*, 230–31.

38. For the "yoke" of 11:28–30 as Roman imperial power, Carter, *Matthew and Empire*, 108–29.

39. And for God (Ps 23) who saves the people from Egyptian (Ps 78:52) and Babylonian (Isa 40:11; 49:9–10) oppression.

40. Suetonius, *Tib.* 32.

41. Dio Chrysostom, *1 Regn.* 13.

emperor Trajan that the emperor is a "shepherd of peoples" who is to "protect flocks, not ... to slaughter, butcher and skin them."[42]

In describing the people as "sheep without a shepherd," Jesus declares that they lack legitimate leadership. This declaration collides with the public transcript that presented the Jerusalem-based leadership as the nation's legitimate leaders since they were allies with and representatives of Rome. Jesus evokes a Hebrew Bible tradition that depicts Israel's leaders as shepherds who fail to represent God's just rule. In Ezekiel 34, for example, such shepherds/leaders rule with "force and harshness," feeding and clothing themselves but not the sheep (Ezek 34:2–3, 8). They neglect the people and have not "strengthened the weak ... healed the sick ... bound up the injured ... brought back the strayed ... sought the lost ... but with force and harshness you ruled them" (34:4, 17–19). Because the elite rulers are in the process of destroying the people, God replaces these leaders. God "will rescue my sheep from their mouths so that they may not be food for them" (34:10). God will gather them together, feed them, heal the sick, and protect them (34:11–22). God will "feed them with justice" (34:16). God will be king through God's agent, "one shepherd, my servant David" (34:23–24). An eschatological age of peace or wholeness comprising security, abundant fertility, and God's presence will follow (34:25–30). Evoking this intertext reveals that the Jerusalem leaders allied with Rome enforce a society contrary to God's purposes. Their rule is illegitimate; their days are numbered.

Differing visions of society are integral to the scenes of conflict between Jesus and these rulers. Jesus conflicts with them over doing mercy on the Sabbath (Matt 12:1–14; cf. Mark 2:23–28), over his authority to manifest God's presence and purposes including against the devil (Matt 1:21–23; 9:1–8; 12:22–45; cf. Mark 2:1–12; 3:20–27), and over their unjustly depriving the elderly of material support (Matt 15:1–20; cf. Mark 7:9–13). The interpretation of Scripture figures prominently in these disputes. Both Jesus and the leaders value the tradition, but they conflict over its interpretation. The interpretation of the biblical traditions was a political act since it involved the control and shape of society. Matthew's Jesus declares that the rulers' leadership and the

---

42. Ibid., 43–44. Philo describes the role of the tutor and adviser Macro in urging the "quarrelsome and contentious" emperor Gaius Caligula to more appropriate public behavior. Philo has Macro refer to the emperor Gaius as the "sovereign of earth and sea" and "a shepherd and master of the flock" (*Leg.* 44, 52).

(unjust) social order that they oversee are contrary to God's purposes; God will "uproot" them (Matt 15:13), an image of judgment and condemnation (Jer 1:10; 12:17).

Having announced God's condemnation of the Jerusalem-based leadership in Matt 15:13, Jesus enacts that condemnation against Jerusalem's temple, the center of their power (21:12–17; cf. Mark 11:15–19). As an instrument of shaping society, the temple secured the elite's socio-political, economic, and religious domination through taxes, buying and selling sacrifices and supplies for temple ritual, administering landed estates, receiving and storing gifts (cf. Matt 15:5), and controlling ritual and festivals.[43] The temple, like others in Rome's world, was part slaughterhouse, worship center, political center, and bank (Josephus, *J.W.* 2.293; *Ant.* 18.60).

Jesus condemns the temple order and practices of changing money and selling sacrifices (Matt 21:12–13). He quotes Isa 56:7 ("a house of prayer") to contrast Isaiah's inclusionary vision incorporating "all peoples" with the elite's exclusionary practices. Jesus enacts this inclusionary vision by healing the blind and lame in the temple (Matt 21:14; cf. Lev 21:16–24; 2 Sam 5:8). Jesus names their temple a "den for robbers/ bandits" (Jer 7:11). The phrase evokes Jeremiah's condemnation of the powerful who seek the temple's protection but contravene God's will with exploitative and oppressive social and economic actions: acting unjustly, oppressing the alien, orphan, and widow, shedding innocent blood, and pursuing other gods (Jer 7:5–6, also 7:9). Their actions meant judgment in 587 BCE. They would likewise for Jerusalem's temple, destroyed, ironically, by Rome in 70 CE (Matt 22:7).

Jesus elaborates the condemnation of the rulers in parables (Matt 21:28—22:14; cf. Mark 12:1–12), foretelling their demise (Matt 21:41; 22:7). The curses of ch. 23 identify the leaders' failures in neglecting "the weightier matters of the law, justice, mercy and faithfulness" (23:23). The Gospel describes them as "evil" (9:4; 12:34) and "tempting" Jesus (16:1–4), thereby (regrettably) applying to them features of the devil (4:1, 3; 13:38–39) and presenting them as the devil's allies and agents. This connection is not surprising since in the temptation scene Matthew deemed the empire to be under the devil's control (4:8; cf. Mark 5:1–20). Matthew's Gospel resists their societal structure by depicting it as opposed to God's purposes.

---

43. Hanson and Oakman, *Palestine in the Time of Jesus*, 131–59.

These forces collide in the scene with Pilate (Matt 27:1–2, 11–26; cf. Mark 15:1–15).[44] As governor, Pilate exercises enormous power as the representative of Roman interests. He rules in alliance with the Jerusalem elite and for their mutual interests in defending the status quo against perceived threats posed by a provincial kingly pretender like Jesus. Thus it is quite false to see the so-called "trial" scene along ethnic lines as a struggle between Jews and Gentiles, or along religious-secular lines in which "religious" Jews need the help of a "secular" ruler to remove a religious opponent. Such divisions are quite inappropriate for imperial dynamics. Oblivious to any imperial dynamics, one interpreter remarkably designates Matthew's Pilate, Rome's representative and chief enforcer of life-and-death imperial power, as "politically neutral"![45] Rather, in this scene ruling elites comprising Jerusalem leaders and the Roman governor work together in a tensive relationship to remove a provincial who threatens their way of structuring the world. Pilate knows that they want him to crucify Jesus, and in addressing Jesus as "king of the Jews," Pilate knows Jesus threatens Rome's authority (Matt 27:11). Only Rome can appoint legitimate (that is, submissive and controllable) kings. But if Pilate agrees too readily to their request, he becomes their pawn. Yet he knows that he needs the alliance with them in order to rule, so he cannot disappoint them. If they are concerned about Jesus, he ought to be also. The outcome is never in doubt. In fact Matt 27:3 indicates Judas's recognition that Jesus is condemned, long before Jesus and Pilate meet.

The real issue that the scene reveals is the process of Jesus' condemnation. It shows how these elite parties negotiate with each other, maintaining their own power, scoring points, taking care of business, and presenting their actions as the will of the people. So, with questions Pilate holds a referendum on who should be set free in an attempt to see whether Jesus or Barabbas has more support (Matt 27:15–19). The Jerusalem leaders manipulate the crowd to shout for Barabbas (27:20–21). Pilate seems to take their advice on Jesus (27:22) but stalls, testing to see how much support there is for Jesus and how much opposition there might be if he crucifies their reputed "king" (27:23–24). He skillfully manipulates the crowd and Jerusalem leaders to beg him (note v. 22, "all of them said") to crucify Jesus. Also skillfully, but quite deceptively, he declares he will do *their* will, thereby disguising the elite's wishes and

---

44. For elaboration, Carter, *Pontius Pilate*, 1–54, 75–99; for Mark, 55–74.
45. Bond, *Pontius Pilate*, 120–37.

masking his control as the people's will (27:24–26). While Pilate washes his hands, Matthew's scene with its focus on all the forces and strategies of the Empire allied against Jesus, God's anointed agent (Son and Christ), exposes Roman justice to be all washed-up.

But they cannot keep him dead. To all appearances Rome's political, economic, cultural, and military power seemed absolute. Its famed military fostered this semblance of omnipotence. In urging Jews not "to take arms against so mighty a power" in 66 CE, for example, Agrippa recognizes Rome's vast power, sanctioned by God, that no one has been able to resist (Josephus, *J.W.* 2.353, 358–94). Yet the conclusion of Matthew's plot reveals the limits of this power. In crucifying Jesus, the empire demonstrates its ultimate power to take life. But the Gospel does not end with Jesus' crucifixion. The angel announces to the women that God has raised Jesus, and they encounter him (Matt 28:6–9; cf. Mark 16:1–7). Resurrection evokes traditions such as Dan 12:1–3 and 2 Maccabees 6–7, whereby this act of justice vindicates faithful opponents of empire and reverses the damage inflicted by empires that act contrary to God's purposes. Acknowledging the missing body, the Jerusalem leaders, namely chief priests and elders, conspire with the soldiers, who were "like dead men" in this place of life, not to tell the governor Pilate but to explain the missing body as theft by the disciples (Matt 28:11–15). In the closing verses, Jesus announces, "All authority in heaven and earth has been given to me" (28:18). God has shared with the risen Jesus life-giving authority over all creation. Rome cannot resist God's empire.

The Gospel's plot is, in James Scott's terms, a "hidden transcript" that contests and dissents from the public transcript or official version of the empire's self-presentation. The story of a crucified provincial whom Rome is unable to keep dead denies ultimate power to Rome, exposes its death-bringing commitments, and celebrates God's greater life-giving power manifested through Jesus' words, works, and resurrection. It is these transformative words and works that are to shape and form the identity and alternative societal existence of Jesus-believers. The Gospel tells a story that guides Jesus-believers in interpreting the present and living accordingly.

Christology: Contesting Imperial Claims

Scholars have examined the origins, historical development, and titular expression of Matthew's Christology.[46] Narrative approaches have criticized an exclusive focus on titles, arguing that the Gospel uses various means to present Jesus' character (words, actions, interactions, etc.) as the plot unfolds, and that narrative contexts supply meaning for titles, whatever their historical traditions.[47] Here, in an extension of narrative approaches, I focus briefly on a cluster of themes that emerge as aspects of Jesus' character.

The Gospel presents Jesus as the agent of God who manifests God's sovereignty, presence, will, and blessing among human beings. Unnoticed by previous Matthean scholarship, this cluster of themes also contests central claims of imperial theology that present Rome and the emperor as agents of the gods, chosen to manifest their sovereignty, presence, will, and wellbeing among human beings.[48] Submission to imperial Rome means submission to the gods. In setting these two sets of different claims together I am not contending that Roman imperial theology is the source of Matthean Christology. My concern is not with origin, but with intertextuality. What happens when these claims interact? I suggest that the Gospel contests Rome's claims, even as it mimics them, by asserting God's purposes encountered in Jesus.

Where are the purposes of the gods found on earth? Who is their agent? According to Virgil, Jupiter ordains Rome to be "lords of the world."[49] A century later, Seneca has Nero ask, "Have I of all mortals found favor with heaven and been chosen to serve on earth as vicar of the gods? I am the arbiter of life and death."[50] Contemporary with Matthew's Gospel, Statius celebrates Domitian who "at Jupiter's command rules for him the blessed world."[51]

In presenting Jesus as God's agent, Matthew contests claims that Rome represents divine purposes, locating such agency in Jesus the "Christ" (Matt 1:1, 17; cf. Mark 1:1), anointed or commissioned to save

---

46. For discussion Carter, *Matthew and Empire*, 57–59; for Mark, Kingsbury, *Christology of Mark's Gospel.*

47. Keck, "Renewal."

48. Carter, *Matthew and Empire*, 57–74.

49. Virgil, *Aen.* 1.281.

50. Seneca, *Clem.* 1.1.2.

51. Statius, *Silvae* 4.3.128–129.

from sins and manifest God's presence (Matt 1:21-23). This commission to enact God's saving presence, confirmed in Jesus' baptism (3:13-17) and temptation (4:1-11), is re-languaged in 4:17 as God's "empire/kingdom" (cf. Mark 1:9-15). Jesus' identity as God's agent is underlined by the terms King (Matt 2:2) and Son (2:15), both of which draw on traditions that emphasized special relationship with God and enact God's reign. Jesus, not Rome or the emperor Domitian, is light for the world (4:15-16).[52]

Claims of agency are closely related to issues of sovereignty. Whose world is it? To whom does the sovereignty of the world belong? Imperial theology asserts Rome's divinely sanctioned rule and claim on human loyalty and production. Jupiter has ordained Rome to rule an empire "without limits."[53] "At Jupiter's command," insists Statius, Domitian "rules for him the blessed world" as "lord of the earth," "ruler of the nations,"[54] and "master of sea and land."[55]

Likewise the Gospel is clear that as God's agent Jesus manifests God's sovereignty. The opening genealogy asserts God's sovereignty over human history in its selective recounting of God's dealings with Israel and the nations (Matt 1:1-17). God's purposes are not manifested here through Rome. This world originates in God's creative work narrated in Genesis 1-3 (Matt 19:4). Jesus originates in God's creative and saving purposes (1:18-25). In announcing the "tensive symbol" of the empire/kingdom of God (4:17; cf. Mark 1:15),[56] Jesus manifests God's sovereignty over this world and its attendant blessings (Matt 5:3-12). The rest of his public ministry elaborates this claim over human lives (4:18-22; cf. Mark 1:16-20), over sickness and demons (Matt 4:23-25; 8:28-36; 12:25; cf. Mark 1:21-34), and over the sea (8:23-27; cf. Mark 4:35-41). Jesus addresses God as Lord of heaven and earth (Matt 11:25) and God grants to him, not to Rome, "all authority in heaven and earth" (28:18).

As God's agent, Jesus manifests God's presence. Philo narrates Gaius Caligula's attempts to co-opt the Jerusalem temple as a place to worship Gaius, "the new Zeus made manifest."[57] Statius identifies Domitian

---

52. Cicero, *Cat.* 4.11; Martial, *Epig* 8.21.
53. Virgil, *Aen.* 1.254, 278-279.
54. Statius, *Silvae* 5.1.37; 3.4.20; 4.2.14-15.
55. Philostratus, *Vit. Apoll.* 7.3.
56. Carter, *Matthew and Empire*, 61.
57. Philo, *Leg. Gai.* 346. For analysis, Carter, *John and Empire*, Appendix.

as "that present Deity," a *deus praesens*.[58] In passages prominent in Matthew (and without parallels in Mark) the Gospel highlights Jesus' role in manifesting divine presence. In Matt 1:23 the unborn Jesus is named Emmanuel, God with us. The citation from Isa 7:14 metonymically evokes Judah's struggles with imperial power involving Israel, Syria, and Assyria, and God's presence with the people (Isa 8:8, 10).[59] In Matt 18:20 Jesus assures disciples that the community of followers gathered for prayer encounters his presence, and through him, God's saving presence. The Gospel closes with the risen Jesus assuring followers, whom he has just sent in mission, that his presence, and that of God, is with them forever (28:20). Throughout his ministry, Jesus Emmanuel disturbs and disrupts the imperial status quo.

Related to agency, sovereignty, and presence are claims about divine will and purpose. Imperial theology asserts that the world under Rome's control is the will of Jupiter and the gods. The Gospel evaluates Rome's world as one of sin from which people need saving (Matt 1:21). Herod, ally and agent of Rome, manifests imperial damage and violence (sinfulness) in protecting this world (ch. 2). The Gospel also evaluates the imperial world as devilish. The devil offers Jesus "all the empires (βασιλείας) "of the world" in return for worship, an offering predicated on the devil's right to assign the world's empires, of which Rome is foremost, to whomever he wishes (4:8; cf. Mark 5:1–20). Jesus forbids his followers to imitate the pervasive domination or "power over" societal structures of the empire: "You know that the rulers of the Gentiles lord it over them and their great ones are tyrants over them. It will not be so among you" (Matt 20:25–26; cf. Mark 10:42–45). The final incompatibility and antipathy are demonstrated in the elite's crucifixion of Jesus.

Matthew's Gospel asserts that Jesus' words and actions manifest God's will, his purposes for the world, saving presence, rule, and sovereignty. Jesus definitively interprets God's will revealed in Scripture. He sums up the tradition with a double command to love God and neighbor, quoting Deut 6:5 and Lev 19:18 (Matt 22:34–39; Mark 12:28–34). Twice he cites Hos 6:6 to indicate God's preference for mercy not sacrifice (Matt 9:13; 12:7). Followers must seek first God's justice or righteousness (6:34). In Matt 5:17–48 Jesus reinterprets six commands clarifying and radicalizing their demands.

---

58 Statius, *Silvae* 5.2.170.

59. Carter, "Evoking Isaiah"; also, *Matthew and Empire*, 93–108.

The last element of the cluster concerns societal wellbeing. Imperial theology boasted that the world's wellbeing results from Roman rule. Various coins, altars (such as Augustus's *Ara Pacis* in Rome), inscriptions, and rhetoric proclaimed big gifts of wellbeing such as peace (*pax, eirēnē*), victory (*victoria, nikē*), social harmony (*concordia*), corn and fertility (*ceres*). Matthew presents Jesus as God's agent in manifesting God's blessing, and societal well-being looks very different. The beatitudes with their double time frame of the now and the not-yet of God's action announce God's blessing on the poor, the powerless, and those who seek justice (Matt 5:3–12).[60] Jesus teaches prayer for God's will, God's empire, and daily bread (6:9–13). His healings, evoking prophetic (Isa 35:5–6) and apocalyptic (2 Bar 29; 73) traditions, reverse the damage caused by, among other things, inadequate food supply and nutrition, and harsh working conditions. His exorcisms set people free from the devilish power behind the empire. His feedings anticipate the eschatological fullness and material abundance of God's reign in contrast with the empire's claims (Matt 14:13–21; 15:31–39; Isa 25:6–10).

While these themes could be elaborated, it is sufficient to note this previously unrecognized intertextuality between imperial theology and Matthew's Christology. The claims collide as the Gospel contests yet imitates imperial claims, and offers its hearers an alternative worldview and societal experience.

Eschatology

Jesus' resurrection is the plot's final scene in which God's sovereignty and Rome's limited power are revealed. Talk of resurrection is, of course, eschatological. That God would raise those who died in faithful relationship to God was a belief that belonged to a cluster of understandings involving the final establishment of God's purposes. This claim of new life and vindication is asserted in contexts of injustice under imperial oppression. It is evident, for instance, in Daniel 12 and 2 Maccabees 7, in the claim of resurrection for those martyred by Antiochus Epiphanes in the second century BCE. Resurrection affirmed that imperial tyranny could not break faithful relationship with God and could not thwart God's purposes. Resurrection ensured participation in the establishment of God's life-giving and just purposes.

60 Carter, "Matthew and the Margins," 128–37; see also Carter, "Power and Identities," and Carter, "Embodying God's Empire."

The Gospel envisions the eschatological establishment of God's purposes and final repudiation of Rome's societal structure. God destroys Rome's world and establishes God's heaven and earth (Matt 19:28; 24:35). In 24:27–31, Matthew presents Jesus' return as the end of all empires, especially Rome's.[61] As I have argued elsewhere, v. 28 makes an unambiguous reference to eagles (not to vultures as ἀετοί = *aetoi* has been mistakenly translated). The verses describe the final battle in which Rome's army, represented by the symbolic eagle that legions carried into battle,[62] is destroyed. Verse 29 denotes judgment on the cosmic deities that Rome claimed sanctioned its power. Jesus the Son of Man returns to establish God's "everlasting dominion . . . and kingship that will never be destroyed" (Dan 7:13–14; cf. Matt 16:27–28).

Interestingly, in depicting God's empire in cosmic terms of overwhelming power, destroyed opponents, and imposed universal rule, this scene imitates conventional assertions of imperial power. It reflects the Gospel's embeddedness in and accommodation to its imperial culture, along with its utilization of imperial biblical traditions like Daniel.[63] Mimicry frequently operates in colonial situations among oppressed groups who know the hybridity of unequal power relations, yearn for the power that they despise, and imitate their oppressors, sometimes to ally with them but often to mock and menace them with visions of their violent downfall.[64] For Matthew, God's empire out-muscles and countermasters Rome's empire.

---

61. Carter, "Are There Imperial Texts in the Class?"

62. Josephus, *J.W.* 3.123; 5.48.

63. Note similar imitation in the parable of the violent king and his son's wedding feast in Matt 22:1–14. Burning cities (22:7) is a common imperial tactic that subjugates and humiliates a defeated people. Titus's troops burned Jerusalem and the temple in 70 CE (Josephus, *J.W.* 2.395–397; 6.249–408). With other Jewish writers (4 Ezra 3:24–36; 4:22–25; 2 Bar 1:1–5; Josephus, *J.W.* 6.96–110, 409–411), Matthew interprets Jerusalem's fall in 70 CE as God's judgment, especially on the Jerusalem leaders for rejecting Jesus. Matthew employs a paradigm from the Hebrew Scriptures that saw various imperial powers as the agents of God's punishment—Assyria (Isa 10:1–7), Babylon (Deut 28–30; Jer 25:1–11), Persia (Isa 45:1–13), the Seleucids under Antiochus Epiphanes (2 Macc 6:12–17)—but were then subjected to God's punishment: Assyria (Isa 10:12–34), Babylon (25:12–14), Antiochus Epiphanes (2 Macc 7:32–36). Matthew evoked this paradigm in quoting Isa 7–9 in 1:23 and 4:15–16; see Carter, *Matthew and Empire*, 93–107.

64. Bhabha, "Of Mimicry and Man."

And in the Meantime? (Ecclesiology)

How are followers of Jesus to live? The Gospel's presentation of Jesus' manifestation of God's rule/empire (Matt 4:17, 18–22; cf. Mark 1:16–20) creates a counter-cultural community committed to God and Jesus with an alternative worldview and set of societal practices. This community, embedded in and subordinated to the empire, is to embody God's reign as an alternative to the empire's societal reality. The Gospel offers strategies, both self-protective and contestive, in which Matthew's people can negotiate imperial demands while maintaining their allegiance to God's purposes manifested in Jesus.

This protective yet contestive way of life forbids violent attacks (Matt 26:52; 5:38–48) and flight (28:18–20) as means of negotiating the power differential. Instead, the readers are to practice non-violent resistance (5:38–48) typical of the calculated and self-protective practices of peasants identified by James Scott.[65] Instead of cowering submission or violent retaliation, Jesus urges a non-violent response to the superior's slap, offering the other check to deflect the intended intimidation and demeaning (5:39). In 5:41 Jesus requires compliance to *angaria*, a custom whereby Rome requisitioned labor, transport (animals, ships), and lodging from subject people. But followers were to subvert imperial authority by carrying the soldier's pack twice the distance, putting the soldier off-balance, in danger of being disciplined for overly harsh conduct. Likewise, in paying taxes followers assumed the common double pose of subordinated groups, namely self-protective public obedience, with a hidden and coded transcript of dissent whereby the taxes, which the Gospel subversively reframes, acknowledge not Rome's sovereignty but God's as lord of heaven and earth (Matt 17:24–27;[66] 22:15–22;[67] cf. Mark 12:13–17).

While some disciples abandon economic activity and social structures to follow Jesus (Matt 4:18–22; 9:9; 19:16–30), there is no general call to separate from family, material, and societal ties. Their social patterns are, however, to contrast with the empire's hierarchical and tyrannical norms. Jesus forbids his followers to imitate the domination behaviors and structures of the "rulers of the gentiles" and "their great men" who

---

65. Scott, *Domination*; Scott, *Weapons of the Weak*; Wink, "Beyond Just War."
66. Carter, *Matthew and Empire*, 130–44.
67. Herzog, "OnStage."

"lord it over" and "rule" others (20:25). Instead, they are to embrace the marginality and humility of the empire's lowest members, slaves, seeking the other's good in imitation of Jesus (20:26–28; cf. 23:11–12; Mark 10:42–45). Followers are to adopt household structures that challenge conventional androcentric, patriarchal, and hierarchical household patterns (Matt 19–20; cf. Mark 10).[68] Their more egalitarian structure (cf. Matt 20:12) reflects that *God* is father (5:16, 45; 6:9; 23:9) not the emperor (*pater patriae*), that Jesus is the only master (23:10), and that all disciples bear a marginal and vulnerable identity as God's children (5:9, 45).

The Gospel consistently warns against the dangers of wealth (Matt 6:24, 33–34; 13:19–22; cf. Mark 4:19). Contrary to Rome's exploitative economics that foreground the quest for wealth, power, and status, Jesus advocates an alternative economic system and a community based in care for the poor. Jesus calls a "rich man" (Matt 19:23, 24), one who has great wealth because he has misused and exploited the poor (so Isa 10:1–3; Ezek 22:6–31; 34:1–22; Amos 5:10–12; Sir 13:2–7, 17–19), to divest and redistribute wealth among the poor (19:21; cf. Mark 10:17–23). Jesus' advocacy of actions to benefit the poor (most of society) contradicts practices that lead the elite, motivated by love of status (*philodoxia*), to engage in self-benefiting acts of patronage, and to ignore or despise the unworthy poor.[69] Jesus' (counter)cultural formation involves a changed identity, societal orientation, and economic activity. Acts of restitution and justice set right inequalities and transform unjust structures, relationships, and practices.

Matthew's Gospel claims that God's blessing and empire especially embrace the poor (Matt 5:3). Citing Psalm 37, Jesus' third beatitude reverses the imperial economic order by promising that the meek will receive the earth or land, the basis of wealth (Matt 5:5). The intertext of Psalm 37 (37:3, 9, 11, 22, 29, 34) depicts the meek as the poor, oppressed by the powerful and dangerous rich (37:7, 12, 14, 20, 32) whom God will destroy (37:9, 13, 20).

The economic practices of Jesus' followers are to include mercy and justice. According to Matt 6:1–18, followers are to practice acts of justice (prayer, almsgiving, fasting) without imitating the "self-regarding" practices of elite patronage concerned with enhancing elite status, reciprocity, creating dependents/clients, love of honor (*philotimia*), and

---

68. Carter, *Matthew and the Margins*, 376–410.
69. For example, Seneca, *Vit. beat.* 24.

reputation (*philodoxa*). Jesus assumes almsgiving (6:2), a word that at its root concerns mercy, a fundamental quality of God's empire exhibited in human interactions (5:7; citing Hos 6:6 in Matt 9:13 and 12:7). Acts of mercy (6:2-4) involve giving to beggars and lending where reciprocity is unlikely (5:42). Prayers for daily bread are often answered in the merciful actions of those who pray (6:11). To fast (6:16-18) is to live justice and mercy in sharing food, housing the homeless, clothing the naked, and comforting the afflicted (cf. Isa 58:6-14; Matt 25:31-46). Jesus commands preaching God's empire, healing the sick, raising the dead, cleansing lepers, and casting out demons without payment (10:7-8). This differentiated way of life for disciples is without anxiety for material goods (food, drink, clothing) since God's justice and reign ensure enough (6:19-34). Yet perseverance, or faithful and active endurance, is always necessary (24:13; cf. Mark 13:13).

One summary of this lifestyle focuses on love for neighbor as for oneself (Matt 22:39; cf 7:12)[70] and love for one's enemy (5:44) in imitation of God's ways (5:45-48). Another summary centers on justice or righteousness (6:34). This commitment to justice, in the midst of Rome's injustice, means observance of Torah-practices (Sabbath, purity, tithes, oaths, etc.) as interpreted by Jesus (5:17-48; 22:37-39). These practices enact justice, mercy, and faithfulness (23:23), basic to the alternative societal order that Jesus reveals as God's reign and purpose.

CONCLUSION

Matthew's Gospel offers Jesus-followers various strategies for negotiating the elite-dominated, socio-political, Roman imperial order. One strategy involves perspective or understanding. They are to understand the imperial system as sinful, devilish, under God's imminent judgment, temporary, and facing destruction. Within it, God's transforming empire is at work, manifesting God's sovereignty, presence, purposes, blessings, and will, mimicking and disputing the similar claims of imperial theology. It is also at work creating and calling followers to an alternative worldview and to a challenging counter-cultural societal experience that embodies God's reign in alternative practices. Until its future eschatological triumph, ironically an imitation of imperial ways that on a cosmic scale attributes the ways of Caesar to God, violent (human)

---

70. Carter, "Love as Societal Vision."

opposition is forbidden. Accommodation, submission, mimicry, and active but self-protective, non-violent resistance, and faithful and hopeful living provide a spectrum of strategies.

BIBLIOGRAPHY

Aristotle. "On the Art of Poetry." In *Classical Literary Criticism*, translated by T. S. Dorsch, 29–75. London: Penguin, 2001.
Arlandson, J. M. *Women, Class, and Society in Early Christianity: Models from Luke–Acts*. Peabody: Hendrickson, 1997.
Barbalet, John. "Power and Resistance." *British Journal of Sociology* 36 (1985) 521–48.
Barclay, John. *Jews in the Mediterranean Diaspora from Alexander to Trajan (323 BCE–117 CE)*. Edinburgh: T. & T. Clark, 1996.
Bhabha, Homi. *The Location of Culture*. London: Routledge, 1994.
———. "Of Mimicry and Man: The Ambivalence of Colonial Discourse." In *Location of Culture*, 85–92.
Bond, Helen. *Pontius Pilate in History and Interpretation*. SNTSMS 100. Cambridge: Cambridge University Press, 1998.
Carter, Warren. "Are There Imperial Texts in the Class? Intertextual Eagles and Matthean Eschatology as 'Lights Out' Time for Imperial Rome (Matthew 24:27–31)." *JBL* 122 (2003) 467–87.
———. "Embodying God's Empire in Communal Practices." In *Preaching the Sermon on the Mount: The World It Imagines*, edited by David Fleer and David Bland, 22–35. St. Louis: Chalice, 2007.
———. "Evoking Isaiah: Matthean Soteriology and an Intertextual Reading of Isaiah 7–9 in Matthew 1:23 and 4:15–16." *JBL* 119 (2000) 503–20.
———. "Honoring the Emperor and Sacrificing Wives and Slaves: 1 Peter 2:13—3:6." In *A Feminist Companion to the Catholic Epistles and Hebrews*, edited by Amy-Jill Levine, 13–43. London: T. & T. Clark, 2004.
———. *John and Empire: Initial Explorations*. London: T. & T. Clark, 2008.
———. "Love as Societal Vision and Fatal Practice in Matthew 22:34–40." In *Biblical Interpretation in Early Christian Gospels*. Vol. 2. *The Gospel of Matthew*, edited by Thomas R. Hatina, 30–44. London/New York: T. & T. Clark, 2008.
———. *Matthew and Empire: Initial Explorations*. Harrisburg: Trinity Press International, 2001.
———. *Matthew and the Margins: A Sociopolitical and Religious Reading*. Maryknoll, NY: Orbis, 2000.
———. *Matthew: Storyteller, Interpreter, Evangelist*. Revised ed. Peabody: Hendrickson, 2004.
———. "Matthew's Gospel: Jewish Christianity, Christian Judaism, or Neither?" In *Jewish Christianity Reconsidered*, edited by Matt Jackson-McCabe, 155–80. Minneapolis: Fortress, 2007.
———. "Matthew's People." In *A People's History of Christianity: Christian Origins*, edited by Richard Horsley, 138–61. Minneapolis: Fortress, 2005.
———. *Pontius Pilate: Portraits of a Roman Governor*. Collegeville: Liturgical, 2003.
———. "Power and Identities: The Contexts of Matthew's Sermon on the Mount." In *Preaching the Sermon on the Mount: The World It Imagines*, edited by David Fleer and David Bland, 8–21. St. Louis: Chalice, 2007.

———. *The Roman Empire and the New Testament: An Essential Guide.* Nashville: Abingdon, 2006.
Castle, Gregory, ed. *Postcolonial Discourses: An Anthology.* Oxford: Blackwell, 2001.
Donaldson, Laura, editor. *Postcolonialism and Scriptural Reading.* Semeia 75. Atlanta: Scholars, 1996.
Duling, Dennis. "Empire: Theories, Methods, Models." In *The Gospel of Matthew in Its Roman Imperial Context,* edited by John Riches and David Sim, 49–74. JSNTSup 276. London: T. & T. Clark, 2005.
Fanon, Franz. *The Wretched of the Earth.* New York: Grove, 1968.
Futrell, Alison. *Blood in the Arena: The Spectacle of Roman Power.* Austin: University of Texas Press, 2000.
Garnsey, Peter. *Famine and Food Supply in the Graeco-Roman World.* Cambridge: Cambridge University Press, 1988.
———. *Food and Society in Classical Antiquity.* Cambridge: Cambridge University Press, 1999.
———. *Social Status and Legal Privilege in the Roman Empire.* Oxford: Clarendon, 1970.
Hanson, K. C., and D. E. Oakman. *Palestine in the Time of Jesus: Social Structures and Social Conflicts.* Minneapolis: Fortress, 1998.
Harland, Philip. *Associations, Synagogues, and Congregations.* Minneapolis: Fortress, 2003.
Hengel, Martin. *Crucifixion.* Philadelphia: Fortress, 1977.
Herzog, William. "OnStage and OffStage with Jesus of Nazareth: Public Transcripts, Hidden Transcripts, and Gospel Texts." In *Hidden Transcripts and the Arts of Resistance,* edited by Richard Horsley, 41–60. Semeia 48. Atlanta: Society of Biblical Literature, 2004.
Horsley, Richard. *Hearing the Whole Story: The Politics of Plot in Mark's Gospel.* Louisville: Westminster John Knox, 2001.
———, editor. *Hidden Transcripts and the Arts of Resistance.* Semeia 48. Atlanta: Society of Biblical Literature, 2004.
Kautsky, John. *The Politics of Aristocratic Empires.* Chapel Hill: University of North Carolina Press, 1982.
Keck, Leander. "Toward the Renewal of New Testament Christology." *NTS* 32 (1986) 362–77.
Kingsbury, Jack Dean. *The Christology of Mark's Gospel.* Philadelphia: Fortress, 1983.
———. *Conflict in Mark: Jesus, Authorities, Disciples.* Minneapolis: Fortress, 1989.
———. "The Figure of Jesus in Matthew's Story: A Literary-Critical Probe." *CBQ* 49 (1987) 57–73.
Kondoleon, Christine. *Antioch: The Lost Ancient City.* Princeton: Princeton University Press, 2000.
Kristeva, Julia. "The Bounded Text." In *Desire in Language: A Semiotic Approach to Literature and Art,* edited by L. Rondiez, 36–63. New York: Columbia University Press, 1980.
Lenski, Gerhard. *Power and Privilege: A Theory of Social Stratification.* Chapel Hill: University of North Carolina Press, 1984.
Liew, Tat-Siong Benny. *Politics of Parousia: Reading Mark Inter(con)textually.* Leiden: Brill, 1999.

Mattingly, David, editor. *Dialogues in Roman Imperialism: Power, Discourse, and Discrepant Experience in the Roman Empire*. JRA Supplementary Series 23. Portsmouth, RI: Journal of Roman Archaeology Supplementary Series, 1997.

Mowery, Robert. "Son of God in Roman Imperial Titles and Matthew." *Bib* 83 (2002) 100–110.

Myers, Ched. *Binding the Strong Man: A Political Reading of Mark's Story of Jesus*. Maryknoll, NY: Orbis, 1988.

Pilgrim, Walter. *Uneasy Neighbors: Church and State in the New Testament*. Minneapolis: Fortress, 1999.

Price, Simon. *Rituals and Power: The Roman Imperial Cult in Asia Minor*. Cambridge: Cambridge University Press, 1984.

Riches, John, and David Sim, editors. *The Gospel of Matthew in Its Roman Imperial Context*. JSNTSup 276. London: T. & T. Clark, 2005.

Said, Edward. *Culture and Imperialism*. New York: Knopf, 1993.

Saldarini, Anthony. *Pharisees, Scribes and Sadducees in Palestinian Society: A Sociological Approach*. Wilmington: Glazier, 1988.

Scott, James. *Domination and the Arts of Resistance: Hidden Transcripts*. New Haven: Yale University Press, 1990.

———. *Weapons of the Weak: Everyday Forms of Peasant Resistance*. New Haven: Yale University Press, 1985.

Segovia, Fernando. *Decolonizing Biblical Studies: A View from the Margins*. Maryknoll, NY: Orbis, 2000.

Stark, Rodney. "Antioch as the Social Situation for Matthew's Gospel." In *Social History of the Matthean Community*, edited by David Balch, 189–210. Minneapolis: Fortress, 1991.

Sugirtharajah, Rasiah. *The Bible as Empire: Postcolonial Explorations*. Cambridge: Cambridge University Press, 2005.

———. *The Postcolonial Bible*. Sheffield: Sheffield Academic, 1998.

———. *Postcolonial Criticism and Biblical Interpretation*. Oxford: Oxford University Press, 2002.

Swain, Simon. *Hellenism and Empire: Language, Classicism, and Power in the Greek World AD 50–250*. Oxford: Clarendon, 1996.

Tilborg, Sjef van. *The Jewish Leaders in Matthew*. Leiden: Brill, 1972.

Webster, J., and N. J. Cooper, editors. *Roman Imperialism: Post-Colonial Perspectives*. Leicester Archaeology Monographs 3. Leicester, UK: University of Leicester, 1996.

Whittaker, C. R. "The Poor." In *The Romans*, edited by Andrea Giardina, 272–99. Chicago: University of Chicago Press, 1993.

Wink, Walter. "Beyond Just War and Pacifism: Jesus' Nonviolent Way." *RevExp* 89 (1992) 197–214.

4

King Jesus and His Ambassadors

Empire and Luke–Acts

CRAIG A. EVANS

IN THE NEW TESTAMENT Gospels, Jesus is acknowledged as king—by his followers and his enemies alike. In Luke–Acts Jesus is implicitly compared to the "benefactors" of his time. This comparison criticizes and at the same time adopts an important political and social epithet. This interesting political dimension is furthered in the book of Acts, where Paul the ambassador is presented as an ambassador of King Jesus. This essay unfolds in three parts: (1) Jesus as king in the Gospels and early Christian literature; (2) Jesus as benefactor; and (3) the apostles as Jesus' ambassadors.

JESUS AS KING IN THE GOSPELS AND EARLY CHRISTIAN LITERATURE

In the New Testament Gospels, the kingship of Jesus is affirmed primarily in his interrogation and execution (which will be considered below). But there are important indications of his kingship elsewhere in the Gospels.

Mark's account of Jesus' entry into Jerusalem only hints at kingship. There is no quotation of Zech 9:9, in which there is mention of Zion's king, and Jesus himself is not called king. The crowds proclaim, "Hosanna! Blessed is he who comes in the name of the Lord! Blessed is the kingdom of our father David that is coming! Hosanna in the highest!" (Mark 11:9–10). What precise role Jesus himself will play in bringing about the "kingdom of David that is coming" is not made clear, at least not in the context of the entrance into Jerusalem. Matthew clarifies the narrative by quoting Zech 9:9 ("Behold, your king is coming to you") and by identifying Jesus as the "son of David" (Matt 21:5, 9). Thus, in Matthew Jesus is king and son of David. Luke does not quote Zech 9:9, but his disciples cry out, "Blessed is the king who comes in the name of the Lord!" (Luke 19:38). Thus, in Luke Jesus is the king. The Fourth Gospel, in its version of the entrance into Jerusalem, also makes Jesus' identity as the king explicit, not only by quoting Zech 9:9 (cf. John 12:15), but by having the crowd cry out: "Hosanna! Blessed is he who comes in the name of the Lord, even the king of Israel!" (John 12:13).

Of course, both the Matthean and Johannine Evangelists proclaim the kingship of Jesus earlier in their respective narratives. Matthew introduces the idea in his infancy account, where the wise men inquire, "Where is he who has been born king of the Jews? For we have seen his star in the East, and have come to worship him" (Matt 2:2). Identifying Jesus as "king of the Jews" (βασιλεὺς τῶν Ἰουδαίων) anticipates his eventual execution as "king of the Jews," thus fulfilling an implicit prophecy. At the beginning of his narrative, the Johannine Evangelist tells us that Nathanael, upon meeting Jesus, declares: "Rabbi, you are the Son of God! You are the King of Israel!" (John 1:49). This confession is very important, for it links the epithets "Son of God" and "King of Israel." Moreover, the epithet "King of Israel," like Matthew's infancy reference to "king of the Jews," anticipates Jesus' official identity on the occasion of his crucifixion.

And finally, both Matthew and John refer to Jesus as king in traditions unique to their respective Gospels. In John, after feeding the five thousand, the multitude attempt to make Jesus king by force (John 6:15).[1] And in Matthew, in the context of the eschatological discourse, the enthroned Jesus is described as the king who judges his enemies and rewards his faithful followers (Matt 25:34, 40).[2]

All four Evangelists are in agreement in affirming the kingship of Jesus at the time of his trial and execution. In Mark, the high priest

---

1. The Greek reads: μέλλουσιν ἔρχεσθαι καὶ ἁρπάζειν αὐτὸν ἵνα ποιήσωσιν βασιλέα ("they were about to come and seize him, that they might make him king").

2. The Greek reads (in v. 34): τότε ἐρεῖ ὁ βασιλεὺς τοῖς ἐκ δεξιῶν αὐτοῦ ("Then the king will say to those on his right ... ").

demands to know of Jesus: "Are you the Messiah, the Son of the Blessed?" (Mark 14:61).[3] Jesus' reply, "I am" (v. 62a), is affirmative: He is indeed the Messiah, the Son of the God.[4] His elaboration, "and you will see the Son of Man seated at the right hand of Power, and coming with the clouds of heaven" (v. 62b),[5] makes clear that Jesus sees himself as God's Anointed who, having received from God kingly authority, will sit at God's right hand (Ps 110:1a; cf. Dan 7:9) and judge his enemies (Ps 110:1b; Dan 7:13-14). The parallel accounts in Matthew and Luke present essentially the same picture, even if they differ at a few points (Matt 26:63-64; Luke 22:67-70).

The kingship of Jesus is affirmed in all four Gospels when Jesus is interrogated by Pontius Pilate, the prefect of Judea. Pilate asks Jesus, "Are you king of the Jews?" (Mark 15:2a = Matt 27:11a = Luke 23:3a = John 18:33). The title "king of the Jews" (ὁ βασιλεὺς τῶν Ἰουδαίων) echoes the title Marcus Antonius and the Roman Senate conferred upon Herod in 40 BCE (Josephus, *J.W.* 1.282: Antonia "resolved to have him made king of the Jews [βασιλέα καθιστᾶν Ἰουδαίων]"; 1.388;[6] cf. *Ant.* 14.9; 15.9; 15.373, 409).[7] Jesus affirms the question, even if his answer appears to be equivocal: "You have said so" (Mark 15:2b =

---

3. The Greek reads: σὺ εἶ ὁ χριστὸς ὁ υἱὸς τοῦ εὐλογητοῦ.

4. The confession to be Messiah, son of God, in the Jewish tradition clearly implies kingship. We see this in Scripture (e.g., 2 Sam 7:14; Pss 2:2, 7; 89:19-21, 26-27) and in traditions that emerge shortly before the time of Jesus and his movement, e.g., "And he (shall be) a righteous king [αὐτὸς βασιλεὺς δίκαιος], taught of God, over them. And there shall be no unrighteousness in his days in their midst, for all shall be holy and their king the Lord's Messiah [βασιλεὺς αὐτῶν χριστὸς κυρίου]" (*Pss. Sol.* 17:32).

5. The Greek reads: καὶ ὄψεσθε τὸν υἱὸν τοῦ ἀνθρώπου ἐκ δεξιῶν καθήμενον τῆς δυνάμεως καὶ ἐρχόμενον μετὰ τῶν νεφελῶν τοῦ οὐρανοῦ.

6. One should note Herod's frank confession before Octavian (soon Augustus), after the latter's defeat of Marcus Antonius: "O Caesar, as I was made king [βασιλεύς] by Antonius, so do I profess that I have used my royal authority in the best manner, and entirely for his advantage; nor will I conceal this further, that you certainly found me in arms, and an inseparable companion of his, had not the Arabians hindered me. However, I sent him as many auxiliaries as I was able, and many thousand measures (*cori*) of corn. Indeed, I did not desert my benefactor [τὸν εὐεργέτην] after the blow that was given him at Actium" (Josephus, *J.W.* 1.388).

7. The statement that Antonius "made" (καθιστᾶν) Herod "king of the Jews" may explain why the Matthean Evangelist words the question of the wise men the way he does: "Where is he who has been born [ὁ τεχθείς] king of the Jews?" In contrast to Herod, whose kingship was the result of Roman appointment, the kingship of Jesus is *by birth*, and a divine birth at that.

Matt 27:11b = Luke 23:3b). Pilate presents Jesus to the crowd as the "king of the Jews," offering to release him (Mark 15:9; cf. John 18:39) and later asking the crowd what to do with the "king of the Jews" (Mark 15:12; cf. John 19:15). Matthew edits the latter two passages, to read "Jesus who is called 'Messiah'" (Matt 27:17, 22), affirming the more appropriate epithet from a Jewish and Christian perspective.

The Fourth Evangelist draws attention to the kingship of Jesus by intensifying the contrast between king Jesus and king Caesar. The opponents of Jesus quarrel with Pilate, lest the governor release him: "If you release this man, you are not Caesar's friend; every one who makes himself a king sets himself against Caesar" (John 19:12). When Pilate asks if he should crucify the Jewish king, the crowd replies: "We have no king but Caesar" (John 19:15). Recognized as king by Nathanael at the beginning of the narrative, nearly forced into becoming king mid-way through the narrative, Jesus is flatly rejected as king by the Jewish rulers at the conclusion of the narrative.

The kingship of Jesus is further affirmed in his abuse and mockery suffered at the hands of the Roman soldiers. They dress Jesus in faux imperial regalia and salute him in imperial language: "Hail, king of the Jews!" (Mark 15:18 = Matt 26:29 = John 19:3).[8] The kingship of Jesus is also affirmed in the crucifixion itself, where a *titulus* (Greek: τίτλος), proclaiming the grounds for punishment (*causa poena*), is posted, reading "The king of the Jews [ὁ βασιλεὺς τῶν Ἰουδαίων]" (Mark 15:26; cf. Matt 27:37; Luke 23:38).[9]

The kingship of Jesus is explicitly affirmed elsewhere in the New Testament. Paul's ministry in Thessalonica is disrupted by opponents who drag the apostle before city officials, charging that he and his companions "are all acting against the decrees of Caesar, saying that there is another king, Jesus" (Acts 17:7). In Revelation, Jesus is twice acclaimed

---

8. The soldiers "clothed him in a purple cloak, and plaiting a crown of thorns they put it on him" (Mark 15:17). The import of the purple cloak is obvious; the "crown of thorns" is supposed to represent the laurel wreath. During the celebration of a triumph, it was customary for Caesar to wear a robe and laurel wreath (cf. Dio Cassius 6.23; 44.11 [Julius Caesar]; Appian, *Bell. civ.* 5.130 [Augustus]; Suetonius, *Tib.* 17.2 "clad in the purple-bordered toga and crowned with laurel" [Tiberius]; Dio Cassius 59.25.3 [Caligula]). For other accounts of such mockery, see Philo, *Flacc.* 36–39; Plutarch, *Pomp.* 24.7–8; P. Louvre 68 1.1–7).

9. Both Matthew and Luke expand Mark's terse "King of the Jews." Matthew reads: "*This is Jesus* the king of the Jews" (27:37), while Luke reads: "*This is* the king of the Jews" (Luke 23:38), with the respective additions placed in italics.

"Lord of lords and King of kings" (Rev 17:14 and 19:16 [with titles reversed]).

Elsewhere in early Christian writings the kingship of Jesus is affirmed. This is especially noted in the account of the *Martyrdom of Polycarp*:

> But when the magistrate persisted and said, "Swear the oath, and I will release you; revile Christ," Polycarp replied, "For eighty-six years I have been his servant, and he has done me no wrong. How can I blaspheme my King who saved me [πῶς δύναμαι βλασφημῆσαι τὸν βασιλέα μου τὸν σώσαντά με]?" (9:3)

> For this one, who is the Son of God, we worship, but the martyrs we love as disciples and imitators of the Lord, as they deserve, on account of their matchless devotion to their own King and Teacher [ἕνεκεν εὐνοίας ἀνυπερβλήτου τῆς εἰς τὸν ἴδιον βασιλέα καὶ διδάσκαλον]. May we also become their partners and fellow-disciples! (17:3)

> Now the blessed Polycarp was martyred on the second day of the first part of the month Xanthicus, seven days before the kalends of March, on a great Sabbath, about two o'clock p.m. He was arrested by Herod, when Philip of Tralles was high priest during the proconsulship of Statius Quadratus, but while Jesus Christ was reigning as King forever [βασιλεύοντος δὲ εἰς τοὺς αἰῶνας Ἰησοῦ Χριστοῦ]. To him be glory, honor, majesty, and the eternal throne [θρόνος αἰώνιος], from generation to generation. Amen. (21:1)[10]

Two more passage should be mentioned:

> You are calloused and don't want to cleanse your hearts and mix your wisdom together in a clean heart, in order that you may have mercy from the great King [παρὰ τοῦ βασιλέως τοῦ μεγάλου]" (Shepherd of Hermas 17:8 [= *Herm. Vis.* 3:9])

> Certainly not! On the contrary, he sent him in gentleness and meekness, as a king might send his son who is a king [βασιλεὺς πέμπων υἱὸν βασιλέα ἔπεμψεν]; he sent him as God; he sent him as a man to men. When he sent him, he did so as one who saves by persuasion, not compulsion, for compulsion is no attribute of God. (*Diogn.* 7:4)[11]

---

10. Translations are based on Lightfoot, Harmer, and Holmes, *The Apostolic Fathers*, 139, 142–43.

11. Translations are based on ibid., 208, 301.

From the accusations leveled against Jesus himself, to the charges brought against the first two or three generations of Christians, it is clear that Jesus was perceived as king and rival to Caesar himself. Of course, this is consistent with his recognition as Messiah and Son of God, which in Jewish tradition, informed by ancient and sacred Scripture, implied kingly status. It is to Luke's distinctive interpretation of this kingly status of Jesus that we now turn.

JESUS AS BENEFACTOR

On the occasion of a dispute over who among them is the greatest, Jesus teaches his disciples: "You know that those who are supposed to rule over the Gentiles lord it over them, and their great men exercise authority over them" (Mark 10:42). The saying reads essentially the same way in the parallel in Matt 20:25.[12] But the parallel in Luke reads differently and in a distinctive way: "The kings of the Gentiles exercise lordship over them; and those in authority over them are called 'benefactors'" (Luke 22:25).[13]

Luke's revision of his Markan source creates a measure of awkwardness. In Mark the transition from 10:42 to 10:43 is natural: "... the Gentiles lord it over them, and their great men exercise authority over them. But it shall not be so among you ... " But in Luke the addition at the conclusion of 22:25, "and those in authority over them are called 'benefactors,'" creates an incongruity with the antithesis in 22:26: "But not so with you ... "[14] Shouldn't the disciples of Jesus seek to be benefactors, or doers of good? As we shall see, they in fact become such in Luke's second volume, the book of Acts.[15]

The tension is resolved, of course, because Luke's readers would readily interpret the reference to "benefactors" in the context of rulers and the mighty, the very people who lord it over others, defining their

---

12. "You know that the rulers of the Gentiles lord it over them, and their great men exercise authority over them."

13. According to the *UBSGNT*[4]: ὁ δὲ εἶπεν αὐτοῖς· οἱ βασιλεῖς τῶν ἐθνῶν κυριεύουσιν αὐτῶν καὶ οἱ ἐξουσιάζοντες αὐτῶν εὐεργέται καλοῦνται.

14. There are several ambiguities in Luke's form of the saying. For discussion of these interpretive difficulties, see Lull, "Servant-Benefactor."

15. Lull ("Servant-Benefactor," 303–4) rightly concludes that the Lukan Evangelist tries to show in Luke-Acts that the Greco-Roman benefactor ideal is exemplified in Jesus and his servants/representatives.

tyrannical rule with the euphemism "benefaction." Luke's readers knew that the epithet "benefactor" (εὐεργέτης) was commonly bestowed on gods, kings, and wealthy and powerful men who contributed to society.

There are many examples from the literature and inscriptions of late antiquity.[16] For example, the people "conceived that (Uranus) who taught such things partook of the nature of the gods [θείας μετέχειν φύσεως], and after he had passed from among men they accorded to him immortal honors [ἀθανάτους τιμάς], both because of his benefactions [εὐεργεσίας] and because of his knowledge of the stars" (Diodorus Siculus, *Discourses* 3.56.5). Hercules too is called "benefactor to mortals and great friend [εὐεργέτης βροτοῖσι καὶ μέγας φίλος]" (Euripides, *Heracl.* 1252).[17]

A good man is "one who takes delight in bestowing benefits [χαίροντα εὐεργεσίαις]—a trait that approaches most nearly to the divine nature [τῆς τῶν θεῶν φύσεως]" (Dio Chrysostom, *2 Regn.* 26).[18] The first-century Stertinius Xenophon is a prominent example, who was honored as εὐεργέτης by the people of Cos with a number of inscriptions.[19] Such thinking as this likely lay behind many of the descriptions of the benefactions of rulers and great men and women. Accordingly, Demosthenes calls Philip II of Macedon, father of Alexander the Great, "Friend, Benefactor, and Savior" of the people of Thessalonica (*Cor.* 43). Although the epigraphic evidence related to Alexander is limited, one can find similar language used in reference to Philip's famous son: "King Alexander ... was especially beneficent [εὐεργέται] to the Greek cities ..." (Diodorus Siculus, *Discourses* 17.24.1); "Alexander mitigated the lot of these unfortunate persons by such benefactions [εὐεργεσίαις] in keeping with his natural kindness" (Diodorus Siculus, *Discourses*

---

16. I depend on the following works: Bertram, "Εὐεργέτης"; Llewelyn, ed., *New Documents* 9; Spicq, "εὐεργεσία, κτλ"; Danker, "Endangered Benefactor"; Danker, *Benefactor*, 323–24; Heisserer, *Alexander*; Lull, "Servant-Benefactor"; Neyrey, *Render to God*, 82–106; Neyrey, "God, Benefactor and Patron"; Nock, "Soter and Euergetes"; and Rajak, "Benefactors."

17. For other examples of inscriptions in honor of various gods as benefactors, see Danker, *Benefactor*, 73–74 (Aphrodite), 176–85 (Isis), 186–91 (Serapis), 192–96 (Asklepios).

18. Text and translation based on Cohoon, *Dio Chrysostom I*, 66–67.

19. See Paton and Hicks, *Inscriptions of Cos*, nos. 46, 84–94, and 345. For discussion of this person, the well known physician of Claudius, who eventually poisoned the emperor, see Deissmann, *Light from the Ancient East*, 253.

17.69.9); Alexander "saw only one hope of gaining his wish, if he might gain the soldiers' great goodwill through beneficence [διὰ τῆς εὐεργεσίας]" (Diodorus Siculus, *Discourses* 17.94.3).[20]

Alexander's successors (esp. Ptolemy and Seleucus and their respective dynasties) are routinely referred to as benefactors and saviors; indeed, several of them adopted these titles as their formal regal names, as seen in the following examples: Ptolemy I Soter (367–282);[21] Ptolemy III Euergetes (284–221);[22] Ptolemy VIII Euergetes II (182–116);[23] Ptolemy IX Soter II (142–80); Antiochus I Soter (280–261); Seleucus III Soter (226–223); Demetrius I Soter (162–150).[24]

The Roman emperors adopted the nomenclature. Julius Caesar (ruled 48–44 BCE) is named "savior and benefactor" in several cities (e.g., *IG* VIII.1835; XII.5, 556; *IGR* 9.57, 303, 305; *CIA* 3.428).[25] Caesar's successor, Octavian, who becomes Caesar Augustus (absolute rule 31 BCE–14 CE), is also frequently called benefactor. In one inscription his full title is given as Αὐτοκράτωρ Καῖσαρ Σεβαστὸς σωτὴρ καὶ εὐεργέτης (*SB* 8897.1): "Emperor Caesar Augustus, Savior and Benefactor." One also thinks of the Priene calendar inscription (*OGIS* 458), which was inscribed and dedicated in honor of "the birthday of the most divine Caesar" (l.4–5; cf. l.17). This inscription proclaims "Augustus, whom (Providence) filled with virtue for the benefit of humans [εἰς εὐεργεσίαν ἀνθρώπων], sending him as a savior [σωτήρ]..." (ll.34; cf. ll.46). There are many other examples (e.g., *IGR* 1.901, 1294; 3.426; 4.201 [because of his benefactions to all humanity, the people of Ilium describe Augustus as "Benefactor" and "Savior"—εὐεργέτην καὶ σωτῆρα]; 4.311, 312; *CIA* 3.575, 576; *IG* 7.1836). Even Philo the Jew speaks of Augustus as "the

---

20. Text and translation based on Welles, *Diodorus of Sicily VIII*, 182–85, 318–19, 390–91.

21. See *SIG* 390.26–30: "... the savior Ptolemy, with godlike honors, and on account of his public benefactions [διὰ τὰς κοινὰς εὐεργεσίας]."

22. One inscribed dedication reads: "May it please the priests of the land that the honors hitherto rendered in the sanctuary (of Osiris) to King Ptolemy and Queen Berenice, gods (and) benefactors [θεοῖς εὐεργέταις]" (*OGIS* 56.20–21; ET based on Spicq, "εὐεργεσία," 110).

23. This king is mentioned in the prologue to Sirach: "When I came to Egypt in the thirty-eighth year of King Euergetes [τοῦ Εὐεργέτου Βασιλέως] and stayed for some time, I found opportunity for no little instruction."

24. All of these dates are BCE.

25. See Taylor, *Divinity of the Roman Emperor*, 267–83; P. Bureth, *Titulatures*, 21–25.

first, the greatest, and universal benefactor [πρῶτος καὶ μέγιστος καὶ κοινὸς εὐεργέτης]" (*Legat.* 149).²⁶

The title "Benefactor" is applied to most of the Julian emperors and their successors. Tiberius, who was emperor during Jesus' ministry, is described as "founder of the city and benefactor of the world [εὐεργέτην τοῦ κόσμου]" (*SEG* 36 [1986] 1092).²⁷ Germanicus, adopted son of Tiberius, complains of honors bestowed on himself, presumably because such practice detracts from his father the emperor. He decrees (19 CE):

> Proclamation of Germanicus Caesar, son of Augustus and grandson of the deified Augustus, Proconsul. Your goodwill, which you display on all occasions when you see me, I welcome, but your acclamations, which for me are invidious and such as are addressed to gods, I altogether deprecate. For they are appropriate only to him who is actually the savior and benefactor [τῶι σωτῆρι . . . εὐεργέτῃ] of the whole human race, my father, and to his mother, my grandmother....²⁸

And of Nero we read: "The good god [ὁ ἀγαθὸς δαίμων] of the inhabited world, besides all the good things with which he benefited [εὐεργέτησεν] Egypt, sent to us Tiberius Claudius Balbillus" (*OGIS* 666.2-7); "To the Savior and Benefactor of the inhabited world [τῷ σωτῆρι καὶ εὐεργέτῃ τῆς οἰκουμένης]" (*OGIS* 668.5); "on account of goodwill I offer benefaction [εὐεργετῶ]" (*OGIS* 814.22-23). In

---

26. For more examples and discussion, see Winter, "Octavian/Augustus"; Schowalter, "Written in Stone."

27. For discussion, see Llewelyn, ed., *New Documents* 9, no. 10.

28. Hunt and Edgar, *Select Papyri*, 2:76-79 (no. 211). There are several examples where officials are called "Benefactor": The governor of Oxyrhynchus, who is petitioned, is called "Benefactor" (P.Oxy. 38.13 [49-50 CE]). The people of Clarus honor Governor Quintus Tullius: "Benefactor of the Greeks and patron of the people" (*SEG* 37 [1987] 958 [61-58 BCE]; for discussion, see Llewelyn, ed., *New Documents* 9.6). Prominent men and women for various services and benefactions are called "Benefactor": "The people of Mallos (honor) Demeas, son of Hermocrates, who has been a public benefactor [κοινὸν εὐεργέτην] and who has held public office for the salvation of the people" (Llewelyn, ed., *New Documents* 9.2 [marble statue base]); "The people (honor) Dionysius, the son of Dionysius, who is a good man with regard to the body of citizens and a benefactor of the people [εὐεργέτην τοῦ δήμου]" (Llewelyn, ed., *New Documents* 9.3); and "The people (honor) Menippus, (son) of Apollonides . . . who is a benefactor and in the interests of the body of citizens zealous and devoted to (their) good and at the head of the fatherland in times of necessity" (*SEG* 37 [1987] 957; for discussion, see Llewelyn, ed., *New Documents* 9.4).

Alexandria the newly acclaimed Vespasian is hailed as "savior and benefactor [σωτὴρ καὶ εὐεργέτης]."[29] Even Herod the Great was known in the Roman Empire as a "Benefactor."[30]

The custom of bestowing the title "Benefactor" on a ruler or on a well respected person in a given city was known to Jews of late antiquity.[31] One Jewish writer speaks of a man "who was the benefactor of the city [τὸν εὐεργέτην τῆς πόλεως], the protector of his fellow countrymen, and a zealot for the laws" (2 Macc 4:2). Another recounts a letter of Ptolemy IV Philopator (ruled 221–203 BCE), who complains of his Jewish subjects in Alexandria: "By maintaining their manifest ill-will toward us, they become the only people among all nations who hold their heads high in defiance of kings and their own benefactors [τοῖς ἑαυτῶν εὐεργέταις], and are unwilling to regard any action as sincere" (3 Macc 3:19). Later, a much repentant Ptolemy warns his followers who wish to destroy the Jews: "You are committing treason and surpassing tyrants in cruelty; and even me, your benefactor [τὸν ὑμῶν εὐεργέτην], you are now attempting to deprive of dominion and life by secretly devising acts of no advantage to the kingdom" (3 Macc 6:24).

The author of the fictive Wisdom of Solomon complains of how the Egyptians treated the Hebrews: "Others had refused to receive strangers when they came to them, but these made slaves of guests who were their benefactors [εὐεργέτας]" (Wis 19:14). Philo described true worshippers as those who "honor God, their Benefactor and Savior" [τὸν εὐεργέτην καὶ σωτῆρα θεόν]" (*Spec.* 1.272). Elsewhere, Philo speaks angrily of the savagery and hypocrisy of Emperor Gaius Caligula, "now looked upon as 'Savior and Benefactor [ὁ σωτὴρ καὶ εὐεργέτης]'; and who was expected to shower down some fresh and everlasting springs of benefits upon all Asia and Europe, so as to endow the inhabitants with inalienable happiness and prosperity" (*Legat.* 22). Josephus also knows the word and concept, making use of εὐεργέτης more than three dozen times[32] and the cognate words εὐεργεσία ("benefaction") and εὐεργετέω ("to benefit") another seventy times or so.

29. As cited by Nock, "Soter and Euergetes," 133 n. 20.
30. Jacobson, "King Herod."
31. McLaren, "Jews and the Imperial Cult."
32. Josephus bitterly complains of the rebels "as though they had been the benefactors and saviors of the city [ὡς εὐεργέται καὶ σωτῆρες τῆς πόλεως]" (*J.W.* 4.146). Implicit in the context is a contrast to the more noble Romans, who had for a long time been friends and genuine benefactors of the Jewish state.

Of course, in the Jewish mind the greatest benefactor is God himself. The "deeds and wonders" (עֲלִילוֹתָיו וְנִפְלְאוֹתָיו) of Ps 78:11 are called "benefactions and wonders" (τῶν εὐεργεσιῶν αὐτοῦ καὶ τῶν θαυμασίων αὐτοῦ) in the Greek version (LXX Ps 77:11). The author of the Wisdom of Solomon speaks of Israel being reminded "lest they should fall into deep forgetfulness and become unresponsive to (God's) kindness [εὐεργεσίας]" (Wis 16:11) and speaks of creation itself, which "in kindness [εὐεργεσίαν] relaxes on behalf of those who trust in" God (Wis 16:24).

Early Christians were also acquainted with the language of benefactor and benefaction. The author of *1 Clement* praises God: "You alone are the Benefactor of spirits and the God of all flesh [μόνον εὐεργέτην πνευμάτων καὶ θεὸν πάσης σαρκός], who looks into the depths, who scans the works of man; the Helper of those who are in peril, the Savior of those in despair; the Creator and Guardian of every spirit" (*1 Clem.* 59:3). In the fictive *Acts of Pilate*, the governor, in a rage, says to the Jews: "Always has your nation been rebellious, and you speak against your benefactors [τοῖς εὐεργέταις ὑμῶν]" (9:2). In this context, of course, the "benefactors" to whom the frustrated governor refers are himself and the rest of the Roman authority.

THE APOSTLES AS JESUS' AMBASSADORS

In the New Testament itself "benefactor" (εὐεργέτης) occurs but once, in the already cited Luke 22:25: "The kings of the Gentiles exercise lordship over them; and those in authority over them are called 'benefactors' [εὐεργέται]."[33] The vocabulary of benefaction (εὐεργετέω, εὐεργεσία, εὐεργέτης) does not occur in the other New Testament Gospels. But it does occur in two important passages in the book of Acts.[34]

In the first passage, the apostles respond to those who arrested and imprisoned them for continuing to proclaim Jesus as Messiah and as resurrected, and for healing in his name (Acts 4:1–22). When asked by

---

33. For an argument that Jesus would have known an Aramaic form of the epithet εὐεργέτης, see Deissmann, *Light from the Ancient East*, 253–54. Deissmann argues that Seleucid and Ptolemaic coins, bearing the inscription εὐεργέτης, were still in circulation in Israel or nearby in the time of Jesus.

34. The only other place in the New Testament where this language occurs is in 1 Tim 6:2, "those who benefit by their service [τῆς εὐεργεσίας]."

what authority Peter had healed the crippled man (cf. Acts 3:1–26), the apostle replied:

> Rulers of the people and elders, if we are being examined today concerning a good deed [ἐπὶ εὐεργεσίᾳ] done to a cripple, by what means this man has been healed [σέσωται], be it known to you all, and to all the people of Israel, that by the name of Jesus Christ of Nazareth, whom you crucified, whom God raised from the dead, by him this man is standing before you well. (Acts 4:8b–10)

In the second passage Peter is again speaking, this time to Cornelius the centurion attached to the Italian cohort in Caesarea Maritima. He had summoned Peter to explain the way of God (Acts 10:1–33). Peter tells the centurion:

> You know the word which he sent to Israel, preaching good news of peace by Jesus Christ (this one is Lord of all),[35] the word which was proclaimed throughout all Judea, beginning from Galilee after the baptism which John preached: how God anointed Jesus of Nazareth with the Holy Spirit and with power; how he went about doing good and healing all that were oppressed [εὐεργετῶν καὶ ἰώμενος πάντας τοὺς καταδυναστευομένους] by the devil, for God was with him. (Acts 10:36–38)

Attentive readers of Luke–Acts in all probability will have recalled the distinctive statement of the Lukan Jesus: "those in authority over them are called 'benefactors'" (Luke 22:25). In the context of Luke 22:24–26, Jesus has admonished his disciples to avoid the examples of the "kings of the Gentiles" who "exercise lordship over" their subjects and desire to be "called 'benefactors.'" But Jesus has not forbidden his disciples *to be benefactors* and to be conveyors of *benefaction*. This is what we see in the book of Acts.

---

35. The RSV translates the parenthetical words, "he is Lord of all," but the Greek text (οὗτός ἐστιν πάντων κύριος) should be rendered "this one is Lord of all," as is rightly argued by Rowe, "Luke–Acts and the Imperial Cult," 291–93. The claim that Jesus is "Lord of all" echoes similar claims made on behalf of the Roman emperors, e.g., Epictetus, *Diatr.* 4.1.12, where of the emperor Nero it is said: ὁ πάντων κύριος Καῖσαρ ("Caesar is Lord of all"); as well as an inscription that reads: ὁ τοῦ παντὸς κόσμου κύριος Νέρων ("Nero is the Lord of the whole world"); and Martial, *Epigramm.* 8.2.5–6, who says Janus promised Domitian that he would become *omni terrarum domino deoque* ("Lord and God of the whole world").

Peter's healing of the crippled man is a benefaction (εὐεργεσία), achieved in the name of Jesus Messiah, whom God has raised up. The ministry of Jesus himself is described in terms of "doing good" and "healing all who were oppressed by the devil."[36] Note that the Lukan Peter does not say "oppressed by Rome" or "oppressed by Rome's client rulers." King Jesus, humanity's true "Benefactor," is not at war with the kings of the earth;[37] he is at war with those agents who represent humanity's truest and most dangerous enemies. The continuing ministry of the risen Jesus is a redemptive ministry, one of seeking and saving. To do this Jesus sends forth his apostles, who, as true emissaries of a king, function as ambassadors. The greatest of these ambassadors in the book of Acts is Paul.

A few times in his letters Paul refers to himself as an ambassador. Three passages are of special interest:

> So we are ambassadors [πρεσβεύομεν] for Christ, God making his appeal through us. We beseech you on behalf of Christ, be reconciled to God. (2 Cor 5:20)

> Pray at all times in the Spirit, with all prayer and supplication. To that end keep alert with all perseverance, making supplication for all the saints, and also for me, that utterance may be given me in opening my mouth boldly to proclaim the mystery of the gospel, for which I am an ambassador [πρεσβεύω] in chains; that I may declare it boldly, as I ought to speak. (Eph 6:18-20)

> Accordingly, though I am bold enough in Christ to command you to do what is required, yet for love's sake I prefer to appeal to you—I, Paul, an ambassador [πρεσβύτης] and now a prisoner also for Christ Jesus—I appeal to you for my child, Onesimus, whose father I have become in my imprisonment. (Phlm 8-10)

In the first passage Paul's use of the verb πρεσβεύω clearly implies an ambassadorial function on the part of himself and the other apostles.

---

36. It should be pointed out that healings were in fact among the benefactions of the Roman emperors. We think of the well-known case where Vespasian, having gained the throne, successfully heals a blind man and a lame man (Suetonius, *Vesp.* 7.2-3).

37. Again see Rowe, "Luke–Acts and the Imperial Cult," 299-300. Rowe concludes that the Evangelist's understanding approximates that of Tertullian, who regarded Caesar as temporal κύριος, but only Jesus as κύριος πάντων (as in Acts 10:36). See Tertullian, *Apol.* 34.1: "I will plainly call the emperor *dominus*, but only in the common manner when I am not forced to call him *dominus* in the sense of God" (as cited by Rowe).

The basic meaning of πρεσβεύω is to be an elder (cf. LSJ), but the context makes it clear that Paul is not referring to himself and others as merely "elders,"[38] but is referring to their work as ambassadors for Jesus the Messiah. Through his ambassadors, God makes his conciliatory appeals to humans (such as those in Corinth).

In the second and third passages Paul describes himself as "an ambassador in chains" and as "an ambassador and now a prisoner." As in modern times, so in antiquity, ambassadors were immune from arrest and imprisonment. But of course Paul is no ambassador in the eyes of the Roman Empire, any more than Jesus is a king. Nevertheless, Paul believes he is an ambassador in the truest sense, for he serves the true King and the true Son of God. Accordingly, he uses the language associated with the tasks of the ambassador: he must speak, declare, appeal, and intercede, to do and say whatever it takes, to make known the gospel, the good news of his king. Moreover, as an ambassador of Jesus, the apostle understood himself as benefactor.[39]

It should also be mentioned that the concept of ambassador does not stand in tension with the status and function of apostle. Indeed, the functions of ambassador and apostle are complementary, for normally ambassadors are "sent" and so, in fact, are apostles.

The language and imagery of ambassador and envoy were known to ancient Israel and its literature: "Then Israel sent messengers [πρέσβεις] to Sihon king of the Amorites, saying . . . " (Num 21:22). In the Greek Bible the term is customarily πρέσβυς. There are many examples in the Old Testament, the Old Testament Pseudepigrapha, Philo, and Josephus.

In the fictive *Letter of Aristeas* we read:

> On the seventh day much more extensive preparations were made, and many others were present from the different cities, among them a large number of ambassadors [πρέσβεις]. When an opportunity occurred, the king asked the first of those who had not yet been questioned how he [could] avoid being deceived by fallacious reasoning. (*Let. Aris.* 275)[40]

---

38. As is the meaning of πρεσβυτέριον in Luke 22:66 and Acts 22:5.

39. On this point, see Joubert, *Paul as Benefactor*; Danker and Jewett, "Jesus as the Apocalyptic Benefactor."

40. See also *Jannes and Jambres* A 3:5–7, part of which reads: "emissaries [πρέσβεις] from the king arrived."

Philo describes the plea of the Jewish people:

> "Do not cause a sedition; do not make war upon us; do not destroy the peace which exists. The honor of the emperor is not identical with dishonor to the ancient laws; let it not be to you a pretence for heaping insult on our nation. Tiberius is not desirous that any of our laws or customs shall be destroyed. And if you yourself say that he is, show us either some command from him, or some letter [ἐπιστολήν], or something of the kind, that we, who have been sent to you as ambassadors [πρέσβεις], may cease to trouble you, and may address our supplications to your master." But this last sentence exasperated him in the greatest possible degree, as he feared lest they might in reality go on an embassy [πρεσβευσάμενοι] to the emperor, and might impeach him. (Philo, *Legat.* 301–302)

Josephus narrates:

> When, therefore, they were thus afflicted, and found no end of the barbarous treatment they met with among the Greeks, they sent ambassadors [ἐπρεσβεύσαντο] to Caesar on those accounts; who gave them the same privileges as they had before, and sent letters to the same purpose to the governors of the provinces, copies of which I subjoin here, as testimonials [μαρτύρια] of the ancient favorable disposition the Roman emperors had towards us ... When these ambassadors had reached Rome, they had opportunity of delivering their letters to Caesar [τὰ γράμματα τῷ Καίσαρα], because they found him reconciled to Herod. (*Ant.* 16.161, 335)

Early Christian literature employs the language as well. Both Ignatius and Polycarp speak of sending an ambassador:

> Since it has been reported to me that in answer to your prayer and the compassion which you have in Christ Jesus the church at Antioch in Syria is at peace, it is appropriate for you, as a church of God, to appoint a deacon to go there on a mission as God's ambassador [εἰς τὸ πρεσβεῦσαι ἐκεῖ θεοῦ πρεσβείαν], to congratulate them when they have assembled together and to glorify the Name. (Ign. *Phld.* 10:1)

> Both you and Ignatius have written me that if anyone is traveling to Syria, he should take your letter along also. This I will do, if I get a good opportunity, either myself or the one whom I will

send as an ambassador [πρεσβεύσοντα], on your behalf as well as ours. (Pol. *Phil.* 13:1)

And Sedrach petitions the archangel Michael:

Hearken to me, O powerful chief, and help me and be my ambassador [πρεσβεῦσαι], so that God may have mercy on the world. (*Apoc. Sedr.* 14:1)[41]

In the book of Acts, Paul functions as ambassador, though he begins his ambassadorial life as an opponent of Jesus and his followers. He addresses his fellow Jews, who had attacked him in the temple precincts, and describes his life prior to his conversion:

I persecuted this Way to the death, binding and delivering to prison both men and women as the high priest and the whole council of elders bear me witness [ὁ ἀρχιερεὺς μαρτυρεῖ μοι καὶ πᾶν τὸ πρεσβυτέριον]. From them I received letters [παρ' ὧν καὶ ἐπιστολὰς δεξάμενος] to the brethren, and I journeyed to Damascus to take those also who were there and bring them in bonds to Jerusalem to be punished. (Acts 22:4–5)

Commissioned with letters (ἐπιστολάς), originating from the highest Jewish authorities, Paul was dispatched to Damascus to seek out and discipline fellow Jews who had embraced the new heresy, bringing them back to Jerusalem to be punished. The imagery of ambassadors in possession of letters from authorities to exact juridical functions is attested in Josephus:

These were the commands he gave them: when there came letters [ἐπιστολαί] from his ambassadors at Rome [παρὰ τῶν ἐν Ῥώμῃ πρέσβεων], whereby information was given that Acme was put to death at Caesar's command, and that Antipater was condemned to die; however, they also wrote, that if Herod had a mind rather to banish him, Caesar permitted him so to do. (*J.W.* 1.166)[42]

---

41. Although the *Apocalypse of Sedrach* probably originated as a Jewish work, it was preserved and glossed in Christian circles.

42. The function of ambassadors bearing letters is quite old. Among the aforementioned meager epigraphic evidence of Alexander the Great we do find at least two inscriptions that refer to this function: "The people decreed: Concerning those things about which ambassadors [οἱ πρέσβεες (*sic*)] give their report, those ambassadors who had been sent [ἀποστάλεντες] to Alexander, and Alexander sent back his order [διαγράφαν] . . ." (*IG* XII, 2, 526 [stoich. 36]; cf. Heisserer, *Alexander*, 38–39);

Even more interesting is Paul's second telling of his Damascus road conversion, which he relates to King Agrippa II:

> And I punished them often in all the synagogues and tried to make them blaspheme; and in raging fury against them, I persecuted them even to foreign cities. Thus I journeyed to Damascus with the authority and commission of the chief priests [μετ' ἐξουσίας καὶ ἐπιτροπῆς τῆς τῶν ἀρχιερέων]. At midday, O king, I saw on the way a light from heaven, brighter than the sun, shining round me and those who journeyed with me. And when we had all fallen to the ground, I heard a voice saying to me in the Hebrew language, "Saul, Saul, why do you persecute me? It hurts you to kick against the goads." And I said, "Who are you, Lord?" And the Lord said, "I am Jesus whom you are persecuting. But rise and stand upon your feet; for I have appeared to you for this purpose, to appoint you to serve and bear witness [προχειρίσασθαί σε ὑπηρέτην καὶ μάρτυρα] to the things in which you have seen me and to those in which I will appear to you, delivering you from the people and from the Gentiles—to whom I send you [εἰς οὓς ἐγὼ ἀποστέλλω σε] to open their eyes, that they may turn from darkness to light and from the power of Satan to God, that they may receive forgiveness of sins and a place among those who are sanctified by faith in me." (Acts 26:11–18)

Again we hear echoes of the language of the functions of the ambassador.[43]

Just as King Jesus performed acts of benefaction, such as "healing all that were oppressed by the devil" (Acts 10:38), so he has called Saul of

---

"King Antigonos to the council and the people of Eresos, greeting: Your ambassadors [οἱ παρ' ὑμῶν πρέσβεις] came to us and spoke, saying that the people, having received the letter [ἐπιστολήν] that we wrote [ἐγράψαμεν] . . ." (IG XII, 2, 526 [stoich. 17]; cf. Heisserer, *Alexander*, 42–43). Functioning as an ambassador of Messiah Jesus, Paul too writes letters, giving instruction to God's people.

43. For examples of πρέσβεις ("ambassadors") and ἐπιτρέπω ("commissioned" or "entrusted") in combination, see Josephus, *J.W.* 1.661; 2.80; *Ant.* 8.365; 20.7, 8. For examples of πρέσβεις or πρεσβεύω ("serving as ambassador") and γράμματα or ἐπιστολάς ("letters") in combination, see Philo, *Legat.* 301–2; Josephus, *Life* 310; *Ant.* 16.161, 335; 17.182, 300; 20.8. For examples of πρέσβεις and ἀποστέλλω ("send") in combination, see LXX Num 21:21; 22:5; Deut 2:26; Isa 39:1 ("the king of Babylonia, sent [ἀπέστειλεν] letters [ἐπιστολάς] and ambassadors [πρέσβεις] and gifts"); Isa 57:9; 1 Macc 9:70; 11:9; 13:14; Josephus, *Ant.* 17.182, 300; 20.8. In an inscription commemorating Nero's letter to Rhodes we find πρέσβεις ("ambassadors"), ἀποστέλλω ("to send"), and ἐπιστολάς ("letters"); cf. *SIG* 810.4, 11.

Tarsus, to open the eyes of the lost, "that they may turn from darkness to light and from the power of Satan to God, that they may receive forgiveness of sins."

Presenting Jesus and his apostles, such as Peter and Paul, in explicitly political terms may strike moderns as strange, moderns who are accustomed to place things political and things religious in carefully separated and isolated spheres. But the world of Jesus and his apostolic ambassadors entertained no such dichotomy. In the ancient world religion and politics were inextricably intertwined, with the king (or Caesar) functioning as priest, offering sacrifice and petitioning the gods. We should bear in mind that the Roman emperor assumed the title, among others, of Pontifex Maximus, or "High Priest."

The proclamation of Jesus as king, who has sent his apostles and ambassadors, to proclaim "good news" (εὐαγγελίου)[44] and to reconcile an estranged world to the one and true God, does indeed envision the mission of the ambassador, who goes forth, bearing the message, will, and letters of his sovereign. The Lukan Evangelist appears to have developed this theme, perhaps more than the other Evangelists.[45]

---

44. The word "good news" or "gospel," whether in the singular (εὐαγγέλιον) or in the plural (εὐαγγέλια), is a highly political word, yet sums up the essence of the message of Jesus himself and the subsequent Christian proclamation. For more on this point, see Evans, "Mark's Incipit."

45. The evangelist's ambassadorial portrait of Paul may well have been part of a legal-political strategy in defense of the apostle. For discussion of this hypothesis, see Mauck, *Paul on Trial*. Mauck argues that Acts was written primarily to defend Paul in his forthcoming trial in Rome (Acts 25:6–12; 28:16–22). The incipits of Luke (1:1–4; cf. Josephus, *Ag. Ap.* 1.1–3) and Acts (1:1–2; cf. Josephus, *Ag. Ap.* 2.1), as well as the quasi-legal statements made by Paul (e.g., Acts 24:3; 26:25; cf. *Diogn.* 1:1), support Mauck's thesis. See also Omerzu, *Der Prozeß des Paulus*. Omerzu argues that Acts 21–25 provide a historically plausible account of Paul's arrest, interrogation, detention, and appeal to the Roman emperor.

BIBLIOGRAPHY

Bertram, G. "Εὐεργέτης." In *TDNT* 2:654–55.
Bureth, P. *Les titulatures impériales dans les papyrus, les ostraca et les inscriptions d'Égypte (30 a.C.–284 p.C.)*. Brussels: Fondation Égyptologique Reine Élisabeth, 1964.
Cohoon, J. W. *Dio Chrysostom* I. LCL. London: William Heinemann, 1932.
Danker, F. W. *Benefactor: Epigraphic Study of a Graeco-Roman and New Testament Semantic Field*. St. Louis: Clayton, 1982.
———. "The Endangered Benefactor in Luke–Acts." In *Society of Biblical Literature 1981 Seminar Papers*, edited by K. H. Richards, 39–48. SBLSP 20. Chico CA: Scholars, 1981.
Danker, F. W., and R. Jewett. "Jesus as the Apocalyptic Benefactor in Second Thessalonians." In *The Thessalonian Correspondence*, edited by R. F. Collins, 486–98. BETL 87. Leuven: Leuven University Press, 1990.
Deissmann, A. *Light from the Ancient East*. London: Hodder & Stoughton/New York: Doran, 1927. Reprint, Peabody, MA: Hendrickson, 1995.
Evans, C. A. "Mark's Incipit and the Priene Calendar Inscription: From Jewish Gospel to Greco-Roman Gospel." *JGRChJ* 1 (2000) 67–81.
Heisserer, A. J. *Alexander the Great and the Greeks: The Epigraphic Evidence*. Norman, OK: University of Oklahoma Press, 1980.
Hunt, A. S., and C. C. Edgar. *Select Papyri*. II. *Non-Literary Public Documents*. LCL 282. Cambridge, MA: Harvard University Press/London: Heinemann, 1934.
Jacobson, D. M. "King Herod: Roman Citizen and Benefactor of Kos." *Bulletin of the Anglo-Israel Archaeological Society* 13 (1993–1994) 31–35.
Joubert, S. *Paul as Benefactor: Reciprocity, Strategy and Theological Reflection in Paul's Collection*. WUNT 2.124. Tübingen: Mohr Siebeck, 2000.
Lightfoot, J. B., J. R. Harmer, and M. W. Holmes. *The Apostolic Fathers*. Rev. ed. Grand Rapids: Baker, 1989.
Llewelyn, S. R., editor. *New Documents Illustrating Early Christianity*. Vol. 9. Grand Rapids: Eerdmans, 2002.
Lull, D. J. "The Servant-Benefactor as Model of Greatness (Luke 22:24–30)." *NovT* 28 (1986) 289–305.
Mauck, J. W. *Paul on Trial: The Book of Acts as a Defense of Christianity*. Nashville: Thomas Nelson, 2001.
McLaren, J. S. "Jews and the Imperial Cult: From Augustus to Domitian." *JSNT* 27 (2005) 257–78.
Neyrey, J. H. "God, Benefactor and Patron: The Major Cultural Model for Interpreting the Deity in Greco-Roman Antiquity." *JSNT* 27 (2005) 465–92.
Neyrey, J. H. *Render to God: New Testament Understandings of the Divine*. Minneapolis: Fortress, 2004.
Nock, A. D. "Soter and Euergetes." In *The Joy of Study: Papers on New Testament and Related Subjects to Honor Frederick Clifton Grant*, edited by S. L. Johnson, 127–48. New York: Macmillan, 1951. Reprinted in *Essays on Religion and the Ancient World*. 2 vols. Edited by Z. Stewart, 2:720–35. Cambridge, MA: Harvard University Press, 1972.
Omerzu, H. *Der Prozeß des Paulus: Eine exegetische und rechthistorische Untersuchung der Apostelgeschichte*. BZNW 115. Berlin: de Gruyter, 2002.
Paton, W. R., and E. L. Hicks. *The Inscriptions of Cos*. Oxford: Clarendon, 1891. Reprint, Hildesheim: Olms, 1990.

Rajak, Tessa. "Benefactors in the Greco-Jewish Diaspora." In *The Jewish Dialogue with Greece and Rome: Studies in Cultural and Social Interaction*, by Tessa Rajak, 373–91. AGJU 48. Leiden: Brill, 1996.

Rowe, C. K. "Luke–Acts and the Imperial Cult: A Way through the Conundrum?" *JSNT* 27 (2005) 279–300.

Schowalter, D. "Written in Stone: A Prayer to Augustus." In *Prayer from Alexander to Constantine: A Critical Anthology*, edited by Mark Kiley, 159–64. London/New York: Routledge 1997.

Spicq, C. "εὐεργεσία, εὐεργετέω, εὐεργέτης." In *TLNT* 2.107–13.

Taylor, L. Ross. *The Divinity of the Roman Emperor*. Philological Monographs 1. Middletown, CT: American Philological Association, 1931.

Welles, C. Bradford. *Diodorus of Sicily VIII*. LCL. London: William Heinemann, 1970.

Winter, E. "Octavian/Augustus als Soter, Euergetes und Epiphanes: Die Datierung des Kalabscha-Tores." *Zeitschrift für ägyptische Sprache und Altertumskunde* 130 (2003) 197–212 + tables XLVI–LI.

5

"I Have Conquered the World"

The Death of Jesus and the End of Empire in the Gospel of John

Tom Thatcher

> [I]n the case of the Fourth Gospel, "passion" is a misnomer; Jesus controls and orchestrates the whole performance.[1]

THIS PAPER WILL ARGUE that the Fourth Gospel's crucifixion story (John 19:16–37) is a carefully crafted response to the foundational premises of imperial power. Specifically, John presents the death of Jesus in a way that is calculated to deny the social values inscribed in the cross, values that reflected the mythical substructure of Roman rule. More than a messy and inefficient means of execution, crucifixion was a carefully staged drama that publicly proclaimed the gospel of conquest. While the New Testament authors deal with the scandal of the cross in a variety of ways, John's response is notable for its complete reversal of everything that crucifixion represents. Indeed, in the Fourth Gospel the normal public meaning of the cross is profaned in a way that makes Caesar and his agents helpless victims of the Christ who conquered the world (John 16:33).[2]

---

1. Ashton, *Understanding the Fourth Gospel*, 189.

2. Throughout this paper, the name "John" will be used synonymously with "the Fourth Evangelist" in reference to that individual who produced the Fourth Gospel as we have it today. The specific identity of this individual, and the issue of whether the current text is a redaction of multiple sources and/or the last in a series of revisions, is irrelevant to this study.

To explore these claims and their implications, I will first highlight the special challenges that the Fourth Gospel presents to any volume on "Empire in the New Testament," then proceed to outline a reading strategy that exposes both the social values of Roman crucifixion and John's techniques for reversing those values. This analysis will, I hope, reveal that John's passion story is grounded in the thesis that Christ is, in every way, greater than Caesar.

THE PROBLEM OF JOHN AND EMPIRE

At first glance, any discussion of the Fourth Gospel's response to empire seems futile, simply because John does not appear to be particularly interested in Rome. In fact, one could readily argue that the Gospel of John is essentially apolitical, on the grounds that the interests of the text are largely theological. Two obvious aspects of John's presentation could be cited in support of this claim, one relating to his treatment of traditional Jesus material that might be used to construct a theory of empire, the other stemming from the overtly christological interests of his narrative.

First, while the Synoptics include many episodes and sayings that might inform a study of Jesus' posture toward Rome—or at least a study of the thinking of the respective Evangelists—John omits most of this material. The Fourth Gospel says nothing, for example, about John the Baptist's admonition that tax collectors and soldiers should not abuse their power (Matt 3:7–12; Luke 3:12–14), about Jesus' ambiguous answer to the question of whether Jews should pay imperial taxes (Mark 12:13–17), about Christ's command that his disciples must not abuse their authority like "the kings of the Gentiles" (Luke 22:25), or about the Sanhedrin's accusation that Jesus is a threat to Rome because he portrays himself as "king" (Luke 23:2).[3] Further, in some cases where John and the Synoptics record the same or similar events, John seems to consciously diminish the political implications of Jesus' words and actions. For example, while Matthew, Mark, and Luke record more than seventy differ-

---

3. For further obvious examples, the Fourth Gospel also omits Herod's execution of the Baptist (Mark 6:16–29), Jesus' assertion that God's children should not be forced to pay temple taxes (Matt 17:24–27), Jesus' prediction that Jerusalem will be "trampled by Gentiles" (Luke 21:24; cf. Mark 13:14), Jesus' promise that the disciples will "sit on thrones judging the twelve tribes of Israel" (Luke 22:29–30//Matt 19:28), Jesus' peculiar counsel, just before his arrest, that the disciples should sell their coats and buy swords (Luke 22:36–38), and Jesus' trial before Herod Antipas (Luke 23:6–12).

ent sayings on "the kingdom of God," the Johannine Jesus refers to the kingdom only twice, both times in the Nicodemus story (John 3). In that context, the obvious political implications of this phrase are thoroughly spiritualized by Jesus' insistence that "seeing/entering the kingdom" follows rebirth "from above by water and spirit" (John 3:3, 5, 12). This view is consistent with John 18:36, where Jesus tells Pilate that his kingdom is "not of this world." Overall, the database for evaluating John's thinking on the Roman Empire appears to be rather impoverished, at least when compared to the rich number of obvious links in the Synoptics.

Second, and perhaps more substantially, one could readily argue that worldly concerns were of little interest to the Fourth Evangelist, who seems to be obsessed with christological reflection and esoteric speculations. Johannine scholarship has traditionally been driven by Clement of Alexandria's (190s CE) famous dictum that John wrote a "spiritual Gospel" (Eusebius, *Hist. eccl.* 6.14.7), a book that focuses more on the theological implications of Christ's career than on its relationship to a specific historical context. Following this precedent, in recent decades scholars have tended to highlight the narrative technique and theological tendencies of the Evangelist, with less concern about the interface between the Fourth Gospel and its imperial context. Those studies that do focus on John's historical background have largely followed in the footsteps of J. Louis Martyn's *History and Theology in the Fourth Gospel* (1968), which reconstructs the Johannine community's conflicts with late-first century Judaism in detail but says next to nothing about John's relationship to Rome. In view of these overriding interests—all of which have produced fruitful and productive readings of the Johannine literature—scholars have tended to portray the Gospel of John as a Jewish document with deeply christological concerns, concerns that left the emperor completely off John's radar screen.

Thus, the paucity of political sayings and scenes in the Fourth Gospel, combined with the overt christological interests of the book, might be taken to mean that John cared very little about the affairs of worldly governments. Yet such a conclusion would reflect a preference for the obvious over an interest in the whole story—less obliquely, John's response to empire should not be measured *quantitatively* (simply in terms of what his story includes or excludes), but rather *qualitatively* (in terms of the way that he interprets the events and characters that he has chosen to bring to the reader's attention). As the narrator explicitly states, the Fourth Gospel seeks to bring the reader to saving faith in Jesus as "the Christ, the Son of God" (John 20:30–31), yet closer inspection of key events from Jesus' career reveals that John's thinking on what it means to be "Son of God" was deeply influenced by the cultural realities of Roman rule. These key events include, for purposes of the present discussion, Jesus' crucifixion and death, which John reinterprets christologically by reversing the imperial rhetoric inherent in the events of public history.

The remainder of this essay will argue that John's crucifixion story may be read at two levels, and that the interplay between these levels defines the christological value of the text (John 19:16–37). Specifically, John subverts the normal public meaning of crucifixion in a way that radically reverses the premises of Roman power and, in the process, asserts that Christ is in every way superior to Caesar. In this respect, one may say that John's Christology is deeply intertwined with his response to Rome, even though he excludes some of the more obvious traditional sayings and stories on the subject.

THE CROSS TELLS A STORY

In John's world, crucifixion was not only a messy and expensive way to dispatch with undesirable people, but also, and much more significantly, a bookmark in the fable of Roman power. Every cross told a story; every story has a moral; the moral of the cross story was calculated to rationalize and maintain the imperial status quo. To explore the story inscribed in the cross, it will be helpful to briefly review Yael Zerubavel's discussion of the "commemorative narratives" that undergird a society's public rituals, and also Michael Foucault's model of "countermemory." Taken together, these approaches offer a reading strategy that exposes both the values latent in Roman crucifixions and John's attempt to reverse those values in his presentation of Christ's death.

In her book *Recovered Roots*, Yael Zerubavel explores ways in which twentieth-century Zionists created an Israeli national heritage by establishing points of (dis)continuity with the history of Judaism. Zerubavel focuses particularly on the cultural values associated with three events that have played a formative role in Israeli consciousness: the mass suicide of Zealot rebels at Masada in 72 CE; the Bar Kokhba Revolt against Rome in 132–135 CE; and, more recently, the violent confrontation between Jewish settlers and Palestinians at Tel Hai in 1920. While the historical details of Zerubavel's discussion are fascinating in their own right, I will restrict my remarks here to her theoretical model, which essentially seeks to explain how these and similar events became significant to Israel's national identity.

Zerubavel argues that the collective consciousness of a society manifests itself in various rituals of commemoration, activities that allow group members to "create, articulate, and negotiate their shared memories of particular events."[4] Put another way, activities that preserve and express social memory both generate and reinforce group values. This is particularly true when the rituals in question rehearse significant occasions and/or events from the group's common past, such as the fireworks celebrations in the United States on the Fourth of July, which commemorate the signing of the Declaration of Independence in 1776. Similarly, in the religious sphere, participation in the Eucharist reinforces the common beliefs of Christian worshippers by symbolically re-enacting Jesus' sacrificial death, a critical event in salvation history.

According to Zerubavel, commemorative rituals derive much of their emotive power from the fact that they tap into myths of origins. Every act of commemoration "reproduces a *commemorative narrative*, a story about a particular past that accounts for this ritualized remembrance and provides a moral message for the group members."[5] When Christians participate in the Lord's Supper, they are aware that they are rehearsing events from the last night of Jesus' life and, further, that these events are recorded in the sacred Scriptures of the church. Similarly, the act of lighting the candles on a menorah at Hanukkah rehearses an ancient story in which the Maccabees earned God's blessing for their faithful refusal to compromise. Individual acts of commemoration, then, serve as indexes for the larger and deeper myths that provide group members with a sense of identity. In a very real sense, the entire gospel story is rehearsed in the Eucharist, in the same way that every citation of the American pledge of allegiance taps into the whole history of the United States.

Of course, no single act of commemoration expresses the total history and value system of a particular culture. Normally, commemorative rituals focus on one major event and, when viewed in isolation, recall only a single chapter of the given society's total image of the past.

---

4. Zerubavel, *Recovered Roots*, 5.

5. Ibid., 6; emphasis original.

Thus, the lighting of advent candles reminds Christian worshippers of the beginning of Jesus' story, while fasting on Good Friday recalls the final days of his life. But one could hypothetically integrate these many subplots into a single unified story, a "master commemorative narrative" built on the framework of the lowest common denominator of social values.[6] In Zerubavel's model, a master commemorative narrative is not an encyclopedic account of all historical events known to all members of a group—not an exhaustive database of the total past—but rather a broad storyline that allows group members to communicate meaningfully about who they are on the basis of what they think has happened. "To fully appreciate the meaning of individual commemorations, then, it is important to examine them within the framework of the master commemorative narrative"[7]—the meaning of the Eucharist is, in other words, ultimately derived from its location in the larger Christian story of salvation history.

Applied to the present discussion, Zerubavel's model suggests that Roman crucifixion was not simply an act of extreme violence but also a form of "ritualized remembrance," a dramatic reenactment of Rome's conquest of the world with pointed propaganda objectives. According to the cross script, every crucifixion tapped into a mythological narrative that might be summarized as follows:

> Many years ago, the gods elevated Rome to a special place of power and authority. The Romans used this privileged position to bring peace and order to the whole world. This thing you see hanging here was once a man, who rose up within an insolent race and dared to threaten the natural order of things by rebelling against Rome. Of course, his insolence inevitably earned him the most extreme form of pain and shame imaginable. Don't try it.

The participants in any specific execution played scripted roles within this collective fable of Roman power. Specifically, the officers overseeing the execution played the part of Caesar's legions, while the victim represented the larger social group of which he was a member. Applied to the case at hand, every Jewish cross was planted in a master commemorative narrative that both rationalized Roman power and discouraged future attempts at innovation. Viewed in this light, the Johannine

6. Ibid.
7. Ibid., 7.

Jesus says nothing remarkable when he compares his forthcoming death to Rome's destruction of the temple in 70 CE (John 2:19–22), for in one sense the story of Jerusalem's past and future destruction was already written into the autobiography of every Jewish crucifixion victim.

While all forms of public execution reflect a society's official vision of justice and order—at the very least by eliminating individuals who engage in taboo behaviors—the cross story was particularly serviceable to Rome's agenda because its plot dramatized the two foundational principles of totalitarian rule: physical deprivation and psychological denigration. As James C. Scott has noted, imperial domination impacts not only the material lives of the oppressed—physical and sexual abuse, seizure of goods and high taxation, laborious work conditions—but also, and perhaps more significantly, the "dignity and autonomy" of subject people.[8] Both elements of domination figured prominently in the cross script, creating a dark storyline that epitomized Rome's power over the bodies and identities of subject people groups.

The extreme brutality of Roman crucifixions—which were sometimes preceded, as in Jesus' case, by torture (see Mark 15:15–20; John 19:1–3)—is evident from the paucity of precise descriptions of the practice in extant ancient literature. Roman authors say very little about the details of this mode of execution, perhaps regarding the topic as an inappropriate theme for polite conversation. Cicero, for example, states explicitly that

> the executioner, the veiling of the head, and the very word "cross" should be far removed not only from the person of a Roman citizen but from his thoughts, his eyes and his ears. For it is not only the actual occurrence of these things or the endurance of them, but liability to them, nay, the mere mention of them, that is unworthy of a Roman citizen. (*Rab. Post.* 5.16)

This is not to say, of course, that Romans viewed such violence as beneath their dignity; Cicero means, rather, that no citizen of the empire should be forced to play a part in the drama of destructive conquest that the cross represented. Indeed, it would be illogical to crucify Romans, for such an act would symbolize Rome's self-destruction, an empire conquering itself.

---

8. Scott, *Domination*, 23.

While modern readers of the Bible, recalling images from Mel Gibson's *The Passion of the Christ*, are most impressed with the gratuitous violence of crucifixions, the Romans viewed the cross not only as an "assault on the body" but also as what Scott calls a "ritual of denigration"—for purposes of the present discussion, "a *commemorative* ritual of denigration," one that reenacted the humiliating subjugation of the victim's people group.[9] Alan Kirk has observed that "torturous deaths—such as crucifixion was—can be highly symbolized forms of violence, with the disfiguring, distending, dismembering, smashing, and perforation of the human body routinized and choreographed to display and enact publicly the socially degraded status of the victim."[10] While Kirk's formulation reflects his own substantial engagement with contemporary social science theory, the ancient Romans were themselves keenly aware of the symbolic element of crucifixion and its potential propaganda value. Indeed, Quintilian notes that "every punishment has less to do with the offense than with the example." Hence, "when we [Romans] crucify criminals the most frequented roads are chosen, where the greatest number of people can look and be seized by this fear" (*Decl.* 274). The violence of the cross went beyond physical punishment to symbolic annihilation; the destruction of the victim's flesh narrated Rome's capacity to suppress every threat to the state's entire sovereignty.

From a Roman perspective, then, scourging and crucifixion were calculated to graphically illustrate the inevitable end of any story that began with resistance to imperial rule. Ironically, Jewish ideology reinforced the values of the cross script in a way that enhanced the propaganda value of the practice. This method of killing could readily be interpreted through Deut 21:22–23, which stipulates that anyone who "hangs on a tree" is under God's curse. While Paul could cleverly play on this text to argue that Christ "became a curse for us" (Gal 3:13), less sympathetic readings would interpret the cross as a symbol of divine judgment. For example, two of the Dead Sea Scrolls—4Q169 3–4 II (*Pesher Nahum*) and 11QT LXIV, 7–13 (*Temple Scroll*)—insist that "the curse of the tree" fell upon the 800 Jewish enemies of Alexander Jannaeus who were crucified as punishment for their participation in a revolt in 88 BCE.[11] In both contexts, the authors of the respective scrolls

---

9. Ibid.
10. Kirk, "Memory of Violence," 192.
11. Fitzmyer, "Crucifixion in Ancient Palestine."

allude to Deuteronomy 21 as evidence that God affirmed the judgment of the earthly authorities by extending his own curse to the condemned. These sentiments are amplified in the Temple Scroll by the assertion that "hanging on a tree" is fit punishment for traitors and those who curse the people of Israel, and in 4Q169 by the application of Nah 2:13 to the victim as well: "'See, I am against you [the one crucified],' says the Lord of hosts" (NRSV). Any witness to a Roman scourging and crucifixion could readily agree that God was not doing much to bring about a happy ending for the victim.

Thus, crucifixions in Roman Palestine not only eliminated dangerous individuals in a highly symbolic way, but also encouraged the subject Jews to perpetuate imperial propaganda within their own community. Indeed, "in any established structure of domination, it is plausible to imagine that subordinate groups are socialized by their parents in the rituals of homage that will keep them from harm." Scott notes, for example, the "cruel paradox of slavery": "it is in the interest of slave mothers, whose overriding wish is to keep their children safe and by their side, to train them in the routines of conformity."[12] One could readily imagine how well this would apply to any Jewish parent who beheld the spectacle of a Jew hanging on a Roman cross just outside the walls of Jerusalem. Nailed to these two embedded narratives, enemies of the state and rejected by God, Jewish crucifixion victims were dehumanized and erased, discouraging any sequel to their stories.

COUNTERING THE CROSS

When crucifixion is viewed as a commemorative ritual that taps into collective memories of Roman conquest for propaganda purposes, one can readily understand why Paul would refer to the cross as a "scandal" (Gal 5:11; 1 Cor 1:22–24). The simple fact that Jesus died by crucifixion carried with it an implied autobiography, suggesting to Gentiles that he was a powerless victim of the state and to Jews that he was cursed by God. Faced with this dilemma, the Evangelists had three options in telling the story of Jesus' demise. First, they could simply deny that such a thing happened, perhaps ignoring the passion story altogether. While it is difficult for modern readers to imagine what the canonical Gospels would look like without Good Friday, this strategy

---

12. Scott, *Domination*, 24.

worked quite well for the authors of the *Gospel of Thomas* and, if such a document existed, Q.[13] Second, the Evangelists could recount the basic events of Calvary while adding elements that would disrupt the logic of the crucifixion plot. This strategy is notable in the Synoptics, which deconstruct the cross script by inserting Jewish apocalyptic elements—eclipse, torn temple curtain, earthquake, resurrection of the righteous dead, testimony of the Gentile centurion (Mark 15:38–39; Matt 27:51–54; Luke 23:44–45)—that bring new and alien implications to the normal meaning of such a story. But the Fourth Gospel's death scene reveals that John preferred a third strategy, one that would essentially admit the public events of the cross while denying their normal commemorative value. To achieve this alternate reading, John produced a narrative that offers a countermemory of Jesus' death.[14]

The term "countermemory" was coined by sociologist Michel Foucault in a discussion of Nietzsche's "genealogical" approach to history.[15] Nietzsche had argued that history books support the current social order by claiming that certain events and individuals are obviously and inherently important to life as we know it. But since every history book can only record a tiny fraction of the total past, what makes a particular incident or person "historical" and worthy of record while others may be forgotten or ignored? Nietzsche answered this question by proposing a "genealogical" mode of historiography, one that would treat all events and cultural institutions as products of complex power relations. For example, a genealogical history of the atomic bombing of Hiroshima would be less concerned with the specific circumstances and details surrounding that event—who built the bomb; who flew the plane; where

---

13. Q11:47–51 might be viewed as an exception, if one views Jesus' citation of "wisdom" (v. 49) as an allusion to his own impending death in the line of the prophets. Even here, however, there is no specific reference to crucifixion, and in fact this pericope would tend to minimize Roman involvement in the death of Jesus by placing responsibility on the shoulders of the Jews.

14. Technically speaking, all early Christian accounts of Jesus' death are countermemories, including Paul's comments on the soteriological meaning of the cross. Hence, a similar argument could be made—and I myself would make such an argument—for the passion stories in Matthew, Mark, Luke, and the Gospel of Peter. As a countermemory, John's account differs only in terms of degree, inasmuch as his style of presentation is essentially limited to commentary on events that most people in the Roman Empire would accept as true—"true" in the sense that they are immanently logical within the public transcript of crucifixion.

15. Foucault, "Nietzsche."

and at what time the bomb struck the city; how much force was released; how many people died—than with the factors that led the United States to develop atomic weapons, the geopolitical motives behind the decision to drop the bomb, and the reasons why that event had such a deep impact on global consciousness when it directly impacted only a tiny percentage of the human race. Of course, such a study would note many of the same facts that appear in more conventional accounts, but would take a radically different approach to the issue of why Hiroshima happened and why this event has subsequently been regarded as "historically significant."

Observing that Nietzsche's approach was radically at odds with the Western tradition of historiography, Foucault noted that any genealogical account would function as a sort of "countermemory," "a transformation of history into a totally different form of time."[16] For purposes of the present discussion, it is important to stress the phrase "a totally different *form* of time" in the preceding quotation. What Foucault calls "countermemories" are not simply different versions of the past; they are, rather, different *ways* of creating a version of the past. Countermemories do not just dispute accepted facts; rather, countermemories *reconfigure* accepted facts by forcing them into a new framework that is radically at odds with the values of mainstream society. Countermemory narratives arrange the common pieces of the history puzzle in ways that create new, and often subversive, images of yesterday.

Close examination of John 19:16–37 reveals that the Fourth Gospel's death story is a "countermemory" in the sense described above. Unlike the author of the *Gospel of Thomas*, John does not deny or ignore Jesus' death; unlike Matthew, he does not attempt to dilute the events of the crucifixion by mixing in unusual apocalyptic signs. Rather, John essentially tells a relatively unremarkable story of a Jewish death on a cross, but reconfigures this public past by viewing these common events through a commemorative framework that radically changes their meaning. Specifically, John's Calvary account affirms all the basic facts of a Roman crucifixion but completely subverts the normal meaning of those events by reversing the imperial propaganda embedded in the cross.

To unpack these claims, I will first note ways in which John 19:16–37 follows the normal logic of a Roman crucifixion, then explore two literary strategies that John uses to subvert the moral of the cross story.

16. Ibid., 160.

This two-level reading—public history and Johannine interpretation—will highlight the primary christological themes of the Fourth Gospel's passion story.

ANOTHER DAY AT CALVARY

For some two centuries now, biblical scholars have been deeply concerned with the problem of the historical Jesus. One major aspect of the debate concerns the events of the cross. While the majority of Jesus scholars believe that the New Testament Gospels are correct to assert that Jesus died by crucifixion—indeed, it is almost impossible to imagine that early Christians would fabricate such a story—there has been substantial disagreement on the details of the passion narrative. Did Roman soldiers really cast lots for Jesus' garments? Was Jesus publicly mocked by the chief priests? Did Pilate affix a placard on the cross that read "King of the Jews"? Any specific answer to each of these questions reflects a larger set of conclusions about the historical value of the Gospels (and various non-canonical documents) as sources for Jesus.

While the question of the Fourth Gospel's historical reliability lies outside the scope of the present essay, I would contend that most first-century readers would have had little difficulty accepting the sequence of events recorded in John 19:16–37. Put another way: whether or not John's death story meets the strict criteria of modern(istic) historical research (it generally does not), most of his contemporaries would likely believe that it was "true" in the sense that it follows the mythological commemorative narrative behind Roman crucifixions. In fact, John goes out of his way to offer logical, indeed obvious, explanations for the events of the cross, while at the same time ignoring the apocalyptic elements of other traditional accounts that some audiences might call into question. Because this is the case, while most first-century readers would be surprised by John's interpretation of the meaning of Christ's death, few would reject the Fourth Gospel's basic database of events surrounding the cross.

John's desire to paint a plausible portrait of the passion is evident, first, from the fact that the specific events he records all fit the fable of Roman power. As noted earlier, every crucifixion rehearsed the physical conquest and psychological denigration of subject peoples. Following this script, each of the six distinct scenes in John 19:16–37 finds an appropriate place in the larger mythical drama of Rome's subjugation of the Jews:

Scene 1: Jesus is Crucified (19:16–18)

John first states the basic fact that Pilate handed Jesus over to his executioners, who forced him to carry his own cross to the site of death and then crucified him. The fact that Jesus must bear the instrument of his own destruction simply magnifies his helpless condition and the impossibility of effective resistance.

Scene 2: The Titulus (19:19–22)

While the charge that Pilate posts over Jesus, "King of the Jews," is ironically appropriate from John's point of view, it also reflects the fact that crucifixions functioned not only, and not even primarily, to punish victims, but rather to humiliate and intimidate entire groups of subject people. In fact, the Jews do not have a "king" because the Romans will not permit them to have one; if, however, they were allowed to have a king, the Romans could put that person on a cross at any time they chose. The reader is unsurprised when the local client authorities, the chief priests, ask for a modification to the *titulus* ("Do not write 'King of the Jews,' but rather, 'This man said, "I am king of the Jews"'"; 19:21) and also unsurprised when Pilate refuses to grant their request. From a Roman point of view, there is no reason to deny the obvious meaning of what is happening.

Scene 3: Casting Lots (19:23–24)

The physical subjugation of the Jews is appropriately symbolized by the fact that Jesus must give even the clothes on his back to Roman soldiers, who divide his possessions among themselves as spoils of conquest while the vanquished Jew looks on.

Scene 4: Jesus' Mother (19:25–27)

Jesus' concern for his mother is striking; at the same time, since the Romans are taking his life, he obviously must find some means to insure her well-being.

Scene 5: Jesus' Last Words and Death (19:28–30)

One could readily imagine that a crucifixion victim would be thirsty, especially if he had previously lost much of his bodily fluid through scourging, and Jesus' dying word, τετέλεσται ("it is finished"), looks like a simple admission of defeat: his movement, and any threat that it may have represented to Roman power, are over.

Scene 6: The Piercing (19:31–37)

Jesus' quick death reflects the efficiency of Roman power and protects the purity of the Sabbath, while the mutilation of his corpse (piercing with a spear) strips him of basic human dignity.

Aside from the general plausibility of the events he records—everything the Romans do in John 19 fits their political agenda nicely—the Evangelist, apparently wishing to assuage any possible doubt, offers a more detailed rationale for two of the six scenes outlined above. First, in scene 3 (John 19:23–24), John intervenes to explain exactly why the soldiers decided to cast lots for Jesus' clothing. While Mark simply notes that the Romans stripped Jesus and threw dice (Mark 15:24), John expands the incident by noting that four soldiers were involved and that one of Jesus' garments, the χιτών (a full length undergarment) was seamless and therefore could not be torn without substantial damage. Realizing this fact, the soldiers discuss the situation and agree to cast lots, each presumably hoping to preserve the value of the garment and secure it as his own (John 19:24). Second and similarly, in scene 6 (John 19:31–37) John goes out of his way to explain exactly why Jesus' legs were *not* broken and why the soldiers stuck a spear into his corpse. Because the Passover Sabbath was about to commence, the Jewish authorities asked Pilate to remove the bodies quickly so as to prevent them from polluting the holy city. Honoring this request, Pilate sent soldiers to break the legs of the victims, thus hastening their deaths (while not reducing their agony). Presumably, the Romans would have done this to Jesus as well, but were surprised to discover that he had expired; to ensure that he was dead, one of the soldiers drove a spear into his side. In both of these instances, John offers entirely rational reasons for specific events on Calvary, reasons that are essentially unsurprising and that fit neatly into the deep logic of Roman crucifixions.

Of course, both the seamless garment and the "water and blood" may reflect significant Johannine theological themes—the former the unity of Christ's message and/or community, the latter the reality of his physical incarnation—and for this reason many scholars have questioned the historical reliability of John's presentation. Without entering that debate, I would argue that John's original readers would have been likely to accept the general outline of the Fourth Gospel's death story, simply because that story follows the underlying logic of the cross script. Jesus, representative of the entire Jewish race, has offended the dignity of Rome by threatening to upset peace and order. Caesar's physical and psychological power over the "king of the Jews" is graphically illustrated by the soldiers' violent destruction of Jesus' body (scourging; crucifixion; thirst) and by the complete dehumanization of his person (divided clothing; inability to care for mother; mutilation of corpse). Whether or not John's account is historically accurate, it is entirely plausible and, indeed, holds back nothing that would tend to mark Jesus as a helpless pawn in the story of Roman power.

Obviously, while the Fourth Gospel's death story essentially follows the plot of the master commemorative narrative behind every Roman crucifixion, John wishes to rewrite the moral of the story. Specifically, John admits the basic sequence of events at Calvary—credible cross stories can only be told so many ways—but reinterprets those events by offering an explicit countermemory interpretation of their meaning. This countermemory is communicated through two literary motifs: the theme of *fulfilled prophecy* and *Jesus' powerful words from the cross*. Taken together, these devices create a second level of meaning within the text of John 19:16–37, a rereading of history that shows that Jesus' death did not quite mean what Caesar thought it meant.

ACCORDING TO SCRIPTURE

As is often noted, all four canonical accounts of Jesus' death are built on the theological premise of 1 Cor 15:3: "Christ died for our sins according to the Scriptures." While John is perhaps less explicitly interested in the "for our sins" part than, say, Mark (see Mark 10:45), his passion play is clearly driven by the notion that Jesus died "according to Scripture." Three of the six scenes in the Fourth Gospel's death story—the lot-casting, Jesus' final words, and the piercing—are explicitly connected to passages from the Old Testament with the formula ἵνα ἡ γραφὴ πληρωθῇ/τελειωθῇ ("so that the Scripture would be fulfilled/completed"; John 19:24, 28, 36–37). Yet John 19 differs from 1 Corinthians 15 in one key respect: while Paul's comment simply reveals that the first Christians connected Christ's death with passages from the Bible, thus incorporating Scripture into the Jesus traditions that they passed on to second generation believers (1 Cor 15:1–3), in the Fourth Gospel prophecy is *a causal force*, a narrative impulse that determines what can and, in fact, what *must* happen on Calvary. In John's countermemory challenge to the public meaning of the cross, the events of Jesus' death were predetermined not by the public transcript of Roman crucifixions, but rather by the imperative that God's word must be fulfilled.

The causative force of prophecy becomes immediately obvious upon closer inspection of the three scenes in which John actually alludes to the Old Testament. As noted above, in each instance the narrated events are entirely unsurprising in the context of a crucifixion, and John twice offers logical explanations for the specific situations that he describes. Yet this logic is immediately subverted by tying the passion to a divine program that Caesar is unaware of and cannot control. As a result, one must read John 19 at two levels—the level of the Roman and Jewish great traditions, and the level of John's countermemory—in order to get the whole story behind the cross.

John first connects Jesus' death to Scripture in the third of the six scenes in his passion account, the lot-casting (John 19:23–25). As noted earlier, witnesses to the crucifixion, including the attending soldiers themselves, would have explained the lot-casting in terms of the fact that Jesus' tunic was seamless and could not be divided (19:23–24). Yet John is not particularly concerned with the reasons why Romans think they do anything and, not trusting the reader's Bible knowledge, proceeds to state explicitly that the soldiers' actions were a fulfillment of Ps 22:18. In fact, John introduces this prophecy in such a way that the soldiers *must* throw dice for Jesus' clothes, whether it would make any sense to do so or not. In Greek, the citation formula at John 19:24 opens with the word ἵνα ("so that"), which is subordinate to the main verb of the sentence, εἶπαν ("they said"): "*So that* the Scripture would be fulfilled [and not because a torn piece of underwear would be worthless] . . . the soldiers said to one another . . ." This grammatical construction adds a new layer of meaning to the soldiers' actions, one that subverts the conventional logic of the cross: while Jesus' nakedness would seem to dramatize the helplessness of the Jews, his executioners are in fact unwitting puppets whose mouths move with God's hand. This impression is strongly reinforced by the awkward phrase "this, then, is what the soldiers did" (οἱ μὲν οὖν στρατιῶται ταῦτα ἐποίησαν) immediately after the Scripture quotation, which in this context can only mean that the Romans are doing just what Christ wants them to do.

Similar language introduces the two texts that John cites at 19:36–37 in connection with the *crurifragium* and the piercing of Jesus' side. Here again, John's explanation of the reason why the thieves' legs were broken and Jesus' legs were not is completely logical from the perspective of the cross script—there would be no need to break the legs of a dead man, and one can readily imagine that Jesus might die quickly after a night of beatings. Indeed, the most problematic feature of this passage is Pilate's sudden willingness to comply with Jewish sensitivities after his stubborn posturing during Jesus' trial (John 18:29–31, 38–39; 19:4–6, 12, 14–15, 19–22). Yet a quick look through the Johannine lens reveals that things are not quite as they appear, for in fact "these things happened (ἐγένετο ταῦτα) so that the Scripture would be fulfilled" (19:36). The Romans did not leave Jesus' legs unbroken because it made sense to do so, nor did they stab him to verify his death; in reality, they did these things because they had to do them.

If the citations of Scripture at John 19:24 and 36–37 add a fatalistic flavor to the story of Christ's death, the reference to prophecy at v. 28 leads one to suspect that the Johannine Jesus is working through a list of "things to do before I die." After committing his mother to the care of the Beloved Disciple (19:25–27), Jesus suddenly realizes that a certain verse remains unfulfilled and says, "I am thirsty." It stands to reason that any crucifixion victim would be thirsty, yet in John's countermemory Christ is no one's victim. Lest there be any doubt, the double repetition of the verb τελειόω at John 19:28–30 clarifies that Jesus is simply finishing a few tasks that must be done before he can go back to the Father.

> μετὰ τοῦτο εἰδὼς ὁ Ἰησοῦς ὅτι ἤδη πάντα τετέλεσται
> After these things, Jesus, knowing that everything *had been finished* already,
>
> ἵνα τελειωθῇ ἡ γραφὴ λέγει Διψῶ …
> said "I am thirsty" so that the Scripture *would be finished* …
>
> οὖν … Ἰησοῦς εἶπεν τετέλεσται
> Then … Jesus said, "*It is finished.*"

The dying word of the Johannine Jesus, τετέλεσται, seems to mean that the Scriptures "finish" with the completion of his mission, which ends with his death on the cross. Because this is the case, Jesus cannot even ask for a drink in the Fourth Gospel without enacting some prophecy. Certainly, his thirst cannot be the result of Roman abuse—indeed, to admit that Jesus was thirsty because of the scourging and the cross would be to admit that Caesar had some small power over Christ's actions, a notion that John cannot accept. Quite the contrary, while all other crucifixion victims must beg their killers for water, Jesus drinks when God tells him to drink and dies when he is ready to die.

John's three references to Scripture, then, create a countermemory of Jesus' death by reversing the values encoded in the cross script. Whereas crucifixions normally re-enacted the story of Roman conquest, every element of Jesus' death follows a divine program that completely supersedes Caesar's claims. While this same theme pervades the Synoptic accounts of Jesus' death, John notably underscores it in three ways to achieve maximum effect. First, while in Mark's account references to Scripture are implicit—Mark's entire death scene is built on Psalm 22, yet he directly cites this text only once, in Jesus' cry of abandonment (15:34; cf. Ps 22:1)—John drapes Old Testament texts over his story like a robe, in each case explicitly drawing the reader's attention to the prophecies that interest him. Second, in two of the three scenes where he quotes Scripture (the lot-casting and the piercing), John cites the Old Testament only after providing a rational reason for the soldiers' actions, a move that highlights the Roman logic of crucifixion only in order to undermine that logic. Third and finally, John accentuates the theme of fulfillment at 19:28 by insisting that Jesus' thirst was a "completion" of Scripture, yet fails to cite any specific Old Testament text. While a number of proposals have been offered, it remains impossible to determine exactly what "prophecy" John has in mind here.[17] Perhaps John was not referring to any specific passage, but rather to the more general point that Jesus' suffering was predetermined by God's plan and not by Pilate's whims.

THE LAST WORDS OF A CONQUERING KING

As noted earlier, the Fourth Evangelist uses two literary motifs to communicate his countermemory reading of the meaning of Jesus' death. The first relates to the theme of prophetic fulfillment, which counters the

---

17. Major proposals include (all quotations NRSV) Ps 22:15, "My mouth is dried up like a potsherd and my tongue sticks to my jaws"; Ps 42:2, "My soul thirsts for God, for the living God"; Ps 63:1, "My soul thirsts for you; my flesh faints for you as in a dry and weary land where there is no water"; and Ps 69:3, "I am weary with my crying; my throat is parched."

moral of the cross script by offering a new causal principle for the events of Calvary: the Romans are not re-enacting their conquest of Palestine, but are rather puppets in a divine plan that transcends the interests of their empire. The second motif relates to John's presentation of Jesus' last words. Specifically, the crucified Christ does not say what he ought to say in such a situation: instead of admitting defeat, he dies by proclaiming victory.

At first glance, a review of the Fourth Gospel's "words from the cross" might seem essentially irrelevant to a discussion of John and empire, simply because the Johannine Jesus has very little to say between the Pilate trial and his final breath. Jesus speaks in only two of the six scenes in John's Calvary story, uttering a total of eleven words. In the Greek text, Christ uses nine words to commit his mother to the care of the Beloved Disciple (19:25–27), two of which are the definite articles ("the") before the words "mother" and "son"; he then says διψῶ ("I am thirsty," one word in Greek; 19:28) and, after taking a drink, τετέλεσται ("It is finished," again one word in Greek; 19:30). Statistically speaking, John's account is similar to that of Mark, where Jesus speaks only ten words at Calvary, yet falls substantially short of the eighty-eight words in Luke's Gospel.[18]

Here again, the Fourth Gospel's presentation must be measured in terms of quality rather than quantity, for closer inspection reveals that John's rendering of Jesus' last words completely reverses the public meaning of crucifixion by allowing Christ to speak from a posture of absolute authority even while hanging on a Roman cross. This strategy is evident both from the larger *context* of the words from the cross—i.e., how these comments connect to Jesus' prior statements about his impending death in the Fourth Gospel—and from the specific *content* of Christ's remarks in John 19:26–30.

First, in terms of *narrative context*, the Johannine Jesus does not need to say as much as his Lukan counterpart simply because he has already said everything that needs to be said long before he gets to Calvary. Specifically here, Christ has already informed a number of Caesar's agents that his death will release a divine power that transcends the claims of every earthly empire. Thus, Jesus has already told the Pharisees that "no one takes my life from me, but rather I myself give it. I have authority to

---

18. This number includes Jesus' comments to the crowds on the way to Calvary, which are attested only in Luke (Luke 23:26–31).

give it, and I have authority to take it back again" (John 10:18). Similarly, Jesus has informed the governor of Judea, in a remarkably casual tone, that Rome has no authority over him save what his own Father has given (19:11). Further, Jesus has already announced in a very public venue (the temple courts, immediately after arresting the attention of Jerusalem through the "triumphal entry"; 12:12–19) that "the ruler of this world"— a moniker that the Passover crowd and any first-century reader would recognize as an appropriate title for the emperor—will be "cast out" (ἐκ- βληθήσεται ἔξω) when Jesus himself is "lifted up," a Johannine euphemism for Christ's violent death (12:31–33; cf. 3:14–15; 8:28). The same insolent spirit pervades Jesus' private assurance to the disciples that the war is over because "I have conquered the world" (16:33), a remarkable claim that apparently refers to his resolve to go to the cross. Against the backdrop of these and similar statements, every word from the mouth of the crucified Christ simply confirms his earlier assertions that a new and true king has invaded Caesar's domain.

Second, in terms of *content*, Jesus' words from the cross are imbued with the same tone of absolute authority that has characterized his discourse throughout the Fourth Gospel. While his comments to Mary and the Beloved Disciple at John 19:25–27 are, as noted earlier, essentially unremarkable—"Behold your son; behold your mother"—the circumstances make them striking. Even after a long night of scourging and several harrowing hearings, Jesus, hanging on the cross, still possesses the presence of mind to provide for his mother's welfare. This fact is all the more significant if, as is often suggested, Mary and the Beloved Disciple are representative figures, symbolizing ideal discipleship or the Johannine Churches: true believers should not be afraid to "stand by the cross" because Jesus is able to provide for them even in his weakest moments.

The content of Jesus' second statement, "I am thirsty" (John 19:28), is so unsurprising in the context of a crucifixion that one wonders why the Evangelist would even mention it. John, however, reveals that these are not merely the words of a dying man whose body has lost most of its fluid, but rather reflect Jesus' awareness that his death is the final act in a divine drama. Notably, John does not use a form of the word πληρόω to describe Jesus' "fulfillment" of messianic prophecy here, but rather the verb τελειόω (ἵνα τελειωθῇ ἡ γραφή), which stresses the theme of "completion." In some sense, Jesus' words on the cross are "finishing" what the sacred Scriptures of Judaism started, a supersessionist claim that inherently challenges the judgment of the religious authorities who demanded his execution.

Finally, and most significantly, John, like Luke, replaces the incoherent death scream of Mark and Matthew (Mark 15:37; Matt 27:50) with a specific statement. Luke's citation of Ps 31:5, "I [Jesus] entrust my spirit to your hands " (Luke 23:46), reflects a confident assurance that Christ will be vindicated by his heavenly Father because he is innocent of any wrongdoing. The Johannine Jesus goes beyond self-defense by proclaiming, "It is finished" (τετέλεσται; 19:30). Here again, any Roman reader could readily accept that Jesus might have said such a thing as he felt his life ebbing away, but in John's countermemory presentation "it is finished" means nothing like "I'm done for," as evident from the aside at 19:28 that he "knew that all was completed (εἰδὼς πάντα τετέλεσται)." The word "all" here may mean that Jesus has fulfilled all the relevant messianic prophecies, or that he has completed all the tasks of his revelatory mission. Most likely, John has both options in view: Jesus has finished his own work by finishing the Old Testament prophecies. In any case, Jesus' dying words in the Fourth Gospel stress that the realities of the cross—the bookmark in Caesar's power story—in no way compromise Christ's ability to achieve his objectives.

THE TWO STORIES

Viewed as a response to Rome, the Fourth Gospel's crucifixion account may be viewed not only as a "countermemory," but also and more specifically as what James C. Scott calls a "profanation" of imperial values. In many instances, oppressed people (like the Fourth Evangelist) publicly affirm the status quo in order to survive, while privately participating in underground behaviors and discussions that create "an alternative moral universe" that reflects their true sentiments. Such expressions are "profane" in the sense that they consciously parody and reverse official religious and political values.[19] Following this model, John's passion story profanes the commemorative narrative behind Roman crucifixion by reversing the plot in a way that makes Caesar and his agents helpless victims of the Christ who conquered the world.

19. Scott, "Protest and Profanation," 17, 20, 29.

Event	Story 1: Public Meaning (Cross Script)	Story 2: Profanation (John's Countermemory)
Scene 1 (John 19:16–18) Jesus carries his cross through town and is crucified.	The Jewish nation, represented by Jesus, is symbolically conquered and subjugated by Rome.	*Jesus is "lifted up" so that he may "cast out the ruler of this world" and grant eternal life to those who believe in him (John 3:14–15; 12:31–33).*
Scene 2 (John 19:19–22) Pilate posts a placard on Jesus' cross that identifies him as "king of the Jews" in three languages.	The Jewish "king" and his subjects are publicly humiliated; the Jewish authorities are powerless to defend their own dignity. Of course, the Romans don't allow the Jews to have a "king," but if they did they could give that individual the same treatment they are now giving Jesus.	*Pilate is ironically correct to observe that Jesus is a "king," although Jesus' kingdom is in fact "not of this world," instead deriving its mandate from the deity who permits the Romans to rule for the time being (John 18:36–37; 19:10–11).*
Scene 3 (John 19:23–24) The Roman soldiers divide Jesus' clothing and cast lots for his seamless tunic.	Roman soldiers reenact Pompey's conquest of Palestine in 63 BCE and, from the perspective of John's late-first-century CE readers, the reconquest and destruction of Jerusalem in 70 CE, dividing the plunder while the helpless Jews look on.	*While the Romans may think that they are casting lots for practical reasons, they are in fact unwitting pawns in Christ's divine drama, fulfilling Ps 22:18.*
Scene 4 (John 19:25–27) Jesus commits his mother to the care of the Beloved Disciple.	Like so many Jewish widows, Jesus' mother is thrown on the mercy of others after her insolent son suffers the just reward for rebellion.	*Even after being scourged and crucified, Jesus is completely capable of providing for the needs of those who are not ashamed of his cross (cf. John 18:1–9).*
Scene 5 (John 19:28–30) Jesus dies after saying "I am thirsty" and "It is finished."	The vanquished Jew admits defeat.	*Jesus returns to the Father after "completing" both the Old Testament Scriptures and his revelatory mission (see John 13:1–3; 16:28)*

Event	Story 1: Public Meaning (Cross Script)	Story 2: Profanation (John's Countermemory)
Scene 6 (John 19:31–37) The soldiers confirm Jesus' death by piercing his side with a spear, producing a flow of water and blood.	The corpse of the Jewish "king" is mutilated, symbolizing the erasure of the most basic human dignities.	*Even after Jesus' death, the Romans can do nothing to him that does not fulfill some prophecy. Thus, they do not break his legs because Scripture says they cannot, and they pierce his side because Scripture says they must.*
	Moral: The Jews are a helpless, subject people; rebellion will lead to annihilation once again.	*Moral: Caesar's agents serve Christ's agenda at every step, proof positive that he has conquered the world.*

As the table above indicates, John 19:16–37 tells two stories, one that recites the creed of the cult of imperial power and a second that profanes and reappropriates Caesar's claims. While the events of public history reenact the drama of Roman conquest, in John's countermemory Caesar falls before a conquering Christ whose agenda is irresistible and whose kingdom transcends every earthly empire. John's theology of the cross emerges from the space between these public and private readings, a history that any emperor could accept married to a confession that Rome cannot withstand.

BIBLIOGRAPHY

Ashton, John. *Understanding the Fourth Gospel*. New York: Oxford University Press, 1991.

Fitzmyer, Joseph A. "Crucifixion in Ancient Palestine, Qumran Literature, and the New Testament." *CBQ* 40 (1978) 498–507.

Foucault, Michael. "Nietzsche, Genealogy, and History." In *Language, Countermemory, Practice*, translated by Donald F. Bouchard and Sherry Simon. Edited by Donald F. Bouchard, 139–64. Ithaca: Cornell University Press, 1977.

Kirk, Alan. "The Memory of Violence and the Death of Jesus in Q." In *Memory, Tradition, and Text: Uses of the Past in Early Christianity*, edited by Alan Kirk and Tom Thatcher, 191–206. SBLSS. Atlanta: Society of Biblical Literature, 2005.

Martyn, J. Louis. *History and Theology in the Fourth Gospel*. New York: Harper & Row, 1968.

Scott, James C. *Domination and the Arts of Resistance: Hidden Transcripts*. New Haven: Yale University Press, 1990.

———. "Protest and Profanation: Agrarian Revolt and the Little Tradition." *Theory and Society* 4 (1977) 1–38.

Zerubavel, Yael. *Recovered Roots: Collective Memory and the Making of Israeli National Tradition*. Chicago: University of Chicago Press, 1995.

6

Paul Confronts Caesar with the Good News

STANLEY E. PORTER

> I know no art, and I only view
> A stone from a wall,
> But I am thinking that stone has echoed
> The voice of Paul.[1]

INTRODUCTION

ONE OF THE MOST important recent transformations in the study of Paul has been from Paul the Jewish religious teacher into Paul the world-citizen within the Roman Empire. There had, of course, been previous study—in fact, much previous study—of Paul within the context of the Roman Empire, and consequently discussion of Paul in relation to such things as his citizenship, his traveling enhanced by the benefits of the *pax Romana*, his missionary strategy in terms of major Greco-Roman cities, and his numerous confrontations with and even imprisonments at the hands of various Roman officials.[2] The transformation that has recently occurred is to see Paul not merely as a figure within the Roman Empire but as a figure who constructively interacts with the Roman Empire in numerous ways related to it as an empire, that is, in terms of its political, social, and economic structures.[3] The results

---

1. Hardy, "In the British Museum."

2. These issues are usually handled within standard introductions to Paul. A good place to start is Bruce, *Paul*.

3. One of those who has led in this recent effort is Richard A. Horsley. See his two

of such study are beginning to become more widely known within the mainstream of Pauline studies. Examples include Neil Elliott's teasing out the political implications of examining Paul's so-called conversion as an act of defiance against Rome,[4] or numerous re-assessments of Paul's theological and practical teaching regarding political issues,[5] or Norman Petersen's reassessment of Paul's supposed social conservatism in his approach to slavery,[6] or Tom Wright's recognition of the importance of the ascendant emperor cult as a fitting backdrop for composition of a number of books of the New Testament,[7] or Stanley Stowers's idea that Romans is addressed to the Romans in order to get their acceptance of Paul's gospel within an Augustan context.[8] These are just some of the many theories being advocated recently in terms of Paul and the Roman Empire. What I wish to pursue in this paper regarding Paul and empire is the relationship of three of Paul's major letters—Romans, and 1 and 2 Corinthians—in relationship to Roman imperialism, especially as this revolves around the emperor cult.

The Roman emperor cult arose out of two major tendencies, and several minor ones. One was the all-too-typical human tendency to want to apotheosize humans of significant abilities, position, or merit. There is a long history of humans doing this, including divinizing ancient rulers, military figures, philosophers, and others. Several of the best known are Hercules,[9] who was welcomed into the pantheon of the gods after his death, and the Egyptian Pharaohs.[10] The second tendency that the Romans directly responded to was the divinization of earlier rulers, especially in the east. Taylor has argued that the Persians divinized their rulers.[11] Although not all scholars have followed her in this, it is widely recognized that such worship became widespread from the

edited volumes: *Paul and Empire* and *Paul and Politics*.

4. Elliott, *Liberating Paul*, 149–67.

5. E.g. Theissen, *Social Setting of Pauline Christianity*; Gorman, *Apostle*, 12, who notes that "There could be nothing more irrational or more un-Roman than to honor—not to mention deify!—a man crucified by the imperial authorities."

6. Petersen, *Rediscovering Paul*.

7. Wright, *Climax of the Covenant*, 140–41.

8. Stowers, *Rereading of Romans*, 21–33.

9. On the apotheosis of Heracles/Hercules, see Graves, *Greek Myths*, 2:200–206.

10. See Ringgren and Ström, *Religions of Mankind*, 41–54, esp. 50, where it is noted that the Pharaoh was seen as divine from earliest times, and the son of the god Re.

11. Taylor, *Divinity*, 247–55.

time of Alexander the Great and his successive Hellenistic rulers of the east, which was transferred to the Roman emperors, at first after their deaths and then increasingly during their own lifetime. Alexander the Great, as ruler in the Temenid line of kings of Macedonia, was seen as descended from Zeus, but undertook a lifetime process of having his divinity recognized in the course of his conquest of the eastern world.[12] One of his legacies was that the Diadochi and their successor Hellenistic kings retained this divinization as a means of retaining social control.[13] For example, Ptolemaic kings were recognized as "god and savior" (IBM 4.906), and the Rosetta stone recognizes Ptolemy V as "being god from god and goddess" (*OGIS* 90). Similarly, the Seleucid kings applied to themselves the term "god," as is seen on their coins.[14] Hence there was an environment in which the deification of leaders was already to be found. As a result, Augustus could have his adopted father, Julius Caesar, divinized, and could be recognized in such a way in the eastern part of the empire, without a threat of this impinging upon his position within the early principate.[15] However, during the first century the emperor cult grew much stronger, until it had become fully entrenched by the end of the century.[16] This recognition of the exalted status of the emperor was reflected in numerous inscriptions, papyrus documents, coins, art and architecture, and the like, as they recognized and paid tribute to the ruler as divinized.

One of the most important pieces of ancient evidence that has been brought into discussion of the New Testament and empire, especially in relation to the emperor cult, is the bilingual calendar inscription from

---

12. For discussion of Alexander and his deification (some say confirmation came at Ammon in Egypt but others later in Bactria), see (among others) Wilcken, *Alexander the Great*, 211–13; Tarn, *Alexander the Great*, 2:347–74; Fox, *Alexander the Great*; Hammond, *Alexander the Great*, but who notes that never outside of Egypt was Alexander seen as an incarnate god (p. 121); Green, *Alexander of Macedon*, who notes that Philip himself was on a similar quest (p. 81).

13. On the divinization of the Hellenistic kings, see Bevan, *House of Seleucus* 2:154–57, on Antiochus IV; Taylor, *Divinity*, 1–34; Green, *From Alexander to Actium*, 396–408.

14. See Deissmann, *Light*, 344–45, esp. n. 1.

15. On Augustus, see Nilsson, *Imperial Rome*, 11–19; Jones, *Augustus*, 150–52.

16. On the emperor cult, see Taylor, *Divinity*, 142–246; Ferguson, *Religions*, 88–98; Price, *Rituals and Power*; Davies, *Rome's Religious History*, 176–85. On the visual artistic evidence, see Strong, *Apotheosis and After Life*.

Asia Minor (*OGIS* 458 for the standard Greek edition).[17] Portions of this inscription in Greek and Latin have been found at Priene (the largest fragments), Apamea Kibotos, Dorylaion, Maionia, and Eumeneia. This inscription was erected at various places in Asia Minor in celebration of Augustus's birthday in 9 BC.[18] This inscription has, rightly, been brought into discussion of the Gospels, especially Mark's Gospel.[19] As will be noted below, there are a number of features of the calendar inscription that Mark's Gospel holds in common to indicate that the Gospel was written in direct confrontation of the imperial cult.[20] So much has become increasingly well-recognized in recent times. The importance of this inscription for studying Paul's letters in relation to the Roman Empire has only been touched upon, but merits further consideration.[21] However, there are numerous other documents from the ancient world that also provide partial glimpses of the kind of thought-world that was given to increasing recognition and veneration of emperors in the imperial cult.

In this paper, I wish to draw upon the conceptual background reflected by these inscriptions to shed light on these three Pauline letters. By doing this, I focus upon one particular aspect of the relationship of Paul's letters to the Roman Empire, while ignoring and passing by a number of other features. Some of the other features that would merit lengthier discussion in another context would be the implied and explicit social relations among those invoked in the letters and Paul's critique of them, other theological and philosophical constructs invoked in the letters, and Paul's social, political, and religious standing in rela-

---

17. This inscription is mistakenly referred to as the Priene inscription, after the place where the largest fragments were discovered, but the inscription is usually studied as a composite from several locations. This inscription can be found in its Greek and Latin forms in Ehrenberg and Jones, *Documents*, no. 98, with some portions not included in *OGIS* 458, and the Latin portions *CIG* 3.3957 = *CIL* 3.12240; *CIG* 3.3902b; *CIL* 3.13651 in Laffi, "Iscrizione." Complete translations (note the importance of this below) are found in Sherk, ed., *Rome and the Greek East*, no. 101, with notes on reconstruction; Danker, *Benefactor*. Photographs of lines 30 and onward are conveniently found in Deissmann, *Light*, figs. 70, 71. Most translations only provide a portion of the document, usually from lines 30 following.

18. This date is not certain, but is the one that most scholars use.

19. For example, a small portion is quoted in Boring, Berger, and Colpe, *Hellenistic Commentary*, 169.

20. As recognized by Evans, "Mark's Incipit"; cf. Evans, *Mark*, lxxxiii–iv.

21. E.g., Wright, "Paul's Gospel."

tion to his audience, among others. Dimensions of some of these ideas will inevitably be touched on in this paper as I discuss the relationship of Paul to the imperial cult, but these are only incidental as they help to inform my major theme.

PAUL'S LETTER TO THE ROMANS

We believe that we live in an age of narrative as an explanation of our relation to the world around us. New Testament studies have become a part of this narrative propensity, especially in relation to the Old Testament.[22] However, narratives have informed cultures from earliest times—not just New Testament scholarship of a sort over the last twenty years—as is seen in the fundamental stories that cultures tell themselves about their being and existence. Such was the ancient world itself. In Paul's letter to the Romans, I believe that we see a fundamental conflict between two highly operative narratives. One of those narratives is that of the imperial cult itself, especially as seen in such a document as the calendar inscription of 9 BC. This was, for the Romans, a new narrative, being told in its fullest and perhaps first form about Augustus. Another narrative is the one that Paul constructed regarding Jesus in his letter to the Romans. This narrative too was a new one, which attempted to capture and then tell the story of who Jesus was in relation to the Roman world of the times. The points of comparison and conflict bear further exploration.

The calendar inscription of 9 BC has rarely—if ever—been studied in regard to its narrative value.[23] The usual means of studying it in relation to the New Testament is to note lexical similarities between a given biblical passage and the inscription. These lexical correspondences are important, as we shall see, but there is more to the inscription than simply the choice and use of these vocabulary items. The inscription weaves a narrative regarding Augustus that is worth examining in more detail. Rather than simply examining a small portion of the inscription—

---

22. Some of the recent works that approach the New Testament from the narrative perspective are Hays, *Faith of Jesus Christ*, Witherington, *Paul's Narrative Thought World*; Wright, *Jesus and the Victory of God*; Riesner, *Paul's Early Period*; Keesmaat, *Paul and His Story*; Grieb, *Story of Romans*.

23. This paper is an exercise in narratology (among other things). For essential works on narratology, see Bal, *Narratology*; Bal, *On Story-Telling*; O'Neill, *Fictions of Discourse*; Stanzel, *Theory of Narrative*; Martin, *Recent Theories of Narrative*.

which is usually done when the inscription is examined with the New Testament in mind—I wish to examine the entire inscription at least in its Greek portion, as reconstructed by scholarship.

The inscription is divided into seven portions. Three of these are in Latin. The Latin portions were found at Apamea Kobotos and Dorylaion, but these are fragmentary and apparently of secondary value in relation to the Greek portions, and so will not be considered further here. The inscription appears to have been known in Greek in Priene, Apamea Kobotos, Maionia, and Eumeneia, with the presumption being that essentially the same inscription was found at each.[24] What is extant seems to be in three portions. The first portion is the edict of the proconsul of Asia, and the second and third portions are the two decrees of the Koinon of Asia. Only the first of these two decrees is sufficiently extant to utilize in reconstructing the full effect of the decree alongside the edict of the governor.

The edict of the proconsul of Asia is damaged, and so the very beginning is no longer extant, although on the basis of the inscriptional tradition it is highly likely that the inscription began with the proconsul identifying himself and announcing his task.[25] The edict follows a particular pattern. The inscription recognizes the significance of the occasion—the birthday of the divine Caesar (IV.4–5)—and places this event within the framework of the natural order, such that the birth of Caesar has maintained and restored natural order (IV.6–8). The inscription then progresses through a series of significant references, first to the natural birth of Caesar (IV.9–10) and then his fortunate and fortuitous life that was beneficial to all (IV.10–14). The inscription then invokes how all of this occurred according to a preordained divine will that has provided for such benefaction (IV.15). This first section of the inscription then lists the particular festal worship events that are to take place in commemoration of Caesar's birthday.

The first decree of the Koinon is intact and begins with standard language regarding a decree ("It has been decreed . . ."). This decree follows a similar pattern to the edict in terms of its reference to Augustus. The decree itself first recognizes the role of Providence in providing Augustus to humanity (VI.33–34). Then there is reference to producing

---

24. That is the way that the fragments have been used in scholarship, with portions only available at one site used to fill in gaps in the inscription at others.

25. See Danker, *Benefactor*, 216.

Augustus to the benefit of humankind, labeling him as a savior who exceeded the hopes of all previous benefactors (VI.35–38). The same kinds of significant references are then made as in the edict, including citation of the beginning of good news occurring with his birthday (VI.40–41), and then the fact that he had bestowed benefits upon various people, including local rulers (VI.45–46). The inscription invokes these benefits within the larger framework of them coming directly from the right hand of the divine Augustus (VI.45–46). The decree then continues with reference to the various specifics of the calendrical celebrations in honor of Augustus's birthday.

There are several features of the inscription to note. One is the common pattern used to present what is said regarding Augustus, before turning to the particulars of how it is that he is to be honored through the celebration of his birthday. I will return to this pattern below.

A second feature is that this particular inscription is not a singular instance, but itself representative of the same inscription that was erected in at least five places in Asia—that is, in five places where fragments of the inscription have been found and recovered. These are not the only inscriptions of this particular nature, however. For example, there was an inscription found at Halicarnassus on the west coat of Asia that was at first thought to be another example of the same inscription, because of the similarity in the language used.[26] When it was first discovered, the resemblance to the decree found at Apamea Kibotos and Eumenia regarding honoring the birthday of Augustus was commented upon. This inscription describes Augustus in terms of father Zeus and savior of the universal race of humans (IBM 4.894).[27] Since then, further inscriptions have been found with somewhat similar preambles as the one noted above, such as at Assos. However, the Halicarnassus inscription, though it does not appear to refer to the same events commemorated by the calendrical inscription of 9 BC, in conjunction with other inscriptions indicates that praise of the emperor was widespread and generally celebrated throughout Asia. This is understandable in the light of the fact that under Augustus the *pax Romana* extended into the East, including the interior of Asia, and brought with it relative peace and orderliness.[28]

---

26. Hirschfeld and Marshall, *Collection*, 64–65.

27. See also Ehrenberg and Jones, *Documents*, no. 98a.

28. Hirschfeld and Marshall, *Collection*, 64–65. On the *pax Romana*, see Petit, *Pax Romana*; Wengst, *Pax Romana*.

A third feature to note is that the edict of the calendrical inscription was instigated by a governor named Paulus Fabius Maximus, who is referred to in VI.4 and VII.80 by name. In IV.30, he states that he issued his edict in both languages, Greek and Latin. Paulus Fabius Maximus was the governor of Asia, probably in 10/9 BC.[29] A noteworthy feature of Paulus Fabius Maximus is that he gained more widespread recognition on account of his erecting the calendrical inscription, and as a result was given divine honors at his death by being recognized at Alexandria Troas as being associated with Apollo Smintheus.[30]

A fourth feature is the fact that there were numerous similar inscriptions venerating the emperors, starting with Julius Caesar and continuing through his successors until Nero.[31] Deissmann notes that there was an inscription erected during the time of Augustus in the city of Tarsus, which read: "Emperor Caesar, son of God, Augustus, the Tarsian people [honor]." As Deissmann states, "Perhaps the young Paul may have seen here the expression Son of God for the first time—long before it came to him with another meaning."[32] However, such similar expressions of veneration of the emperor were found throughout the empire, from the time of Julius Caesar on. I think that it is virtually certain that they had an impact upon Paul. I will note some of those inscriptions in areas that Paul visited.[33] Julius Caesar was widely heralded as savior, benefactor (*IG* VII.1835; *CIA* 3.428; *Inschriften von Olympia* 365; *IG* XII.5.556), and even god (*IG* XII 5.557) in Greece. In Asia, the language is similar, and perhaps even more pronounced. He was described as god at Lesbos (*Ath. Mitt.* 13 [1888] 61), as benefactor at Chios (*IGR* 4.929), and as savior and benefactor (*IGR* 4.57), creator (*IG* XII 2.165b) and also god (*IG* XII 2.35b; *IGR* 4.33) at Mytilene. At Pergamum, he was depicted as savior (*IGR* 4.304), benefactor (*IGR* 4.307), and savior and benefactor

---

29. See Sherk, *Rome and the Greek East*, 127, nn. 2, 5.

30. Taylor, *Divinity*, 273.

31. I note only those who would have lived roughly contemporaneously with Paul (apart from Julius Caesar).

32. Deissmann, *Bible Studies*, 167 n. 1, citing W. H. Waddington, *Voyage archéologique en Grèce et en Asie Mineure*, III.2 (Paris: Didot, 1870), no. 1476 (p. 348).

33. This means that I am not going to cite inscriptions or papyri from Egypt, where they are in abundance, or Africa, Spain, etc. I cite these inscriptions according to standard abbreviations, and from the following sources: Taylor, *Divinity*, 267–83; Ehrenberg and Jones, *Documents*; Charlesworth, *Documents*; Smallwood, *Documents*; Danker, *Benefactor*. Cf. Evans, *Mark*, lxvii–lxviii, who cites mostly papyri from Egypt.

(*IGR* 4.303, 305, 306). There was an inscription at Ephesus erected by the cities of Asia to honor Caesar as "manifest god" and "common savior of human life" (*SIG*³ 760).

Evidence of divinization of Augustus is even more widespread, extending throughout the empire.[34] On Crete at Lyttus, Augustus was depicted as god (*IGR* 1.1007). In Athens, there was an inscription on the Acropolis in a shrine to the goddess Roma and the savior Augustus (*CIA* 3.63; see also *CIA* 3.34) and to Augustus as creator (*CIA* 3.30). There were also inscriptions to Augustus as savior in Olympia (*Inschriften von Olympia* 366), savior and god in Olympia (*Inschriften von Olympia* 53), savior and benefactor in Thespiae (*IG* VII 1836), savior and creator in Pontus (*IGR* 4.314), god and benefactor in Hypata (*SIG*³ 778), god in Melos (*IG* XII 3.1104), and "son of god" in Nicopolis (*CIG* 1810), Thera (*IG* XII 3.469),[35] and Sardes (*Sardis* 7.1 no. 8). In Galatia, an inscription was erected by the league of the Galatian cities to both the god Augustus and the goddess Roma (*OGIS* 533), and in Neapolis there was an inscription that contains the oath to be taken by one at this altar to Augustus, in which Augustus is listed along with all of the other gods and goddesses to which one is to swear allegiance (*IGR* 3.137). In Pisidia, Augustus was hailed as savior and benefactor (*IGR* 3.426), in Tlos in Lycia as god, creator, and savior (*IGR* 3.546), and in Myria in Lycia as "god Augustus, son of god, Caesar, emperor of the earth and sea, benefactor and savior of the entire world" (*IGR* 3.719). Augustus was called god along with Poseidon and Aphrodite at Cilicia (*IGR* 3.921), and god on Cyprus (*IGR* 3.932, 973, 994; *CIG* 2629). In Mytilene, there was a temple to Augustus with a decree honoring him, and copies of this decree were to be placed also in Pergamum, Actium, Brundisium, Tarraco, Maissilia, along with other places (see *IGR* 4.39). In numerous Mytilene inscriptions, Augustus was heralded as god (IGR 4.38, 42, 59, 60, 63, 64, 68, 114; *IG* XII 2.168), as well as Zeus (*IGR* 4.95). In Ilium, he was called "emperor Caesar, son of god, god Augustus," benefactor and savior (*IGR* 4.201). In Pergamum, Augustus was called god (*IGR* 4.309, 315, 317, 318), god, benefactor, and creator (*IGR* 4.311), and "son of god" and "god Augustus" (*Inschriften*

---

34. There is also evidence of divinization of Augustus's family members, such as his son Gaius. See, e.g., *CIA* 3.444; *SIG*³ 1065; *IG*² II.3.3250.

35. According to Taylor (*Divinity*, 271), Wilamowitz-Möllendorf made the suggestion that the use of the Greek article in the genitive singular, τοῦ (*tou*), may have indicated divinity.

von Pergamon 381). Other references to Augustus as god are found at Samos (*IGR* 4.975, 977), Myrina Caesarea (*IGR* 4.1173), Cyme (*IGR* 4.1302), Hierocaesarea (*IGR* 4.1304), Smyrna (*IGR* 4.1444), and Ancyra (*OGIS* 533), and in both Greek and Latin prologues to the *Res Gestae Divi Augusti*, portions of which have been found at Ancyra in Galatia, Pisidian Antioch, and Apollonia in Pisidia (*IGR* 3.159 for the texts from Ancyra and Pisidia). The evidence, especially throughout Asia Minor, for the deification of Augustus would have been hard to avoid, especially as it was found in most urban centers of the area.

Tiberius was recognized as a benefactor at Pergamum (*IGR* 4.320, but before the death of Augustus), son of the god Augustus at Gytheion in Laconia (*SEG* 11.922), and god and the son of the god Augustus at Lapethus in Cyprus (*OGIS* 583) and Myra in Lycia (*IGR* 3.721). Gaius Caligula was recognized in Athens as the new Ares (*CIA* 3.444) and son of Ares (*CIA* 3.444a). He was said to be son of the god Augustus and a new god at Halasarna (*IGR* 4.1094), and was recognized as a god at Mytilene (*IGR* 4.67).

Claudius was called son of the new Zeus at Ahat (*MAMA* 6.250), and savior and benefactor at both Aezani in Phrygia (*IGR* 4.584) and Athens (*IG* II/III2 3274). In a lengthy inscription from Acraephia in Boeotia, Nero was repeatedly called "Lord Nero," the one with foreknowledge, and savior, Zeus the savior, and Zeus the liberator, and "Lord Augustus" (*SIG*³ 814). Nero was also called son of the god Claudius at Rhodes (*Syll*³ 810), the son of the greatest of gods (*IM* 157b), and the young Apollo (*IG* II/III² 3278). In two unusual inscriptions, Nero was called the "good god Asclepius Caesar" (*IGR* 4.1053)[36] and the new Apollo in Athens (*IG* II/III² 3278).

My contention is that Paul was very familiar with the widespread use of terms that divinized the Caesars when he wrote his letter to the Romans. This is not, so far as I know, a particularly contentious statement to make. He only had to have his eyes open as he traveled throughout and repeatedly within Asia Minor.[37] Paul's travels took him to a variety

---

36. See Deissmann, *Light*, 345 n. 4 for discussion.

37. This raises the question of general literacy, and in particular Paul's literacy. On Paul's education, see Porter and Pitts, "Paul's Bible," where it is argued in the light of recent research that Paul received a grammatical education in Tarsus before going to Jerusalem for his rabbinical training. The article also makes the point that most people in the Greco-Roman world were subjected to a literate culture, and needed to have access to writing, even if they were not literate.

of places within the Greco-Roman world where such inscriptions were erected. I have merely noted the places above that were in the ambit of Paul's travels. These places included primarily Greece and Asia Minor. These inscriptions preserve ample record of language of divinization as part of the emperor cult, presented in public form for all to see. One of the features of inscriptions—as opposed to papyri (although the papyrological evidence is widespread as well)—is that these documents were written as permanent representations of edicts, decrees, and the like. In the light of this widespread evidence, I wish to go further and suggest the possibility that Paul had in fact seen many such inscriptions, and may have even seen, or at least knew of the kind of material contained within, the calendar inscription found at Priene and other sites. In the course of his travels Paul had been close by or possibly even passed through several of the sites that had a form of the calendar inscription. These places include Dorylaeum, which may have been visited on his way from Pisidian Antioch to Troas on the second missionary journey, Priene, which was located close to Ephesus (and not too far from Miletus) and could have been visited on his second journey or during his lengthy stay in Ephesus on his third missionary journey, or Apamea Kobotos, which was in Phrygia near Laodicea and Colossae and could have been passed through on his third missionary journey. Any one or more of these cities could have been visited before Paul wrote his letter to the Romans, probably after visiting Corinth on his third missionary journey.[38] Even if he did not actually visit these places, Paul was within the vicinity, and, along with the other evidence of widespread reference to the emperor as a form of god, would have no doubt taken notice of such language. However, I believe that there is a stronger influence than simply incidental references to the divinization of the emperor—Paul seems to know of the narrative that is found in the calendrical inscription. In the light of his having the name Paul, as did the one who commissioned and erected the calendar inscription and the last proconsul to be himself given divine honors, I believe that there is even a possibility that Paul is styling himself as the new erector of a new inscription to the true Lord, Jesus Christ.

The Pauline letter form takes a fairly standard pattern. Whether one sees this as consisting of three, four, or five parts, all agree that there is

---

38. For discussion of the date of composition, see McDonald and Porter, *Early Christianity*, 451, where a date around AD 56 or 57 is suggested as reasonable.

the Pauline letter opening. Within this letter opening, there are some variations that can and do take place. For example, Paul expands the section on the addressee in 2 Cor 1:2.[39] In the opening to his letter to the Romans, Paul does something that he does not do in any other letter that he writes. He crafts the most extensive introduction of the portion of the opening that specifies the sender. His playing on the similarity of his name with the sponsor of the calendar inscription, his patterning of what he says in the opening, and his address of the letter to the Romans all point toward Paul consciously writing a letter to the Romans that confronts them with the nature of who the true "Lord" is.

The opening of the letter to the Romans, I believe, follows a similar narrative pattern to the one found in the calendrical inscription. This could be merely coincidental, but the pattern itself helps to explain some of the features of the letter opening in ways that other explanations do not.

Prescript

The letter is written by "Paul, slave of Christ Jesus, called apostle,[40] designated for the good news of God." The prescript with Paul listed first is typical of the Pauline letter form and is found elsewhere in his letters.[41] Similarly, the reconstruction of the letter by the proconsul, Paulus Fabius Maximus, begins with his name at the outset as well, as one would expect in the letter form, even if it is inscribed on stone.

Like any Roman of the time, Paul would have had three names: a *cognomen* by which he was addressed (Paul), a *praenomen* and a *nomen*, both of which are unknown to us. We do know that he had an alternative name or *supernomen*, Saul. The name Paul was a common one as a *cognomen*, and had the sense of "small," whether used pejoratively in terms of size or as a term of affection.[42] Paulus Fabius Maximus had a

---

39. On the Pauline letter form, see McDonald and Porter, *Early Christianity*, 380–86, esp. 380–82; and Porter and Adams, eds., *Paul and the Ancient Letter Form*.

40. Some have questioned whether a single or double attribute is noted here: "called apostle" or "called" and "apostle." See Jewett, *Romans*, 101.

41. Romans is one of only five letters where Paul has no co-sender, the others being Ephesians and the Pastoral Epistles.

42. See Hemer, "Name," esp. 183, who notes that many *cognomina* were pejorative, although the widespread use of the feminine form (Paulina) indicates use of the name Paul as a term of endearment.

name that had a superficial resemblance to Paul's name, although Paulus was the proconsul's "obsolete rare *praenomen* ... which was occasionally revived as an archaizing fashion."[43] Paulus Fabius Maximus had a name that also indicated being from the tribe of Fabius (*nomen*), a well-known tribe with members such as the orator M. Fabius Quintilianusis, and a *cognomen* of Maximus, meaning "great" or "large" (equivalent to the Greek μέγας or μάκρος).[44]

I cannot help but think, whether Paul was writing with conscious reference to Paulus Fabius Maximus or not, that he was playing on his own name whenever he wrote his letters, and especially in his letter to the Romans. Paul begins his letter by essentially stating: "Little Paul, slave of Christ Jesus..." By contrast, if he has his eye on Paulus Fabius Maximus, he is positioning himself in relation to the great or large Paul from the Fabian tribe.[45] The (soon to be seen to be ironic) contrast of position is further supported by Paul's use of passive words to describe himself. He is not only a slave of Christ Jesus, but he is "called" by another, a "sent one" (apostle) sent by another, and "one set apart" by another, for the purpose of the good news of God. Paulus Fabius Maximus, by contrast, is actively "ordering" the erection of the decree and "ordering" the edict to be written upon it.

From the start, Paul seems to have captured the apparent power differential between the proconsul of the Roman government and the servant of God. Paulus Fabius Maximus fashioned himself as a great man who was doing a noble and worthy deed in erecting the calendrical inscription throughout Asia in commemoration of the birthday of Caesar Augustus. So his contemporaries also styled him, on the basis of his receiving divine honors. Paul, on the other hand, fashions himself not

---

43. Ibid.

44. The fact that the transition from Paul's Jewish *supernomen* to his Roman *cognomen* occurs in Acts 13:9 has raised the question of the relation of Paul's name to that of the Roman proconsul, Sergius Paulus (13:7). Like some of the time, Sergius Paulus is addressed by *nomen* and *cognomen* (his full name may have been Quintus Sergius Paulus [see Bruce, *Acts*, 297], but no Roman is addressed by all three names in the New Testament [Hemer, "Name," 182]). It has been suggested that Paul's name was given to him after his first convert, but this is unlikely, as Paul would have had his Roman name from birth. See Conzelmann, *Acts*, 100.

45. Some may question whether Paul was up to such "humor." Note that Paul uses a number of literary figures in his letters, including Romans, such as personification, apostrophe, hyperbole, and litotes, among others.

as great and mighty, but as a slave, one who was called, sent, and determined on the basis of another—his God—to bring the "good news."

Fulfilled Order

The second major feature of the calendrical inscription letter and decree was how the birthday of the divine Caesar was a joyful and blessed event on the basis of its coming about as part of the natural order. The letter from Paulus Fabius Maximus describes the birthday as, if not the beginning of nature, the beginning of all things in terms of usefulness, by his restoring that which was disordered. The decree itself speaks of providence sending a savior for humanity who has set everything in order. Paul recognizes a similar kind of setting of the natural order right, or fulfillment of the divine order, in the way he heralds the coming of the "good news." The term "good news," also rendered in translations of the calendrical inscription as "glad tidings," is not used in the inscription until later in the decree itself (reconstructed in line 37 and partial in line 40). In the inscription, the "good news" concerns the birthday of Augustus.

For Paul, the "good news" that God proclaims is the coming of Jesus Christ. Paul styles himself as one set apart for God's good news. This good news, he says, consists of three major elements. One is that it was promised beforehand, the second is that it was given through prophets, and the third was that it was contained in the holy writings or Scriptures. Paul's approach to the good news is to trump the assertion of Paulus Fabius Maximus in the calendrical inscription. The inscription reveals a tension between wanting to attribute all that is good to the coming of Augustus, while no doubt also recognizing that Augustus was not the first of the great rulers and leaders. Thus Paulus Fabius Maximus casts the recognition in terms of restoring the natural order. His coming was a fulfillment, but was also a necessity in the light of circumstances.[46] Paul goes further and places the coming of Christ Jesus within the context of not just having been anticipated or hinted at by God, but having been promised beforehand by God. God's promise was not merely something revealed in the present circumstances—as is hinted at in the calendrical inscription—but was, Paul says, mediated through God's own proph-

---

46. It has been noted by a number of commentators that ruler cults were less of a theological structure than they were a pragmatic approach to society. See Wilcken, *Alexander the Great*, 212–13; Taylor, *Divinity*, 35, 237, 238.

ets and contained in the holy writings or Scriptures (that is, the Old Testament). Paul is clear elsewhere in Romans that one of the advantages of the Jewish people was that they had been given the divine words of God (see Rom 3:2). Here Paul invokes these words from the outset of his letter to provide proclaimed and written proof that the coming of Jesus Christ as the "good news" was not merely a circumstantial and coincidental recognition brought about by exigency, but a foretold and confirmed event that had been heralded in advance, and was contained within personal first-hand and written documentation.

Natural Birth

One of the major features of the calendrical inscription is that it was erected to clarify and regulate the Roman calendar on the basis of the birthdate of Augustus (thus correcting the Julian calendar). Hence, the physical birth of Augustus is an important feature of the proclamation by Paulus Fabius Maximus and the edict itself. Several times the birthday of the god, Augustus, is mentioned in the two major panels. In the edict of the proconsul, he states that the world would in fact have been a very different place in both appearance and result if Augustus had not been born. The edict itself states that the producing of Augustus was the culmination of life on earth.

References to the earthly life of Jesus Christ have often been discussed with regard to Paul's letters.[47] A number of scholars have claimed that Paul's knowledge of the earthly life of Jesus was nearly non-existent, because he does not refer to a number of events, teachings, or other features that they believe Paul should have cited if he had had such knowledge. More particularly, the reference in Rom 1:3 to Christ Jesus being begotten from the seed of David according to the flesh has struck scholars as unusual, in regard to both the perceived general lack of references to Jesus' earthly life in Paul's letters and what is perceived to be unusual wording in this verse.[48] This is not the place to discuss in lengthy detail how much Paul knew about the life of Jesus. A few simple facts can be laid out, however. One is that, whereas Paul might not cite the words of Jesus as frequently as one might have hoped or even expected, he does in fact have knowledge of both specific words of Jesus and, much

---

47. Much of this discussion stems from R. Bultmann and his influential dismissive interpretation of 2 Cor 5:16. See his *Theology of the New Testament*, 1:238–39.

48. E.g., see Dunn, *Romans*, 1.11–12.

more importantly, major teaching events within Jesus' life. Paul knows, for example, that Jesus was human (Rom 9:5), was born of a woman (Gal 4:4), had brothers (1 Cor 9:5; Gal 1:19), ate the night he was betrayed (1 Cor 11:23–25), testified before Pilate (1 Tim 6:13), was crucified and died on a cross (Phil 2:8 among many), was buried (1 Cor 15:4), was raised from the dead (1 Cor 15:4 and others), and was seen by Peter and others (1 Cor 15:5–7), among other statements. Paul also seems to know of many of Jesus' significant teaching passages, including statements found in the Sermon on the Mount (see Rom 12:14, 17, 18–19), Jesus' teaching on the Lord's supper (1 Cor 11:23–25), Jesus teaching on divorce (1 Cor 7:10), and Jesus' beliefs about his return (1 Thess 2:15–16 and elsewhere).[49] In fact, I think that it is worth noting that we know far more from Paul's letters about the earthly life of Jesus than we can gather from many, if not most, of the inscriptions regarding Augustus, certainly from what we know from the calendrical inscription.[50] Seen within the context of comparison with the calendrical inscription, Paul's reference here to Jesus' being in the line of David makes good sense. Even if one were to concede that Paul does not speak about the earthly life of Jesus as much as one would like, it is understandable that Paul would invoke the knowledge that he did have if he were self-consciously imitating (or even mimicking) the calendrical inscription or similar documents. This would also account for why what is said here is unusual for Paul. In only one other place does Paul refer to Jesus as being in the line of David (2 Tim 2:8). Paul is clearly concerned here in the opening of Romans to let his readers know that the "good news" that he is speaking of is found in a figure who is certainly a human being, even though god's son (on this designation, see below). More particularly, he is a human being who has a specific lineage. Just as Octavian had been adopted by Julius Caesar, so Jesus is depicted as from the seed of David in so far as his fleshly or human side was concerned.

---

49. See Porter and Bedard, *Unmasking the Pagan Christ*, 122–24.

50. Here is the place to mention the importance of the *Res Gestae Divi Augusti* for our knowledge of Augustus. Even so, we must keep in mind that this relatively short document covers a reign of forty years, often speaks in generalities, and overlooks a number of details, and in fact was written and commissioned for erection by the featured figure Augustus himself, at the end of his life when he was 75 years old. A convenient edition with translation is by Shipley in the Loeb Classical Library.

Good Fortune

The next stage in the narrative is to attribute good fortune to the emperor's earthly life. The edict of the governor Paulus Fabius Maximus said that people considered the coming of Augustus as the beginning of life and of living. He says that, in terms of both private and public life, everyone was better off, especially those living in Asia, on account of Augustus. The decree itself similarly states that Augustus had exceeded everyone's hopes and expectations through his benefaction to humanity, which far exceeded anything previously received, and would not be exceeded in the future. The calendrical inscription makes it clear that the good fortune that has fallen on all of humanity because of the divine Augustus is on account of all of the good things that he has done.[51] In other words, it is in what he does that he proves his divine character. A person who is able to right the social order, turn chaos to regulation, and provide beneficence to others is deemed to be one worthy of praise.

Paul turns this formulation on its head by specifying what it is that distinguishes Jesus Christ as the "good news" for humanity. Paul's statement indicates that God designated Christ Jesus as the son of God in power on the basis of the spirit of holiness as evidenced in the resurrection from the dead, and that as a result Jesus Christ is our Lord. This one statement is full of language that confronts and contradicts the imperial cult by appropriating the very language used of the deified Caesars for Jesus Christ. Paul states that deification is based on more than simply the fact that the Caesar was the biggest benefactor or the most powerful general or the right person on the scene to restore social order. Paul lays out a number of factors that identify Jesus Christ as the ruler who trumps Caesar. First, he states that Jesus Christ was designated in a particular way. The calendrical inscription at the outset mentions the goodwill of the gods, but does not actually state in particular terms the criteria by which one is designated as divine (apart from simply being Caesar). The word that Paul uses, ὁρισθέντος (*horisthentos*), is one that indicates a formal circumscription and designation, and this designation was the result of an act by another, in this case, God.

Second, Paul states that Jesus Christ was designated "son of God." This language, as we have seen above, was very common in the imperial

---

51. Augustus's ability to bring peace and restore order to the world was also commended in his own statue, with representations on his breastplate. See Mackay, *Ancient Rome*, fig. 15.

cult language of the first century, from Augustus to Nero, and is used by Paul twice of Jesus Christ in just these few opening verses of Romans. The calendrical inscription itself does not explicitly state that Augustus was "son of god," but it does state that it commemorates the "birthday of the god" (lines 40–41).

Third, Paul goes further and states that Jesus Christ was designated son of God "with/in power." The calendrical inscription emphasizes that Augustus is commended for what he has done, especially by restoring social order and establishing peace in the empire. By stating that Jesus Christ is designated son of God "with/in power," Paul seems to be indicating that the title being given to Jesus Christ is not simply an honorific in recognition of a position or even accomplishments, but a designation with force and substance to it, even an indication that carries the assertion of an essential character.

Fourth, Paul indicates that there is an essential character to this designation when he says that it came about on the basis of the spirit of holiness. There has been much debate whether this is an unusual (that is, unique) term for the Holy Spirit, a circumlocution for the Holy Spirit, or some other spirit, such as Jesus' spirit.[52] Here is not the place to explicate proto-trinitarian beliefs in the New Testament, but one of the subthemes of this opening of Romans is the interplay between the figures that later theology would designate as the Trinity: God, Jesus Christ, and the Holy Spirit.[53] While Paul does not go into detail to parse the nature of the Trinity, here and elsewhere he recognizes a differentiated function of members of the godhead, including here the work of the spirit of holiness in empowering the designated son of God.

Fifth, Paul states that this was related to the resurrection from the dead. The function of the preposition ἐκ (*ek*) in this passage has been widely debated. There are those who would say that the resurrection was the means by which Jesus' divinity was established, while others would not take ἐκ as causal but as temporal, indicating the time from which it was recognized that he was "son of God."[54] In the light of the context here in Romans and in conjunction with what I see as possible conscious

---

52. See Moo, *Romans*, 49–50.

53. I emphasize this in my forthcoming commentary, *Romans*. My use of the term proto-trinitarian (see Porter, "Hermeneutics," 122 n. 59) has been picked up by Fee, *Pauline Christology*, 63.

54. See Cranfield, *Romans*, 1:62.

reflection of the calendrical inscription, I believe that the resurrection of the dead is seen as the time from which the powerful designation as "son of God" was clearly manifested. Paul has previously noted that the good news concerning Jesus Christ had already been designated through the prophets and in the Old Testament, concerning God's son as one who came through the seed of David. This is a fitting parallel to the calendrical inscription's celebration of the birthday of Caesar. The calendar inscription is not celebrating the birthday of Augustus as the date at which everyone recognized him as divine, but is now acknowledging him as divine (when he was already 50 years old) from the beginning since he is now fully recognized as such through his actions.

Sixth, Paul appositionally explicates Jesus Christ as "our Lord." The term "lord" was also one that had a history of being used of divine figures. This language is found in some of the imperial cult language, but is also used in the Septuagint as the most frequent word used to translate the name for God in Hebrew.[55] The use of the full name of Jesus Christ and describing him as "our Lord" serves several purposes in this context. Recent scholarship has wanted to see the designation Jesus Christ as simply Paul's name for the figure of Jesus. However, I think that Paul still uses two names and their ordering to indicate a perspective on Jesus.[56] When Christ appears before Jesus, as it does in Rom 1:1, the divine character is often seen to be emphasized—Paul is contrasting his status as slave with the exalted Christ. Here in v. 4, Paul follows his more usual order, but also the order that he has used in presenting Jesus—from the line of David and designated son of God. He recapitulates this in the title that would indicate divinity to both Jew and Gentile: "Lord."

Divine Benefit

The next stage in the narrative of divine assertion is to note the benefits that come about through divine beneficence. In the edict regarding Augustus, Paulus Fabius Maximus states that this was the result of the divine will and cannot be repaid by human beings, sentiments echoed by the edict itself. The calendrical inscription places these benefits in terms of material prosperity, including such things as an orderly society.

---

55. See Kramer, *Christ*, 156.

56. On some of the related issues, see Kramer, *Christ, passim*.

Paul, however, sees the divine benefit in terms of what we receive through the Lord Jesus Christ. He states that "we" receive grace and apostleship. Whereas the calendrical inscription speaks only of a tangible and secularized benefit of divinization, Paul transforms the benefit accrued from divine status into that of both spiritual and material spheres. The first is that we are to receive grace. Paul does not state here in the letter what this grace means, but in some ways it may well be at least the early Christian correlate of the kind of secular prosperity and order that Paulus Fabius Maximus speaks of when he notes the kinds of benefactions that have resulted from Augustus.[57] Paul states that the greatest benefaction of humanity is the graciousness of God. The second feature is that of a vocational calling. Again, this is stated in parallel with the calendrical inscription. The inscription speaks of the kinds of social benefits gained by the recognition of the birthday of the divine Caesar. Paul speaks of a social benefit with reference to a specific calling. Just as Paul himself characterized himself as a called apostle, that is, one sent out by God at his divine command, so Paul recognizes the general call to apostleship, those who are sent out under God's calling, as the common benefit of those who follow the Lord Jesus Christ.

Worship and Obedience

The major narrative pattern of the calendrical inscription ends with words of worship and obedience. Paulus Fabius Maximus speaks of the recognition of the significance of the birthday of Augustus as a type of "religious observance" that will have general benefit to all in its being recognized. Similarly, the decree itself calls for proclamations and festivals that recognize this special date. All of these are placed within the context of the widespread recognition throughout Asia of the importance of these celebrations.

As one might imagine, Paul transforms the kind of obedience that is expected into what he calls "obedience of faith in all the nations for the name" of Jesus Christ. This is not, as in the calendrical inscription, an occasion for social merry-making, even if it commemorates better time-keeping and better social order. For Paul, we have received in order to fulfill a worshipful obedience that extends beyond festive occasions to faith itself. Paul is calling for obedience that results in faith. The faith that

---

57. On grace as a benefit of benefaction, see deSilva, *Honor*, 121–56.

he is speaking of here is not entirely clear. It may be the faith of those who are obedient, or, assuming that those who are obedient already have faith as demonstrated by their obedience, it may be the faith of those to whom "we" are apostles. Whereas the calendrical inscription was promulgated widely with physical examples erected in a number of places within Asia, Paul transcends regional boundaries by calling for obedience that calls for faith in all the nations or groups of people. Paul recognizes that his Roman audience is already among those who are the ones who have been called by Jesus Christ (the motif of Jew and Greek being included in God's call to faith is found throughout Romans; see 1:16).

What Paul has said in the letter opening is, essentially, that there is "good news" from God to be experienced. However, this good news does not focus upon or originate with Augustus—or any other emperor for that matter—but with the coming of Jesus Christ into the world. Just as the various edicts and inscriptions have announced celebratory days regarding various emperors, including Augustus with his calendrical inscription, Paul announces without the fanfare of public office that, as a slave of Christ Jesus, he is nevertheless called to announce this authentic good news. This good news was promised beforehand through the prophets and in the holy Scriptures, and thus is in accord with not just happenstance but divine purpose. The good news is regarding God's son, who was in the line of David in his earthly existence, and who was designated "son of God" in a powerful way by the Holy Spirit, as was indicated by his resurrection from the dead. This figure—whose human and divine origins are clearly demarcated (unlike the distinguishing features of the Caesar, apart from bringing material prosperity)—is Jesus Christ our Lord. On the basis of this, we have received divine favor and a calling to apostleship that results in obedient worship as we promote faith among the nations on his behalf, and the Roman Christians recognized—if not before they had read this salutation, certainly by the time they got to the end of it—that there was only one Lord, and he was not Caesar Augustus, but Christ Jesus. Thus, the letter to the Romans is delivered to the heart of the empire with the bold statement that there is only one true Lord, Jesus Christ.

If what I have outlined is correct, this helps us to make sense of several other important parts of Paul's letter, not least Romans 13. Romans 13:1–7 is notoriously difficult in the history of interpretation, because interpreters have typically cast this passage as demanding unqualified obedience to the state. This is predicated upon the belief that Paul was one who was not an opponent or antagonist of the Roman hierarchy and establishment. If what I have presented above is correct regarding how he begins his letter to the Romans, nothing could be further from the truth. Paul is in fact a political opponent of the Roman regime, who does not hesitate to send a missive into the midst of the Roman Empire proclaiming another figure as the Lord God, Jesus Christ.

If this is the case, then it makes it even more difficult to understand Rom 13:1–7 as teaching unqualified obedience to the state.[58] There have, of course, been numerous people and groups who have invoked Romans 13 as a means of maintaining social and political control, while perpetrating numerous unconscionable acts that should make genuine followers of Jesus Christ cringe in horror. Many have. As a result, there are a number of interpretive reactions that have attempted to come to terms with the meaning of this problematic passage. One is to restrict the call to unqualified obedience simply to the Roman situation—an interpretation that misses the point, as I have demonstrated in my treatment of the opening of Romans. Others believe that Paul's comments are addressed to enthusiasts in the Roman church—an explanation that does not address the heart of the interpretive issue. Some believe that the passage either was not written by Paul or was a later interpolation, and therefore not part of the original letter to the Romans—solutions that have no textual support. Others take it as establishing an ideal ethic—even if it cannot be followed. Finally, some believe that, despite what it teaches regarding unqualified obedience, there are circumstances that call for Christian disobedience—ultimately a counsel of despair for interpretation.[59] Though a number of interpreters continue to recognize problems with the traditional interpretation, most recent interpreters go to even more extreme efforts to justify such an explanation.[60]

I believe that in the light of how Paul opens his letter to the Romans, what Paul is saying in Rom 13:1–7 is consistent with his epistolary opening. The letter to the Romans is set within a context in which there is

---

58. In this section on Romans 13, I follow a proposal I made a number of years ago. See Porter, "Romans 13:1–7."

59. See Ibid., 116–17. The history of some important interpreters is found in Reasoner, *Romans in Full Circle*, 129–42. This work shows, among other things, that many theologians have not been particularly good biblical interpreters.

60. As a recent example, see Elliott, "Romans 13:1–7," who takes the passage as a warning against supersessionism.

only one true Lord, Jesus Christ. He is the one who comes about as a result of the natural order instigated by God as revealed through his previous prophetic announcements. His natural birth in the line of David was a continuation of this ordered world, but resulted in his revelation, through his being designated son of God in power and the resurrection, as the Lord Jesus Christ. The response is one of obedience of faith by all the nations. This opening would make it very difficult, I believe, for Paul to turn around and say that, in terms of the realia of political survival within the empire, even though we believe there is only one Lord, Jesus Christ, we are to offer unqualified obedience to the Roman state. In fact, I do not believe that that is what Paul is stating at all in Romans 13—but quite the opposite. In this passage, Paul argues for two important concepts in relation to the theme of Roman imperialism. On the one hand, he calls the authorities themselves to account. He calls for them to be just authorities who are rightly exercising their divinely instigated powers. On the other hand, he calls for Roman Christians, and by implication other Christians within the authority of the empire, to recognize the Lordship of Jesus Christ that does not necessarily result in unqualified obedience to Rome, but that might result in disobedience, if such a context warranted it.

Paul defines obedience in Romans 13 in terms of willing submission, with the unstated though clearly implied assumption that this obedience is only appropriate to a power that warrants such obedience, that is, to a just power but not to an unjust one. For Paul, if all authority comes from God, who rules justly, an authority that wishes to rule as a divine instrument of justice must rule consistently with God's justice. As a result, Paul's discussion in Rom 13:1-7 is concerned with obedience to just authorities, as there are no other authorities to whom one must be obedient. Unjust authorities are not due obedience, but fall outside the parameters that Paul defines.

Romans 13:1 opens with Paul's command to "let every soul be obedient to the superior authorities." "Every soul" includes both Jews and Gentiles, a motif that Paul has developed from the outset of the letter. In Rom 13:1-7, Paul uses a number of different terms that fall within the semantic field of words of obedience. The word translated here "be obedient" (ὑποτάσσω, *hupotassō*) is one of those words. Many commentators have taken the word for obedience here as if it were a strong word implying unqualified obedience, and their translations often render it with language of strong subjection (i.e., be subject to . . .). Within the range of obedience words available, there are some that have a stronger sense of command than does this word. This word for obedience has a range of meanings, from being compelled to voluntary or willing submission of one's rights. In instances of voluntary or willing submission, there is often an assumed recognition of a larger factor that makes subjection expedient or that can render it invalid.[61] Thus, Josephus speaks of subordinating oneself servilely (J.W. 4.175), or subordinating oneself by acknowledging another as master (J.W. 2.433). Epictetus (1.4.19) recommends against making oneself obedient to another. Ps.-Callisthenes (1.22.4) says that it is proper for a wife to be subject to her husband. In the New Testament, the kind of submission spoken of is usually voluntary. Luke 2:51 says Jesus was obedient to his parents and Jas 4:7 calls upon his readers to submit themselves to God and stand against the devil. Hebrews 2:7 asks whether it is not more reasonable to submit to one's spiritual father, as one would to an earthly one, and 1 Pet 5:5 says that the younger are to be obedient to the older, which is part of a proper humble attitude. Thus, this word for obedience seems to include willing subordination.

Paul states further that every soul is to be subordinate to the "authorities." Some have tried to see these authorities as angelic powers, or anything other than earthly authorities, but the fact that Paul advocates paying taxes to them (v. 6) indicates a form of earthly authority. Paul is not speaking simply of authorities, but authorities that he designates as, according to most translators, "governing authorities." Most scholars interpret this as referring to either the supreme authority, that is, the Roman emperor, all authority of the state, or simply government authority in general.[62] What is usually not discussed is the meaning of the word translated "governing" (ὑπερέχω, *huperechō*). This word has two major uses.[63] One is to designate superiority in position, rank, or order. Most commentators take the usage in this sense, for which there is much evidence. For example, Polybius (289.4.9) refers to rulers who have superior rank, Pausanias (6.3.16) speaks of honoring the things of superior strength, Diogenes Laertius (6.78) mentions men of superior position arriving, and 1 Tim 2:2 speaks of those in superior positions.

---

61. See Porter, "Romans 13:1–7," 120–22.
62. Ibid., 122.
63. See ibid., 123–24.

There is a second sense of the word worth considering, however. This is a metaphorical extension of the first sense and indicates superiority in quality. There are also examples of this usage. Isocrates (4.95) speaks of cities that are superior being blotted out, Daniel 5:11 (LXX) refers to Daniel surpassing all the wise men of Babylon, and Sir 33:7 speaks of one day being superior to others.

The question is which of these two senses applies to Rom 13:1. There are three uses of the participle form of this verb besides the example in Rom 13:1. All of these occur in Philippians. In Phil 3:8 Paul states that he considers "all things worthless according to the superiority of the knowledge of Christ Jesus our Lord." Here Paul's contrast is not between a positionally superior knowledge and a positionally inferior knowledge, but a qualitatively different knowledge, that is, between things worthless and things valuable. In Phil 4:7, Paul calls the peace of God superior to all understanding. This is not just a positional superiority but a qualitative superiority. The last example is Phil 2:3. Here Paul commends the Philippians to regard others as superior to themselves. Several commentators endorse the positional sense here,[64] and this may be right in light of Paul's directives regarding humility as seen in the dignity and respect shown to others. However, the qualitative sense may also be worth considering here as indicating not just that they occupy a superior status, but that they genuinely have a qualitatively superior position. This would seem to make better sense of genuine humility as evidenced in the example of the incarnation, death and exaltation of Jesus Christ.

The usage elsewhere of the word "superior" and the context in Rom 13:1 make the qualitative sense far more likely. On the one hand, it would be strange if Paul were commanding obedience to those who are positionally superior, when they would occupy such a position of superiority anyway. On the other hand, in the light of Paul's confronting the Romans with the true Lord, Jesus Christ, the Roman Christians' reaction might be that while they may be compelled by force to be subordinate to the positionally superior leaders, they now know the real Lord and so are not going to be obedient to any authority except Jesus Christ. Paul says that they should submit themselves to those authorities that are qualitatively superior, that is, just authorities.

This understanding of the verse makes the best sense of the rest of the passage. Paul gives reasons why obedience to just authorities should

---

64. Following a long list of interpreters is Fowl, *Philippians*, 77.

occur. One is that there is no legitimate authority except as that authority is put in place by God. This is what makes sense of Rom 13:3. Rulers, Paul says, are not a cause of fear for those who do good works, but for evil. But it is only just authorities and rulers about whom one can say this. The only way not to have fear of authority and to be able to count on receiving praise from them is if they are just and honorable. Only a just authority can be a minister of God for good purpose. No corrupt authority can guarantee that if one does evil there will be punishment, or that punishment will not be given to those who do good.[65]

Thus, from start to nearly finish, the book of Romans is Paul's attempt to indicate in the face of Roman imperialism the nature of the true Lord, Jesus Christ, and what the good news of his lordship might indicate for those who wish to follow him in the obedience of faith.

FIRST AND SECOND CORINTHIANS

First and Second Corinthians were some of the earliest letters studied regarding the relationship of Paul's letters to the Roman Empire.[66] No doubt on the basis of the history of interpretation of the letter to the Romans, study of Romans for its political sensitivities came late on the scene. The traditional view of the letter to the Romans was that it was Paul's thoughtful and considered theological reflection. This had an impact on how the book was viewed even when the political turn occurred in Pauline studies. This was not the case for Paul's letters to the Corinthians. As a result, they provided early fertile ground for examination of some of the elements of empire that have come to be associated with Paul and his response to Rome. The Corinthian letters in some ways continue a theme introduced above, but in another sense go in a different direction than does Romans.

There has been much recent work on the Corinthian letters and how they relate to the notion of the benefaction system, patronage, and social order. The general tenor of thought is that Paul is confronted with the results of the Greco-Roman patronage system as exemplified by the socially diverse church at Corinth, and he sees the results of such an outworking of the social differentiation. First Corinthians is in many

---

65. For development of this argument, see Porter, "Romans 13:1–7," 124–36.

66. E.g., Theissen, *Social Setting of Pauline Christianity*; Marshall, *Enmity in Corinth*; Chow, *Patronage and Power*; Wire, *Corinthian Women Prophets*.

ways a work that addresses issues that are at play in the Corinthian church. There are, for example, the issues of allegiance to various leaders and hence social stratification and differentiation (1 Cor 1:12-13). The bulk of the letter itself is given over to a series of episodes where it is arguably the case that there is abuse of the Roman social structure for the benefit of some within the church. As a result, Paul is compelled to condemn: the powerful man who is apparently sleeping with his father's wife (1 Cor 5:1), the rich among the Corinthians who are taking others of the church to court (1 Cor 6:1), various forms of sexual impropriety no doubt brought on and encouraged by position and status, including having sex with prostitutes (1 Cor 6:12-16) and sexual malpractices among married couples (1 Cor 7:1-5), the politically motivated people who eat food offered to idols (1 Cor 8:1), the flaunting of social status at the Lord's supper (1 Cor 11:20-21), and those who take pride in spiritual gifts and their manifestation (1 Cor 12:1).[67] Similarly in 2 Corinthians, Paul seems to call for an abandonment of distinctions that would restrict the apostolic ministry to certain ones who occupy positions of favor (2 Cor 4:1) and endorses the universal call for humans to be reconciled to God (2 Cor 5:20).

As a result of such passages, one is tempted to argue that Paul was a social and cultural egalitarian in relation to the Roman Empire. Whereas Rome endorsed a patronage system with the gods at the head, mediated through the great benefactor the emperor down through various levels of social and economic hierarchy, Paul advocated an overthrow of such distinctions, in which certain people believed that they were entitled on the basis of status, power, and wealth to benefit over and from others. In some ways, this is correct, but, I believe, only incidentally. For what Paul is really advocating, I think, is the replacement of one hierarchy with another. Just as he advocated to the Romans that the true "good news" was found in the coming of the Lord Jesus Christ, not Augustus—an instance of a replacement empire, with the true divine ruler taking the place of the false—so Paul argues in the Corinthian letters not for no hierarchy, but for a divine hierarchy. This is seen in two significant passages.[68]

The first passage is 1 Corinthians 7 in regard to marriage. The situation seems to be one regarding whether it is better for one to marry or

---

67. Some of these are discussed in more detail in Chow, *Patronage and Power*, chs. 3 and 4.

68. See Danker, *Benefactor*, 362.

not, and if one is married whether that is a preferable state to be in. Paul says that if people do not have self-control, it is better for them to marry than to burn with passion. In this context, he says, it is better for a wife not to leave her husband. He attributes this not just to his instructions but to those of the Lord (1 Cor 7:10). Paul next moves to a related situation of a man with an unbelieving wife who consents to live with him, stating that she should not be sent away. After just having claimed a word from the Lord regarding a wife leaving her husband, he now claims not a word of the Lord but his own statement as authoritative (1 Cor 7:12). After further explication, Paul turns to the situation of virgins. Again, he recognizes that he does not have a command of the Lord, but he gives his own opinion as one who is trustworthy by the mercy of the Lord (1 Cor 7:25). This progression indicates that Paul is not replacing authority with no authority, or hierarchy with no hierarchy. To the contrary, just as he indicated in Romans that he is replacing a false "son of god" with the true "son of God," Paul reflects a hierarchy that seems to flow from the Lord to Paul to the Corinthians. One could probably expand this and say that Paul would recognize God as the ultimate authority, Jesus Christ as the mediator between God and humanity (cf. 1 Tim 2:5), Paul as his trustworthy communicative servant (1 Cor 7:25), and, at the bottom of the hierarchy, those in the church.

Paul reflects a similar ecclesial hierarchy in 2 Corinthians 8. This passage is in the context of the collection that Paul was taking up for the church in Jerusalem. He makes clear to the Corinthians that the Macedonians, probably including the Philippian church and others, were very generous in their support. Even though they were poor financially, they begged to be a part of the collection, and Titus had been sent to them to complete this work that Paul had begun elsewhere. In other words, from a position of authority, Paul instructs the Corinthians that they are to take the role of benefactors of others, the saints who are in need (in Jerusalem). Paul puts their potential benefaction in terms of how they have already been the recipients of benefaction from the Lord Jesus Christ (2 Cor 8:9). He states—in language with some similarities to the opening of Romans—that they know the grace of our Lord Jesus Christ, who became poor for their ultimate benefit. Although Paul says that he is not commanding this (2 Cor 8:8), he does state that he is giving his opinion in this matter (2 Cor 8:9), and that it is to their advantage to be a part of the collection and to bring it to completion. So, he says, "now finish doing it also" (2 Cor 8:11). There is again a clear hierarchy of beneficence, one that begins with the Lord Jesus Christ and passes through Paul to the believers in Corinth and then to the believers in Jerusalem.

Paul does not advocate a rejection of hierarchy, but does endorse the proper hierarchy. Paul engages in empirical replacement, whereby the imperial cult that originated with the patronage and beneficence of the emperor and was translated down through the authority structures to the common people was not eliminated, but was replaced by a divine hierarchy. The divine hierarchy originated with the one true God, whose son the Lord Jesus Christ commanded and worked through Paul to the church at Corinth and through them to other saints.

CONCLUSION

There are various ways that one might classify Paul on the basis of the analysis I have offered above. From one perspective, and contra Barth,[69] Paul may well look like an early advocate of civil disobedience. Paul, according to this reading, replaces the position of Caesar with that of the Lord Jesus Christ, and as a result a new moral accountability is in place that demands appeal not to status, whether imperial or otherwise, but to God. From another perspective, Paul may well look like an insurrectionist or even a revolutionary—or at least a covert revolutionary. He does not call for an out and out rebellion against Roman authority, even though he states in not uncertain terms that there is only one Lord, Jesus Christ, not Caesar. One's obedience is to Jesus Christ, and to Caesar only in so far as what is demanded is just. From a final perspective, Paul is neither a civil disobedient nor a quiet revolutionary, but he is simply a thinking follower of the Lord Jesus Christ. Paul recognizes that the coming of Jesus Christ into the world from the line of David and as the son of God with power as manifested from the time of his resurrection changes everything—and it certainly changes how one views the political, social, and economic structures in which one lives. For Paul, there is no such thing as a quiescent bifurcation between Christian proclamation and day-to-day life. Just as there was no separation between religion and politics in the divinization of the emperor in the imperial cult, so for Paul there was no unhealthy divide between serving God and the state. One could only serve the state by following the Lord Jesus

---

69. See Reasoner, *Romans in Full Circle*, 137.

Christ. For the Romans this meant obedience to the empire where warranted in the return of good for good and punishment of evil for evil. For the Corinthians this meant rejecting a hierarchy of obedience that was based on privilege and power inherited from the imperial power structures, and replacing them with the structures inaugurated through the instigation of the Lord Jesus Christ as the son of God.

BIBLIOGRAPHY

Bal, M. *Narratology: Introduction to the Theory of Narrative*. Translated by C. Van Boheemen. Toronto: University of Toronto Press, 1985.

———. *On Story-Telling: Essays in Narratology*. Edited by D. Jobling. Sonoma, CA: Polebridge, 1991.

Bevan, E. *The House of Seleucus*. 2 vols. London: Edward Arnold, 1902.

Boring, M. E., K. Berger, and C. Colpe. *Hellenistic Commentary to the New Testament*. Nashville: Abingdon, 1995.

Bruce, F. F. *The Acts of the Apostles*. 3rd ed. Grand Rapids: Eerdmans, 1990.

———. *Paul: Apostle of the Heart Set Free*. Grand Rapids: Eerdmans, 1974.

Bultmann, R. *Theology of the New Testament*. 2 vols. Translated by K. Grobel. London: SCM, 1951, 1955.

Charlesworth, M. P. *Documents Illustrating the Reigns of Claudius and Nero*. Cambridge: Cambridge University Press, 1939.

Chow, J. K. *Patronage and Power: A Study of Social Networks in Corinth*. JSNTSup 75. Sheffield: JSOT Press, 1992.

Conzelmann, H. *Acts of the Apostles*. Hermeneia. Minneapolis: Fortress, 1987.

Cranfield, C. E. B. *A Critical and Exegetical Commentary on the Epistle to the Romans*. ICC. 2 vols. Edinburgh: T. & T. Clark, 1975, 1979.

Danker, F. W. *Benefactor: Epigraphic Study of a Graeco-Roman and New Testament Semantic Field*. St. Louis: Clayton, 1982.

Davies, J. P. *Rome's Religious History: Livy, Tacitus and Ammianus on their Gods*. Cambridge: Cambridge University Press, 2004.

Deissmann, A. *Bible Studies*. Translated by A. Grieve. Edinburgh: T. & T. Clark, 1923.

———. *Light from the Ancient East*. 4th ed. Translated by L. R. Strachan. London: Hodder and Stoughton, 1927.

deSilva, D. A. *Honor, Patronage, Kinship and Purity: Unlocking New Testament Culture*. Downers Grove, IL: InterVarsity, 2000.

Dunn, J. D. G. *Romans*. WBC 38A, B. Dallas: Word, 1988.

Ehrenberg, V., and A. H. M. Jones. *Documents Illustrating the Reigns of Augustus and Tiberius*. 2nd ed. Oxford: Clarendon, 1955.

Elliott, N. *Liberating Paul: The Justice of God and the Politics of the Apostle*. Sheffield: Sheffield Academic, 1995.

———. "Romans 13:1–7 in the Context of Imperial Propaganda." In *Paul and Empire: Religion and Power in Roman Imperial Society*, edited by Richard A. Horsely, 184–204. Harrisburg, PA: Trinity Press International, 1997.

Evans, C. A. *Mark 8:27—16:20.* WBC 34B. Nashville: Nelson, 2001.

———. "Mark's Incipit and the Priene Calendar Inscription: From Jewish Gospel to Greco-Roman Gospel." *JGRChJ* 1 (2000) 67-81.

Fee, G. D. *Pauline Christology.* Peabody, MA: Hendrickson, 2007.

Ferguson, J. *The Religions of the Roman Empire.* Ithaca: Cornell University Press, 1970.

Fowl, S. E. *Philippians.* Grand Rapids: Eerdmans, 2005.

Fox, R. Lane. *Alexander the Great.* London: Dial, 1974.

Gorman, M. J. *Apostle of the Crucified Lord: A Theological Introduction to Paul and His Letters.* Grand Rapids: Eerdmans, 2004.

Graves, R. *The Greek Myths.* Vol. 2. Harmondsworth: Penguin, 1960.

Green, P. *Alexander of Macedon 356-323 B.C.: A Historical Biography.* Berkeley: University of California Press, 1991.

———. *From Alexander to Actium: The Historical Evolution of the Hellenistic Age.* Berkeley: University of California Press, 1990.

Grieb, A. K. *The Story of Romans: A Narrative Defense of God's Righteousness.* Louisville: Westminster John Knox, 2002.

Hammond, N. G. L. *Alexander the Great: King, Commander and Statesman.* 3rd ed. London: Bristol Press, 1989.

Hardy, Thomas. "In the British Museum" (1914). In *Selected Poems*, edited by David Wright, 166. London: Penguin, 1978.

Hays, R. B. *The Faith of Jesus Christ: The Narrative Substructure of Galatians 3.1—4.11.* 2nd ed. Grand Rapids: Eerdmans, 2002.

Hemer, C. J. "The Name of Paul." *TynBul* 36 (1985) 179-83.

Hirschfeld, G., and F. H. Marshall. *The Collection of Ancient Greek Inscriptions in the British Museum Part IV.* Oxford: Clarendon, 1893-1916. Reprint, Milan: Cisalpino, 1979.

Horsley, Richard A., ed. *Paul and Empire: Religion and Power in Roman Imperial Society.* Harrisburg, PA: Trinity Press International, 1997.

———, editor. *Paul and Politics: Ekklesia, Israel, Imperium, Interpretation.* FS Krister Stendahl. Harrisburg, PA: Trinity Press International, 2000.

Jewett, R. K. *Romans.* Hermeneia. Minneapolis: Fortress, 2007.

Jones, A. H. M. *Augustus.* London: Chatto & Windus, 1980.

Keesmaat, S. C. *Paul and His Story: (Re)Interpreting the Exodus Tradition.* JSNTSup 181. Sheffield: Sheffield Academic, 1999.

Kramer, W. *Christ, Lord, Son of God.* London: SCM, 1966.

Laffi, U. "Le iscrizione relative all'introduzione nel 9 a.C. del nuovo calendario della Provincia d'Asia." *SCO* 16 (1967) 5-98.

Mackay, C. S. *Ancient Rome: A Military and Political History.* Cambridge: Cambridge University Press, 2004.

Marshall, P. *Enmity in Corinth: Social Conventions in Paul's Relations with the Corinthians.* WUNT 2.23. Tübingen: Mohr Siebeck, 1987.

Martin, W. *Recent Theories of Narrative.* Ithaca: Cornell University Press, 1986.

McDonald, L. M., and S. E. Porter. *Early Christianity and Its Sacred Literature.* Peabody, MA: Hendrickson, 2000.

Moo, D. J. *The Epistle to the Romans.* NICNT. Grand Rapids: Eerdmans, 1996.

Nilsson, M. P. *Imperial Rome.* Translated by G. C. Richards. London: Bell, 1926.

O'Neill, P. *Fictions of Discourse: Reading Narrative Theory.* Toronto: University of Toronto Press, 1996.

Petersen, N. *Rediscovering Paul: Philemon and the Sociology of Paul's Narrative World*. Philadelphia: Fortress, 1985.

Petit, P. *Pax Romana*. London: Batsford, 1969.

Porter, S. E. "Hermeneutics, Biblical Interpretation and Theology: Hunch, Holy Spirit or Hard Work?" In *Beyond the Bible: Moving from Scripture to Theology, with essays by Kevin J. Vanhoozer and Stanley E. Porter*, by I. Howard Marshall, 97–127. Grand Rapids: Baker Academic, 2004.

———. *Romans*. Sheffield: Sheffield Phoenix, forthcoming.

———. "Romans 13:1-7 as Pauline Political Rhetoric." *FN* 3 (1990) 115–39.

Porter, S. E., and A. W. Pitts. "Paul's Bible, His Education and His Access to the Scriptures of Israel." *JGRChJ* 5 (2008) 9–40.

Porter, S. E., and S. A. Adams, editors. *Paul and the Ancient Letter Form*. Pauline Studies 6. Leiden: Brill, 2010.

Porter, S. E., and S. Bedard. *Unmasking the Pagan Christ: An Evangelical Response to the Cosmic Christ Idea*. Toronto: Clements, 2006.

Price, S. R. F. *Rituals and Power: The Roman Imperial Cult in Asia Minor*. Cambridge: Cambridge University Press, 1984.

Reasoner, M. *Romans in Full Circle: A History of Interpretation*. Louisville: Westminster John Knox, 2005.

Riesner, R. *Paul's Early Period: Chronology, Mission, Strategy, Theology*. Translated by D. Stott. Grand Rapids: Eerdmans, 1998.

Ringgren, H., and A. V. Ström. *Religions of Mankind: Today and Yesterday*. Translated by N. L. Jensen. Edited by J. C. G. Greig. Edinburgh: Oliver & Boyd, 1967.

Sherk, R. K. editor. and trans. *Rome and the Greek East to the Death of Augustus*. TDGR 4. Cambridge: Cambridge University Press, 1984.

Shipley, F. W., translator. *Res Gestae Divi Augusti*. Loeb Classical Library 152. Cambridge, MA: Harvard University Press, 1924.

Smallwood, E. M. *Documents Illustrating the Principates of Gaius, Claudius and Nero*. Cambridge: Cambridge University Press, 1967.

Stanzel, F. K. *A Theory of Narrative*. Translated by C. Goedsche. Cambridge: Cambridge University Press, 1984.

Stowers, S. K. *A Rereading of Romans: Justice, Jews, and Gentiles*. New Haven: Yale University Press, 1994.

Strong, E. *Apotheosis and After Life: Three Lectures on Certain Phases of Art and Religion in the Roman Empire*. London: Constable, 1915.

Tarn, W. W. *Alexander the Great: II. Sources and Studies*. Cambridge: Cambridge University Press, 1948.

Taylor, L. R. *The Divinity of the Roman Emperor*. 1931. Reprint, Atlanta: Scholars Press, n.d.

Theissen, G. *The Social Setting of Pauline Christianity: Essays on Corinth*. Translated by J. H. Schütz. Philadelphia: Fortress, 1982.

Wengst, K. *Pax Romana and the Peace of Jesus Christ*. Translated by J. Bowden. London: SCM, 1987.

Wilcken, U. *Alexander the Great*. Translated by G. C. Richards. New York: Norton, 1967.

Wire, A. C. *The Corinthian Women Prophets: A Reconstruction through Paul's Rhetoric*. Minneapolis: Fortress, 1990.

Witherington, B., III. *Paul's Narrative Thought World: The Tapestry of Tragedy and Triumph*. Louisville: Westminster John Knox, 1994.

Wright, N. T. *The Climax of the Covenant: Christ and the Law in Pauline Theology.* Edinburgh: T. & T. Clark, 1991.

———. *Jesus and the Victory of God.* Minneapolis: Fortress, 1996.

———. "Paul's Gospel and Caesar's Empire." In *Paul and Politics: Ekklesia, Israel, Imperium, Interpretation*, edited by Richard A. Horsley, 160–83. FS Krister Stendahl. Harrisburg, PA: Trinity Press International, 2000.

7

"This Was Not an Ordinary Death"

Empire and Atonement in the Minor Pauline Epistles

MATTHEW FORREST LOWE

"EVEN TO UNBELIEVERS LIKE myself," writes the protagonist of the P. D. James novel *Children of Men*, "the cross, stigma of the barbarism of officialdom and of man's ineluctable cruelty, has never been a comfortable symbol."[1] This fictional historian's assessment is accurate: while the offensive character (*skandalon*: Rom 9:33; 11:9; 1 Cor 1:23; and especially Gal 5:11) of the cross in the New Testament draws much of its force from Deuteronomic law,[2] crucifixion itself was a distinctively Roman form of execution, grimly staking the empire's claims of power over life and death. As Richard Horsley and Neil Silberman put it,

> No less than the other powerful forms of visual communication used by the Romans, crucifixion was meant to convey a message ... the cross and the Corinthian column were the two sides of the Roman experience. One offered shade and shelter to all those who would accept the Roman world's logic and structures of power; the other systematically transformed anyone branded as an enemy of the Roman order from a living, breathing person into a

---

1. James, *Children of Men*, 50. Ironically echoing this statement, the book's cruciform symbolism was largely absent when it was produced as a film (Universal; dir. Alfonso Cuarón) in 2006.

2. As in Gal 3:13's use of Deut 21:22–23 ("for it is written, 'Cursed is everyone who hangs on a tree'" [NRSV]).

bruised, bloated, almost unrecognizable corpse. Crucifixion was as much communal punishment and state-sponsored terrorism as it was judicial vengeance against a particular crime.[3]

These authors join James' protagonist in connecting the terror and cruelty of the cross to the expression of imperial power; so, I would argue, did Paul. I will seek to show here that in the minor (shorter) epistles—Galatians, Ephesians, Philippians, Colossians, 1 and 2 Thessalonians, 1 and 2 Timothy, Titus, and Philemon—Paul sought out ways of *contextualizing* and *circumscribing* Rome's power, largely through his appropriation of language and imagery from two very different frameworks: the traditions of the Old Testament on the one hand, and the ideology of Rome on the other. But Paul's rhetoric is not one of syncretism or fusion; in the process of demonstrating how the rubrics of empire deconstruct, he favors a new message that he views as very much in line with the acts of God in the Old Testament. At the heart of that message is the death of Christ—"even death on a cross"—which will form the focus of this study, as atonement intersects with empire in Paul's thought.

This is hardly the first time that Paul's interaction with Rome has been noted in the Bingham Colloquia. This Colloquium marks the tenth anniversary of the Colloquium that produced the volume *Life in the Face of Death: The Resurrection Message of the New Testament*, in which Peter Bolt's essay described Rome's imperial power as "a two-edged sword—with both the power to save life and the power to kill." Despite the lofty ideals of imperial rhetoric, Bolt continued, "to live under Rome's rule was to live under the shadow of death."[4] More recently, Sylvia Keesmaat chose imperial contexts as the subject of her study of Paul's use of Scripture in the shorter epistles,[5] a contribution which I admire but will try not to duplicate despite the obvious overlap in primary sources. Here, I think it quite appropriate to assemble these witnesses in underscoring how Paul appropriates both Old Testament and Roman imagery in order to construct a counter-imperial theology, based around the atonement: essentially, resurrected life in the face of imperial death.

One potential stumbling block must be addressed before considering the individual letters of the "minor" Pauline corpus. In surveying the broadest and most numerous sampling of New Testament documents

---

3. Horsley and Silberman, *Message and the Kingdom*, 86.
4. Bolt, "Life, Death, and the Afterlife," 54–55.
5. Keesmaat, "In the Face of Empire."

among this Colloquium's presentations, this essay bears a substantial part of the burden shared by the contributors of many other years, a challenge invited by the Colloquium's own customary structure. Systematic movement through the New Testament presupposes some degree of basic unity, both of canon and of thought or worldview, between its books. Given that authorship even within the Pauline (or deutero-Pauline) corpus is heavily disputed,[6] how can any claim of unanimity be made regarding the New Testament as a coherent whole?[7]

At the very least, the "systematic" movement mentioned above hints at Marilyn McCord Adams's possibility of maintaining the New Testament documents as "*a variety of loosely integrated systematic proposals* which—insofar as Scripture is authoritative—demand the Christologian's serious consideration," in that a shared theological agenda can be confidently proposed.[8] Warren Carter goes somewhat further, locating among the New Testament authors a variety of strategies for "negotiating" the imperial world.[9] The goal that I have outlined above entails arguing significantly beyond the common-agenda and negotiation-strategy levels; in showing Paul's thoughts on the atonement as a rubric that appropriates and deconstructs those of Rome, we can give

---

6. Common Pauline authorship is assumed for the duration of this essay; for a balanced opposing view, see Gorman, *Apostle*, who argues that Paul is "more or less directly responsible for eleven of the thirteen letters" bearing his name, excluding 1 Timothy and Titus (41 n. 2, summarizing later discussion, 87–89). Even those who choose to doubt Paul's authorship should readily admit that similar imperial contexts—and similar thoughts on Christology, at least to an extent—would have been keenly felt by anyone attempting to write in imitation of Paul.

7. Many biblical theologians have struggled with related issues of canonical unity; the Scripture & Hermeneutics series, edited by Craig G. Bartholomew and Anthony C. Thiselton, and in particular, *Out Of Egypt*, edited by Bartholomew, Moller, Thiselton, and Healy, and *Canon and Biblical Interpretation*, edited by Bartholomew, Hahn, Parry, and Seitz, provide a fine range of current opinions.

8. Adams, *Christ and Horrors*, 23 (italics hers). Just previously, Adams asserts that the New Testament documents reflect "*an attempt to resystematize*, to offer complementary and overlapping theological interpretations of, Jesus' human career" (22, italics hers again), but even this definition fails to address the fact that Paul and the authors of Hebrews and Revelation are seldom directly concerned with the details of Jesus' "human career" ministry. How Adams can continue to refer to the "loose integration" of material as *Scripture* with a capital *S* is also in doubt.

9. Carter, *Roman Empire and the New Testament*, 1, 15, and elsewhere, as well as in his contribution to the present volume.

some direction to a New-Testament-wide theology of the cross in the face of empire.

GALATIANS: THE OFFENSE OF THE CROSS

The process of identifying God's messiah with the crucified Jesus was not easy for Paul. In Luke's first rendering of the events following Paul's conversion, Ananias credits Jesus with sending him to Saul to restore Saul's sight—but the disciple evidently feels he must further reinforce Jesus' identity as "the Lord," the source and speaker of Paul's vision, and the giver of the Holy Spirit (Acts 9:17). This clarification is underscored by Paul's repetition of his own initial question (Acts 9:5: "Who are you, Lord?") and Jesus' response, in the retellings in Acts 22:8 and 26:15. Paul's impulse to address Jesus as Lord (*kyrie*) is apparently immediate, as is a context of repentance, shown especially through Ananias's words in 22:16. But it would likely have taken a bit longer to understand the repercussions of seeing a crucified Jew as the agent of God, as God incarnate. How can Paul incorporate a cause of ritual curse and a humiliating form of execution into his theology?

Here in Galatians, the cross itself already forms the basis of a language of repentance and discipleship. Too often studies of Gal 5:22–26 yield only "the fruit of the Spirit," all but ignoring the shocking words of 5:24: "those who belong to Christ Jesus have crucified the flesh with its passions and desires." How can Paul refer to the Roman torture device as an instrument of purification? Though the cross continues to cause persecution (6:12), it is also somehow a foundation (apparently the *only* valid foundation) for boasting, in that the cross belonging to "our Lord Jesus Christ" is now the means "by which the world has been crucified to me, and I to the world" in Paul's postscript (6:14). Scandal!

Yet Paul uses such positive language of the cross for more than its initial, theological shock value. Being "crucified with Christ" (Gal 2:20) means that Christ lives in and through Paul; the Son of God loved and "gave himself" for the apostle—enabling him to speak of this as an act of *redeeming* (*exēgorasen*, 3:13–14; *exagorasē*, 4:5) and through redemption comes adoption into the people with whom God communes and fights against enemies (Deut 9:3; 20:4). The atoning death of God's messiah and Son restores this relationship by his "becoming a curse for us" (Gal 3:13), entering the situation of the cursed in all its darkness and evil. Put another way,

Because crucifixion renders its victim ritually cursed and so cast into outer darkness, excluded from the people of God and cut off from the God Who goes in and out with them (Deuteronomy 21:23; Galatians 3:13), crucifixion appears decisively to defeat Jesus' claim to be the Messiah. But if Christ comes to save human persons from the ruinous power of horrendous evil, then crucifixion is precisely the sort of thing that would make his mission successful. If God takes God's stand with the cursed, the cursed are not cut off from God after all![10]

It is possible to make many of these arguments without reference to Rome; yet it is the empire's very involvement in the crucifixion that makes the arguments so curious. The Romans did not invent crucifixion; it was practiced as a method of torture and execution in time periods and places both before and after the Roman era, and in various forms, not necessarily even involving a conventional cross.[11] The Old Testament records examples of crucifixion (on trees) in Josh 8:29 (the king of Ai) and 10:26 (the kings of Hebron, Jarmuth, Lachish, Eglon, and—eerily—Jerusalem, all evidently postmortem).

But in Paul's Mediterranean, first-century-CE world, crucifixion was a distinctly Roman tool of social control,[12] or in Horsley and Silberman's description cited above, the most blatant example of "state-sponsored terrorism." The Romans perfected the process, using trees, single beams, and "variously shaped crosses" to destroy those who threatened the all-important *pax Romana*; as Michael Gorman concludes, "there could be nothing more irrational or more un-Roman than to honor—not to mention *deify!*—a man crucified by the imperial authorities."[13] But in Galatians, Rome's method of cruel execution is unveiled as a means to an end: Jesus' crucifixion becomes the paramount execution of God's plan. That is, the (Roman) cross of Christ emerges as Paul's hermeneutical lens for reading, interpreting, and drawing ethics from Scripture.

10. Adams, *Christ and Horrors*, 41.

11. Hengel, *Crucifixion*, 22–23, cited in Maslen and Mitchell, "Medical Theories," 185–88. Noting mass-crucifixion accounts from Seneca (4 BCE–65 CE) and Josephus (37–ca.100 CE), in which victims were hung upside down, impaled by their genitals, or in other positions according to the Roman soldiers' whim, the authors define crucifixion broadly as being suspended "from a cross *or similar structure* until dead" (185, emphasis added).

12. Maslen and Mitchell, "Medical Theories," 185.

13. Gorman, *Apostle*, 12 (italics his). Gorman includes a photo of a first-century sculpture of a single-beam crucifixion on the previous page.

Nor was Paul alone in shaping his exegesis around the cross; later Christian writers followed his example. Reading Gal 3:13, Chrysostom (344/354–407, fl. 386–407 CE) remarks that "just as by dying he snatched from death those who were going to die, so also when he suffered the curse he released them from the curse."[14] Epiphanius (ca. 315–403) writes that the incarnation "and the cross fulfilled the plan for the loosing of the curse."[15] What Paul modeled for these writers was essentially a *cruciform exegesis*, allowing the cross to transform his view of the Scriptures and the world around him; the cross even marks his signature, as he writes in his postscript that he carries "the marks of Jesus branded on my body" (Gal 6:17). The audacity of this claim, linking the fulfillment of Scripture to the suffering inflicted by the empire, would have shocked Paul's readers, especially those among his Jewish audiences. Perhaps it should continue to shock—or scandalize—modern eyes and ears as well.

EPHESIANS: A POWER MYTH APPROPRIATED

Ephesians has received little attention amid the recent explorations of Paul's imperial contexts. It benefits from no direct treatment in studies such as Richard Horsley's *Paul and Empire*, and warrants only a single reference out of all the essays in his subsequent volume, *Paul and Politics*.[16] If there is imperial material here, its influences are likely subtle—but not necessarily untraceable. Particularly promising is the language of the "powers," a frequent subject of study in Paul and the rest of the New Testament that finds a major locus in Ephesians.[17] Clinton Arnold and Walter Wink have argued independently that the author's terminology, while imprecise, is intended to be all-inclusive. In Arnold's words, Christ's supremacy over "'all things' and the powerful rule of the Lord are repeatedly asserted throughout the whole of the epistle . . . the author leaves no doubt whatsoever in the minds of the readers that any conceivable hostile 'power' is outside and independent of Christ's

---

14. Chrysostom, *Hom. Gal.* 3:13; cited in Edwards, ed., *Galatians*, 42.

15. Epiphanius, *Pan.* 42.12.3 (Second Refutation of Marcion), cited in Edwards, ed., *Galatians*, 42.

16. The sole exception in the second book comes in Wright's mention of Eph 1:19–22 in "Paul's Gospel."

17. The work of Walter Wink has proved influential in New Testament scholarship; see his *Naming the Powers*. For examples of similar work specific to Paul and to Ephesians, see Arnold, *Ephesians*, and *Powers of Darkness*.

dominion."[18] Wink locates a comparably universal scope in the "comprehensive" list of Eph 6:12 ("rulers" [*archas*]; "authorities" [*exousias*]; "cosmic powers [*kosmokratoras*] of this present darkness"; and "spiritual forces [*pneumatika*] of evil in the heavenly places"). This list, according to Wink, could have been intended to include even "the spirit of empire, which perpetuates itself through a succession of rulers and which was so powerful, in the case of Rome, that it was able to sustain the madness of three emperors in one century."[19] Previous scholarship thus presents ample precedent for considering earthly, political forces among the New Testament's pantheon of powers.

More recently, Timothy Gombis has proposed that portions of Ephesians (1:20—2:22, and the allusion to Psalm 68 in 4:8-10) should be read in light of the divine warfare myths of the ancient Near East. Interpreted through this paradigm, Paul's arguments catalog the triumphs of God in Christ, vindicating the claim of Christ's exaltation as Lord (Eph 1:20-23, supported in 2:1-22) and celebrating Christ's triumphant ascent in 4:8-10.[20] "By his death," writes Gombis, "Christ has triumphed over the divisive effects of the enemy powers ... the ascent of Christ is the triumphant procession of the conquering Warrior to his throne, from which he will bless his people with gifts."[21]

While convincing, Gombis's arguments are not comprehensive enough to address the multiple levels of "powers" that Paul acknowledges; but Gombis's repeated use of the theme of *triumph* hints at a viable adaptation for his research. His main concern is to show that Ephesians owes a debt to the ideology of divine warfare, myths of power and exaltation that the Old Testament traditions frequently imitated and appropriated. God-as-divine-warrior fought against (and triumphed over) mythological enemies identified variously as Rahab, Leviathan, River, and Sea, paralleling Canaanite and other ancient Near-Eastern mythic accounts; the victorious warrior role was at times transferred at least partially to

---

18. Arnold, *Ephesians*, 129.

19. Wink (*Naming the Powers*, 54–55) also indicates that for the entire New Testament, the "imprecise, liquid, interchangeable" language of power would have been used and interpreted in the "most comprehensive sense," representing both heavenly *and* earthly powers, denoting human *and* structural dimensions (9, 100–101).

20. Gombis, "Ephesians 2," and "Cosmic Lordship."

21. Gombis, "Cosmic Lordship," 377, 379.

Israel's kings, with Psalm 68 as one of many examples.[22] Some interpreters have even used this psalm to posit God's kingly rule over the earth as explicitly imperial in nature.[23] But while the New Testament authors could easily have inherited from their Scriptures an understanding of their Lord as a reigning (imperial?) warrior, this is not the only ideology they were familiar with.

A re-reading of Ephesians 4 and its power-myth Old Testament referent shows a subtle awareness of Rome's presence and power. Arnold rightly cautions against strictly political appraisals of the powers,[24] as such analyses fail to account for the elasticity of the "power" chords struck by the New Testament. But if we plug in the applications of Wink's argument for the empire as a power simultaneously spiritual and structural, the image of Christ's victorious ascent takes on another layer of meaning. Having invoked Ps 68:18 in Eph 4:8 ("Therefore it is said, 'When he ascended on high he made captivity itself a captive'") as a description of Christ, the author employs the terms *ascended* and *descended* through the next two verses, terms which have given interpreters almost as much trouble as the apparent misquotation here (4:8b, "'he gave [*edōken*] gifts to his people,'" where the original has God receiving [LXX: *elabes*] gifts in tribute, not giving them). Does the reworking of Old Testament language indicate a polemic against Jewish uses of the same psalm,[25] a Pentecost-oriented understanding of Christ's ascent (in resurrection) and descent (as the gift-giving Spirit),[26] or crucifixion as descent with resurrection as triumphant ascension?[27]

This final option becomes more compelling when we recall the letter's first-century social context. The emphasis on themes of triumph

---

22. Isa 27:1 and Ps 29 can also stand as representative texts of the Divine Warrior's role.

23. Roberts, "Enthronement," 685: "the surrounding nations would come up to Jerusalem to pay tribute to this imperial God," citing Ps 68:30–33.

24. Arnold, *Powers of Darkness*, 173.

25. So Moritz, *Profound Mystery*, 71–85; also cited in Gombis, "Cosmic Lordship," 370.

26. So Caird, "Descent of Christ," 535–45. Gombis ("Cosmic Lordship," 370–71) rightly critiques the direct identification of Christ with the Spirit.

27. See, for example, Barth, *Broken Wall*, 262–63. In "Cosmic Lordship" (372), Gombis appeals to Barth's *Ephesians 1–3*, 433, to counter the "in-descent" proposal that Christ descended back to earth via the Spirit.

shared by Gombis[28] and Markus Barth[29] takes on sharper focus in light of the images of triumph that the early Christian communities would have known: as the Romans perfected earlier practices of crucifixion, so they developed the ancient Near Eastern traditions of victory-procession into magnificent events of ceremony and propaganda. Though the imperial senate rarely granted the right to a *triumphus* parade,[30] the events themselves were memorable, and were commemorated in coins and architecture depicting subjugated enemies, captured spoils of war, and the endorsement of deities such as the personified Roma and Oikoumenē (Rome and the civilized world), and winged Nikē (victory).[31] Where the divine warfare myths culminated in ascent to a divine throne, the climax of imperial triumphs came at the ascent of Rome's Capitoline hill, where the captive opponents were ceremonially executed.[32] The image was obviously a familiar one to Paul, who uses triumph terminology explicitly to highlight his own role as Christ's suffering follower—and prisoner!—in 2 Cor 2:14 ("thanks be to God, who in Christ always leads us in triumphal procession" [*thriambeuonti*]) and as further mockery of the "powers" in Col 2:15 (below).[33] When Ephesians states that Christ

28. In addition to the examples already provided, see Gombis, "Cosmic Lordship," 375: "the author portrays Christ as the victorious Divine Warrior who has the right to give gifts to his people because of his triumphs."

29. Barth's language in *Broken Wall* is even more helpful to our purposes here: "Ephesians adds triumphantly that what imprisoned men, Christ made a (i.e., 'his') prisoner through the resurrection" (262).

30. Kreitzer, *Striking New Images*, 129, complies a list of at least eight such events for victorious generals and emperors: Julius's quadruple triumph (45 BCE: Gaul, Egypt, Pontus, Africa); Augustus's triple (27 BCE: Illyrium, Egypt, Actium); two for Tiberius (8–7 BCE and 12 CE: Germany and Pannonia, with the second repeated for Germanicus, 17 CE); Claudius (Britain, 44 CE); Nero (Tiridates, 62–63 CE); and most notably for New Testament audiences, Vespasian and Titus (June 71, celebrating the fall of Jerusalem, September 70 CE).

31. Head, "Mark," attests to the impact of the triumph in positing Mark and Josephus as co-spectators at Vespasian and Titus's parade. For the effects of numismatic propaganda, see Kreitzer, *Striking New Images*, 76–98, 135–40, on personified deities and the *Gaul, Germania*, and *Judea Capta* coins; and Esler, "Rome in Apocalyptic and Rabbinic Literature." Esler's essay summarizes and develops his work in "God's Honour and Rome's Triumph."

32. Kreitzer, *Striking New Images*, 142–44, uses this feature to modify previous scholarship on Paul's use of triumph imagery in Colossians.

33. Knowles offers an in-depth exploration of Paul's use of triumph and its implications for ministry in "Triumph and Captivity, Sacrifice and Sufficiency," the second chapter of his *We Preach Not Ourselves*, 75–111.

"ascended on high" and "made captivity itself a captive," the letter's first readers would surely have recognized the reworked psalm of divine triumph, but they would have seen more than one tradition appropriated: the author shrewdly superimposes a Roman image as an overlay. Christ leads his captives in an almost unmistakably imperial triumph.

Commentators ancient and modern have found the same thematic language in other imperial venues, such as the gladiatorial arena. Ignatius (ca. 35–107 CE), under Roman military guard from Smyrna, would later imitate Paul's tone in writing to the Ephesian churches, "I am a convict; you have been freed. I am in danger; you are safe," before adding the telling remark, "You are the route for God's victims"—an acknowledgment of the city's position on the route by which criminals were led to supply Rome's amphitheater.[34] Wink depicts early Christians as rebels who denied the emperor's power by acknowledging a higher power, and thus entered "into the power-game on the empire's terms and lost, and the rules of the game required their liquidation." He goes on:

> When Christians knelt in the Colosseum to pray as lions bore down on them, something sullied the audience's thirst for revenge. Even in death these Christians were not only challenging the ultimacy of the emperor and the "spirit" of empire but also demonstrating the emperor's powerlessness to impose his will even by death. The final sanction had been publicly robbed of its power. Even as the lions lapped up the blood of the saints, Caesar was stripped of his arms and led captive in Christ's triumphal procession. His authority was shown to be only penultimate after all.[35]

Seeing both sides of triumph and captivity, experiencing (whether personally or vicariously) the status of both victor and victim, Paul, Ignatius and their Ephesian readers[36] would have found a christocentric

---

34. The contrasting first-person, second-person language resembles Paul's "If we are being afflicted, it is for your consolation and salvation" and "So death is at work in us, but life in you" (2 Cor 1:6 and 4:12, NRSV), as well as the application of Ps 44:22 in Rom 8:36, "For your sake we are being killed [TNIV: "we face death"] all day long." See Ign. *Eph.* 12.2, cited in Richardson, trans. and ed., *Early Christian Fathers*, 91.

35. Wink, *Naming the Powers*, 111.

36. To qualify a sweeping statement on these early Christian authors and audiences: certainly the Ephesian letters attributed to Paul and Ignatius would have been intended for larger audiences, perhaps in a circular-letter format. Even if the authenticity of both epistles is questioned, no more than a single generation elapsed between the two, and the similarities in tone have already been noted. Richardson, who makes

recasting of the triumph to be an *appropriate* image—if not always a positive one. Themes of divine enthronement ideology drawn from the Old Testament are surely present in Ephesians, but they are adapted to match the triumphal processions of the day. Though Roman victors may continue to parade their captives as a demonstration of their prowess, Christ is already the true *triumphator*, whose lordship supersedes both that of Caesar and whatever spiritual powers may lie behind Rome's rule. N. T. Wright has noted that Old Testament images of human and divine kingship form "one of the 'echo chambers' within which Paul uses the word *lord* of Jesus";[37] I suggest that in complementary fashion, demonstrations of power in Roman military practice formed another such "echo chamber." When Christ's death and resurrection—in Ephesians 4, his descent and ascent, with captivating powers in tow—are phrased as a "victorious siege"[38] and a triumph over his opponents, the implications for the theology of the atonement are profound.

PHILIPPIANS: NO ORDINARY DEATH

If captivity supplied part of the thematic content of Ephesians, the experience is even more fundamental to Philippians, as Paul wrote from under Roman guard. Whether Paul's chains (Phil 1:7) are literal or not, and whether the Praetorian Guard (1:13) refers to that in Rome or another form of custody in Ephesus or Caesarea, his imprisonment is imperial.[39] This context informs at least three images in the letter: citizenship, peace, and the crucifixion as the focal point of the Christ-hymn in Philippians 2.

---

more general comments about the resemblance between Ignatius's frank quality and Paul's, dates Ignatius's letter and subsequent martyrdom broadly within Trajan's 98–117 CE reign (*Early Christian Fathers*, 74–75). More specific to Pauline authorship on this issue, Elliott, "Anti-Imperial Message," 180, claims that Paul "uses the metaphor of the triumphal procession more sparingly" than the putative author(s) of Colossians and Ephesians. While the current proposal cannot prove conclusively that Colossians and Ephesians are Pauline, it does serve to strengthen the thematic and literary relationships between the two letters and the language of 2 Corinthians.

37. Wright, "Paul's Gospel," 168.

38. Arnold, *Ephesians*, 160: the church receives its gifts "as a direct result of *Christ's victorious siege* against the principalities and 'powers'" (citing Eph 4:8, cf. 1:19–22; italics added).

39. Oakes, "God's Sovereignty," 127.

Citizenship

Peter Oakes amply demonstrates Paul's confidence that the gospel is sovereign over his own imprisoned situation as well as the Philippian believers' context of suffering (as in Phil 1:29–30), just as God exercises sovereignty over the Roman authorities through Christ.[40] Paul's appeal takes the form of a metaphor that the Philippians should find familiar. When he asks them to "live your life in a manner worthy of the gospel of Christ," the verb is *politeuesthe*, or "live as a citizen." Some translations render the phrase as the TNIV does, "as *citizens of heaven* live in a manner worthy," acknowledging a link to the cognate *politeuma* (citizenship or commonwealth) in 3:20 (NRSV): "But our citizenship is in heaven, and it is from there that we are expecting a Savior, the Lord Jesus Christ."[41] One commentator uses evidence from Acts (16:12, 20, 21, 36–40) to support the idea of the Philippians' pride in their Roman citizenship, and Paul's reference to his own citizen status to expedite his release while imprisoned there.[42] Though some may overestimate the degree of Paul's own pride on this count,[43] the challenge of his two connected references was not overlooked by ancient interpreters: Clement of Alexandria (150–211? CE), commenting on Phil 3:20, noted that to be mindful of heavenly citizenship was to live as an expatriate.[44] As closely as Paul may have related to the members of his congregations, his travels and imprisonments must have taught him a degree of expatriated disconnection that would have served him well in meeting his own challenge.

Peace

As with many of his letters, Paul greets his church with "Grace to you and peace from God our Father and the Lord Jesus Christ" (Phil 1:2). He underscores the divine origin of that blessing as he closes this epistle, however, naming "the peace of God" as that which guards the Philippians'

---

40. Ibid., 126–27.

41. Kent, "Philippians," 118 and 120 n. 27: the cognate "makes it clear that the citizenship Paul had in mind was not Roman but heavenly." Still, the essential metaphor is one of Roman origin.

42. Ibid., points then to the challenge of living up to a "vastly more significant citizenship" in 3:20.

43. See Eisenman, *James*, 24, where Paul "almost makes a religion out of loyalty to Rome" in Rom 13:1–7.

44. Clement of Alexandria, *Strom.* 3.95, cited in Edwards, ed., *Galatians*, 277.

"hearts and your minds in Christ Jesus" (4:7),[45] and promising them that "the God of peace will be with you" as they imitate Paul's own example (4:9). But to leave this as a purely spiritual benediction is to miss the irony of the letter's provenance: peace is a questionable commodity for a prisoner of an empire maintained by "conquest, subjugation, and intimidation."[46] Marius Victorinus (fourth century CE) would later connect God's peace to a state of security and rest, while Ambrosiaster notes that the call *to* peace is made *by* the God of peace, a virtue that so characterizes God that God will not "by the terror of his manifested power . . . force even the unwilling into subjection."[47] For Paul and for later Christian writers, Rome's peace is inimical to the peace called for by God.[48]

The Crux of the Christ-Hymn

The early church recognized the importance of the cross as the place of a historical and violent event. Philippians 2:6–11 is the foremost example of the New Testament's hymnic and devotional materials concerning the crucifixion;[49] when the passage drew commentary from the church fathers, they were quick to point out Paul's emphasis on the brutality of the cross, evident in his appropriation of the hymn. Tertullian (ca. 155–230 CE) finds a key indicator of Christ's human mortality where Paul "adds

---

45. Gorman, commenting on the connection between peace and joy (rejoicing) in 4:4–7, adds that for "an imprisoned apostle and a persecuted church, the two belong together" (*Apostle*, 446).

46. Ibid., 8 ("It was, in other words, peace through war"), 8–12, and 108, where the author compares the Jewish contextual meaning of peace ("right relations among humans and between humans and God") to the Greco-Roman context: "imperial rule and the cessation of internal and external conflict."

47. Edwards, ed., *Galatians*, 282, 284, citing Marius Victorinus, *Epistle to the Philippians* 4.7, and Ambrosiaster, *Epistle to the Philippians* 4.9. Though both writers speak primarily of peace on a spiritual level, note how each statement blurs the heavenly/earthly distinction, effectively borrowing from both Jewish and Roman contexts as Gorman outlines them above.

48. Compare Chrysostom's remark on Eph 4:3, from *Hom. Eph.* 9.4.1–3: the "bond of peace" is "not a chain that bruises" (as Roman chains can); in Edwards, ed., *Galatians*, 159.

49. Longenecker, *New Wine*, 12, 15, cites Phil 2:6–11 as the "most obvious" of early confessional materials. Among his exegetical questions when he considers the passage in greater depth (29–30) is, "Who are those 'in heaven and on earth and under the earth' who are to bow before that name?"

the heavily laden words *even unto the death of the cross*. For he would not exaggerate the atrocity in extolling his power in a conflict which he knew to have been imaginary or a mere fantasy."[50] Tying the borrowed hymnic image to Paul's own use of Deut 21:23 in Gal 3:13, Chrysostom later remarked that Christ had humbled himself *twice*: first in "taking the form of a slave," and then again in dying such an ignominious death. "And in death he appeared to be a reprobate. This was not an ordinary death."[51]

Not all commentators chose to highlight Rome's involvement in Jesus' death; Paul himself does not explicitly mention the empire here either. But as in Galatians, so here: the cross, vividly evoked in Phil 2:6–11 as a too-familiar place of death, is more than just a tool for execution; it shapes the face of humility. To be obedient to death on a cross is to be obedient to Rome, to the empire's power over life and death. This obedience does not equate to unquestioning assent. Keesmaat finds in Paul's rhetoric in Romans and Galatians an attempt to reorient his readers' search for justice from one story to another—drawing them from Caesar's "imperial narrative" to "the story of Israel as reinterpreted in light of the story of Jesus."[52] Especially in Galatians, this reorienting process addresses theodicy from a perspective of suffering for the sake of the counter-imperial gospel.[53]

Ephesians 4 phrased the crucifixion and resurrection as descent and ascent; Philippians plots a similar arc for Christ, as God

> also highly exalted him
>   and gave him the name
>   that is above every name,
> so that at the name of Jesus
>   every knee should bend,
>   in heaven and on earth and under the earth,
>   and every tongue should confess
>   that Jesus Christ is Lord,
>   to the glory of God the Father. (Phil 2:9–11, NRSV)

---

50. Tertullian, *Marc.* 5.20.4–5, cited in Edwards, ed., *Galatians*, 249; italics in original.

51. Chrysostom, *Hom. Phil.* 8.2.5–11, cited in Edwards, ed., *Galatians*, 250. Many further comments on the voluntary, honorable, kenotic, and exemplary nature of Christ's humiliation can be collected from ibid., 246–50.

52. Keesmaat, "Psalms," 139.

53. Ibid., 157–58, drawing in part from N. T. Wright and Richard B. Hays.

But who are those who are to bow, and how is Christ's name "above every name"? Even these questions can find imperial-context responses—though those are not the only possible answers. Again, a more nuanced view is called for. Some of the apparent opponents are spiritual, or perhaps ontological: this is one of several passages where early Christian interpreters saw enemies such as *enmity* wounded or slain (Eph 2:15–16), *captivity* led as a captive (Eph 4:8), and *death* itself put to death (Phil 2:8).[54] But this second half of the Christ-hymn, the song that Oakes attributes directly to Paul, is also deliberately styled to evoke the ascent and exaltation of the Roman emperor[55]—even as it plots an arc exactly *opposite* to Caesar's ascension, as Christ has descended to the status of *servant* or *slave* before his crucifixion, resurrection, and exaltation.[56] In asserting Jesus Christ's position as lord over the cosmos and even the underworld, Paul is using imagery borrowed from Isaiah to supersede and rewrite even the emperor's claims of ultimate power.[57]

Whenever Paul's churches read about, or made reference to, the cross; whenever *we* read or refer to it; indeed, whenever we use descriptors such as *crucial*, *excruciating*, and especially *cruciform*, the atonement carries a reminder of empire. Is it even possible to speak of the atonement without this "death on a cross" from Philippians? Eugene Lemcio equates the two, identifying "atonement theology" with the "theology of the cross."[58] If they are equivalent or synonymous,[59] then to investigate any form of atonement theology is to be reminded of Rome—for the cross imprints the stamp of the empire on any theology that issues from it.

---

54. See Chrysostom, *Hom. Eph.* 5.2.16; Jerome (ca. 345–420 CE), *Comm. Eph.* 2.4.8; and Epiphanius, *Ancoratus* 92, in Edwards, ed., *Galatians*, 141, 163, 250. The connections between these passages would seem to be strengthened by the fact that Eph 2:15–16 yields the only explicit mention of the cross in this letter.

55. Oakes, "God's Sovereignty," 133–35.

56. I am indebted to Craig Evans for pressing me to think further on this point.

57. Oakes, "God's Sovereignty," 134, 136, citing Isa 45.

58. Lemcio, "Gospels," 133.

59. I see little reason why they should not be equivalent in this corpus; the canonical Gospels certainly attest an atonement theology that draws more broadly from Christ's incarnation, not just from his death. I appreciate Warren Carter's input on this point.

COLOSSIANS: RULERS DISARMED

The imperial context of Colossians has already received definitive and imaginative treatment in Brian Walsh and Sylvia Keesmaat's *Colossians Remixed*. Here, I hope only to fill in a few of the places where they have left an idea sketched out, particularly in two places where the empire comes into close contact with Paul's statements on the atonement: the christological hymn of Col 1:15–20, and the triumph imagery of Col 2:14–15.

He Is the Image; Peace through the Blood of His Cross

Like Phil 2:6–11, a portion of the second chapter of Colossians is widely held to be an adaptation of an early christological confessional statement, though its apparent lack of poetic structure has often kept it from being regarded as a proper hymn; even as formulaic prose, its proclamation clearly consists of the supremacy of Christ's person (1:15–18a) and his work (18b–20) in both cosmic and ecclesiological contexts.[60] Walsh and Keesmaat maintain that the passage is poetic, and treat it accordingly. They offer a targum (an "extended translation and expansion that attempts to read the world through the eyes of the text, allowing the Scripture to resonate with and confront our changing cultural reality") that brings out a number of the portion's implicit emphases: conflict between images, supremacy and sovereignty, and reconciliation by grace through the cross.[61] Though the targum and the authors' explanatory comments are too lengthy to reproduce here, these emphases reward further examination pertaining to Rome and the cross.

First, that Christ is identified as "the image (*eikōn*) of the invisible God" is highly significant for Paul—and for Walsh and Keesmaat, who contrast the "image-saturated" world of imagination-capturing logos (true of both Rome, with its sustaining myth of *pax Romana*, and the modern corporate world's advertising myths) with Christ, "the source

---

60. Longenecker, *New Wine*, 13, 16–17, classifying the passage as a *homologia* (a "formulaic confessional portion"). Oakes's analysis of Philippians' main argument, above, is remarkably similar, with the addition of the imperial context.

61. Walsh and Keesmaat, *Colossians Remixed*, 85–89. The targum is certainly extended and expanded, perhaps to the point of becoming a full-blown midrash (as Michael Knowles has pointed out to me). Some 110 words in the Greek and 128 in English (NRSV) fill three and a half pages of poetry in *Colossians Remixed*. Attempting to "read the world through the eyes of the text" remains problematic as a model, though it is explained previously by the authors.

of a liberated imagination/a subversion of the empire."[62] Christ's role as God's image-bearer is never far removed from his atoning work, as it is the divine image-representative himself who is hung on a cross (and resurrected), thus setting a pattern for all who would follow in *his* image. To use the Greek term to adapt the English truism: the *eikōn* doesn't fall far from the tree.[63]

Second, Christ is supreme, or sovereign; he is "before all things, and in him all things hold together" (Col 1:17). All the power and authority of "the institutionalized power structures," whether civil, economic, social, or religious, is "derived at best/parasitic at worst."[64] The crucified lord is revealed as supreme—even over Wink's "spirit of empire."

Third, this revelation occurs through the crucifixion and resurrection, events that are the means of reconciliation: "through him God was pleased to reconcile to himself all things, whether on earth or in heaven, by making peace through the blood of his cross" (Col 1:19–20). "It all happens on a cross . . . at a state execution . . . at the hands of the empire that has captured our imagination."[65] The authors underscore the same phenomenon we have seen at work in the other letters surveyed so far: the (Roman) cross governs Paul's interpretation of atonement and empire.

Triumphing over Them

In his next chapter, Paul returns[66] to a rare but familiar theme. Colossians 2:14–15, mentioned above in the context of Paul's triumph imagery, tells the reader that with the obstacles of the "written code" and past tres-

---

62. Ibid., 85–86, and (for the sustaining myths of empires ancient and modern) 52, 61–63.

63. With apologies for being a bit too cute, and especially to those who have little tolerance for Greek-English puns.

64. Walsh and Keesmaat, *Colossians Remixed*, 86.

65. Ibid., 88–89. The lines that follow reveal a targumic intertextuality with Phil 2:6–11: "it all happens through blood/not through a power grab by the sovereign one."

66. Reading canonically here, I do take seriously Ben Witherington's caution as he introduces 1 Timothy: he warns that canonical readings of Pauline texts tend to "over-read shorter documents on the basis of longer, more prominent ones," as when Romans is used as a guide and a "key measuring rod of Paulinicity." He recommends treating documents independently before moving to "intertextual, interrelational and canonical sorts of questions," but fails to see how difficult this task can be when intra-canonical influence is *part of the point of a study*, as I believe it is here. See Witherington, *Titus, 1–2 Timothy and 1–3 John*, 169 n. 4.

passes removed, even nailed to the cross, Christ "disarmed the rulers and authorities and made a public example of them, triumphing over them in it." Kreitzer theorizes that Paul owes his image here to Nero's victory over Tiridates in 63 CE, as it would have been celebrated in triumph in Rome.[67] But to evoke an image is not to agree with its message. Kreitzer says elsewhere that "the Roman concept of apotheosis moved a man from earth toward heaven, whereas the Christian concept of incarnation moved God from heaven toward earth, but the two are similar in that they both deal with the relationship between the human and the divine";[68] here we must disagree. Where the Roman triumph exalted a man at the height of his military power who would soon be (or had already been) divinized, Paul's portrayal of Christ's triumph contains an arc exactly opposite, similar not to apotheosis but to the pattern glimpsed in Philippians and Ephesians. Christ disarms the rulers and authorities at his moment of greatest weakness; he makes "a public example of them" (lit. "exposed them with openness," *edeigmatisen en parrēsia*) when he was himself exposed; and he triumphs over them when it seems the other way around.

But again, we must ask: who are the "rulers and authorities"? Walsh and Keesmaat are quite clear on their interpretation of the verse: the disarmament was an exercise of Christ's "sovereignty, his rule over the empire. This rule was established on the cross and confirmed in the resurrection. Rome could not keep Jesus in a grave sealed by the empire."[69] Again, the view of the powers I am arguing for here—including the rulers (*archas*) and authorities (*exousias*), the first two groups mentioned in the list of Eph 6:12—is intended to nuance and complement other models. The powers were not necessarily *exclusively* imperial in nature. But given the connections here in Colossians between image, supremacy, triumph, and cross, it would seem that Paul included the imperial authorities as opponents disarmed by Christ—even if his own life and death indicated otherwise.

---

67. Kreitzer, *Striking New Images*, 123–25.
68. Ibid., 97–98.
69. Walsh and Keesmaat, *Colossians Remixed*, 154–55.

1 AND 2 THESSALONIANS: "PEACE AND SECURITY"

A number of features relevant to imperial contexts can be briefly noted in the Thessalonian correspondence. The members of Paul's congregation have reportedly turned away from idols "to serve a living and true God" (1 Thess 1:9), one of several barbs from Paul's letters directed at the practice; here, idol worship serves to highlight positive characteristics of Paul's divine patron, who (unlike the other patron gods) is both living (*zōnti*) and true (*alēthinō*).[70] God is also identified as the one who calls the Thessalonians "into his own kingdom [*basileian*] and glory" (1 Thess 2:12). *Basileia* appears infrequently in Paul; customarily rendered *kingdom*, it can be better translated as *dominion*, meaning both the governing power and the realm itself—"the place in which God's rule is exercised,"[71] and as such, an alternative to the kingdom or empire of Caesar. There is also some indication that the persecution in which the Thessalonian church is suffering (1 Thess 2:14; 2 Thess 1:5) has a Greco-Roman, rather than Jewish, source. The strongest locus of imperial content, however, lies in 1 Thess 4:13–18, with a related clause a few verses later, in 5:3.

Meeting the Lord at His Arrival: Loaded Political Terms

Paul renders the *parousia*—the "coming (alternative translation *presence*, or *arrival*) of the Lord" in 4:15—in imperial key, in clear imitation of the visitation of the emperor or another such royal guest. With his congregants worrying about the fate of those among their number who have died, Paul reassures them: "For the Lord himself, with a cry of command, with the archangel's call and with the sound of God's trumpet, will descend from heaven, and the dead in Christ will rise first," before those still living also go out to meet him (4:16–17). John Crossan and Jonathan Reed propose that the *parousia*, so often a mainstay of millennial thought in the modern church, is an imperial event that Paul adapts as a metaphor.

---

70. The most commonly referenced passage on idols is 1 Cor 8; the dual adjectives parallel "blessed and only" as descriptors for Christ in 1 Tim 6:15. "Living" is itself a distinctive of 1 Tim (3:15; 4:10).

71. Wanamaker, *Thessalonians*, 107–108. Kingdom terminology is of course more common to the Synoptic Gospels; but for a proposal that *John's* language, while less prone to explicit kingdom references, is more "basileic" than many scholars will admit, see Anderson, *Fourth Gospel and the Quest for Jesus*, 52–54.

A ruler making a formal urban visitation to Thessalonica, as in many ancient cities, would pass the tombs and mausoleums of the outlying cemeteries before entering the city proper, meeting "first the elite dead before any meeting with the elite living."[72] The metaphor is indeed eschatological, as Paul anticipates the final visitation that will vindicate his message and the suffering of his readers. But as the emperor remained present between visits (through coins, statues, and other images), Paul argues that Christ is already present with the Thessalonians, even when he is physically absent.[73] The confident *expectation* of God-in-Christ's final state-visit was the "state" in which Paul asked the believers to live.

But what does it mean for Paul to use this metaphor? Is Christ's visitation to resemble, supersede, or replace the visitation of the emperor?[74] In borrowing from imperial language here and elsewhere, Paul is using "heavily loaded political terms": Karl Donfried identifies *parousia, kyrios* (lord) and *apantēsis* (the "meeting" Paul refers to in 1 Thess 4:17, connoting "the actions of the greeting committee as it goes forth from the city to escort the royal person or dignitary into the city for his official visit") as language belonging to the imperial court.[75] To use such terms entailed risk for both author and recipients. When Paul *transfers* political language from Caesar to Jesus, who in his view is "the only God who ever walked the earth," he makes a political statement, not just a theological one: in this emperor-friendly, pluralistic city whose status as a "free city" was precarious, to undermine Caesar was to threaten the hierarchical

---

72 Crossan and Reed, *In Search of Paul*, 168–69.

73. Ibid., 170–71; thus the authors translate *parousia* as "return," hoping to avoid "translations for *parousia* that in any way imply a prior absence" (171). Oakes, "God's Sovereignty," 138–39, offers a similar view of visitation-hope in Philippi: "The Christians are like members of a colony such as Philippi, defended from a distance by the ruler of the city to which they ultimately belong ... [they] have a better citizenship than that of Rome, defended by a stronger saviour than that of Rome." Witherington, *Thessalonians*, xv, would likely dispute this comparison, as he insists that the Thessalonian audience is not composed of colonials as those of Philippi and Corinth would have been; instead, he looks for parallels in John of Patmos's situation, writing to the heavily pressured and persecuted.

74. Shrewd questions from Crossan and Reed, *In Search of Paul*, 171, who point to the *parousia* as both *consolation* and *confrontation*.

75. Donfried, "Cults of Thessalonica," 34; the *apantēsis* description is Witherington's (*Thessalonians*, 138), who earlier notes the use of *parousia* for the visitation of a *deity*, coming in deliverance (91).

network of inter-city patronage, to arouse fears of imperial censure and the end of benefaction.[76]

"The cost of 'freedom' and the Pax Romana in one's city was unswerving loyalty to the emperor," Witherington observes.[77] He rightly emphasizes "freedom" as a component of Paul's rhetoric in this letter, for empire and the ability to speak freely do not coexist easily. Paul reports earlier that despite undeservedly poor treatment in Philippi and continuing opposition in Thessalonica, he and his coworkers still "had courage in our God to declare to you the gospel" (1 Thess 2:2). The term translated "had courage" is drawn from *parrēsia*, which in democratic Greece "meant 'freedom of speech.' Paul treats his converts and congregations as persons and places where free speech is appropriate and in order."[78] In his later letter to the Colossians, Paul would provide a christological foundation for this liberty of *parrēsia*: the same word is the "openness" with which Christ "exposed" the rulers and authorities in Col 2:15. Whether Paul makes this connection in this earlier letter can be debated; certainly the opposition he mentions here would have highlighted the *lack* of real freedom among the imperial cities where he lived and wrote.

Pax et Securitas

Shortly after Paul's heavy co-opting of imperial language in 1 Thessalonians 4, he elaborates on the timing of the expected visitation of Christ the deliverer: "For you yourselves know very well that the day of the Lord will come like a thief in the night. When they say, 'There is peace and security,' then sudden destruction will come upon them" (1 Thess 5:2–3a). The saying of "peace and security" has proven to be a difficult issue—as has the identity of those saying it. As he indicated regarding Paul's use of "kingdom" above, Charles Wanamaker says that this statement is "not typical of Paul"; the concept of the "false cry of peace" is one he attributes not to apocalyptic thought (despite the destructive threats in 5:3) but to the prophetic tradition.[79] Witherington agrees that there are Old Testament prophetic echoes here, but also marks the inscrip-

---

76. Witherington, *Thessalonians*, 3, 6–7, 40.
77. Ibid., 7.
78. Ibid., 77, esp. n. 68.
79. Wanamaker, *Thessalonians*, 180.

tions "all over the empire" attributing the arrival of *pax et securitas*—or *eirēnē* and *asphaleia*—to Rome and the emperor Augustus; this verse, then, represents Paul's critique of the slogans of the *pax Romana*.[80]

How penetrating is this critique meant to be? Donfried describes it as a "frontal" or "direct attack," "an assault" on *Pax et Securitas* as an imperial program; he borrows from W. H. C. Frend's account of Paul's motive as one of startling bitterness.[81] Neil Elliott concurs that Paul's intent is subversive, but sees him lampooning the Augustan propaganda with an ironic inversion: a similar dynamic is at work in the triumph of 2 Cor 2:14–15, where Paul is publicly a humiliated captive, and yet also a living manifestation of God's power.[82] Paul's actual motive may be difficult to discern, but his strategy remains effective: he marshals Old Testament prophetic traditions to rebuff the empire's powerful propaganda, making an ironic defensive move, rather than a scalding attack. Paul comes to parry Caesar, not to braise him.

I provide a brief example by returning to the ideology of divine warfare, reviewed above as relevant to Ephesians. Ephesians 4:8 appropriates Psalm 68; here I appeal to a related text, Psalm 29. Dominated by the praises ascribed to God, largely for the raw power of God's voice, the psalm concludes (29:10–11), "The LORD sits enthroned over the flood; the LORD sits enthroned as king for ever. May the LORD give strength to his people! May the LORD bless his people with peace!" Carroll Stuhlmueller finds that even this early psalm, in its apparent mimicry of other ancient Near-Eastern myths (such as Baal's position as storm-god), "actually parodies Baal worship, since power and enthronement are granted exclusively to Yahweh."[83] Circumscribing the power of the (apparently) untamed storm is an *inclusio* of God's *strength* (Ps 29:1, 11),[84] resulting in *peace* for his people. As Patrick Miller comments on the psalm's theological and political polemic, "in Canaanite mythology, Baal was enthroned over the conquered flood or primordial waters of chaos. Here is affirmed

---

80. Witherington, *Thessalonians*, 146–47; the Thessalonian statue of Augustus (p. 5) may have inspired this critique. Alert linguists will notice that the English word *asphalt* can be traced to *asphaleia*—perhaps paving the way to peace and security?

81. Donfried, "Cults of Thessalonica," 34, 43; Donfried, "Assembly of the Thessalonians," 144. Also see Frend, *Martyrdom*, 96.

82. Elliott, "Strategies of Resistance," 119.

83. Stuhlmueller, "Psalms," 405.

84. Ibid.

the universal kingship of the Lord, who dethrones all other powers and is the only one able to grant *security and peace*."[85]

I do not insist that 1 Thess 5:3 contains any explicit allusions to Psalm 29, though the word pairs (strength and peace; peace and security) are tempting; the Thessalonian correspondence does not even merit an essay in a recent volume devoted to hearing the psalms in the New Testament, nor is Psalm 29 itself considered at any point in the collective survey.[86] I merely suggest that this is the type of text, or more broadly the type of ideology, that Paul might have had in mind when he attempted to counter the imperial program of peace and security. This tentative proposal is further strengthened by the theophanic quality of Paul's language throughout 1 Thessalonians 4–5 and into 2 Thessalonians 1,[87] and by what I hope are convincing parallels in the language of dethroning opposing powers. A strong precedent also exists for defending the appropriation of Psalm 29 elsewhere in the New Testament. Clinton McCann has argued convincingly that another theophanic event, the angelic proclamation of Jesus' birth in Luke 2:8–12, is not a direct quotation but is "certainly reminiscent" of the enthronement psalm,[88] an echo made more forceful here by shared context: Luke 2 and 1 Thessalonians 4–5 both announce the impending arrival of a king who will rival Caesar. At the very least, then, this psalm's ideological mindset is *appropriate*; at most, it is in some way *appropriated*. As Paul's critique is so closely related to the co-opted imperial language he employs to describe the coming visitation of Christ, the crucified and resurrected deliverer, the dual ideological background is perhaps worthy of further study.

---

85. Miller, "Psalms," 825, italics mine.

86. Moyise and Menken, *Psalms in the New Testament*, mentioned above in discussion of Philippians.

87. Witherington, *Thessalonians*, 141, echoing Mic 1:3 ("the Lord is coming out of his place, and will come down and tread upon the high places of the earth") in 1 Thess 4:16, a high point of both eschatological and court language; and 195, where Witherington cites parallels to Acts 7:30, Ps 104:4, and increasingly, Isa 2, 29, 30, 44, and 66.

88. McCann, *Theological Introduction to Psalms*, 164. With an allusion or at least a preservation of "the same movement as in Psalm 29," McCann continues, Luke "makes a powerful theological affirmation. God is being enthroned in the birth of Jesus!" The same view of Jesus as a fulfillment of the Psalter's core theology can be applied here to the *parousia*, remembering whose image of visiting royalty is being appropriated.

TITUS AND 1 AND 2 TIMOTHY: SAVIOR, KING, DESPOT

Here we alter the canonical order slightly, in order to place Titus—the earliest of Paul's pastoral letters, and the least likely to be pseudepigraphic—at the forefront,[89] so as to begin an emphasis on the titles that appear in the Pastoral correspondence.

Savior

The first few lines of the letter reflect a change from Paul's usual opening, with relevance for the imperial environment: the titles normally common to Paul's greetings are absent (with the exception of *Christ*) until the end of 1:3, where God is referred to as *Savior*, a title also ascribed to Jesus in 1:4. The same title (*sōtēr, sōtēros*) appears six times in Titus—more than any other Pauline letter, and accounting for one in every four uses of the word in the entire New Testament—while the customary title for Jesus, *lord* (*kyrios*), is never used. Witherington finds extensive use of a language of soteriology in the Pastorals, while it is avoided in earlier Paulines except the chronologically latest, Philippians (as in 3:20, mentioned above: "our citizenship is in heaven, and it is from there that we are expecting a Savior, the Lord Jesus Christ").[90]

As with the expectation of the divine deliverer's visitation in 1 and 2 Thessalonians, *sōtēr* is a common descriptor for a god who rescues, heals, or otherwise intervenes for those who require help: Zeus and Artemis were both termed this way, as were some human benefactors, and the LXX offers further examples, especially common among the psalms.[91] Witherington's judgment that soteriological language is "dou-

---

89. Following Witherington, *Titus, 1–2 Timothy and 1–3 John*, 86: Titus, ca. 64–65 CE, is most likely genuine, for who but Paul would send a mission letter to *Crete*?

90. Witherington (*Titus, 1–2 Timothy and 1–3 John*, 103–5) wonders if the comparative lack of savior-language in 2 Timothy "reflects the more dangerous situation and Roman setting of that letter" (103 n. 46). A question for Witherington in response might be this: should modern readers draw the same conclusion of the earlier Paulines that largely avoid such soteriological terms? Note, too, that even Phil 3:20 supports its *sōtēr* reference with the more common *kyrios*.

91. Witherington, *Titus, 1–2 Timothy and 1–3 John*, 102–5. He attributes the use of "more Hellenistic language" of gods and epiphanies to Luke, as Paul's influential amanuensis: the "hand and diction" in Titus and 1 Timothy are Luke's, though the voice is Paul's (102). Given such a broad basis for a language of soteriological intervention, one wishes Witherington would explore further the overlap with terms of *patronage* (which might well serve as a vehicle for much soteriological thought in Roman contexts), as he begins to do when God is spoken of as a *benefactor* (156, on Titus 3:4).

bly appropriate"[92] because of its dual background could be taken further still: it is doubly *appropriated* when used to refer to Christ. The initial reference to Christ as *sōtēr* finds fullest (and perhaps most Trinitarian) expression here:

> But when the goodness and loving kindness of God our Savior appeared, he saved us, not because of any works of righteousness that we had done, but according to his mercy, through the water of rebirth and renewal by the Holy Spirit. This Spirit he poured out on us richly through Jesus Christ our Savior, so that, having been justified by his grace, we might become heirs according to the hope of eternal life. (Titus 3:4–7)

A number of Pauline emphases are discernible here: justification by grace, the questionable righteousness of works, the significance of baptism, and the Spirit's related role. Most relevant to empire and atonement are two points. First, what the NRSV renders "loving kindness" is literally *philanthrōpia*, love to/for humans (perhaps *humankindness*?). This term draws from the language of Roman patronage[93]—and is thus entirely appropriate (and worth appropriating!) to savior-language as well. This first point leads to the second: both God and Jesus Christ are called *our savior* here, contextualizing God's benefaction and reminding the reader that God's patronage and intervention are not without horrific cost. Though it is not mentioned explicitly, the phrase *through Jesus Christ our Savior*, followed closely by justification, is a quiet reference to the cross.

King

Paul's doxological statement early in 1 Timothy (1:17) presents another unusual descriptive title: "the King of the ages, immortal [*aphthartō*, lit. "incorruptible"], invisible, the only God." George Knight points out that this is not a frequent term for God in the New Testament,[94] especially in Paul. Yet it is followed near the end of the letter with the massive honorific, "the blessed and only Sovereign, the King of kings and Lord of lords" (1 Tim 6:15, and on into v. 16); and in even closer proximity, Paul urges his reader(s) to pray for, intercede on behalf of, and even express

92. Ibid., 104.
93. As has already been noted: ibid., 156.
94. Knight, *Pastoral Epistles*, 104. Compare also discussion of *basileia* in 1 Thess 2:12, above, with this reference and with the phrase "his [heavenly] kingdom" in 2 Tim 4:1 and 4:18.

thanksgiving (!) for "kings and all who are in high positions, so that we may lead a quiet and peaceable life in all godliness and dignity" (1 Tim 2:1–2, with the endorsement of "God our Savior" and Christ Jesus, the self-giving ransom, in vv. 3–6). While this would seem to lead to undue degrees of collaboration with the empire, Knight cautions that Rome did provide "a measure of peace and tranquility" for early Christian ministry, citing evidence from Acts and the Prison Epistles. "Perhaps," he continues, "Paul has in mind the words of Jer. 29:7 (LXX 36:7): 'Seek the welfare of the city where I have sent you into exile . . .'"[95] God's role as king has an Old Testament precedent that evidently informs his people's intended interaction with other (rival) kings.

Despot

Carrying forward a measure of 1 Timothy's emphasis on divine kingship, 2 Tim 2:3 has Timothy and Paul serving as soldiers under Christ's command; yet in enduring their suffering, they have the promise that they will "also reign with him" (2:12). Among its other titles, however, the letter also carries one designation that may trouble modern eyes. In the reference in 2:21 to believers as vessels "useful to the owner of the house, ready for every good work," the house-owner (TNIV: "the Master") is a term borrowed from Greco-Roman domestic life: *despotē*, or *despotēs*, the source of the English word *despot*. Normally conveying the status of lord or master, as over slaves (1 Tim 6:12; Titus 2:9; 1 Pet 2:18), the term is also used to describe authority, as with the title "Sovereign Lord" with references to both God and Jesus Christ.[96] Similar issues of translation arise in the benediction of 1 Tim 6:15–16: only here in the New Testament is God called *dynastēs*, "Sovereign," a term normally used to refer to human rulers in Luke and Acts, but used here for a counter-rhetorical function.[97] Christ's resurrection remains synonymous with Paul's gospel, for which he suffers "hardship, even to the point of being

---

95. Ibid., 117, citing Phil 1:12–13, Paul's report on the gospel's influence among the imperial guard. Though Paul does see this as providential, it was only *after* being imprisoned that he apparently learned to give thanks for this.

96. Used to refer to God: Luke 2:29; Acts 4:24; Rev 6:10; to Christ: 2 Pet 2:1; Jude 4. Despite semantic shifts, it remains difficult for modern Christians to use the same word to describe Christ that has been used to describe modern dictators.

97. See Witherington, *Titus, 1–2 Timothy and 1–3 John*, 294–98.

chained like a criminal" (2 Tim 2:9).[98] But serious risk is involved when language normally reserved for human masters and rulers is borrowed to speak of God and of Christ. Counter-rhetoric is only effective when it remains distinctive from both its sources and its opposition.

PHILEMON: A PRISONER OF CHRIST

The other Prison Epistles, along with portions of the Pastorals, share with Paul's letter to Philemon the knowledge of imprisoned suffering: here Paul calls himself both an "old man" and "a prisoner of Christ Jesus" (Phlm 9). It is from this background that Paul makes his "appeal on the basis of love," during his "imprisonment for the gospel" (Phlm 9–10, 13). What is the nature of his appeal? His first goal is for Philemon to forgive his runaway slave Onesimus; his second, more subtle objective is the slave's manumission. Paul places a "roundabout" request for Onesimus' freedom—and the freedom that Christ accomplishes for the early Christian community—within the context of the Deuteronomic tradition, and more specifically the Jubilee narrative of liberation from captivity and slavery. "It is no wonder, then," Keesmaat says, "that in the letter to Philemon Paul calls for the fundamental shape of that story to be reflected in the life of the early church,"[99] including even the common household relationships of master and slave—relationships now made *uncommon* by a shared bond of obedience (Phlm 21) to Christ.

Beyond Keesmaat's attention to the work Christ has performed and its place within the narratives of Israel and the early church, can anything more about Philemon be said, specific to empire and atonement? There is the basic observation to be made again: Paul's own captivity is likely enforced by Rome. Walsh and Keesmaat explore Paul's advice through a creative exercise, crafting a letter from Onesimus to Paul that reports on the reception of the letters to the Colossians and Philemon, and arguing in the process for a broader "ethic of liberation," informed by Christ's death on the cross.[100]

---

98. Compare Paul's rejoinder in the same verse ("But the word of God is not chained") to Phil 1:13; 3:10–11.

99. Keesmaat, "In the Face of Empire," 209.

100. Walsh and Keesmaat, *Colossians Remixed*, 201–19; Jesus is "the One who came to bring salvation to Israel and bring God's new kingdom of peace to both Israel and the whole world through his death on the cross and his rising from the dead" (205).

But another facet of the master-slave dynamic reveals just how disruptive, how truly subversive, such an ethic would have been. Albert Harrill's examination of Rome's hierarchical society shows that a *personalized* understanding of power was integral to the empire: the relative qualities of honor (*dignitas*) and mastery (*auctoritas*) that distinguished the master from his slave were the same traits that sustained the role and governance of the emperor, as when Augustus was "proclaimed the ultimate guarantor (*auctor*) of peace and stability after decades of civil war."[101] That is, the empire's societal structure and the integrity of the *pax Romana* itself were subject to the same rules as master and slave: a distinctively Roman ideology of mastery.[102] To proclaim a crucified lord instead of Caesar, and to use this claim as the analogical basis for manumission,[103] was to disrupt the proper channels of power. No wonder Paul left his request implicit! If his letter had fallen into the wrong hands, his analogies alone could have caused further imperial entanglements for Paul and for Philemon's household.

THE CRUCIFORM RUBRIC

Michael Gorman asserts that for Paul, "the death of Christ is not only revelatory, representative, and redemptive ... but also paradigmatic. The essence of believing existence is conformity to the crucified Christ, or cruciformity," a term Gorman identifies with the "law of Christ" (Gal 6:2; 1 Cor 9:21), or the "narrative pattern of the crucified Messiah."[104] I believe Gorman is on target when he refers to Christ's death as paradigmatic, and comprehensively so; the questions I have attempted to address here are perhaps more specific, in asking *how* the cruciform paradigm works when applied to the interpretation and application of Scripture and to the annexation of Roman imperial imagery.[105] I would

101. Harrill, *Slaves in the New Testament*, esp. 23.

102. Ibid., 25-26.

103. I thank David Huctwith and the other participants in Craig Evans's course "Christian Origins and the Roman Empire," for helping me to clarify this analogy during discussion on June 1, 2007, leading up to the Colloquium.

104. Gorman, *Apostle*, 140-41, references several passages used here including the Phil 2 Christ-hymn, but employs Gal 3:13—which I have argued is literally crucial to Paul's cruciform Scripture reading—as a text for the promise of the Spirit.

105. "Annexation" is admittedly a strong word, but accurate nonetheless. One could speculate that Paul lost little sleep over arrogating terminology that belonged to an arrogating empire.

argue that that the cross shapes a rubric for Paul's exegesis of both text and culture, and that the result is a *dialectic* rubric, following in part from examples proposed by Walter Brueggemann for studying the Old Testament. Evaluating what he refers to as the *core* and *counter testimony* in the Old Testament, Brueggemann suggests three dialectic pairs (*covenant* and *exile*; *hymn* and *lament*; and *presence* and *theodicy*) as rubrics for further exploration.[106] Brueggemann could just as easily have substituted *empire* for exile, rendering the first pair as *covenant* and *empire*, as nearby empires were often the forces that shaped and enforced Israel's exilic experiences.[107]

Rome's role in shaping the minor Pauline epistles—and the New Testament as a whole—is just as forceful, but often implicit. Though first-century Palestinian Jews and Christians were technically no longer living in exile, their land and their lives belonged to Rome; Paul's developing theology of the atonement had to take the empire's control into account. Where Brueggemann has seen the Old Testament prophets take a dramatic stand against the "mythic claims of the empire," exposing its gods as powerless and exalting "YHWH the sovereign one" in their place,[108] Paul has Christ disarming "the rulers and authorities" to make "a public example of them, triumphing over them" in the cross (Col 2:15), a scandalous but subtle message meant only for those with eyes to read—and decode. Paul borrows from Rome's banks of words and images, but rarely ends up in debt to them, in part because he finds another lending source in the traditions of the Old Testament; he can apply ideologies of divine warfare and supremacy to defend against Rome's ideologies of power and mastery. Even crucifixion, used by Rome to communicate the price of dissent, can be appropriated from one ideology to another. Christ's cross evokes (perhaps even *invokes*) both God's covenant and Rome's empire, not reconciling the two, but juxtaposing them, allow-

---

106. Brueggemann, "Biblical Theology Appropriately Postmodern," 101–3. These three pairs are, of course, designed with postmodern readings in mind.

107. As Brueggemann himself has pointed out repeatedly: see *Prophetic Imagination*, where true reality is shaped by the "God who is as yet unco-opted and uncontained by the empire" (27), while later prophetic voices, including that of Jesus, serve to dismantle the surrounding empire's favorite images (76–83). Another example comes from the structure of Brueggemann's *Reverberations of Faith*: empire does not appear as one of the book's 100 "topics of theological interest," but each historical superpower Israel faced receives its own entry!

108. Brueggemann, *Prophetic Imagination*, 16.

ing Paul to drop hints about how one circumscribes the other. Empire is here the *antithesis* of covenant, the counter-theme among biblical-theological themes that can be traced through the Old Testament and New Testament.

Finally, to cite another "NT": N. T. Wright makes a similar claim about the status of empire relative to God's reign. If Paul casts Jesus as "Lord" as a rival to Caesar, then Jesus' "empire" competes with Rome's:

> This counter-empire can never be merely critical, never merely subversive. It claims to be the reality of which Caesar's empire is the parody. It claims to be modeling the genuine humanness, not least the justice and peace, and the unity across traditional racial and cultural barriers, of which Caesar's empire boasted.[109]

Witherington uses this excerpt from Wright to highlight the importance of allegiance to Christ as Lord: in the course of reassuring his congregants concerning the fate of martyred friends, Paul is "making some remarkable christological and eschatological assertions," but is "also busily deconstructing the extant pagan value system so that his converts will not lapse back into allegiance to it."[110] Yet after quoting Wright, Witherington immediately returns to calling Paul's message subversive.[111] Certainly it could have been read that way; but as Wright says, it is never *merely* subversive. To those with eyes to see and read carefully, Paul is indeed borrowing from the rubrics of the Old Testament, and deconstructing those of the empire—but he uses many of the pieces to build his own interpretive rubric, in the shape of the cross of Christ.

BIBLIOGRAPHY

Adams, Marilyn McCord. *Christ and Horrors: The Coherence of Christology*. Current Issues in Theology Series. Cambridge: Cambridge University Press, 2006.

Anderson, Paul N. *The Fourth Gospel and the Quest for Jesus: Modern Foundations Reconsidered*. LNTS (JSNTSup) 321. New York: T. & T. Clark, 2006.

Arnold, Clinton E. *Ephesians, Power and Magic: The Concept of Power in Ephesians in Light of its Historical Setting*. Cambridge: Cambridge University Press, 1989.

———. *Powers of Darkness: Principalities and Powers in Paul's Letters*. Downers Grove, IL: InterVarsity, 1992.

Barth, Markus. *Ephesians 1–3*. AB 34. Garden City, NY: Doubleday, 1974.

---

109. Wright, "Paul's Gospel," 182–83, referring mainly to Phil 2.
110. Witherington, *Thessalonians*, 140.
111. Ibid., 141.

———. *The Broken Wall: A Study of the Epistle to the Ephesians*. Philadelphia: Judson, 1959.
Bartholomew, Craig et al., editors. *Canon and Biblical Interpretation*. SH 7. Grand Rapids: Zondervan. 2006.
Bartholomew, Craig et al., editors. *Out Of Egypt: Biblical Theology and Biblical Interpretation*. SH 5. Grand Rapids: Zondervan, 2004.
Bolt, Peter G. "Life, Death, and the Afterlife in the Greco-Roman World." In *Life in the Face of Death: The Resurrection Message of the New Testament*, edited by Richard N. Longenecker, 51–79. MNTS. Grand Rapids: Eerdmans, 1998.
Brueggemann, Walter. "Biblical Theology Appropriately Postmodern." In *Jews, Christians, and the Theology of the Hebrew Scriptures*, edited by Alice Ogden Bellis and Joel S. Kaminsky, 97–108. SBLSymS 8. Atlanta: SBL, 2000.
———. *The Prophetic Imagination*. Philadelphia: Fortress, 1978.
———. *Reverberations of Faith: A Theological Handbook of Old Testament Themes*. Louisville: Westminster John Knox, 2002.
Caird, G. B. "The Descent of Christ in Ephesians 4:7–11." In *Studia Evangelica II–III*, edited by F. L. Cross, 535–45. TUGAL 87–88. Berlin: Akademie-Verlag, 1964.
Carter, Warren. *The Roman Empire and the New Testament: An Essential Guide*. Abingdon Essential Guides. Nashville: Abingdon, 2006.
Crossan, John Dominic, and Jonathan L. Reed. *In Search of Paul: How Jesus' Apostle Opposed Rome's Empire with God's Kingdom*. San Francisco: HarperSanFrancisco, 2004.
Donfried, Karl. "The Assembly of the Thessalonians: Reflections on the Ecclesiology of the Earliest Christian Letter." In *Paul, Thessalonica, and Early Christianity*, 139–62. Grand Rapids: Eerdmans, 2002.
———. "The Cults of Thessalonica and the Thessalonian Correspondence." In his *Paul, Thessalonica, and Early Christianity*, 21–48. Grand Rapids: Eerdmans, 2002.
Edwards, Mark J. editor. *Galatians, Ephesians, Philippians*. ACCS: New Testament 8. Chicago: Fitzroy Dearborn, 1999.
Eisenman, Robert. *James the Brother of Jesus: The Key to Unlocking the Secrets of Early Christianity and the Dead Sea Scrolls*. New York: Penguin, 1997.
Elliott, Neil. "The Anti-Imperial Message of the Cross." In *Paul and Empire: Religion and Power in Roman Imperial Society*, edited by Richard A. Horsley, 167–83. Harrisburg: Trinity Press International, 1997.
———. "Strategies of Resistance and Hidden Transcripts in the Pauline Communities." In *Hidden Transcripts and the Arts of Resistance: Applying the Work of James C. Scott to Jesus and Paul*, edited by Richard A. Horsley, 97–122. Atlanta: SBL, 2004.
Esler, Philip F. "God's Honour and Rome's Triumph: Responses to the Fall of Jerusalem in 70 CE in Three Jewish Apocalypses." In *Modelling Early Christianity: Social-Scientific Studies of the New Testament in its Context*, edited by Philip F. Esler, 239–58. New York: Routledge, 1995.
———. "Rome in Apocalyptic and Rabbinic Literature." In *The Gospel of Matthew in Its Roman Imperial Context*, edited by John Riches and David C. Sim, 9–33. JSNTSup 276. New York: T. & T. Clark (Continuum), 2005.
Frend, W. H. C. *Martyrdom and Persecution in the Early Church: A Study of a Conflict from the Maccabees to Donatus*. Oxford: Blackwell, 1965.
Gombis, Timothy G. "Cosmic Lordship and Divine Gift-Giving: Psalm 68 in Ephesians 4:8." *NovT* 47 (2005) 367–80.

———. "Ephesians 2 as a Narrative of Divine Warfare." *JSNT* 26 (2004) 403–18.
Gorman, Michael J. *Apostle of the Crucified Lord: A Theological Introduction to Paul and His Letters*. Grand Rapids: Eerdmans, 2004.
Harrill, J. Albert. *Slaves in the New Testament: Literary, Social and Moral Dimensions*. Minneapolis: Augsburg Fortress, 2006.
Head, Ivan. "Mark as a Roman Document from the Year 69: Testing Martin Hengel's Thesis." *JRH* 28 (2004) 240–59.
Hengel, Martin. *Crucifixion in the Ancient World, and the Folly of the Message of the Cross*. Translated by J. Bowden. London: SCM, 1986.
Horsley, Richard A., ed. *Paul and Empire: Religion and Power in Roman Imperial Society*. Harrisburg: Trinity Press International, 1997.
Horsley, Richard A., and Neil Asher Silberman. *The Message and the Kingdom: How Jesus and Paul Ignited a Revolution and Transformed the Ancient World*. Minneapolis: Fortress, 1997.
James, P. D. *The Children of Men*. New York: Knopf, 1992.
Keesmaat, Sylvia C. "In the Face of Empire: Paul's Use of Scripture in the Shorter Epistles." In *Hearing the Old Testament in the New Testament*, edited by Stanley E. Porter, 182–212. MNTS. Grand Rapids: Eerdmans, 2006.
———. "The Psalms in Romans and Galatians." In *The Psalms in the New Testament*, edited by Steve Moyise and M. J. J. Menken, 139–61. New Testament and the Scriptures of Israel Series. London: T. & T. Clark, 2004.
Kent, Homer A., Jr. "Philippians." In *The Expositor's Bible Commentary*, edited by Frank E. Gaebelein, 11:95–159. Grand Rapids: Zondervan, 1978.
Knight, George W., III. *The Pastoral Epistles: A Commentary on the Greek Text*. NIGTC. Grand Rapids: Eerdmans; Exeter: Paternoster, 1992.
Knowles, Michael P. *We Preach Not Ourselves: Paul and Preaching in the Presence of God*. Grand Rapids: Brazos, 2008.
Kreitzer, Larry J. *Striking New Images: Roman Imperial Coinage and the New Testament World*. JSNTSup 134. Sheffield: Sheffield Academic, 1996.
Lemcio, Eugene E. "The Gospels within the New Testament Canon." In *Canon and Biblical Interpretation*, edited by Craig Bartholomew et al., 123–45. SH 7. Grand Rapids: Zondervan, 2006.
Longenecker, Richard N. *New Wine into Fresh Wineskins: Contextualizing the Early Christian Confessions*. Peabody, MA: Hendrickson, 1999.
Maslen, Matthew W., and Piers D. Mitchell. "Medical Theories on the Cause of Death in Crucifixion." *Journal of the Royal Society of Medicine* 99 (2006) 185–88.
McCann, J. Clinton, Jr. *A Theological Introduction to the Book of Psalms: The Psalms as Torah*. Nashville: Abingdon, 1993.
Miller, Patrick D. "Psalms." In *The HarperCollins Study Bible, NRSV*, edited by Wayne A. Meeks, 797–937. SBL Annotated Edition. San Francisco: HarperSanFrancisco, 1993.
Moritz, Thorsten. *A Profound Mystery: The Use of the Old Testament in Ephesians*. NovTSup 85. Leiden: Brill, 1996.
Moyise, Steve, and M. J. J. Menken, editors. *The Psalms in the New Testament*. New Testament and the Scriptures of Israel Series. London: T. & T. Clark, 2004.
Oakes, Peter. "God's Sovereignty over Roman Authorities: A Theme in Philippians." In *Rome in the Bible and the Early Church*, edited by Peter Oakes, 126–41. Carlisle: Paternoster; Grand Rapids: Baker Academic, 2002.

Richardson, Cyril C., trans. and ed. *Early Christian Fathers.* LCC vol. 1. New York: Collier/Macmillan, 1970.

Roberts, J. J. M. "The Enthronement of Yhwh and David: The Abiding Theological Significance of the Kingship Language of the Psalms." *CBQ* 64 (2002) 675–86.

Stuhlmueller, Carroll. "Psalms." In *The HarperCollins Bible Commentary*, edited by James L. Mays, 394–446. Revised ed. San Francisco: HarperSanFrancisco, 2000.

Walsh, Brian J., and Sylvia C. Keesmaat. *Colossians Remixed: Subverting the Empire.* Downers Grove, IL: InterVarsity, 2004.

Wanamaker, C. A. *The Epistles to the Thessalonians: A Commentary on the Greek Text.* NIGTC. Grand Rapids: Eerdmans; Exeter: Paternoster, 1990.

Wink, Walter. *Naming the Powers: The Language of Power in the New Testament.* Philadelphia: Fortress, 1984.

Witherington, Ben. *1 and 2 Thessalonians: A Socio-Rhetorical Commentary.* Grand Rapids: Eerdmans, 2006.

———. *Letters and Homilies for Hellenized Christians. I. A Socio-Rhetorical Commentary on Titus, 1–2 Timothy and 1–3 John.* Downers Grove, IL: IVP Academic; Nottingham: Apollos, 2006.

Wright, N. T. "Paul's Gospel and Caesar's Empire." In *Paul and Politics: Ekklesia, Israel, Imperium, Interpretation: Essays in Honor of Krister Stendahl*, edited by Richard Horsley, 160–83. Harrisburg: Trinity Press International, 2000.

8

Running the Gamut

The Varied Responses to Empire in Jewish Christianity

Cynthia Long Westfall

THIS PAPER EXPLORES THE relationship between the Roman Empire and the Jewish Christian corpus in the New Testament, excluding the Gospels, which includes Hebrews, the General Epistles, and Revelation.[1] The relationship between the Roman Empire and any book in the New Testament offers an interesting challenge. The first question to ask is, "What counts for evidence in locating the relationship between empire and the New Testament?" I propose that there are three criteria, any of which could count for evidence. The first would be authorial intention: Did the author intend to interact with the Roman Empire either in accommodation or confrontation in what is written? Authorial intent is difficult to ascertain, but that can be helped by the second criterion: "Would the recipients read a given passage or phrase as a negotiation or confrontation of empire?" The third criterion is as important as the first two: "Would the Roman authorities perceive a passage or phrase to be addressing empire; especially, would a given statement offend the authorities or be considered subversive to the empire?" This may be the most pertinent question, because an author may claim that Christian

---

1. See the discussion of the constitution of the Hebrew mission in terms of identity, geography, leadership and canon in Westfall, "The Hebrew Mission," 189–91. See also Dunn's chart in *Unity and Diversity*, 265, though Dunn places the Johannine literature and Jude in an additional category as "Hellenistic Christianity," and Revelation is identified as a separate category of apocalyptic literature. He also treats 2 Peter as institutionalization in the early church.

behavior is submissive or command the recipients to behave as good citizens of a city, but then define or qualify behavior in such a way that the Roman Empire would consider it illegitimate. Some would suggest that some of the practices that are addressed in the empire genre were not peculiar to Roman rule, but had their origin in local practices, the ancient Mediterranean and Eastern culture, or virtually all civilization, so that the Roman Empire cannot be held responsible. However, the empire utilized local customs and cultures to accomplish its goals, and neither the Old Testament nor the New Testament was shy about holding an oppressive conqueror responsible for many of the challenges that the people of God faced.

The study of the Roman Empire in the New Testament often involves the analysis of the text through various lenses or models of the social sciences. An extensive study of empire in any given text would involve utilizing a series of tools on each text that uncover, for example, each of the eight means highlighted by Warren Carter through which the Roman Empire exercised political, economic, social, military, and religious power.[2] However, the literature of early Jewish Christianity in the non-Pauline epistles has a tendency to display the negotiation of one aspect of empire more distinctively than others, so that I will identify and utilize one lens to view each epistle. James is analyzed with an economic model, 1 Peter is analyzed with a social model, 2 Peter, Jude, and the Johannine Epistles are analyzed in relation to the ethical values of the empire, and Hebrews is analyzed with a religious/political model. Finally, Revelation is viewed as running the gamut of the concerns that Jewish Christianity faced as it negotiated a perilous path among the Roman Empire, Judaism, and Gentile Christianity.

JAMES AND THE ECONOMIC CONTROL OF THE EMPIRE

James has been surrounded by controversies concerning its authorship, content, and message. However, its scathing critique[3] of economic condi-

---

2. See Carter, "Proclaiming (in/against) Empire," 153–54. The eight means were economic control, taxes and tributes, Roman military power, war, pervasive patronage, imperial theology, rhetoric, and Roman "justice."

3. Elsa Tamez characterizes James as "subversive" and reads James from the viewpoint of liberation theology in *The Scandalous Message of James*. *Colossians Remixed*, by Walsh and Keesmaat, is reminiscent of Tamez's work and the reading of other liberation theologians, though the relationship is not generally explicit.

tions under the Roman Empire is consistent with the tensions among the peasants in Palestine that eventually provoked the war against Rome and preceded the destruction of the temple in 70 CE.[4] It is also consistent with conditions throughout the empire in places such as Syria and possibly Egypt.

According to S. Dyson, the Jewish revolt against the Roman Empire occurred because of rapid Hellenization and Romanization acculturation.[5] It was too much too fast, where Rome imposed a new administrative structure, governors, and taxation, and confiscated the land for the soldier-farmers: the new aristocracy. As Duling observed, "politically, urban ruling strata needed large bureaucracies and military establishments and exploited peasants."[6] It was an agrarian economy where an aristocracy or the upper strata were the ruling class, which needed many peasants in the lower strata to support it. This relationship involved exploitation.

The recipients of James addressed by the author could potentially be identified with a number of economic groups. However, the text identifies the Christian faith with the poor (Jas 2:5) and the congregation as a whole is described as exploited and abused by the rich (Jas 2:6). The letter begins with how to handle trials, and the specific trials the author addresses in the letter are the struggles of poverty and oppression.[7] Rich landowners and merchants are also addressed directly (Jas 4:13–17; 5:1–7), though the address to the rich in Jas 5:1–7 is probably a rhetorical diatribe or apostrophe directed at non-Christians. The most plausible picture is a congregation that was primarily in the lower economic stratum of rural day laborers[8] and urban artisans, some of whom were drawn to the commercial opportunities offered in the empire.[9] Some of those artisans could have moved or been in the process of mov-

---

4. There is no specific crisis in view but a state of affairs. While James is consistent with conditions preceding the Bar Kochba revolt, the pivotal crisis of the destruction of the temple with the violent use of military force in Palestine may have cast more of a shadow over the depiction of the rich and powerful.

5. Dyson, "Native Revolts."

6. Duling, "Empire: Theories, Methods, Models," 53.

7. As states Keener, *Bible Background Commentary*, 690.

8. The reference to the wages of day laborers rather than slave labor may indicate a Palestinian destination.

9. Davids, *James*, 30, suggests that the shortage of land together with the influx of Hellenistic goods attracted many to trade.

ing into the top of the lower strata, comparable to Roman freedpersons who owned land and were involved in trading, banking, as well as artisan work, but could not move into the higher orders because of servile origins.[10] Nevertheless, this segment of the lower strata could achieve great wealth and sometimes became benefactors. Therefore the congregation could be economically diverse while belonging to the 99 percent of the population in the lower strata, sandwiched between the elite in the upper strata who exploited them and the expendables (Jas 2:2–4), over whom they in turn held a position of economic and social status and power.

James characterizes three people groups according to their economic status: the poor, the merchants, and the rich. The descriptions of the "poor" coincide well with economic descriptions of the 99 percent in the lower strata. He gives an example of "a poor person in filthy clothes" (Jas 2:2) who is depicted as marginalized and insulted in the congregation. Another example of an expendable is the brother or sister without clothes and daily food in 2:15. Barely higher than expendables, the rural day laborers are particularly presented as an oppressed group in Jas 5:4:

> Look! The wages you failed to pay the workers who mowed your fields are crying out against you. The cries of the harvesters have reached the ears of the Almighty.

This group of day laborers grew significantly over a century before, when the Roman general Pompey first seized and controlled Judean territory and left many Jewish peasants landless. Consequent exorbitant taxation under the Roman system would have added to the number of landless poor who worked on feudal-like estates or became day laborers who showed up in the market place, something like migrant workers, as in the parable of the workers in the vineyard in Matt 20:1–16. Though the subsistence living of the day laborers and the control of the land by the elite is recognized as exploitation, James further claims that the poor are not being paid their wages. James's accusation that the innocent are condemned and murdered by the rich most likely extends beyond day laborers to any lethal use of power against the powerless of the lower strata (Jas 5:6). James claims that the readers, as members of the lower strata, are all victims of economic exploitation by the rich elite (Jas 2:6).

---

10. Alföldy, *Social History*, 109–26, gives a pyramidal analysis of the Roman Orders where the upper strata (after Caesar) consist of senators (*ordo senatorius*), the equestrian order (*ordo equester*), the local (urban) elites (*ordo decurionum*), and the emperor's slaves and freedpersons (*familia Caesaris*); see the chart on 146.

Furthermore, James places the readers in the lower strata when he claims that the rich subject them to what Warren Carter calls "Roman justice" when they are dragged before a court that "protected elite members and took harsh action against threats to the structures" (Jas 2:6).[11]

In Jas 4:13–17, James (perhaps rhetorically) addresses merchants, and in 5:1–6, he addresses wealthy landowners. In the light of the economic models of the Roman Empire, it is tempting to suggest that James addresses first the urban rich and then the rural rich, since they are juxtaposed. However, the scenario also fits ambitious artisans who possessed enough resources to take advantage of the opportunities that the Roman Empire had to offer—and many in Palestine had those kinds of resources. The merchant or potential merchant in 4:13 makes entrepreneurial plans to travel to a city, start a business, work for only a year, and expects or assumes a profit in that period of time. This may reflect the particular Palestinian concern of the author. Since Greek rule began under Alexander, Jews had been taking part in a voluntary dispersion because this kind of opportunity in parts of the Greek and Roman Empires offered greater economic gain than Israel offered. Consequently, Alexandria became the largest location of Jews outside Palestine. Therefore the group of people who functioned as merchants included people from both the upper and lower strata. Contrary to what is often asserted, the fledgling church in Israel or Syria needed no significant time to develop this kind of problem with wealth. Perhaps the group of merchants should be more characterized by their entrepreneurial attitudes, plans, and actions rather than their economic status, which could vary significantly.

It may be simplistic to assume that every reference to the rich in James reflects the upper strata. The "rich" described in Jas 1:10–11, where

---

11. Carter, "Proclaiming (in/against) Empire," 154. Keener, *Bible Background Commentary*, 694, writes, "Roman laws explicitly favored the rich. Persons of lower class, who were thought to act from economic self-interest, could not bring accusations against persons of higher class, and the laws prescribed harsher penalties for lower-class persons convicted of offenses than for offenders from the higher class." Blomberg, *Jesus and the Gospels*, 23, reflects the traditional perspective when he claims that Rome implemented "perhaps the most enlightened and advanced judicial processes of antiquity. It had its tyrants and despots to be sure, along with various breaches of conduct, but due process of law brought justice, at least for citizens, more consistently than in other empires." Perhaps the key phrase here is "at least for citizens." What worked in Paul's favor as a Roman citizen discriminated against most Jewish Christians and other local populations.

the rich person's position is contrasted with the poor person's position, may primarily refer to those in the congregation who had relatively more economic power and status than others in "humble circumstances" in the congregation—a person in "humble circumstances" tends to classify wealth on the pragmatic basis of comparison—someone is perceived as rich who has significantly more possessions than others in a given group.[12] Similarly, if the preferential treatment of the "rich" person in the rhetorical example in Jas 2:2 reflected an actual pattern of behavior, it could include persons who were potential benefactors, including artisans or merchants in the lower strata—they certainly would be a target for those raising funds.[13] On the other hand, the description in James's rhetorical example signals a member of the upper strata. Gold rings and fine clothes marked great wealth and status.[14] Even more, the context of the court and lawsuits indicates that James was targeting the upper strata (Jas 2:6). The upper strata could initiate lawsuits against social inferiors, but social inferiors could not initiate lawsuits. The Jewish Law rejects this kind of distinction as immoral, so that if the venue is Palestine, the text depicts a corruption of the Jewish court by Roman practice, presumably through the collusion of the local elite: wealthy urban and rural Jews. James goes further in 5:1–6 and accuses rich landowners of hoarding in a way that reflects Jesus' teaching on storing up treasure in Matt 6:19–20: their stockpiled goods are rotted, clothing is moth-eaten, and gold and silver are corroded (Jas 5:2–3). They are living in luxury and self-indulgence while withholding the wages of the day laborers (Jas 5:4–5). Again, the withholding of wages from the poor for even a day was expressly forbidden in the Jewish Law, which says that when the poor cry out to

---

12. Some recent commentators have suggested that the rich in Jas 1:9–11 are non-Christian because of the omission of "brother" in referring to the rich, the rich in the rest of the epistle consistently seem to form a wicked class, and there is no spiritual future mentioned (Martin, *James*, 25–26; Maynard-Reid, *Poverty and Wealth*, 40–47). However, it is probable that ὁ πλούσιος is a modifier of ὁ ἀδελφός in direct parallel with ὁ ταπεινός. If so, in 1:10 the rich are called to a biblical humility in the context of faith, in which they value others more than themselves. This is a more appropriate address to believers with more resources rather than those involved in exploitation, corruption, hoarding, and murder.

13. As Blomberg, *Neither Poverty nor Riches*, 151, asserts, while 2:1–4 could represent a hypothetical situation, the "historical verisimilitude" and the subsequent argument in 2:5–7 ("but you have insulted the poor") indicate that it is an actual pattern of occurrence.

14. Keener, *Bible Background Commentary*, 694.

complain about it, God will act (Deut 24:14–15; Lev 19:13; Prov 11:24; Jer 22:13; Mal 3:5). In Judea, this would be considered further evidence of the corruption of the Jewish local elite by the Roman Empire. The accusation that they had condemned and murdered the innocent culminates the charges of exploitation (Jas 5:6). Building tensions between the poor and rich Jewish landowners because of these practices resulted in Jewish patriots slaughtering the rich Jewish landowners during the revolt.[15]

James directly criticized the entitlement and pride inherent in the Roman Empire's economic system and blasted the exploitation of the poor. As Carter says, the empire was concerned with the exercise of power: "Who gets what and why?" (p. 94). The system was intentionally set up so the upper strata controlled the power, wealth (land, slave labor, rents, taxes), and status. James directly confronted the practice of basing status and power on wealth by reversing the status of the rich and poor. In Jas 1:9-11, the poor were told to take pride in their high position and the rich were told to take pride in their humiliation. The high position of the poor refers to the spiritual blessings and position the believer receives in this life as well as the material and spiritual eschatological blessings.[16] This is particularly clear in 2:5, where James states that God has chosen the poor to be rich in faith and to inherit the kingdom. The humiliation of the rich is the recognition of the transience of wealth and life in general (Jas 1:10–11), an evaluation that James also apples to the merchants (4:14). This view of reversed status is further reinforced in Jas 2:1–7, where James insists that an expendable poor person be given the same status and honor in welcome and seating in their meetings as the rich person—this was truly revolutionary in a society where greeting and seating indicated one's status in the synagogues and banquets (cf. Luke 11:43, 14:7–11).[17] While the poor are characterized as being rich in faith, the rich are characterized by societal patterns of abuse. In addition, the pride of the entrepreneurial spirit of the merchants fostered by the opportunities of the Roman Empire is criticized. James cautions

---

15. Ibid., 691.

16. See Blomberg, *Neither Poverty nor Riches*, 149. However, Davids appears to see the position as eschatological (Davids, *James*, 76).

17. In Luke 11:43 and 14:7–11, the importance of status and honor in the greeting and seating is of particular importance for Pharisees. One's seat signifies one's importance in relation to the others present. Public buildings such as the amphitheatres also had seating by status.

his readers against a "practical atheism" that plans and expects profit without leaving room for God's sovereign will and the unpredictability of life (Jas 4:13–17).[18] Finally, James confronts the abuses of the wealthy landowners in a prophetic style, promising judgment where they are fattened for the day of slaughter and their flesh will be eaten like fire (Jas 5:1–6). There is no question that James is directly confronting the economic power structure of the empire, calling believers to operate outside of the economic value system and pronouncing severe judgment on the exploitation by the rich.

James's criticism of the rich and his advocacy for the poor were both criticisms of the local Jewish elite and a denunciation of the exploitation by the Roman Empire. These conditions and similar reactions led to the Palestinian revolt against Rome. However, though James denounced exploitation in a manner worthy of the Old Testament prophets, his form of resistance to the empire was non-violent active resistance. He challenged the position and power of the wealthy and granted equal or greater honor and status to the poor believer. He challenged the arrogance of the entrepreneurial spirit of materialism that was prevalent in the empire. The Roman authorities would have found this to be subversive. The counter-cultural challenge of James, which includes fellowship across social boundaries, and advocacy for the powerless, the poor and the oppressed should continue to be hallmarks of our interaction within our church, society, and government.

FIRST PETER AND SOCIAL MARGINALITY IN THE EMPIRE

The social system of the Roman Empire provides the context of the argument in 1 Peter. The text identifies the readers as Christian Gentiles who are suffering primarily because of social alienation—the suffering of dishonor.[19] The text identifies the author as "Peter, an apostle of Jesus Christ." Tradition held that the Jewish/Galilean Christian Peter was writing from Rome in the early or mid 60s, close to the Neronian persecution. Though the letter is often held to be pseudonymous, the text would still appeal to whatever traditional context the early church had formulated about Peter by use of his name in the espistolary opening. The context

---

18. Adamson, *James*, 180.

19. As argued by Campbell, *Rhetoric of 1 Peter*. However, Campbell's treatment of the value of honor as a compositional key goes beyond using the social value as a lens.

of Peter's life and situation is meant to frame the letter's information and exhortation.[20]

The social identity of individuals within the Roman Empire was closely related to economic status, but not identical to it. David deSilva asserts, "The patron-client relationship is the basic building block of Greco-Roman Society."[21] Patronage involved personal connections between patrons and clients, consisting of favors and loyalty as well as privilege and dependency. The principle of reciprocity that existed between patrons and clients permeated all levels of society and relationships, from Caesar on down to slaves. A person's worth within the social system was that person's honor, which is the "affirmation of one's worth by one's peers and society, awarded on the basis of the individual's ability to embody the virtues and attributes that his or her society values."[22] Since the Roman Empire utilized the patron-client relationship as a means to exercise power, honoring the established authorities was one of its basic building blocks, and the system was supported by the threat of irrevocable dishonor for ingratitude, disloyalty, or non-conformity.

Honor came in knowing one's place or identity (birth, social class and status, wealth, and patronage), conforming to society's expectations and essential values consistent with one's place, and competing for honor with one's social peers. However, honor was defined somewhat differently for women and slaves. Female so-called honor was the primary female virtue of "shame," comprised of defferential behavior, modesty, and chastity that enhanced the honor of the male head of household (cf. Sir 26:10–16; 42:9–12; 4 Macc 18:6–8; Thucydides, *Hist.* 2.45.2).[23] Slaves

---

20. According to tradition, Peter died in the mid to late 60s, crucified upside down. Critical discussion often finds 1 Peter to be pseudonymous because the Greek vocabulary and style is considered to be too polished for a Galilean fisherman, and often places the letter during the Domitian reign in the late 80s or early 90s. Others suggest it reflects the hostilities under Trajan in the 110s. However, there is nothing in the text that indicates direct official persecution.

21. deSilva, "Patronage," 766.

22. deSilva, "Honor and Shame," 518.

23. Barton, "Social Values," 1129, 1130. Some have tried to say that shame indicated women's high value, but this argument falls short of the reality where women were valued so little that infanticide practiced on female infants was so wide-spread that there was a shortage of females in the Roman Empire. As Rodney Stark suggests, the decline of the Roman population was due to the widespread infanticide of female infants, and the common practice of primitive methods of abortion, which resulted in the deaths of women and infertility (Stark, *Rise of Christianity*, 115–22). He concludes,

in the Roman Empire could be found at all economic levels, but they had no honor. Slavery has been described as a "dynamic process of alienation and dishonor termed *social death* . . . Social death means denying a person all dignity (as understood in that particular culture) and ties of birth in both ascending or descending generations . . . Although they are not biologically dead, slaves, in effect, are socially dead to the free population."[24] Therefore, in the rhetoric of the Greco-Roman culture, women and slaves represented the end of the line as far as patronage and honor was concerned—in the Roman Empire, they were socially defined by their dependency. Household codes originated with ancient moralists to define the authority relationship between the *paterfamilias* and the groups within the household (wives, children, and slaves) in order to produce order in society as a whole.[25]

Peter addresses three primary social challenges of marginalization that the Christians are facing that are sources of suffering: the group as a whole is experiencing deep rejection and public disgrace through insults and other forms of attack (1 Pet 3:8—4:19);[26] slaves are subject to indignity, harsh treatment, and physical and sexual abuse (1 Pet 2:18–25);[27] and women are vulnerable and threatened in their marital relationships, particularly in marriages to unbelievers (1 Pet 3:1–7).[28] As members of a group under attack, slaves and women have a double stigma and are the members of the group most vulnerable to suffering and abuse, particularly when the *paterfamilias* is not a Christian.

"In the final analysis, a population's capacity to reproduce is a function of the proportion of that population consisting of women in their childbearing years, and the Greco-Roman world had an acute shortage of women" (122).

24. Harrill, "Slavery," 1125.

25. See Keener, "Family and Household," 353, for a brief introduction to household codes.

26. See Westfall, "Relationship," 117–23, where it is shown that the topic in 1 Pet 3:8—4:6 is speech.

27. The physical abuse experienced by slaves in the Roman Empire was not limited to beating, which is mentioned as a specific example in 1 Pet 2:30, but included routine sexual violation for both males and females. Margaret MacDonald documents the common sexual violation of slaves and the break-up of slave families in the Roman culture ("Slavery"). The sexual violation and breakup of families were two of the primary reasons for the slave's dishonor.

28. Campbell, *Rhetoric of 1 Peter*, 147, suggests that the address to wives is longer than the address to husbands "probably because of the potential explosiveness within a marriage where the wife has converted to Christ and the husband has not."

Barth Campbell suggests that a major development of Peter's epistolary discourse is "how Christian sufferers who are publicly disgraced can nevertheless bear honor."[29] As he argues, "The Christian community . . . was perceived by the indigenous ethnic and/or religious majorities somehow to be a threat to the established order."[30] The dominant culture responded with rejection that took the form of a continuous stream of insults, challenging with hostile questions, slandering, and maligning believers, and ultimately blaspheming. People who did this represented the dominant cultural system in which the believers had to exist as a subculture. Peter responded to this challenge in 1 Pet 1:1—2:10, establishing that the believers who were alien residents and visiting strangers in the Roman Empire had honor as members of the household of God. This identity was strengthened by metaphors drawn from the identity of Israel in the Old Testament: they were rejected by people but chosen by God to be a temple, a chosen people, a royal priesthood, a holy nation, and a people belonging to God (1 Pet 2:4–5, 9). Peter established the readers' value outside of the social system of the dominant culture—what was disgrace in the eyes of the Roman Empire was honor in the eyes of God and in the community of faith. That non-conformity was exactly why they were perceived as a threat to the established order. It required an identity and life pattern that Peter understood from his experience as a Jew living under harsh Roman rule, which he could explain and transfer to the readers—the conditions of the Jewish Diaspora were applied to the Gentile believers.[31]

Peter's commands were to submit to "every authority instituted among people" including the emperor and the governors sent by the king, and to honor everyone, particularly the emperor (1 Pet 2:13–17). This command to submit must be read within the context of his militant resistance of the society's values through non-conformity and the pos-

---

29. Ibid., 37.

30. Ibid., 107.

31. See Martin, *Metaphor and Composition*, 192. Martin sees ἐλεύθεροι in 1 Pet 2:16 as political: "Because of the significant theological tradition behind this term many commentators deny it has any political connotation in this passage. However, I argue it does have political connotation in this context that contains political terms drawn from the Diaspora and discusses various groups of aliens." It is interesting that Campbell, along with other commentators, appears to compartmentalize metaphor, theological tradition, and political connotations (*Rhetoric of 1 Peter*, 117 n. 60). Clearly, what is metaphoric can be political—particularly in the view of a despotic empire.

session of the citizenship of a kingdom that was in competition with the empire. After stepping outside of the patronage system and taking a stance that could only be perceived by those who were outsiders to the faith but insiders to the empire as disloyal, his definition of submission and the client's obligation to honor had become seriously constrained. Submission to authority in 1 Peter is a limited commitment of respect or deference to authorities in the correct application of Roman justice (1 Pet 2:14) and working for the public good.[32] This fell far short of the imperial definition and demands of submission, but met ethical demands.

The fact that Peter instructed household slaves and wives directly would be seen as usurping the prerogative of the head of the household. It also implied that slaves and women had moral responsibility and choice that was unparalleled in the dominant culture and so was a way of resistance because it seized initiative from the powerful.[33] The submission of household slaves to masters (1 Pet 2:18–25) was constrained in the same way as the believer's submission to governing authorities with more radical results.[34] Yes, the household slaves were to submit themselves to their masters with all respect, whether they were considerate or harsh, but the slaves' submission was embedded in the general command for the believer to honor everyone, which implied that honor was no longer based on one's status or value in the eyes of society.[35] Furthermore, the believer's identity and value in Christ was applied to the slave who had no honor or social existence in the eyes of the empire. More than that, the household slaves were shown to be potentially the ultimate models of Christ's example. They were told to suffer for doing good because,

32. See Campbell, *Rhetoric of 1 Peter*, 108–14.

33. See Jobes, *1 Peter*, 206.

34. In 1 Pet 2:18, οἰκέται is used to refer to household slaves rather than the term δοῦλοι, which is favored by Paul in the household codes. This connects the slaves explicitly to the spiritual house of God (οἶκος πνευματικός) in 1 Pet 2:5.

35. The discourse of honoring everyone (1 Pet 2:17) is continued with the specific application of household slaves honoring their masters, formally signaled by the use of the participle ὑποτασσόμενοι in 1 Pet 2:18 and 3:1, as well as συνοικοῦντες and ἀπονέμοντες in 3:7 rather than a finite verb. Furthermore, 3:1 and 3:7 are marked with ὁμοίως. Therefore, the household code is embedded in a general command, which subverts the hierarchical application. There are structural similarities to Eph 5:22, where the wives' submission is embedded in a general command to be filled with the Spirit (5:18)—only in the case of the wife, the verb is missing entirely so that it is further embedded in the participial phrase to submit to one another in 5:21.

"To this you were called, because Christ suffered for you, leaving you an example, that you should follow in his steps" (1 Pet 2:21). Then Peter proceeded to give parallels between the abused slave and the passion of Christ (1 Pet 2:22-25).[36] In the same way that Mark reversed the shame of the crucifixion of Christ so that it was the glory of the cross, Peter reversed the shame of the slave. A slave no longer had to submit because of social inferiority and degradation—he or she was called to walk in the footsteps of Jesus and be a model of Christ-like behavior to the whole suffering community. This redefinition of the slave's identity struck at the heart of the patronage system and the value of honor in the Roman Empire—everything was turned on its head, and yet a Christian slave who took Peter's teaching to heart would be an ethical and economic pillar in the household.

Whereas an abused slave had a mission of modeling Christ to the Christian community through submission and enduring suffering, women had a mission of winning their husbands to faith through submission (3:1-6).[37] In the cultural context, this was an oxymoron. A woman was required to adopt her husband's religious beliefs; the suggestion that a wife should have a religious agenda for her husband was disruptive of the social order; it was not submissive behavior.[38] On the other hand, the "moral division of labor" of the dominant culture of the Roman Empire was upheld in the subsequent instructions. Women were to pursue sexual purity, reverence, modest dress, a gentle and quiet spirit, and culturally respectful address to their husbands, which overtly communicated the expected domestic female submission. However, it lacked similar motivation. They were to pursue this behavior in a proactive way without "giving way to fear" (1 Pet 3:6). In the culture, women

---

36. The association of the household slave with Christ through the suffering servant in Isaiah (1 Pet 2:22; Isa 53:9) may have been formative for Peter's theology.

37. David Schroeder identified the household codes as ethical teaching that identified them as part of the mission of the church in a specific social context (Schroeder, *Haustafeln*, 26). Leonhard Goppelt similarly suggests that conformity to the social institutions of society define "doing good" in the structure of that society (Goppelt, *Erste Petrusbrief*, 6, 41, 59, 177). But see MacDonald, *Early Christian Women*, for a more specific discussion of the evangelizing potential of household relations in both 1 Cor 7:12-16 and 1 Pet 3:1-6 (189-204). See also Rodney Stark's discussion of exogamous marriage and secondary conversion as well as Christian women's fertility rates in the spread of early Christianity in Stark, *Rise of Christianity*, 111-17.

38. See Plutarch, *Mor.* 140D, 144D-E. See also Balch, *Let Wives Be Submissive*, 65-80, 85, 96-97, 99.

were held to be fearful while men were held to be courageous. However, Peter equips vulnerable women to behave differentially with courage, that is, without being motivated by intimidation or worry. Significantly, the believing men are not enjoined to a complementary moral division of labor. On the contrary, they are told to live with their wives or females in a considerate way since women are vulnerable, and to give honor to their wives as fellow heirs of the grace of life.[39] The instructions both to the wife and to the husband are formally embedded along with the instructions to slaves in the general command to honor one another, so that they are specific applications as to how believers are to honor one another in relationships that are hierarchical in the culture. As in the case of slaves, women whose virtue is their shame in the Roman Empire are called to courageous mission driven by a different set of motivations and are to be awarded honor or equal value by their husbands because of their identity in Christ.[40] Peter has reversed the honor–shame language in such a way that he has shown that women in the Christian community are to be the social peers of men.

Peter offered honor to those who were dishonored in the dominant society. He offered value to slaves who were not considered to be persons. He offered honor and value to women who had no honor and relatively little social currency. It is difficult to ascertain from the text if either Peter or the readers saw his directions as subversive of the empire. After all, the text is often presented as being supportive of the Roman Empire and the governing officials. However, there is evidence that Roman culture found the Christian social status of slaves and women threatening and reprehensible.[41] Furthermore, the Christian practice

---

39. There is some question as to whether the reference that is usually translated as "wife" may rather refer to a class "the female": since γυναικεῖος (feminine, female) is used substantively rather than γυνή (woman, wife), which is used in vv. 1–6. Those who take it as a class conclude that it would refer to all of the women in the household under a man's authority. See Jobes, *1 Peter*, 207; and for example, Achtemeier, *1 Peter*, 217. However, in the larger context of honoring everyone, γυναικεῖος could also refer to all women in the Christian community.

40. See Stark's discussion on the higher status of women in Christian circles: Stark, *Rise of Christianity*, 95–128.

41. As Margaret MacDonald notes, Celsus specifically criticized the effect that Christianity had on the wider social order (MacDonald, *Early Christian Women*, 110–11). Celsus complained, "By the fact that they themselves admit that these people are worthy of their God, they show that they want and are able to convince only the foolish, dishonourable and stupid, and only slaves, women and little children" (*C. Cels.* 3.44). So

of Christian women having an intention to convert the husband and subsequent children would have been decried as subversive wherever detected, as would the evangelistic activities of slaves. Peter's teaching contributed to the attraction of women and slaves to Christianity in significant numbers. It would suggest that they recognized the non-violent active nature of the resistance.

JUDE AND 2 PETER, THE JOHANNINE EPISTLES, AND EMPIRE VALUES

At first glance, the five short epistles that precede Revelation have little to say about empire. All five address the problem of deviant disciples or false teaching within the Christian community, so the focus is internal rather than external. However, all five epistles attempt to create distance between the readers and the false teachers by depicting the false teachers as representatives of the mindset and morality of the Gentile "world" that will be judged apocalyptically.

Virtue or morality was a concern and interest of philosophers such as Plato, Xenophon, and the Stoics, and there was a great deal of ethical discourse in the Greco-Roman culture, which was reflected in speeches, inscriptions, gravesites, statues, and memorials but also in aphorisms encountered in ornaments, gymnasia, and city walls.[42] However, "the good" reflected the prevailing social expectations and ideals of the Roman Empire. The virtues that are listed honor the superiority of the upper strata and the wealthy, such as military generals, office holders, doctors, and judges, and there is a vast gulf that separates superior men from their inferiors.[43] Religious and moral self-development or progress, and social ambition for status and promotion in rank were considered virtue, though balanced in theory by moderation. As Mark Strom states, "for

---

the status/worth/honor that women and slaves found in Christianity was ridiculed. It was threatening because they took Christian teaching as the authority and basis of their lives, which undermined their traditional authorities: "But whenever [the low status Christian teachers] get hold of children in private and some stupid women with them, they let out some astounding statements, as, for example, that they must not pay any attention to their father and school-teachers, but must obey them; they say that these talk nonsense and have no understanding..." (*C. Cels.* 3.55).

42. See Charles, "Vice and Virtue Lists." For examples of ethical discourse in the Greco-Roman culture, see Hesiod, *Theog.* 77–79, 240–64; Aristophanes, *Ran.* 5.145; Seneca, *Brev. Vit.* 10.4.

43. See Carter's description of elite versus non-elite values in *Roman Empire*, 8–11.

most people, high and low, morality was shaped by their social experiences of obligation and virtue."[44] The social systems described of rank, friendship, patronage, honor, and reciprocity informed the ethical/moral behavior, prioritizing serenity, order, and stability in civic life and the household. Such a definition of morality failed to address the central Jewish moral concerns, and it accounts for some of the accusations against Christians of gross immorality and crimes against humanity. Christian condemnation of practices such as infanticide and abortion failed to conform to the family values of the Roman Empire, Christian refusal to worship the emperor was immoral because it was disloyal, and their refusal to worship local gods was a failure of one's civic duty and no less than immoral atheism.

In common with Paul, the authors of the non-Pauline epistles applied characteristic Jewish polemics against three general categories of Gentile behavior: the rejection of God (evidenced among Gentiles as the worship of false gods/idols), greed, and sexual immorality.[45] However, rather than targeting Gentiles directly, they accused the false teachers that threatened the Christian community of identifying with the world and exhibiting characteristic Gentile sins. "Many deceivers have gone out into the world" (2 John 7), "those people belong to the world" (1 John 4:5), and they speak the language of the world (1 John 4:5). As Steven Smalley argues, the "world" is "human society, temporarily controlled by the power of evil, organized in opposition to God."[46] The Roman Empire embodied the preoccupation with what is temporal and corruptible in a system that supported and attempted to control human society. Pagan authors such as Tacitus, Suetonius, Juvenal, and Seneca confirm the immorality and greed of the Greco-Roman world. By identifying the false teachers with Gentile immorality, the New Testament writers created distance between the readers and the false teachers. They also created or reflected distance between the readers and the imperial theology of the Roman Empire.

44. Strom, *Reframing Paul*, 146.

45. James Dunn explains the origins of Paul's condemnation of idolatry, greed, and sexual immorality in humankind as coming from typical Jewish polemics directed against Gentiles, such as Wis 11–15 (Dunn, *Theology of Paul*, 91–93).

46. Smalley, *1, 2, 3 John*, 81. While the "world" might be "human nature incapable of attaining to God unless it is recreated by His Spirit," and "the absence of the otherworldly" as argued by Raymond Brown, pious Judaism saw an inevitable progression from the absence of God to idolatry and immorality (Brown, *Epistles of John*, 325).

Although the authors of the five epistles did not accuse the false teachers of idol worship, they repeatedly accused them of denying Christ and, at times, of slandering celestial beings (2 Pet 2:10; Jude 8). However, in Wisdom and other Jewish polemics, idolatry originates from failing to recognize God (Wis 13). As Dunn summarizes,

> The point is that human creatures need their gods. As creatures they will always be dependent on someone or something for their fulfillment as creatures. If not God, then something altogether baser. Without God they become subservient to their own desires.[47]

For the authors of the five epistles, the denial of Jesus (2 Pet 2:1; Jude 4) or the denial of the essential nature of Jesus (1 John 2:22–23; 4:2–3; 5:10, 21; 2 John 7–9) places the false teachers on the same trajectory as the Gentiles who fail to recognize God. As 1 John 2:23 states, the failure to recognize Jesus is the failure to recognize God: "No one who denies the Son has the Father; whoever acknowledges the Son has the Father also" (cf. 2 John 7). Perhaps the essential connection between the denial of God and idolatry explains the cryptic closing of 1 John. After repeatedly confronting and exposing false teaching about the nature of Jesus, the author ends with "Dear children, keep yourself from idols" (1 John 5:21).

Jude juxtaposes sexual immorality with the denial of "Jesus Christ our only sovereign and Lord" (Jude 4) in a similar way that Wis 14:12 juxtaposes idolatry and fornication: "The idea of making idols was the origin of fornication, their discovery corrupted life." The sexual immorality of the false teachers is a particular concern of Jude. He cryptically compares their behavior to Israel after leaving Egypt, the angels who had sexual relations with women in Gen 6:1–6, and Sodom and Gomorrah (Jude 5–7). Second Peter similarly characterizes the false teachers: "their idea of pleasure is to carouse in broad daylight...With eyes full of adultery, they never stop sinning; they seduce the unstable" (2 Pet 2:13, 14; see also 2:17–18). The indictment of the culture of the empire becomes clear when Peter says that after the false teachers escaped the corruption of that world by knowing Jesus, and then again became entangled in

---

47. Dunn, *Theology of Paul*, 92. It is important to note that Dunn is describing how Paul drew his theology from the book of Wisdom, and that I am not suggesting that the authors of the non-Pauline epistles have necessarily read Paul, but that they also are drawing from Wisdom or a similar source.

it and overcome—they were dogs returning to their vomit. The world represented by the Roman Empire is equated to vomit.

In 1 John, John warns the readers not to love the world or anything in the world. The desires of the world are the cravings of sinful people, the lust of the eyes, and the pride of life (1 John 2:15–17). The confrontation of sexual immorality is woven together with the condemnation of pride and greed—and ambition was considered to be virtuous in the Roman value system. Third John was written against Diotrephes, whose desire "to be first" caused him to reject "the elder," to refuse to receive others, and even excommunicate those who did receive them (3 John 9–10). Jude cryptically compares the false teachers in their selfishness and greed with Cain and Balaam, calling them shepherds who only feed themselves. Peter accuses the false teachers of exploiting the readers in their greed (1 Pet 2:3). "They are experts in greed—an accursed brood!" who followed the way of Balaam by prophesying for pay (2 Pet 2:14–15). The false teachers are described as ambitious, selfish, and prideful, and motivated by a desire for money. Though the authors draw parallels with Old Testament figures, the behavior is consistent with the dominant culture's virtue of social ambition for status and promotion in rank.

The judgment of the false teachers' deceptions about Christ, sexual immorality, and greed would culminate in their apocalyptic destruction along with all the ungodly at the coming of Christ, which is particularly emphasized in Jude and 2 Peter (Jude 14–16; 2 Pet 2:1–10, 3:1–14). Therefore, the authors pass judgment on the Roman Empire's claim to faith, righteousness, and peace and the creed that Rome was to be an empire without end (Virgil, *Aen.* 1.279).[48]

Ethics and values are not prevalent topics in the empire genre, but this kind of confrontation of the Roman Empire in Jewish Christianity has a deep root in the Old Testament and Hebrew literature, and comes to full flower in Revelation. The idolatry, sexual immorality, and greed of the Roman Empire are primary reasons for its ultimate destruction.

HEBREWS AS A CHALLENGE TO ROMAN REALITY

Hebrews represents a distinct challenge because its author and recipients are unknown, so that reading it in the light of its context involves a

---

48. For a brief summary of imperial theology and claims of the "eternal Rome," see Carter, *Roman Empire*, 83–85, 88–89.

certain amount of speculation. However, Hebrews can be convincingly portrayed as an exhortation written by an educated Hellenistic Jew to a group or church composed of Jewish believers whose world is falling apart.[49] Their past has included public humiliation, imprisonment, and seizure of property, which indicate the shame of weakness and vulnerability within the society and a record of conflict with governing officials.[50] Now, the recipients appear to be in mortal danger. They are clearly under pressure (10:22–39), where they have *not yet* experienced bloodshed (Heb 12:4). The portrayal of humans "held in slavery by their fear of death" (Heb 2:15), and the different aspects of death that dominate ch. 11 indicate mortal danger where the recipients are desperately in need of mercy and grace in their "time of need" (Heb 4:16).[51] The author believes that they are in danger of hardening their hearts (Heb 3:7–19) by rejecting their spiritual foundation (Heb 5:11—6:6), regressing in growth (Heb 6:7–12) or sinning and rejecting God in their crisis (Heb 10:26–39). What kind of crisis could be threatening the readers? Two good suggestions for the circumstances of the readers are an imminent persecution of Christians located in Rome,[52] or the impending violence and destruction and the subsequent disruption of Jewish communities in the Eastern Empire resulting from the Jewish uprising in Palestine and the suppression of the revolt by the Roman Imperial Army between 67 and 73 CE.[53] Either choice indicates that the context

---

49. See Lane, *Hebrews 1–8*, lxi. See also Lane, "Hebrews: A Sermon in Search of a Setting," 16.

50. Luke Timothy Johnson notes their experience of shame and real physical suffering (Johnson, *Hebrews*, 33–38).

51. For the aspects of death that dominate ch. 11, see Westfall, *Discourse Analysis*, 256–57.

52. The location of the recipients in Rome comes from Heb 13:24: "Those from Italy send you their greetings." For an argument for a Roman destination, see Lane who suggests the edict of Claudius in 49 CE as the occasion (Lane, *Hebrews 1–8*, lxiii–lxvi). See also, for example, Bruce, *Hebrews*, 3–14. However, there are several other contexts that could account for this phrase, including the location of the author. It is difficult to believe that a Roman Christian community would be so totally disrupted as to lose all information about the epistle.

53. Attridge notes that a Palestinian location was the common opinion of ancient commentators and is now defended by many "moderns" (Attridge, *Hebrews*, 9). While the temple in Jerusalem was destroyed in 70 CE, Masada was not captured until 73 CE. Jewish communities were under attack, not only from the army, but also from local populations in the Eastern Empire. Jewish Christians would not be distinguished from other Jews as targets. The circumstances that caused the loss and recovery of the existence and location of the Dead Sea Scrolls offer a possible parallel.

of Hebrews anticipated a confrontation with the Roman Empire. The subsequent confrontation presumably was disruptive enough to cause the loss of all information about the epistle so that there was no tradition connected with it—one assumes that Rome won the encounter insofar as the church did not survive to tell the tale. Such disruption would be more likely linked to the disastrous impact of the revolt and suppression than persecution in Rome or the expulsion of the Jews.

However, Hebrews does not counter-attack the Roman Empire directly. Rather, the author redefines the reader's existence so that the Roman Empire does not define reality for the believer. David deSilva has done a socio-rhetorical commentary on Hebrews and outlined the rhetorical strategy where, among other things, he describes how the author is insulating the community from society's pressure.[54] As described above, honor and shame were the primary tools of social control in the ancient world. The author challenges the shame of their past experiences, first by giving them worthy models who chose a lower status (aliens and sojourners) for the sake of attaining more lasting honor and advantages, namely the promises of God (Heb 10:32—12:2). Second, the writer does it by reinterpreting the hostility of the unbelievers in a more honorable light for the persecuted: "The believers' experiences of ridicule, trial, loss of status and property, and endurance of continued reproach [are seen] as God's training or discipline of his adopted children" and part of their partnership with Christ (12:1–11).[55]

However, probably the most powerful tool the author utilizes is imagery or metaphor, where he places the believers' existence in the unseen heavenly kingdom. The nature of the imagery indicates that the readers are facing more than shame and pressure. The believers are placed in the heavenly tabernacle, and their life is depicted as running a race in the middle of a festival assembly of all the righteous and heavenly beings located in heavenly Jerusalem. In the central section of the epistle (4:11—10:25), the author has reframed the readers, existence by explaining the heavenly realities through the institutions of Judaism. The priesthood, the tabernacle, the covenant, and the law are used to describe Jesus' priesthood, the heavenly tabernacle, the new covenant, and the internal law. The familiar icons of their religious history "are vehicles that carry the readers from the familiar physical and material objects and events of

54. deSilva, *Perseverance*, 64–68.
55. Ibid., 67.

their heritage to the unseen realities behind them, and ultimately into the presence of God."[56] They are to follow Jesus into the heavenly tabernacle (10:19-22) and their worship of praise and their godly actions towards others become their priestly sacrifice (12:28; 13:13-16).[57] The believers' struggles and service are viewed as an athletic contest and priestly ministry in the context of their location in the invisible heavenly kingdom of God (12:1-29). In the light of the believers' reception of such a kingdom, and on the basis of Jesus' suffering "outside the camp," they are to "go to him outside the camp, bearing the disgrace he bore. For we do not have an enduring city, but we are looking for the city that is to come" (Heb 13:13-14).

The author has equipped the readers to negotiate their relationship with a hostile empire and the mounting hostility of Judaism. The injunction near the end to go to Jesus outside of the camp and bear the disgrace that he bore occurs with an assertion that believers have an altar that the Jewish priests (those who minister at the tabernacle) have no right to access. This would indicate a certain separation of Jewish Christians from Judaism due to increased hostility from the Jews, hence the believers share in Jesus' disgrace. If the context for Hebrews is located in or near Palestine between the revolt and the destruction of the temple, this is exactly what happened. Jewish Christians refused to take part in the revolts, whether out of teaching on non-violence or the warnings to flee to the hills in the Olivet Discourse (Matt 24:15-21). Consequently, tensions increased between Christianity and Judaism that led to the "Parting of the Ways." Jewish Christians were placed in a vulnerable and untenable position between rising Jewish opposition to Christianity and Roman retaliation against Jews that spread throughout the empire. As the people of faith in Hebrews 11 exemplify, they are never to find their status in the society of the Roman Empire—instead they are foreigners and strangers who *have* found a country of their own that will not be shaken, and who have a city "already and not yet" that rivals Rome and replaces the earthly Jerusalem. The climax of the chapter on faith indicates that the ultimate examples of faith are the people who were tortured, jeered and flogged,

---

56. Westfall, *Discourse Analysis*, 241.

57. The fact that the center of worship is always called the "tabernacle" is significant, and the discussion of the temple as a political force is relevant to Hebrews. The contemporary reader assumes a separation between church and state that was not true in the ancient world. For a discussion of the political nature of temples, see Carter, *Roman Empire*, 64-82.

imprisoned in chains, stoned, sawn in two, without clothes, destitute, persecuted, mistreated, and homeless: the world was not worthy of them (Heb 11:36–38). As far as resistance to the empire goes, the argument of Hebrews is geared to equip the believer to resist sin and endure opposition from the Roman Empire to the point of shedding blood (12:4). Rome has been denied the privilege of defining reality for believers and is stripped of the clout of its military power over anyone who values their loyalty to Jesus over their own life.

REVELATION CONFRONTING THE EMPIRE

Unlike the General Epistles and Hebrews, Revelation has been central in the empire genre. Revelation has a plethora of references and imagery that the readers would have understood as referring to the Roman Empire, so only broad generalizations will serve here in this brief summary. Revelation confronts the empire at many of the same points as each of the general epistles, running the gamut of different facets of resistance that are particularly portrayed in the letters to the seven churches. However, Revelation also dramatically confronts the military power of Rome directly. The confrontation between Christianity and Rome is finally "gloves off"—and I use the word "finally" because Revelation is located on a trajectory that represents not only Christianity's alienation and resistance to empire, but the peculiar plight of Jewish Christianity.

Revelation is the New Testament document that is most critical of the empire, and considered by the majority of recent scholars to be written at the end of the first century. The last quarter of the first century was characterized by increasing pressure on Christianity, but particularly on Jewish Christianity. Jewish Christianity was caught in the crossfire of hostility from Jews, the official actions and policies of the Roman Empire towards both Christians and Jews, and unofficial public hostility. As John Riches argues, the temple's destruction in 70 CE was a "massive shock" to the Jewish community, followed by "an urgent need to strengthen and support their community's sense of identity." This was "an acute crisis . . . clearly precipitated by the loss of one of the key markers of Jewish identity: the Temple and its cult."[58] Whatever the attitude of the Jewish author of Revelation toward the temple, the ripple effects of its destruction affected every Jew in the empire by association with the

---

58. Riches, "Introduction," 1.

community, if nothing else. One of those ripple effects was a growing alienation, rejection, and eviction of the Jewish Christians who were still living in Jewish communities all over the empire, and even attending Jewish synagogues. This provides the context for the scathing phrase "the synagogue of Satan who say they are Jews but are not" (Rev 2:9; 3:9).

In addition to Jewish hostility, the Jewish Christians were the targets of imperial and public hostility towards Jews. The Roman victory in Palestine was followed by retaliatory policies including punitive taxation that were imposed on all Jews, and being a Jewish Christian hardly made one exempt. Because of its peculiar position of being marginalized by the Jewish community, the Roman Empire, and eventually Gentile Christians who would require Jewish Christians to conform to Gentile Christianity, the voice of Jewish Christianity in Revelation represents faith on the margins better than in any other New Testament book.

Pressure to worship the emperor, and persecution from both the dominant society and Judaism, had picked up generally and are reflected in the letters to the seven churches. John was in exile in Patmos as a result of Roman authority,[59] and several passages in Revelation indicate that believers had suffered from court trials and martyrdom (Rev 2:13; 6:9–11; 16:6; 17:6; 18:24; 20:4). John also anticipated persecution (2:10; 3:10), but that may indicate a wave of public policy emanating from Rome that had not yet reached the recipients in Asia Minor, or it had not yet been implemented by the local officials. Most likely, the Domitian persecutions (reign 81–96 CE) were the precipitating crisis or the close context for Revelation, and certainly the attacks from Nero (reign 54–68 CE) cast a long shadow over the author's experience of Rome and Empire.

Revelation is a combination of genres: epistolary, prophetic, and apocalyptic in its nature, though not pseudonymous. As a letter, it was written possibly as a circular letter to seven churches in Asia Minor: Ephesus, Smyrna, Pergamum, Thyatira, Sardis, Philadelphia, and Laodicea. It is in the direct address to the recipients that the author highlights his primary concerns that are addressed in the rest of the book—the follow-

---

59. Cassidy qualifies the professed exile by Roman authority as "distinctly possible" (Cassidy, *Christians and Roman Rule*, 106). However, any exile for the sake of the gospel at this point would indicate that it was under the auspices of Roman government. Perhaps Cassidy allows that the exile could be by a local authority, but the local elite is considered here to be part of the Roman system of authority.

ing prophecy is completely relevant to the circumstances, problems, and needs of the seven churches that are articulated in Revelation 2–3. The author is concerned about all of the issues of conflict with the empire that Hebrews and the General Epistles confront and more. The remarks to the seven churches demonstrate a serious concern with pressure and compromise including issues of poverty (Rev 2:8–9), materialism (Rev 3:17–18), attacks through slander, rejection, persecution, imprisonment and martyrdom (Rev 2:9b–10, 13), idolatry (Rev 2:14b, 20b), and sexual immorality (Rev 2:14a, 20–23).[60] These issues are addressed throughout the subsequent prophecy primarily by its barely veiled indictment of and prediction of future destruction of the Roman Empire and the victory and sovereignty of God and Jesus Christ over all competition. John's pervasive use of Old Testament allusions brings forward not only the Judaic expectations of deliverance and the Day of the Lord, but also associate the Roman Empire with the line of imperial power and oppression throughout the Old Testament, specifically including Babylon, but also other empires such as Assyria, Greece, and Persia.

Revelation is apocalyptic in the use of compositional styles, which include a narrative framework, recapitulation, dualism, angelic mediation, complex imagery, and the extensive use of symbols including numerology. The genre had been popular for approximately three hundred years, and examples include *2 Enoch*, selections from the Dead Sea Scrolls, *4 Ezra*, *2 Baruch* and *Sib. Or.* 5, and also parts of Ezekiel and Daniel.[61] According to Paul Hanson, the use of the apocalyptic genre occurs within an oppressive social, political, and economic situation when "any effort at reform based on the standards of justice and compassion associated with God's reign are repulsed by violence and persecution."[62] It is political by nature, and often the symbolism is a cryptic coded message of hope and liberation that is written in such an obscure way that it shields the true meaning from the oppressors.[63] However, John's references to Rome are transparent, and probably the genre is used for its

60. Again, notice the close association of sexual immorality and idolatry.

61. See a discussion of the apocalyptic roots of Revelation in Howard-Brook and Gwyther, *Unveiling Empire*, 46–86. See also Collins, "Apocalyptic Literature."

62. Hanson, "Prophetic and Apocalyptic Politics," 57.

63. This is Norman Beck's more general definition of "cryptograms," which are more general symbols that he finds throughout the New Testament (Beck, *Anti-Roman Cryptograms*). See Beck's analysis of the background and content of Revelation in 133–39.

"intrinsic evocative power" rather than to keep the criticism of Rome secret.[64] Who could miss the reference to the whore of Babylon sitting on seven hills (Rev 17:9)?[65] The readers were used to numerology and probably interpreted the number of the beast (666) as referring to Nero (Rev 13:18), perhaps indicating that Nero's crimes were being repeated by Domitian so as to identify him as a type of Nero.[66] But more than that, in a context where Rome was considered to be eternal and invincible, all of the references to social, political, economic, and military power would have been read in a Roman context.

The imagery and symbols of the prophecy would have been understood by the readers and the Roman authorities as criticism of Rome, and the prediction of its destruction came at the height of its power.[67] The criticism includes Roman economic exploitation and materialism (Rev 13:6; ch. 18), persecution and martyrdom of believers, as well as general violence toward humanity (Rev 6:9–10; 16:6; 17:6; 18:24), and blasphemy and idolatry (which are associated with sexual immorality) (Rev 13:5–6; 13:12b–14; 18:7b).[68] Therefore, the responsibility for the challenges that the seven churches faced is placed on the Roman Empire and the origin of the empire was demonic (Rev 12:9–17; 13:2b, 4). God responds to Rome's abuses with a series of destructions including earthquake, fire, plague, famine, internal conflict, violence, and Christ at the head of a heavenly army. The climax of the predictions of Rome's destruction occurs in the lament in Revelation 18: "Fallen! Fallen is Babylon the Great!" (Rev 18:2). A catalogue of Rome's crimes as the political and economic hub of the "earth" follows. Imperial triumphalistic theology and power is pitted directly against the power, sovereignty, and victory of God in Christ. They are competing kingdoms with conflicting claims.

The seven churches are called to resist the Roman Empire on every front in which they are challenged without compromise. They are not called to guerilla warfare or accommodation to the evils of the culture,

---

64. So states Collins, *Crisis and Catharsis*, 124. See also Beck, *Anti-Roman Cryptograms*, 138–39.

65. As Aune, *Revelation 17–22*, 944–45, states, it "would be instantly recognizable as a metaphor for Rome."

66. See David Aune's discussion in *Revelation 6–16*, 770–73.

67. See Collins, "Satan's Throne."

68. See Cassidy's brief description of Revelation's criticism of Rome in *Christians and Roman Rule*, 109–14.

but to the salvation that lies with God alone. Loyalty to God involves overcoming the considerable hardships, persecution, suffering and death, not tolerating wickedness, idolatry and sexual immorality, and fleeing or "coming out" of the power structures and materialism of Rome:

> Come out of her, my people,
> So that you do not share in her sins,
> So that you will not receive any of her plagues.
> For her sins are piled up to heaven,
> And God will remember her crimes. (Rev 18:4–5)

The seven churches are offered hope and liberation by the apocalyptic message, but perhaps not in the way we would intuitively expect. Along with promises to those who overcome, there is a radical call to repentance, and a disturbing recognition that believers are caught up in entangling alliances with the empire. The resistance to Rome begins with self-examination and self-denial of the churches as a whole and individuals within the churches in the areas of materialism, violence, idolatry, and immorality (cf. Rev 22:10–16). There is no triumphalistic escape from suffering, persecution, and possible death in this life, there is only loyalty to God at any price.

While the readers would have understood the prophecy as referring to the Roman Empire, it is clear that the second coming of Jesus did not occur with the end of the Roman Empire. Some have concluded that Rome could not have been the referent of the prophecy, and virtually each generation has suggested its own identity of the beast/antichrist, and declared the previous generation as mistaken. However, the message is more about encouragement to believers and how they respond to the pressures that they face—Revelation is particularly written to give hope to people who are besieged, marginalized, and oppressed. Rome represents oppressive ungodly power wherever it is located. The believers' response to injustice, persecution, immorality, idolatry, and wickedness should be no compromise.

CONCLUSION

Jewish Christianity may provide the clearest resistance to the Roman Empire in the New Testament. It drew directly from the traditions of Judaism and the relationship of Judaism with the past empires including Egypt, Assyria, Babylon, Persia, and Greece. Jewish Christianity occupied an increasingly difficult position as hostility built between the Roman Empire and Christianity, pressure built between the Roman Empire and Judaism, and alienation built between Jewish Christians and Jews. Therefore, the challenges that Jewish Christianity faced and addressed are particularly informative in understanding how the early Christians resisted the pressures from the Roman Empire. James addressed economic issues including exploitation, materialism, and poverty; 1 Peter secured honor and dignity for the powerless; 2 Peter, Jude, 1, 2, and 3 John stressed the ethics and values that set God's kingdom apart; and Hebrews challenged the Roman view of reality and kingdom. Revelation addressed the spectrum of issues in the other books, but was sharpened by persecution and martyrdom. John held the Roman Empire responsible for idolatry, blasphemy, sexual immorality, persecution, exploitation, and materialism. The Roman Empire was described as in competition with God's sovereignty and would be destroyed. The believer's response to an oppressive empire begins with personal repentance that disassociates from the patterns of abuse and includes non-violent active resistance. Positively, believers find their position, value, and reality in the kingdom of God.

BIBLIOGRAPHY

Achtemeier, P. J. *1 Peter*. Hermeneia. Minneapolis: Fortress, 1996.
Adamson, *The Epistle of James*. NICNT. Grand Rapids: Eerdmans, 1995.
Alföldy, Géza. *The Social History of Rome*. Totowa, NJ: Barnes & Noble, 1985.
Attridge, Harold W. *The Epistle to the Hebrews*. Hermeneia. Philadelphia: Fortress, 1989.
Aune, David E. *Revelation 6–16*. WBC. Nashville: Nelson, 1998.
———. *Revelation 17–22*. WBC. Nashville: Nelson, 1993.
Balch, David L. *Let Wives Be Submissive: The Domestic Code in 1 Peter*. SBLMS 26. Atlanta: Scholars, 1981.
Barton, S. C. "Social Values and Structures." In *Dictionary of New Testament Background*, edited by Craig A. Evans and Stanley E. Porter, 1127–34. Downers Grove, IL: InterVarsity, 2000.
Beck, Norman A. *Anti-Roman Cryptograms in the New Testament: Symbolic Messages of Hope and Liberation*. New York: Lang, 1997.
Blomberg, Craig L. *Jesus and the Gospels*. Nashville: Broadman & Holman, 1997.
———. *Neither Poverty nor Riches: A Biblical Theology of Possessions*. Downers Grove, IL: InterVarsity, 1999.
Brown, Raymond E. *The Epistles of John: Translated with Introduction, Notes and Commentary*. AB. New York: Doubleday, 1982.
Bruce, F. F. *The Epistle to the Hebrews*. Grand Rapids: Eerdmans, 1990.
Campbell, Barth L. *Honor, Shame and the Rhetoric of 1 Peter*. SBLDS 160. Atlanta: Scholars, 1998.

Carter, W. "Proclaiming (in/against) Empire Then and Now." *Word & World* 25.2 (2005) 149–58.

———. *The Roman Empire and the New Testament: An Essential Guide.* Nashville: Abingdon, 2006.

Cassidy, Richard J. *Christians and Roman Rule in the New Testament: New Perspectives.* Companions to the New Testament. New York: Crossroad, 2001.

Charles, J. D. "Vice and Virtue Lists." In *Dictionary of New Testament Background*, edited by Craig A. Evans and Stanley E. Porter, 1252–57. Downers Grove, IL: InterVarsity, 2000.

Collins, Adela Yarbro. *Crisis and Catharsis: The Power of the Apocalypse.* Philadelphia: Westminster, 1984.

———. "Satan's Throne: Revelations from Revelation." *BAR* 32.3 (May/June 2006) 26–39.

Collins, J. J. "Apocalyptic Literature." In *Dictionary of New Testament Background*, edited by Craig A. Evans and Stanley E. Porter, 40–45. Downers Grove, IL: InterVarsity, 2000.

Davids, Peter. *The Epistle of James.* NIGTC. Grand Rapids: Eerdmans, 1982.

deSilva, David A. "Honor and Shame." In *Dictionary of New Testament Background*, edited by Craig A. Evans and Stanley E. Porter, 518–22. Downers Grove, IL: InterVarsity, 2000.

———. Patronage." In *Dictionary of New Testament Background*, edited by Craig A. Evans and Stanley E. Porter, 766–71. Downers Grove, IL: InterVarsity, 2000.

———. *Perseverance in Gratitude: A Socio-Rhetorical Commentary on the Epistle "to the Hebrews."* Grand Rapids: Eerdmans, 2000.

Duling, Dennis C. "Empire: Theories, Methods, Models." In *The Gospel of Matthew in Its Roman Imperial Context*, edited by John Riches and David C. Sim, 49–74. JSNTSup 276. London: T. & T. Clark, 2005.

Dunn, James D. G. *The Theology of Paul the Apostle.* Grand Rapids: Eerdmans, 1998.

———. *Unity and Diversity in the New Testament: An Inquiry into the Character of Earliest Christianity.* 2nd ed. Harrisburg, PA: Trinity Press International, 1990.

Dyson, S. "Native Revolts in the Roman Empire." *Historia* 20 (1971) 239–74.

Goppelt, Leonhard. *Der Erste Petrusbrief.* MeyerK. Göttingen: Vandenhoeck & Ruprecht, 1978.

Hanson, Paul D. "Prophetic and Apocalyptic Politics." In *The Last Things: Biblical and Theological Perspectives on Eschatology*, edited by Carl E. Braaten and Robert W. Jenson, 43–66. Grand Rapids: Eerdmans, 2002.

Harrill, J. A. "Slavery." In *Dictionary of New Testament Background*, edited by Craig A. Evans and Stanley E. Porter, 1124–27. Downers Grove, IL: InterVarsity, 2000.

Howard-Brook, Wes, and Anthony Gwyther. *Unveiling Empire: Reading Revelation Then and Now.* Maryknoll, NY: Orbis, 1999.

Jobes, Karen H. *1 Peter.* BECNT. Grand Rapids: Baker, 2005.

Johnson, Luke Timothy. *Hebrews: A Commentary.* NTL. Louisville: Westminster John Knox, 2006.

Keener, Craig. *Bible Background Commentary: New Testament.* Downers Grove, IL: InterVarsity, 1993.

———. "Family and Household." In *Dictionary of New Testament Background*, edited by Craig A. Evans and Stanley E. Porter, 353–68. Downers Grove, IL: InterVarsity, 2000.

Lane, William L. *Hebrews 1–8.* WBC. Dallas: Word, 1991.
———. "Hebrews: A Sermon in Search of a Setting." *SWJT* 28 (1985) 13–18.
MacDonald, Margaret E. *Early Christian Women and Pagan Opinion: The Power of the Hysterical Woman.* Cambridge: Cambridge University Press, 1996.
———. "Slavery, Sexuality and House Churches." *NTS* 53 (2007) 94–113.
Martin, Ralph P. *James.* WBC. Waco, TX: Word, 1988.
Martin, Troy W. *Metaphor and Composition in 1 Peter.* SBLDS 131. Atlanta: Scholars, 1992.
Maynard-Reid, Pedrito U. *Poverty and Wealth in James.* Maryknoll, NY: Orbis, 1987.
Riches, John. "Introduction." In *The Gospel of Matthew in Its Roman Imperial Context*, edited by John Riches and David C. Sim, 1–8. JSNTSup 276. London: T. & T. Clark, 2005.
Schroeder, David. *Die Haustafeln des Neuen Testaments.* Grundrisse zum Neuen Testament 4. Göttingen: Vandenhoeck & Ruprecht, 1982.
Smalley, Steven S. *1, 2, 3 John.* WBC. Waco, TX: Word, 1984.
Stark, Rodney. *The Rise of Christianity.* San Francisco: HarperSanFrancisco, 1997.
Strom, Mark. *Reframing Paul: Conversations in Grace and Community.* Downers Grove, IL: InterVarsity, 2000.
Tamez, Elsa. *The Scandalous Message of James: Faith without Works Is Dead.* New York: Crossroad, 1985.
Walsh, Brian J., and Sylvia Keesmaat. *Colossians Remixed: Subverting the Empire.* Downers Grove, IL: InterVarsity, 2004.
Westfall, Cynthia Long. *A Discourse Analysis of the Letter to the Hebrews: The Relationship between Form and Meaning.* London: T. & T. Clark, 2005.
———. "The Hebrew Mission: Voices from the Margin?" In *Christian Mission: Old Testament Foundations and New Testament Developments*, edited by Stanley E. Porter and Cynthia Long Westfall, 187–207. MNTS. Eugene, OR: Pickwick, 2010.
———. "The Relationship between the Resurrection, the Proclamation to the Spirits in Prison and Baptismal Regeneration: 1 Peter 3.19–22." In *Resurrection*, edited by Stanley E. Porter, Michael A. Hayes, and David Tombs, 106–35. JSNTSup 186. Sheffield: Sheffield Academic, 1999.

9

The Church Fathers and the Roman Empire

GORDON L. HEATH

IN HIS RECENT BOOK on the history of the British Empire, *Empire: The Rise and Demise of the British World Order and the Lessons for Global Power* (2003), Niall Ferguson identifies obvious parallels between the British Empire at the peak of its power and the United States today. He goes on to claim "in truth, there is only one power capable of playing an imperial role in the modern world, and that is the United States. Indeed, to some degree it is already playing that role."[1] Such parallels are interesting, and the call for America to take up the mantle of imperial power—for the benefit of the world—is highly provocative and contentious.[2]

Just what is a Christian to think about empire? The essays in this book are timely, for they compel us to look once again at the New Testament writings for guidance, texts that were written at the height of one of the greatest empires the world has ever seen. I consider it a privilege to be able to present a brief response to these provocative and insightful papers, but to be honest, I also come with fear and trepidation. I am not a biblical scholar. I am a historian. My discipline is usually more concerned with Acts 29 and following than with the contents of the Old and New Testaments. However, despite my lack of qualifications with

---

1. Ferguson, *Empire*, 367.

2. The following are just a few of the numerous works critiquing U.S. foreign policy, especially as it relates to notions of empire: Albright and Woodward, *Mighty and the Almighty*; Chapman, "Imperial Exegesis"; Mandelbaum, *Case for Goliath*; Northcott, *Angel Directs the Storm*; Singer, *President of Good and Evil*.

regards to the discipline of biblical studies, I am a historian interested in imperialism and Christianity.

Because of my obvious bias for the study of history, my focus in this response will be to survey briefly the earliest church fathers' attitudes to the Roman Empire.[3] My rationale is simple: these papers make specific claims about the biblical authors and empire. I want to use the church fathers as a foil to the claims being made in these essays, and to use the Church fathers' responses to empire as clues as to how the earliest Christians understood empire.

PRESENTATIONS

While much of post-Holocaust New Testament studies has dealt with Paul's relationship to Judaism,[4] a great deal of the contemporary literature on empire and the New Testament has been shaped by post-Christendom attitudes and assumptions, as well as by the breakup of Western empires. The disestablishment of the church, and an increasingly post-Christian *Zeitgeist* in the West, has led to many questioning the assumptions that undergirded the old religious establishment. The postwar breakup of European empires, once deemed to be providentially established to civilize and Christianize the world, has also led to an outpouring of Edward Said-like criticisms of Western imperialism and even of the idea of empire itself.[5] The rise and development of Liberation Theology and the emphasis on *praxis* contributed to the growing consensus that the New Testament Jesus could not be used as a supporter of repressive systems or empires. In fact, it was claimed, revolutionaries had more in common with Jesus than did the powerful established churches. For instance, John Howard Yoder notes in his *The Politics of Jesus* (1972) that the 1960s radicals saw Jesus more like themselves than as a supporter of the elites.[6] The time was ripe for people to take a fresh new look at Jesus, and to

---

3. I realize that there are numerous other texts that do not belong to the orthodox tradition, such as the various Gnostic writings. While many of those writings self-identify as Christian, this response will not focus on them. Of course, the Gnostic view of empire would be an interesting topic for a future study.

4. See Horsley, *Paul and the Roman Imperial Order*, 1–2.

5. Said, *Orientalism*, is a "classic" in post-colonial studies.

6. Yoder, *Politics of Jesus*, 11.

proclaim a Jesus that was radically different from the dominant one that had been presented for over a thousand years.[7]

Recent scholarship maintains this trajectory. Over the past two decades or so, a number of books have been published on the Roman Empire and the New Testament.[8] Klaus Wengst's *Pax Romana and the Peace of Jesus Christ* (1987) pointed out that the imminence of the kingdom of God challenged the assumptions of the *pax Romana*. Neil Elliott's *Liberating Paul: The Justice of God and the Politics of the Apostle* (1994) provocatively outlined the political implications of Paul's theology. More recently, Richard Horsley[9] and Warren Carter[10] have led the way with numerous books and articles that explore the political implications of the contents of the New Testament. William R. Herzog II, John Dominic Crossan, Jonathan L. Reed, Anthony Gwyther, Wes Howard-Brook, Ched Myers, Norman Beck, Gary Gilbert, Richard Cassidy, and numerous others have also begun to take seriously the contention that the New Testament writings have a great deal to say about politics and empire, then and now.[11]

The papers in this volume continue this trajectory. While they are certainly not as outspoken as Horsley when he critiques the "depoliticized Jesus of American imperial culture"[12] or as inflammatory as Elliott when he refers to the "Pauline legacy as an ideological weapon of death,"[13] they all agree that the canonical writings contain material that addresses imperial concerns. The first two papers illustrate how empire building for human aggrandizement was frowned upon in the Old Testament. The papers on various New Testament books all argue

---

7. For instance, see Brandon, *Jesus and the Zealots*; Griffiths, *New Testament and the Roman State*.

8. Conferences have also dealt with the subject. For instance, the panel topic "Paul and the Roman Imperial Order" was a part of the 2000 Annual Meeting of the Society of Biblical Literature.

9. Horsley, ed., *Paul and Empire*; Horsley, ed., *Paul and Politics*; Horsley, *Jesus and Empire*; Horsley, ed., *Paul and the Roman Imperial Order*.

10. Carter, *Matthew and Empire*; Carter, *Roman Empire*.

11. Herzog, *Parables*; Herzog, *Jesus, Justice, and the Reign of God*; Crossan and Reed, *In Search of Paul*; Gwyther and Howard-Brook, *Unveiling Empire*; Myers, *Binding the Strong Man*; Beck, *Anti-Roman Cryptograms*; Gilbert, "List of Nations"; Cassidy, *Christians and Roman Rule*; Cassidy, *John's Gospel in New Perspective*.

12. Horsley, *Jesus and Empire*, 148.

13. Elliott, *Liberating Paul*, 9.

that there is a great deal of imperial material in the canonical writings, and some contend that, to use the words of Carter, the "Roman Empire comprises not the New Testament background but its foreground" (p. 90). The claims made range from the biblical authors merely using imperial imagery to express Christian convictions to the biblical authors making covert, subversive statements to undermine claims of Roman hegemony (with some papers arguing for a bit of both). But, as noted above, my intention is to examine briefly the earliest church fathers' view of empire as a foil to these claims.

THE CHURCH FATHERS

The typical "decline paradigm" in church history is that the church lost its pristine purity after Emperor Constantine's profession of faith and the subsequent Christianization of the Roman Empire in the fourth century. As noted above, contemporary scholars assume and claim that the New Testament writers were opposed to empire. But were the earliest Christians as anti-empire as recent scholars claim? And was the supportive posture towards the empire after Constantine that much of a shift from the attitudes of the earliest church fathers about the empire? This response argues that, if the church fathers are any indication, in both cases the answer is no.

Roland Bainton notes that there was an element of criticism of Rome in early Christian literature (he argues that this was one of the reasons for early Christian pacifism). But that criticism did not include an outright rejection of the benefits of Roman rule.

> The Patristic judgment upon the empire was qualified.... Christian apologists, in order to parry the charge of calamity-bringing so often leveled against their religion, quarried in the classical literature which recorded and bemoaned Roman decadence. Tertullian and Minucius Felix took over from Horace the contention that the fratricide of Romulus had injected a virus of corruption into the Roman blood stream, while Lactantius borrowed from Sallust the theme that Rome by destroying Carthage lost the stimulus of rivalry and fell prey to dissension, cruelty, ambition, pursuit of luxury, and debauchery. The process by which Roman rule had been acquired was subjected to scathing denunciation. ... At the same time, the early Church did not follow the book of

Revelation in identifying Rome with Antichrist. The blessings of the Roman peace were appreciated.[14]

This appreciation that Bainton is referring to was two centuries before Constantine. The following two sections briefly illustrate the tension in the writings of the church fathers. As will be seen below, there are examples that indicate that they supported and appreciated the empire, but there are also examples that indicate that such appreciation did not mean that they were blindly subservient to the imperial powers.

Supportive of the Empire

Use of Military Metaphors

While it seems that the New Testament ideal was non-violence (Matt 5–7), the treatment of Roman military personnel and the use of military metaphors is interesting. Jesus praised the centurion (Matt 8:5–13), John the Baptist did not order soldiers to quit service (Luke 3:14), Peter baptized the centurion Cornelius (Acts 10), and Paul was silent about the jailer who became converted (Acts 16). John described visions of war (and a violent Christ at that) in Revelation. Paul used metaphors of soldiers in Eph 6:10–17 and 2 Tim 2:3. As Harnack notes, there are numerous military references in the earliest Christian writings:

> We find in the earliest Christian writings all of the following: the soldier, weapons of various kinds, wages (cf. the serious word of Rom. 6:23, "The wages of sin is death"), discipline, the wreath, gifts (*donativa*), imprisonment, pillage, fortification, bulwark, military onslaughts, and the heretics, who like cunning foes sneak into the houses and take away women as captives (2 Tim. 3:6).[15]

Clement of Rome (ca. 95–100 CE) continued the use of military metaphors. In *1 Clement* he urged his Christian audience to "act the part of soldiers" who served under generals.[16] Clement of Alexandria (ca. 150–215) used the military metaphor "soldiers of peace"[17] and referred

---

14. Bainton, *Historical Survey*, 74–75.
15. Harnack, *Militia Christi*, 39.
16. *1 Clem.* 37. Unless noted otherwise, all references in footnotes to early Christian writings below are from Roberts and Donaldson, eds., *Ante-Nicene Fathers*.
17. Clement of Alexandria, *Protr.* 11.

to Jesus as the "great General" and "Commander-in-chief."[18] Tertullian (ca. 155–ca. 240) paralleled the Christian life with life in the Roman military.[19]

These references did not create a militaristic community that acted out the violent images of Revelation: the earliest Christians did not take up the sword when persecuted. Nevertheless, Adolf Harnack argues that this use of military imagery had a logic of its own and shaped opinions and attitudes over the centuries. At the very least, it seems that these references indicate that there was not an outright rejection or condemnation of Roman imperial military life.

References to the Old Testament

The essays presented here from the Old Testament argue that the example of David and the teaching of the prophet Isaiah are decidedly anti-empire. While that may be the case, Tertullian used Old Testament examples to provide guidance for working within an imperial context, not to condemn the idea of imperialism or the political reality of the empire.[20]

Roman rule and Roman military life were considered by Tertullian to be riddled with idolatry, and he considered such idolatry to be a "principal crime of the human race."[21] In *On Idolatry* he provided instruction for Christians in the midst of pagan festivals by pointing out some Old Testament examples of people who lived in a similar context. Tertullian pointed to Shadrach, Meshach, and Abednego in Babylon who were obedient to the ruler but drew the line at idolatry.[22] He also noted Daniel's submission to Darius, as long as he could be free in the practice of his religion.[23] The general principle was that Christians should be subject to "magistrates, princes and powers" so long as they kept themselves "sepa-

---

18. Clement of Alexandria, *Paed.* 8.

19. Tertullian, *Mart.* 3.

20. While the example provided here is from Tertullian and his concern for idolatry, Clement of Alexandria's praise for Moses' prowess as a great military leader is another example of how the Old Testament was not necessarily read for its anti-imperial sentiments. See Clement of Alexandria, *Strom.* 1.24. Louis J. Swift notes that Old Testament references to God-sanctioned warfare made it difficult for the church fathers to reject all forms of warfare. See Swift, *Early Fathers on War*, 20–21.

21. Tertullian, *Idol.* 1.

22. Ibid., 15.

23. Ibid.

rate from idolatry."[24] In regards to what offices Christians could hold, Tertullian pointed out that while the Patriarchs Joseph or Daniel may have served kings without committing idolatry, it would be very hard to do so in the Roman Empire.[25] Nevertheless, he did not completely rule out the possibility.

Positive Actions and Statements

The above examples suggest an attitude to the empire that was not explicitly hostile. Even taking into account rhetorical flourish and apologetic aims,[26] the following examples of overt actions and statements show that the earliest church fathers (and at least some early Christians) had quite a positive view of the empire.

One important piece of evidence to consider is the account of Christians serving in the Roman army, and the response of the church fathers to such service. Certainly not all Christians supported such a practice, least of all Tertullian who wrote *On the Crown* against such a practice. Before the 170s there is no evidence of Christians serving in the Roman Army. Since slaves could not serve in the army, nor could Jews, one can see why the early church, composed largely of Jews, slaves, and women, did not have to confront the problem of Christians in the army.[27] By the 170s, however, there is an account of Christians serving in the "Thundering Legion" of Marcus Aurelius.[28] The story is told by Eusebius in his *Ecclesiastical History* of how Christians in the legion prayed and the army was rescued by a thunderstorm (other accounts say

---

24. Ibid.

25. Ibid., 17.

26. For a discussion of the uses of rhetoric among the church fathers, see Sider, *Ancient Rhetoric*; Kinzig, "Greek Christian Writers"; Satterthwaite, "Latin Church Fathers."

27. Cadoux, *Early Christian Attitude to War*, 16. During this time Christians were also too small a movement to even begin to think about being in a position of power and influence, and thus had no need to determine their view on the subject. See Swift, *Early Fathers on War*, 29.

28. Edward Ryan argues that the changing conditions in the empire (large-scale military operations, declining population that made recruits scarce, Rome on the defensive, and everything being at stake) led to pressure on Christians to serve. See Ryan, "Rejection of Military Service," 12.

an Egyptian magician saved the army).²⁹ The column of Marcus Aurelius contains the account of the Thundering Legion.³⁰

As noted above, Tertullian argued in *On the Crown* against service in the military (his primary objection was that there was too much idolatry in the military for a Christian to serve). However, Clement of Alexandria stated that after conversion, soldiers, like sailors and farmers, were to continue in their service and obey their commander.³¹ Here we have two opposing statements by two church fathers.

By the third century numerous accounts of military martyrs such as Marinus (260), Maximilian (295), Marcellus (298), Dasius (303), Tipasius the Veteran (303), and Julius the Veteran (303) indicate the increasing numbers of Christians serving in the army. Military inscriptions also indicate that Christians served in the army prior to Constantine.³²

In these cases it appears that some Christians did not see the New Testament as being necessarily anti-empire. While their presence in the military may have led to criticism, the church fathers' statements on the blessings of empire and the necessity of Christian support for the empire no doubt contributed to the conviction that it was acceptable to serve in the army. It is to these statements that we now turn.

Clement of Rome stated that Christians were loyal to the emperor and empire and prayed for stability and for wisdom for the emperor.³³ Polycarp declared that the imperial rulers were "ordained of God" and needed to be honored.³⁴ Justin Martyr (ca. 100–ca. 165) stated that Christians were loyal citizens and prayed for the emperor.³⁵ Irenaeus (ca. 130–ca. 200) stated that the ruling authorities were established by

---

29. Eusebius, *Hist. eccl.* 5.5.

30. For further discussion of this account, see Fowden, "Pagan Versions"; Rubin, "Weather Miracles."

31. Clement of Alexandria, *Protr.* 10.

32. Helgeland, "Christians in the Roman Army," 161.

33. *1 Clem.* 60–61. (The *Ante-Nicene Fathers* set does not have 60–61—see Clarke, *First Epistle of Clement*.) "[G]rant that we may be obedient to thy almighty and excellent name, and to our governors and rulers on earth. Thou, Lord, hast given them the authority of the Kingdom by thy excellent and unutterable might, that we . . . may be subject to them, in no respect opposing thy will. To them, Lord, grant health, peace, concord, stability, that they may administer the rule given them by thee without offence."

34. *Mart. Pol.* 10.

35. Justin, *1 Apol.* 17.

God, and that all must submit to their authority.[36] He also claimed that God had established such authorities due to the need to restrain sin, and gave the sword to the governing authorities so that the fear of the sword would bring about a degree of justice.

> Earthly rule, therefore, has been appointed by God for the benefit of nations, and not by the devil, who is never at rest at all, nay, who does not love to see even nations conducting themselves after a quiet manner, so that under the fear of human rule, men may not eat each other up like fishes; but that, by means of the establishment of laws, they may keep down an excess of wickedness among the nations. And considered from this point of view, those who exact tribute from us are "God's ministers, serving for this very purpose."[37]

This argument, it should be noted, was made in response to Gnostic claims that the powers of the world—Rome included—were created by the devil. Irenaeus opposed such a view and defended the position that God had established ruling authorities—Rome included—and because of that they must be obeyed.

Cyprian of Carthage (d. 258) expressed the inevitability of war,[38] stated that the decline of military forces within the empire was a sign of God's punishment,[39] and prayed for the success of the imperial armies in warding off enemies.[40] Origen's (ca. 185–ca. 254) response to Celsus, a pagan philosopher and critic of Christians, was also sympathetic to the empire.[41] Celsus accused the Christians of being parasites because they did not fight for the Roman Empire, but still benefited from its armies. Origen's response was that Christians were loyal and that the Christian vocation was different from the pagan vocation: pagans were involved in temporal warfare, but Christians were involved in spiritual warfare, and exercised a "priesthood" on behalf of the empire. In this regard, there was a co-ordination between the *pax Romana* and the *pax Christiana*.

---

36. Irenaeus, *Haer.* 5.24. In 4.36 Irenaeus provided the same interpretation of Romans 13.

37. Irenaeus, *Haer.* 5.24.

38. Cyprian, *On Morality* 2.

39. Cyprian, *Demetr.* 3, 17.

40. Ibid., 20.

41. This summary of Origen's response to Celsus is taken from Campenhausen, "Christians and Military Service," 165–67.

Origen also understood the empire to have been providentially arranged so that the gospel could more easily be preached.[42] What happens, Celsus asked, when everyone becomes a Christian and no one will fight in the army? Origen had no real answer. For him the idea of everyone (or the majority) being Christian was not really foreseeable.

Perhaps the one writer who best demonstrates the differences between contemporary attitudes to empire and early Christian attitudes to empire is Tertullian. Tertullian has been coined the first Puritan for his commitment to a pure and biblical church, one not tainted by idolatry and philosophy (he is the one who stated "what does Jerusalem have to do with Athens?"). He noted in his *Apology* that, while Christians could not profess Caesar to be god-like in any way, they did offer prayers for the emperor.

> Without ceasing, for all our emperors we offer prayer. We pray for life prolonged; for security to the empire; for protection to the imperial house; for brave armies, a faithful senate, a virtuous people, the world at rest, whatever, as man or Caesar, an emperor would wish.[43]

As for those who claimed the Christians' prayers were faked in order to escape persecution, he said that there were two reasons for such prayers to be sincere. First, Christians were enjoined by their Scriptures to pray for their rulers. His reference was to 2 Tim 2:2 and the admonition to pray for kings, rulers, and powers.[44] Second, he also noted how there was another reason for Christian prayers for the empire: the empire was holding back disaster.

> There is another and a greater necessity for our offering prayer in behalf of the emperors, nay, for the complete stability of the empire, and for Roman interests in general. For we know that a mighty shock impending over the whole earth—in fact, the very end of all things threatening dreadful woes—is only retarded by the continued existence of the Roman empire. We have no desire, then, to be overtaken by these dire events; and in praying that their coming may be delayed, we are lending our aid to Rome's duration.[45]

---

42. Origen, *Cels.* 2.30.
43. Tertullian, *Apol.* 30.
44. Ibid., 31.
45. Ibid., 32. Athenagoras, *Leg.* 32 (ca. 177) echoes this concern for the benefits of

As one commentator puts it, Tertullian believed that Christians were citizens like any other citizen (in fact, because of their high moral caliber, he considered them to be better citizens than most), and in Tertullian's opinion the "Roman State is *their* State; that which damages the State also damages them; that which is beneficial to the State is beneficial to them also."[46] As for the emperor, Tertullian argued that Christians held him in "reverence and sacred respect" and that he was "called by ... [the] Lord to his office."[47] In fact, he went so far as to say that "Caesar is more ours than yours" since it was the Christian God who "appointed him" to his office.[48] Tertullian was even willing to call him Lord, but only in what he called "the common acceptance of the word," not when it meant "Lord as in God's place."[49] In Tertullian's other writings we see the same attitude to the Roman authorities. In *On Idolatry* he referred to Romans 13, 1 Pet 2:13–14, and Titus 3:1 when he urged his readers to obey the authorities (note that he did not make a distinction between "qualitatively superior authorities," something that Porter claims Paul was doing in Romans 13).[50] As noted above, however, this obedience ended when idolatry was required. When he wrote *To Scapula* in order to address the persecution of Christians, he reminded the Roman governor that the Roman authorities had nothing to fear from Christians, for the

> Christian is enemy to none, least of all to the Emperor of Rome, whom he knows to be appointed by his God, and so cannot but love and honour; and whose well-being moreover, he must needs desire, with that of the empire over which he reigns so long as the world shall stand—for so long as that shall Rome continue.[51]

He went on to say that Christians sacrificed for the safety of the emperor and prayed for the well-being of the empire.

Rome: "For who are more deserving to obtain the things they ask, than those who, like us, pray for your government, that you may, as is most equitable, receive the kingdom, son from father, and that your empire may receive increase and addition, all men becoming subject to your sway? And this is also for our advantage, that we may lead a peaceable and quiet life, and may ourselves readily perform all that is commanded us."

46. As quoted in Swift, *Early Fathers on War*, 24.
47. Tertullian, *Apol.* 33.
48. Ibid.
49. Ibid., 34.
50. Tertullian, *Idol.* 15.
51. Tertullian, *Scap.* 2.

What is noteworthy about Tertullian's view of empire is that his primary concern was idolatry—not empire *per se*. Not surprisingly, he also did not seem to envision the possibility of any other political reality but empire. D. R. Griffiths notes that the New Testament writers had a very different view of empire than we do today. He writes:

> The New Testament writers lived under an autocratic government in which they themselves had no semblance of political power or responsibility. The choice between them was acceptance of the Roman Empire or anarchy and chaos. There were certain features in the life of the Empire which proved helpful for the diffusion of Christianity... These aspects of contemporary life were accepted by the early Christians with gratitude.[52]

As outlined above, Tertullian and the other church fathers continued this positive view of the empire.

Criticism of the Empire

In his discussion of the role of empire in the shaping of Christology, Joerg Rieger states that what is not surprising is how Christians were influenced by the empire. Rather, what is surprising is how they still managed to "develop resistance" to the imperial powers.[53] The following sections outline some of this resistance.

Prophecy of Its Demise

Despite Irenaeus's exhortations to be obedient to the authorities that God had appointed, he pointed to the prophecy of Daniel and the book of Revelation to remind his readers that someday Rome would fall.[54] The context is a refutation of Gnostic denials of the Old Testament God, and an assertion that the prophecies of the Old Testament and the Lord Jesus both had their origins in God the Father. Whether or not a critique of

---

52. Griffiths, *New Testament and the Roman State*, 126–27.

53. "What is particularly interesting is not that Christians were influenced by the logic of empire—after all, the empire was like the air they breathed; what is remarkable is that some of them were able to recognize the ambivalence of empire and to develop resistance. Without achieving complete independence from empire—an illusionary goal then as now—some of the earliest theologies and Christologies managed to refuse conforming to the expectations of empire" (Rieger, *Christ and Empire*, 28).

54. Irenaeus, *Haer.* 5.26.

Rome was on his mind, such a claim certainly challenged the popular idea that Rome would exist forever.

Warning of Judgment for Its Sins

Justin wrote his *First Apology* to the Roman Emperor Titus. He informed the emperor that Christians were loyal and obedient, as Jesus had instructed them to be when he said "Render therefore to Caesar the things that are Caesar's and to God the things that are God's." However, he also warned the emperor that he was not immune to God's judgment.

> Whence to God alone we render worship, but in other things we gladly serve you, acknowledging you as kings and rulers of men, and praying that with your kingly power you be found to possess also sound judgment. But if you pay no regard to our prayers and frank explanations, we shall suffer no loss, since we believe (or rather, indeed are persuaded) that every man will suffer punishment in eternal fire according to the merit of his deed, and will render account according to the power he has received from God, as Christ intimated when He said, "To whom God has given more, of him shall more be required."[55]

This threat of God's judgment on unjust rulers was echoed by others.

As noted above, Irenaeus counseled obedience to the political powers considered ordained by God. The authorities were able to bear the sword and execute justice without punishment from God, for in acting justly they were acting as God's agents. However, this was not counsel that provided the state with unlimited power with no moral constraints. Rather, Irenaeus made it clear that the authorities themselves would be judged for their own sins because God judges everyone: rulers included.

> But whatsoever ... [rulers] do to the subversion of justice, iniquitously, and impiously, and illegally, and tyrannically, in these things shall they also perish; for the just judgment of God comes equally upon all, and in no case is defective.[56]

Tertullian went further than Irenaeus, and in *To Scapula* he actually wrote to a Roman Proconsul in Carthage and threatened him with God's judgment if he did not stop the persecution of Christians. He attempted

---

55. Justin, *1 Apol.* 17.
56. Irenaeus, *Haer.* 5.24.

to make it clear that Christians loved their enemies and were friends of the emperor. Nonetheless, he wrote that he felt compelled to write to the Proconsul out of a concern for him and other enemies of Christians.[57] Why concern? Because God will bring judgment down on all who mistreat his people, for "no state shall bear unpunished the guilt of shedding Christian blood."[58] A great deal of the short letter is filled with descriptions of the often-grisly deaths of those punished by God. The warning was clear: back off or face God's judgment. As for Christians, they did not mind the persecution, for the Roman persecution led to their "glory."[59] In his commentary on Romans, Origen addressed the question: what about unjust rulers who persecute Christians? His response was the following:

> Nobody will deny that our senses—sight, sound and thought— are given to us by God. But although we get them from God, what we do with them is up to us . . . God will judge us righteously for having abused what he gave us to use for good. Likewise, God's judgment against the authorities will be just, if they have used the powers they have received according to their own ungodliness and not according to the laws of God.[60]

Once again, the message was that God's judgment was coming for those who persecuted the church. Cyprian echoed these sentiments when he declared that the certainty of future divine vengeance made the Christians patient in the midst of persecution.[61]

Counsel to Refuse to Serve in the Army (or as Magistrates)

The question of Christians and Roman military service is a contentious one for those seeking to identify early church pacifism, and there is no consensus in sight. Why? First, there is a problem with sources. There is a paucity of sources and in the ones that do survive there are contradictory accounts (e.g., Celsus critiques Christians for not serving in the

---

57. Tertullian, *Scap.* 1. He also wrote that he was not trying to scare him, but simply warn him. "We who are without fear ourselves are not seeking to frighten you, but we would save all men if possible by warning them not to fight with God." See Tertullian, *Scap.* 4.

58. Tertullian, *Scap.* 3.

59. Ibid., 5.

60. Origen, *Comm. Rom.* 5.92, 94, as noted in Bray, ed., *Romans*, 324.

61. Cyprian, *Demetr.* 17.

army at the same time as Christians were serving in the "Thundering Legion"). Second, the stakes are high. Everyone wants the early church to be on their side. Third, the problem of biases is always a factor, and in the case of early Christians in the army, John Helgeland argues that one's confessional viewpoint usually determines the outcome of one's research.[62] However, my goal in this section is far more modest than to settle the early church pacifism debate. My purpose in this section is simply to provide examples of Christian opposition to service in the imperial army. The larger question as to whether or not all—or most—Christians were pacifists will remain unanswered.[63]

Clement of Alexandria was critical of the violence of the Romans and their gods,[64] and exhorted Christians to be peaceful people.[65] Hippolytus (ca. 170–ca. 236) said that Christians must not execute people, must not enter the army as a catechumen or baptized Christian, and he opposed the oaths and army lifestyle.[66] Cyprian rejected dual morality for the state and individuals,[67] and declared that after the reception of the Eucharist "the hand is not to be stained with the sword and bloodshed."[68] Origen made it clear that while Christians would pray for the empire's success on the battlefield, they would not physically fight on it.[69] Unlike Tertullian (who emphasized idolatry more than violence), Origen eschewed the violence associated with military service because he was convinced Christ prohibited it.[70]

Tertullian is a critical source for determining early Christian involvement in the military. While he conceded that Christians served in the army, he wrote against the practice. As noted above, the problem of idolatry was central for Tertullian, and he argued against serving in the army or as a magistrate because there was no way to avoid implicating

62. Helgeland, "Christians in the Roman Army."

63. For helpful (but dated) summary of the church fathers and war, see Swift, *Early Fathers on War*.

64. Clement of Alexandria, *Protr.* 3.

65. Clement of Alexandria, *Paed.* 1.12.

66. Hippolytus, *Trad. ap.* 16.

67. Cyprian, *Don.* 6.

68. Cyprian, *Pat.* 14.

69. "We do not indeed fight under . . . [the emperor], although he require it; but we fight on his behalf, forming a special army—an army of piety—by offering our prayers to God." See Origen, *Cels.* 8.73.

70. Ibid., 3.8.

oneself with the idolatry so intimately and inseparably associated with military and political life.[71] The issue of bloodshed was also an important one, and he contended that Christians were not to shed blood, and thus should not serve in the army or as a magistrate.[72]

Martyrdom

The greatest resistance to empire was the refusal of early Christians to submit to the demands of the empire in regards to idolatry. The consequence was persecution. The well-known martyrdom account of Polycarp, Bishop of Smyrna, is a classic (but there were many more accounts written to inspire the faithful who might have to follow the same path[73]). A portion of it reads:

> And the Irenarch Herod . . . met him, and taking him up into the chariot, they seated themselves beside him, and endeavoured to persuade him, saying, "What harm is there in saying, Caesar is Lord, and in sacrificing, with the other ceremonies observed on such occasions, and so make sure of safety?" . . . Then, the proconsul urging him, and saying, "Swear, and I will set thee at liberty, reproach Christ"; Polycarp declared, "Eighty and six years have I served Him, and He never did me any injury: how then can I blaspheme my King and my Saviour?"[74]

Polycarp's refusal to confess "Caesar is Lord" is a clear example of the point made by the papers on the New Testament in this volume. Thatcher claims the crucifixion account turns on its head the imperial version of who is Lord; Carter states how "Matthew contests claims that Rome

---

71. Tertullian, *Idol.* 15–19. The issue of idolatry was the sole issue that Tertullian dealt with in *De coronis militis*, his treatment of whether or not Christians should serve in the military (he said "no" due to the pervasive idolatry).

72. "But how will a Christian man war, nay, how will he serve even in peace, without a sword, which the Lord has taken away? For albeit soldiers had come unto John, and had received the formula of their rule; albeit, likewise, a centurion had believed; still the Lord afterward, in disarming Peter, unbelted every soldier. No dress is lawful among us, if assigned to any unlawful action" (ibid., 19).

73. "Martyrdom was also a literary phenomenon. Texts helped to create the martyr ethos and governed its interpretation. Historians now distrust many surviving accounts. They are often demonstrably late: incidents that occurred in the second or third centuries are recorded in documents written in the fifth or sixth. The surviving *acta*, *martyria* and *passiones* shroud their early components in a complex interweaving of heavily edited material" (Rousseau, *Early Christian Centuries*, 159).

74. *Mart. Pol.* 8, 10.

represents divine purposes, locating such agency in Jesus the 'Christ'" (p. 109); Westfall notes how imperial "triumphalistic theology and power is pitted directly against the power, sovereignty, and victory of God in Christ" in Revelation (p. 254); Evans identifies the kingship of Jesus in Luke; Porter outlines how the letter to the Romans identifies the true Lord; and Lowe argues that in Ephesians "Christ leads his captives in an almost unmistakably imperial triumph" (p. 206). In all these instances the critical issue was the identity of Lord Jesus and the claims of Lord Caesar. The New Testament writers made it clear that it was one or the other; the church fathers and the examples of early Christian martyrs reflected that conviction when they refused to confess "Caesar is Lord." Whether covertly or overtly, the New Testament writers challenged the imperial authority's claims of ultimate loyalty, and in this regard were successful in inculcating convictions that would lead to the martyrdoms of the second, third, and fourth centuries. Of course, the reasons for the Roman persecution of Christians were more complex than I am presenting here, and varied due to time, place, and personality of rulers.[75] Be that as it may, at the core of the issue for Christians was the refusal to commit idolatry by recognizing anyone but Jesus as Lord, and by the second century this conviction was far from a covert teaching—it was openly written about and confessed to emperors (Justin Martyr) and local rulers (Tertullian).

What is noteworthy is that while we may see these refusals to confess Caesar as Lord as examples of anti-empire sentiment (and certainly the Roman authorities did), the church fathers did not. As Swift notes, the critical issue for the early Christians was not imperial power, but the issue of idolatry. And when "the issue of idolatry was solved at the time of Constantine . . . the principal source of opposition to the state was removed."[76]

CONCLUSION

In summary, while there was not unanimity among the church fathers in regards to every issue related to empire, there are some salient points that can be drawn from this brief survey. First, the church fathers contin-

---

75. For further details on the persecution of early Christians, see Frend, *Martyrdom*.
76. Swift, *Early Fathers on War*, 25.

ued the trajectory of the New Testament writers when they unanimously refused to worship any Lord but Jesus. Within the pages of the New Testament, Christians found an ideological framework that not only necessitated their non-participation in certain civil and religious events (such as proclaiming "Caesar is Lord"), but also sustained them and gave them hope in the midst of often-brutal persecution or lonely alienation when they did not participate in the normal functions of Roman life. However, this refusal to say "Caesar is Lord" must not be confused with an anti-empire attitude.

Second, there was a remarkable degree of sympathy for the empire. Prayers for the health and welfare of the emperor, prayers for imperial victories on the battlefield, and appreciation for the fact that the empire aided the spread of the faith all indicate that the church fathers appreciated the benefits of empire. Their instruction for Christians to obey their rulers by "rendering to Caesar what is Caesar's" only reinforces the impression that the church fathers were far from revolutionaries seeking to overthrow imperial rule, and they seemed quite content to have the empire continue for the foreseeable future. Of course, the positive view of empire was always in tension with the ever-present violence and idolatry, something that the Christians needed to avoid.

Here we need to pause and note that we must be careful not to project back into the early centuries of the church contemporary anti-imperial assumptions. I agree with Carter when he states that method is a "fundamental issue in exploring how the gospels of Matthew and Mark negotiate the Roman Empire" (p. 90). As demonstrated in these papers, postmodern, social science, and other methodologies (or critical theories) have been used to uncover what may be covert anti-Roman sentiments in the New Testament writings.

At the risk of sounding like a Luddite, I have to say that I am not sold on every particular critical theory within the postmodern world. In the most basic sense, postmodern and postcolonial theories were born out of a noble desire to hear (and liberate) the voices of the disenfranchised, the oppressed, and the constructed "other." Written mainly by those who were increasingly alienated from their religion of birth (Judaism), and who were in the process of losing the legal protection that came from that association, the canonical writings provide what seems to be an obvious testing ground for such theories.

However, the drawback of some theories is that the intention of the biblical author becomes, at best, a secondary concern, or at worst, an irrelevant (or unknowable) matter. Frederick Crews, in *Postmodern Pooh*, provides a humorous but scathing critique of many modern literary theories that, when applied to the Winnie the Pooh stories, reveal a children's story full of same sex marriage (Piglet moves in with Pooh), misogyny (Kanga's oppressed state at home), abuse (Piglet's behavior is obviously a sign of an abusive past), and even imperialism (Pooh's attempts to steal honey from the bees).

I have no desire to go into the wars over postmodernism in my discipline,[77] other than to say that I am concerned about the intention of the authors. It seems pretty clear that John had the Roman Empire in mind when he penned Revelation. But what about other authors and their intentions? For instance, did John intentionally construct the crucifixion account as a counter-memory to the dominant narrative of Roman supremacy?

Certain theories related to empire and the New Testament are predicated not just on the assumption that the New Testament writers were anti-empire, but that their anti-empire sentiments were similar to late twentieth-century anti-imperial sentiments. In other words, one could take theories or studies related to twentieth-century opposition to imperialism, transport them back 1900 years and superimpose them on a completely different people, period, and problem. Carter leans heavily on postcolonial studies for his look at Matthew, and Thatcher relies on Foucault's model of "countermemory" in his reading of John. In each case, the assumption is that the biblical author's attitudes to empire mirrored those of twentieth-century opponents of empire. But what if the New Testament writers appreciated the benefits of empire? While the Neronian persecution was brutal, it was not empire-wide. And, as Carter notes, there is "no evidence" that the empire subjected "late first-century followers of Jesus to daily, life-or-death persecution" (p. 91). So why would they be so anti-empire? We assume that they would be because we are. In fact, some contemporary scholars—writers of the papers presented

---

77. For some examples of criticisms of postmodernism in the history academy, see Evans, *In Defense of History*; Appleby, Hunt, and Jacob, *Telling the Truth*. For a defense of postmodernism in the academy, see Stone, *Constructing the Holocaust*. For a helpful and brief summary of recent developments regarding postmodernism in the history academy, see Curthoys and Docker, *Is History Fiction?*, chs. 7–11.

here included—indicate surprise if there is even a hint of pro-empire sentiment; the assumption, of course, is that the biblical authors should be appalled with empire, not appreciative of it. But was that the case? A look at the church fathers suggests that they were not as anti-empire as many suppose and hope.

Third, a look at the church fathers helps deal with contemporary debates over contentious passages such as Romans 13. As Porter notes, this passage has been a point of contention for those who struggle with Paul's alleged subservience to the empire and command to obey "no matter what." Neil Elliott is one such person. In regards to Romans 13, he writes:

> That we should allow these verses to thwart even the most modest inquiries into our government's complicity in repression and murder is a staggering betrayal, not only of the oppressed, but also of the holy man who traced his apostolate from city to city with his own blood. Only the arrogant presumptions of our own privilege have allowed us to hear these verses as a sacred legitimation of power.[78]

However, even a casual reading of the church fathers indicates that there was never a sense that Romans 13 indicated a "no matter what" policy in regards to obedience. Obedience and respect were usually qualified by limits, such as the avoidance of idolatry. Remember, the ones with such a positive view of empire were also the ones refusing to submit to aspects of Roman rule and writing critiques of Roman power. My hunch is that the church fathers would have been amazed, saddened, and angered by the misreadings of Romans 13 that defend blind adherence to the state. But my hunch is also that they would have been quite surprised at our inability to see the relative benefits of Roman rule and the New Testament imperative to submit to the authorities.

Fourth, we need to see that the progression to Constantine and a Christian empire was not so farfetched or such a radical departure from earlier years. In fact, much of what was necessary for a Christian empire was expressed long before Constantine: belief in a divinely appointed emperor, obedience to the state expected, support for imperial victories on the battlefield, and the conviction that there was a providential role for the state to benefit the church. As Swift notes, "The change that occurred [with Constantine's conversion] represents a major shift rather

---

78. Elliott, *Liberating Paul*, 226.

than a reversal in Christian thinking, a shift that was made possible by earlier ambiguities and disagreements concerning the use of coercion and made necessary by the altered political circumstances in which Christians now found themselves."[79]

To conclude, in her discussion of Christians and violence, Lisa Cahill asks two questions relevant to this topic.[80] What is the way of discipleship as established by Jesus according to the Scriptures? How can Christians, and the Christian community, integrate their religious identities with their membership in a particular culture and civil society? The church fathers addressed those questions in the earliest years of Christianity, and in the context of the Roman Empire. The answer for them, in part, seems to be expressed well in the words of the anonymous *Letter to Diognetus*: "They [Christians] dwell in their own countries, but simply as sojourners. As citizens, they share in all things with others, and yet they endure all things as if foreigners."[81] To use a modern phrase, they had dual citizenship. They were good citizens, appreciative of the empire, and loyal to the emperor, but never completely a part of the empire, for their ultimate loyalty lay elsewhere (much to the chagrin of the imperial authorities). That was the tension then, as it is today.

---

79. Swift, *Early Fathers on War*, 29.
80. Cahill, *Love Your Enemies*, 40.
81. *Diogn.* 5.

BIBLIOGRAPHY

Albright, Madeleine, and Bill Woodward. *The Mighty and the Almighty: Reflections on America, God, and World Affairs*. New York: HarperCollins, 2006.

Appleby, Joyce, Lynn Hunt, and Margaret Jacob. *Telling the Truth about History*. New York/London: Norton, 1994.

Bainton, Roland. *A Historical Survey and Critical Re-evaluation*. Nashville: Abingdon, 1988.

Beck, Norman A. *Anti-Roman Cryptograms in the New Testament: Symbolic Messages of Hope and Liberation*. New York: Peter Lang, 1997.

Brandon, S. G. F. *Jesus and the Zealots: A Study of the Political Factor in Primitive Christianity*. New York: Scribner's, 1967.

Bray, Gerald, ed. *Romans*. Downers Grove, IL: InterVarsity, 1998.

Cadoux, C. John. *The Early Christian Attitude to War*. New York: Seabury, 1982.

Cahill, Lisa Sowle. *Love Your Enemies: Discipleship, Pacifism, and Just War Theory*. Minneapolis: Fortress, 1994.

Campenhausen, Hans von. "Christians and Military Service in the Early Church." In *Tradition and Life in the Church*, translated by A. V. Littledale, 160–70. London: Collins, 1968.

Carter, Warren. *Matthew and Empire: Initial Explorations*. Harrisburg, PA: Trinity Press International, 2001.

———. *The Roman Empire and the New Testament: An Essential Guide*. Nashville: Abingdon, 2006.

Cassidy, Richard J. *Christians and Roman Rule in the New Testament: New Perspectives*. New York: Crossroad, 2001.

———. *John's Gospel in New Perspective: Christology, and the Realities of Roman Rule*. Maryknoll, NY: Orbis, 1992.

Chapman, Stephen B. "Imperial Exegesis: When Caesar Interprets Scripture." In *Anxious about Empire: Theological Essays on the New Global Realities*, edited by Wes Avram, 91–102. Grand Rapids: Brazos, 2004.

Clarke, W. K. Lowther. *The First Epistle of Clement to the Corinthians*. London: SPCK, 1937.

Crews, Frederick. *Postmodern Pooh*. New York: North Point, 2001.

Crossan, John Dominic, and Jonathan L. Reed. *In Search of Paul: How Jesus' Apostle Opposed Rome's Empire with God's Kingdom*. San Francisco: HarperSanFrancisco, 2004.

Curthoys, Ann, and John Docker. *Is History Fiction?* Ann Arbor: University of Michigan Press, 2005.

Elliott, Neil. *Liberating Paul: The Justice of God and the Politics of the Apostle*. Maryknoll, NY: Orbis, 1994.

Evans, Richard. *In Defense of History*. London: Granta, 1997.

Ferguson, Niall. *Empire: The Rise and Demise of the British World Order and the Lessons for Global Power*. New York: Basic, 2003.

Fowden, Garth. "Pagan Versions of the Rain Miracle of A.D. 172." *Historia* 36 (1987) 83–95.

Frend, W. H. C. *Martyrdom and Persecution in the Early Church: A Study of a Conflict from the Maccabees to Donatus*. New York: New York University Press, 1967.

Gilbert, Gary. "The List of Nations in Acts 2: Roman Propaganda and the Lukan Response." *JBL* 121 (2003) 497–529.

Griffiths, D. R. *The New Testament and the Roman State*. Swansea: John Penry, 1970.
Gwyther, Anthony, and Wes Howard-Brook. *Unveiling Empire: Reading Revelation Then and Now*. Maryknoll, NY: Orbis, 2001.
Harnack, Adolf. *Militia Christi: The Christian Religion and the Military in the First Three Centuries*. Philadelphia: Fortress, 1981.
Helgeland, John. "Christians and the Roman Army A.D. 173–337." *Church History* 43 (1974) 149–63, 200.
Herzog, William R., II. *Jesus, Justice, and the Reign of God*. Louisville: Westminster John Knox, 2003.
———. *Parables as Subversive Speech: Jesus as Pedagogue of the Oppressed*. Louisville: Westminster John Knox, 1994.
Horsley, Richard A. *Jesus and Empire: The Kingdom of God and the New World Disorder*. Minneapolis: Fortress, 2003.
———, editor. *Paul and Empire: Religion and Power in Roman Imperial Society*. Harrisburg, PA: Trinity Press International, 1997.
———, editor. *Paul and Politics: Ekklesia, Israel, Imperium, Interpretation*. Harrisburg, PA: Trinity Press International, 2000.
———, editor. *Paul and the Roman Imperial Order*. Harrisburg, PA: Trinity Press International, 2004.
Kinzig, Wolfram. "The Greek Christian Writers." In *Handbook of Classical Rhetoric in the Hellenistic Period, 330 BC–AD 400*, edited by Stanley E. Porter, 633–70. Leiden: Brill, 1997.
Mandelbaum, Michael. *The Case for Goliath: How America Acts as the World's Government in the Twenty-First Century*. New York: Public Affairs, 2005.
Myers, Ched. *Binding the Strong Man: A Political Reading of Mark's Story of Jesus*. Maryknoll, NY: Orbis, 1988.
Northcott, Michael. *An Angel Directs the Storm: Apocalyptic Religion and American Empire*. London: Tauris, 2004.
Rieger, Joerg. *Christ and Empire: From Paul to Postcolonial Times*. Minneapolis: Fortress, 2007.
Roberts, Alexander, and James Donaldson, eds. *Ante-Nicene Fathers*. 10 vols. Christian Literature Publishing Company, 1885. Reprint, Peabody, MA: Hendrickson, 2004.
Rousseau, Philip. *The Early Christian Centuries*. London: Longman, 2002.
Rubin, H. Z. "Weather Miracles under Marcus Aurelius." *Athenaeum* 57 (1979) 357–80.
Ryan, Edward. "The Rejection of Military Service by the Early Christians." *Theological Studies* 13 (1952) 1–32.
Said, Edward. *Orientalism*. New York: Vintage, 1979.
Satterthwaite, Philip E. "The Latin Church Fathers." In *Handbook of Classical Rhetoric in the Hellenistic Period, 330 BC–AD 400*, edited by Stanley E. Porter, 671–94. Leiden: Brill, 1997.
Sider, Robert Dick. *Ancient Rhetoric and the Art of Tertullian*. Oxford: Oxford University Press, 1971.
Singer, Peter. *The President of Good and Evil: The Ethics of George W. Bush*. New York: Dutton, 2004.
Stone, Dan. *Constructing the Holocaust: A Study in Historiography*. London/Portland: Vallentine Mitchell, 2003.
Swift, Louis J. *The Early Fathers on War and Military Service*. Wilmington, DE: Michael Glazier, 1983.

Wengst, Klaus. *Pax Romana and the Peace of Jesus Christ*. Philadelphia: Fortress, 1987.
Yoder, John Howard. *The Politics of Jesus*. Grand Rapids: Eerdmans, 1972.

Modern Authors

Achtemeier, P. J., 243, 256
Ackroyd, P. R., 63, 86
Adams, M. M., 199, 201, 226
Adamson, J. B., 237, 256
Albright, M., 259, 280
Alföldy, G., 233, 256
Anderson, P. N., 215, 226
Appleby, J., 277, 280
Arlandson, J. M., 94, 116
Arnold, C. E., 202–4, 207, 226
Ashton, J., 140, 163
Attridge, H. W., 248, 256
Aune, D. E., 254, 256
Avram, W., 280

Bainton, R., 15, 16, 262, 263, 280
Bal, M., 168, 193
Balch, D. L., 118, 242, 256
Barbalet, J., 97, 116
Barclay, J., 91, 116
Barth, K., 192
Barth, M., 204, 205, 226, 227
Bartholomew, C. G., 199, 227, 228
Barton, S. C., 238, 256
Beck, N. A., 253, 254, 256, 261, 280
Bedard, S., 179, 195
Begg, C. T., 63, 66, 86
Bellis, A. O., 227
Berger, K., 167, 193
Bertram, G., 126, 138
Bevan, E., 166, 193
Bhabha, H., 99, 100, 113, 116
Biddle, M. E., 75, 82, 86
Bland, D., 116, 117

Blenkinsopp, J., 68, 72, 77, 78, 84, 86
Blomberg, C. L., 234–36, 256
Boda, M. J., 4, 5, 6, 56, 65, 68, 78, 81, 83, 86
Bolt, P. G., 198, 227
Bond, H., 106, 116
Bonnard, P. E., 78, 86
Boring, M. E., 167, 193
Bouchard, D. F., 163
Braaten, C. F., 257
Brandon, S. G. F., 261, 280
Bray, G., 280
Brown, R. E., 245, 256
Bruce, F. F., 164, 176, 193, 248, 256
Brueggemann, W., 56, 84, 86, 225, 227
Bultmann, R., 178, 193
Bureth, P., 127, 138

Cadoux, C. J., 265, 280
Cahill, L. S., 279, 280
Caird, G. B., 204, 227
Campbell, B. L., 237, 239–41, 256
Campenhausen, H., 267, 280
Carr, D. M., 56, 67, 82, 86
Carter, W., 6, 7, 90–94, 96, 101, 103, 104, 106, 108, 110–16, 199, 211, 227, 231, 234, 236, 244, 247, 250, 257, 261, 262, 276, 277, 280
Cassidy, R. J., 252, 254, 257, 261, 280
Castle, G., 99, 117
Chapman, S. B., 259, 280
Charles, J. D., 244, 257

Charlesworth, M. P., 171, 193
Childs, B. S., 56, 63, 83, 86
Chow, J. K., 189, 190, 193
Clarke, W. K. L., 266, 280
Clements, R. E., 56, 59, 63, 66, 76, 78, 86, 87
Clines, D. J. A., 89
Clough, A. A., 24, 53
Coggins, R. J., 56, 87
Cohoon, J. W., 126, 138
Collins, A. Y., 253, 254, 257
Collins, J. J., 257
Collins, R. F., 138
Colpe, C., 167, 193
Conrad, E. W., 61, 66, 87
Conzelmann, H., 176, 193
Cooper, N. J., 99, 119
Cranfield, C. E. B., 181, 193
Crews, F., 277, 280
Cross, F. L., 227
Cross, F. M., 49, 53, 67, 87
Crossan, J. D., 215, 216, 227, 261, 280,
Curthoys, A., 277, 280

Danker, F. W., 126, 133, 138, 167, 169, 171, 190, 193
Davids, P., 232, 236, 257
Davies, G. I., 56, 58, 59, 87
Davies, J. P., 166, 193
Davies, P. R., 86
Deissmann, A., 126, 130, 138, 166, 167, 171, 173, 193
deSilva, D. A., 183, 193, 238, 249, 257
Docker, J., 277, 280
Donaldson, J., 263, 281
Donaldson, L., 99, 117
Donfried, K., 216, 218, 227
Dorsch, T., S., 116
Duling, D., 94, 117, 232, 257
Dumbrell, W. J., 59, 87
Dunn, J. D. G., 178, 193, 230, 245, 246, 257

Dyson, S., 232, 257

Edgar, C. C., 128, 138
Edwards, M. J., 202, 208–11, 227
Ehrenberg, V., 167, 170, 171, 193
Eisenman, R., 208, 227
Elliott, N. 165, 185, 193, 207, 218, 227, 278, 261, 280
Emmerson, G., 78, 82, 87
Esler, P., 205, 227
Evans, C. A., 7–9, 56, 87, 137, 138, 167, 171, 194, 256, 257, 275
Evans, R., 277, 280

Fanon, F., 99, 100, 117
Fee, G. D., 181, 194
Ferguson, J., 166, 194
Ferguson, N., 259, 280
Fitzmyer, J., 147, 163
Fleer, D., 116, 117
Fohrer, G., 58, 87
Foucault, P. M., 9, 143, 149, 150, 163, 277
Fowden, G., 266, 280
Fowl, S. E., 89, 188, 194
Fox, R. L., 166, 194,
Frend, W. H. C., 218, 227, 275, 281
Friedman, R. E., 89
Futrell, A., 94, 117

Gaebelein, F. E., 228
Gardiner, A., 26, 28, 53,
Garnsey,, P., 94, 96, 117
Giardina, A., 119
Gilbert, G., 261, 281
Gombis, T. G., 203–5, 227, 228
Goppelt, L., 242, 257
Gordon, R. P., 39, 53, 86
Gorman, M. J., 165, 194, 199, 201, 209, 224, 228
Graves, R., 165, 194
Green, P., 166, 194
Greig, A. C. G., 195
Grieb, A. K., 168, 194

Modern Authors

Griffiths, D. R., 270, 281
Gwyther, A., 253, 257, 261, 281

Hahn, S., 199
Hallo, W. W., 19, 53, 89
Hammond, N. G. L., 166, 194,
Hanson, K., C., 105, 117
Hanson, P. D., 253, 257
Hardy, T., 164, 194
Harland, P., 94, 117
Harmer, J. R., 124, 138
Harnack, A., 263, 264, 281
Harrill, J. A., 224, 228, 239, 257
Hatina, T. R., 117
Hayes, M. A., 258
Hays, R. B., 168, 194, 210
Head, I., 205, 228
Healy, M., 199
Heath, G., 15, 16
Heisserer, A. J., 126, 135, 136, 138
Helgeland, J., 266, 273, 281
Hemer, C. J., 175, 176, 194
Hengel, M., 117, 201, 228
Herzog, W. R., 114, 117, 261, 281
Hess, R. S., 59, 87
Hicks, E. L., 126, 138
Hirschfeld, G., 170, 194
Holmes, M. W., 124, 138
Hoppe, L. J., 59, 75, 76, 87
Horsley, R. A., 90, 98, 117, 164,
    193, 194, 196–98, 201, 202,
    227–29, 260, 261, 281
Howard-Brook, W., 253, 257, 261,
    281
Hunt, A. S., 128, 138
Hunt, L., 277, 280

Ishida, T., 88

Jackson-McCabe, M., 117
Jacob, M., 277, 280
Jacobson, D. M., 129, 138
James, P. D., 197, 198, 228
Jenson, R. W., 257

Jewett, R. K., 133, 138, 175, 194
Jobes, K. H., 241, 243, 257
Jobling, D., 193
Johnson, L. T., 248, 257
Johnson, S. L., 138
Jones, A. H. M., 166, 167, 170, 171,
    193, 194
Jones, B. W., 89
Joubert, S., 133, 138

Kaminsky, J. S., 227
Kang, S. M., 80, 87
Kaplan, M. M., 57, 87
Kautsky, J., 94, 118
Keck, L., 108, 118
Keener, C., 232, 234–36, 239, 257
Keesmaat, S. C., 168, 194, 198, 210,
    212–14, 223, 228, 229
Kent, H. A., Jr., 208, 228
Kiley, M., 139
King, L. W., 20, 53
Kingsbury, J. D., 102, 103, 108, 118
Kinzig, W., 265, 281
Kirk, A., 147, 163
Knight, G. W., 221, 222, 228
Knoppers, G., 86
Knowles, M. P., 205, 228
Kondoleon, C., 93, 118
Kramer, W., 182, 194
Kreitzer, L. J., 205, 214, 228
Kristeva, J., 92, 118
Kuschke, A., 88

Lack, R., 78, 87
Laffi, U., 167, 194
Lane, W. L., 248, 258
Lemcio, E. E., 211, 228
Lenski, G., 94, 118
Levenson, J. D., 59, 60, 87
Levine, A. J., 116
Liebreich, L. J., 82, 87
Liew, T. B., 90, 118
Lightfoot, J. B., 124, 138
Lipschitz, O., 56, 87

Llewelyn, S. R., 126, 128, 138
Longenecker, R. N., 209, 212, 227, 228
Longman, T., 80, 87
Louis, M., 163
Lowe, M. F., 12–15
Lull, D. J., 125, 126, 138

MacDonald, M. E., 239, 242, 243, 258
MacKay, C. S., 180, 194
Mandelbaum, M., 259, 281
Marshall, F. H., 170, 194
Marshall, I. H., 195
Marshall, P., 189, 194
Martin, R. P., 235, 258
Martin, T. W., 240, 258
Martin, W., 168, 194
Martyn, J., L., 142
Maslen, M. W., 201, 228
Mattingly, D., 90, 118
Mattingly, G. L., 89
Mauck, J. W., 137, 138
Maynard-Reid, P. U., 235, 258
Mays, J. L., 60, 87, 229
McCann, J. C., 219, 228
McDonald, L. M., 174, 175, 194
McLaren, J. S., 129, 138
Meeks, W. A., 228
Melugin, R. F., 86, 88
Mendenhall, G., 44, 53
Menken, M. J. J., 219, 228
Milgrom, J., 57, 87
Miller, P. D., 80, 87, 218, 219, 228
Mitchell, P. D., 201, 228
Moller, K., 199
Moo, D. J., 181, 194
Moran, W. L., 24, 53
Moritz, T., 204, 228
Mowery, R., 90, 118
Moyise, S., 219, 228
Moytl, A. J., 17, 28, 53
Myers, C., 90, 118, 261, 281

Neyrey, J. H., 126, 138
Nilsson, M. P., 166, 194
Nock, A. D., 126, 129, 138
Northcott, M., 259, 281

Oakes, P., 207, 208, 211, 212, 216, 228
Oakman, D. E., 105, 117
Ollenburger, B. C., 59, 60, 76, 87
Omerzu, H., 137, 138
O'Neill, P., 168, 194
Oswalt, J., 56, 59, 61, 78, 87, 88

Parry, R, 199
Paton, W. R., 126, 138
Petersen, N., 165, 195
Petit, P., 170, 195
Pilgrim, W., 92, 118
Pitts, A. W., 173, 195
Polan, G. J., 78, 88
Porteous, N. W., 59, 82, 85, 88
Porter, S. E., 10–12, 89, 173–75, 179, 181, 185, 187, 189, 194, 195, 228, 256–58, 269, 275, 278, 280, 281
Pratt, R., 39, 53
Price, S. R. F., 94, 118, 166, 195

Quinn-Miscall, P. D., 65, 76, 88

Rajak, T., 126, 139
Reasoner, M., 185, 192, 195,
Reed, J. L., 215, 216, 227, 261, 280
Reid, D. G., 80, 87
Rendtorff, R., 67, 88
Richards, K. H., 138
Richardson, C. C., 206, 229
Riches, J., 90, 117, 118, 227, 251, 257, 258
Rieger, J., 270, 281
Riesner, R., 168, 195
Ringgren, H., 165, 195
Ristau, K., 86
Roberts, A., 263, 281

Modern Authors

Roberts, J. J. M., 60, 65, 81, 83, 88, 204, 229
Rondiez, L., 118
Rousseau, P., 274, 281
Rowe, C. K., 132, 139
Rubin, H. Z., 266, 281
Ryan, E., 265, 281

Said, E., 99, 100, 118, 260, 281
Saldarini, A., 103, 118
Satterthwaite, P. E., 265, 281
Sawyer, J. F. A., 56, 75, 88
Schowalter, D., 128, 139
Schroeder, D., 242, 258
Scott, J. C., 96–98, 100, 108, 113, 118, 146, 148, 160, 163
Segovia, F., 99, 118
Seitz, C. R., 56, 59, 61, 66, 67, 69, 75, 76, 83, 87, 88, 199
Sherk, R. K., 167, 171, 195
Sherlock., C., 80, 88
Sider, R. D., 265, 281
Silberman, N. A., 197, 198, 201, 228
Sim, D. C., 90, 117, 118, 227, 257, 258
Singer, P., 259, 281
Smalley, S., 245, 258
Smallwood, E. M., 171, 195
Sparks, K. L., 24, 26, 27, 44, 53
Speiser, E. A., 19, 53
Spicq, C., 126, 127, 139
Spykerboer, H. C., 76, 88
Stansell, G., 64, 88
Stanzel, F. K., 168, 195
Stark, R., 94, 118, 238, 242, 243, 258
Stone, D., 277, 282
Stowers, S. K., 165, 195
Ström, A. V., 165, 195
Strom, M., 244, 245, 258
Strong, E., 166, 195
Stuart, D. K., 2, 3, 15, 24, 34, 35, 38, 45, 53
Stuhlmueller, C., 218, 229
Sugirtharajah, R., 99, 100, 118

Swain, S., 94, 119
Sweeney, M. A., 56, 58, 82, 83, 86, 88
Swift, L. J., 264, 265, 269, 273, 275, 278, 279, 282

Tamez, E., 231, 258
Tarn, W. W., 166, 195
Taylor, L. R., 127, 139, 165, 166, 171, 172, 177, 195
Thatcher, T., 9, 10, 14, 163, 277
Theissen, G., 165, 189, 195
Thiselton, A., 199
Tomasino, A. J., 82, 88
Tombs, D., 258

Van Boheeman, C., 193
Van Ruiten, J. T. A. G. M., 87, 88
Van Tilborg, S., 103, 119
Vermeylen, J., 86–88
Vervenne, M., 87, 88
Von Rad, G., 34, 53, 60, 89

Waddington, W. H., 171
Walsh, B. J., 212–14, 223, 229
Wanamaker, C. A., 215, 217, 229
Webb, B. G., 56, 66, 76, 89
Webster, J., 99, 119
Weinfeld, M., 60, 89
Welles, C. B., 127, 139,
Wengst, K., 170, 195, 261, 282
Wenham, G., J., 59, 87
Westermann, C., 68, 78, 82, 89
Westfall, C. L., 14, 15, 230, 239, 248, 250, 258, 280
Whittaker, C. R., 94, 119
Whorf, B., 30
Wilamowitz-Möllendorf, U., 172
Wilcken, U., 166, 177, 195
Williamson, H. G. M., 56, 57, 59, 63, 67, 82, 83, 89
Wilshire, L. E., 75, 76, 89
Wilson, A., 76, 89
Wink, W., 119, 202–4, 206, 213, 229
Winter, E., 128, 139

Wire, A. C., 189, 195
Wiseman, D. J., 24, 53
Witherington, B., 168, 195, 213, 216–22, 226, 229
Woodward, B., 259, 280
Wright, G. E., 28, 53
Wright, N. T., 165, 167, 168, 195, 196, 202, 207, 210, 226, 229

Yoder, J. H., 260, 282
Younger, K. L., 19, 53

Zerubavel, Y., 9, 143–45, 163

Ancient Sources

OLD TESTAMENT

Genesis
1–3	109
6:1–6	246
15:12–16	37

Exodus
3:1	104
15	80
17:14	38
19:5–7	79

Leviticus
19:13	236
19:18	111
21:16–24	105

Numbers
1	44
21:22	133
26	44
27:15–23	104

Deuteronomy
6:5	111
9:3	200
12	52
20:1–20	3, 35
20:4	200
21	147
21:22–23	147
21:23	201, 210
24:14–15	236
30:4	78
32:8	30
33	80
34:23–24	105

Joshua
8:29	201
10:26	201

1 Samuel
14	42

2 Samuel
5:2	104
5:8	105
8	45
24	2, 3, 39, 40, 44–46, 49, 51
24:1–17	36
24:10	50

1 Kings
18	51

2 Kings
14:23	54
15:2	54
15:19–20	54
15:29–30	54
17:3–6	55

1 Chronicles
21	2, 3, 39, 40, 44–46, 48, 49, 51

1 Chronicles (cont.)

21:7	50
21:8	50

Ezra

1:2	22

Job

1–2	50

Psalms

2	59, 60, 102
2:11–12	82
4:8–10	203
22	157
22:1	157
22:18	155, 161
29	218, 219
29:1	218
29:10–11	218
29:11	218
31:5	160
37	115
37:3	115
37:7	115
37:9	115
37:11	115
37:12	115
37:13	115
37:14	115
37:20	115
37:22	115
37:29	115
37:32	115
37:34	115
48	59
68	203, 218
68:18	13, 204
77:11 (LXX)	130
78:11	130
109:6	50
110	60
110:1a	122
110:1b	122
132	60

Proverbs

11:24	236

Isaiah

1–39	57, 58, 66, 70
1–5	57, 60, 82–84
1	57–59
1:1	57, 66
1:2–20	58
1:4	58, 70
1:7–8	57
1:8	58
1:9	57
1:21–31	58
1:21	58
1:26	58
1:27	58
2–5	58, 59
2	59
2:1–5	58, 81
2:1	57, 58, 66
2:2b–3a	58
2:3b–4	58
2:5	83
4	59
4:2–6	59, 81
4:3–4	59
4:5–6	59
5:1–7	59
5:16	70
5:19	70
5:24	70
6–39	4, 5, 56, 60, 65–67, 70, 82–84
6	57, 60, 61, 64, 67, 70, 77, 82, 83
6:1	55, 57, 60, 66
6:2	61
6:3	61, 70
6:5	60
6:13	61, 70
7–39	4, 61, 63, 64

Isaiah (cont.)

7–12	61
7	55
7:1–6	61
7:1	62, 66
7:3	61, 62
7:4–9	64
7:4	61
7:9	62
7:14	61, 110
8:7–8	62
8:8	110
8:10	110
9:6–7	65
9:7	61
10:1–3	114
10:5–14	31
10:17	70
10:20	70
11:1–12	65
12:6	70
13–35	63, 64
13–23	63, 64
13:1–22	63
14:28	66
16:4–5	65
17:7	70
17:12–14	63
18:1–7	63
18:1	63
19:24–25	35
23:1–18	63
23:13	63
24–27	64
24:12	64
25:6–10	111
26:1	64
28–33	64
28:16	64
29:1—31:9	64
29:15	64
29:19	70
29:23	70
30:1	64
30:8–11	70
30:12	70
30:15	64, 70
30:18	64
31:1	64, 70
32:1–2	65
34–35	64
35:5–6	111
36–39	61
36–37	64
36:1–2	61
36:1	57, 66
36:2	61
36:8–10	62
36:36	62
37:1–7	62
37:2	62
37:4	58
37:6	61
37:14–20	63
37:21–35	63
37:23	70
37:31–32	58
37:32	61
38:7–8	61
39	61, 64, 66, 77, 83
39:5–7	66
40–55	4, 5, 57, 66–68, 70–73, 76–79, 82–84
40–48	84
40	66, 69
40:1–11	67, 70, 83
40:1–2	67
40:1	67, 73, 79
40:2	68, 75
40:9–10	73
40:9	68, 69, 73
40:9c	67
40:10–11	68
40:10	67, 71
40:11	67
40:12—49:13	67–69, 75
40:12–31	67, 70
40:12–17	69

Isaiah (cont.)

40:12–16	69
40:18–20	69
40:22–24	69
40:25–26	69
40:25	70
40:27	67–70, 75
40:29–31	69
41–55	72
41–48	5, 71, 72, 77
41	72
41:8	67, 68, 72
41:14	68, 70, 75
41:16	68
41:17	68
41:20	68, 70
41:21	68, 83
41:27	68
42	72, 74
42:1–7	72
42:6	72, 74
42:18–25	71
42:24	68
43–48	71
43:1	68
43:3	68, 70
43:14	68, 70, 71
43:15	68, 70, 83
43:22	68
43:28	68
44:1–2	67
44:1	68
44:2	68
44:5	68
44:6	68, 83
44:21	67, 68
44:23	68
44:24—45:7	76
44:26	68
44:28	68, 71, 72, 78
45:1–3	72
45:1	71, 78, 83
45:3	68
45:4	67, 68
45:11	68, 70
45:13	71, 72, 78
45:15	68
45:17	68
45:19	68
45:25	68
46:1	71
46:3	68
46:8–12	71
46:13	68
47–48	72, 78
47	71
47:4	68, 70
48	71
48:1–22	71
48:1	68
48:2	68, 71
48:12	68
48:14	72
48:17	68, 70
48:20	68, 71
48:22	71
49–55	5, 72, 75, 76, 77, 84
49–54	69
49	72, 74
49:1–12	73
49:1–6	74
49:3	68, 73, 74
49:5	68
49:6	68, 72, 74
49:7	68, 74
49:7ab	70
49:13	69, 73
49:14—54:17	68, 75
49:14–26	67
49:14	5, 68–70, 73, 75, 76
49:26	68
50	74
50:4–9	74
50:10	74
51:1–8	71
51:3	68, 73
51:5	71
51:7	70

Ancient Sources

Isaiah (cont.)

Reference	Pages
51:9—52:6	71
51:9	71
51:11	68
51:12	70, 73, 75
51:13	70
51:16	68
51:17	68, 75
52–54	74, 75, 76
52–53	74, 76
52:1–2	75
52:1	68
52:2	68
52:7–10	70, 73, 76
52:7	68
52:8	68, 73
52:9	68, 73
52:10	71, 73
52:11–12	72
52:12	68
52:13–15	75
52:13	73, 74
52:14	73
52:15	74
53	75
53:1	74
54	75
54:1–17	70
54:2–3	76
54:4	70
54:5	68, 70, 76
54:7	76
54:14	76
55–66	5
55	76
55:3–5	83
55:5	68
55:6–7	76
56–66	4, 57, 77, 78, 80–85
56	77
56:1–2	79
56:3–8	78
56:7	105
56:8	68, 77
56:9—59:15a	81
56:9—58:14	81
57:15	82
58:1	68
58:6–14	115
58:14	68
59:1–15a	81
59:15b–21	80
59:16	80, 82
59:17	80
59:18	80
59:20	68, 80
59:21	80
60–62	78, 84
60	80
60:1–22	80
60:3	80
60:6–7	82
60:9	68
60:14	68
60:16	68
61	79, 80, 85
61:1–3	79
61:1	79
61:3	68
61:4–9	78, 79
61:7	79
61:8	79
61:8b	79
61:9	79
61:10–11	79
61:11	79
62	80
62:1–12	80
62:1	68
62:2	80
62:6	68
62:7	68
62:11	68
62:12	82
63:1–6	80
63:1	82
63:3–4	80
63:5	80, 82

Isaiah (cont.)

63:6	80
63:7—66:6	81
63:7—64:12	81
63:7	68
63:16	68
64:10	68
65:1—66:6	81
65:9	68
65:18	68
65:19	68
66	58
66:7–24	78
66:7–22	78
66:8	68
66:10	68, 82
66:13	68
66:19	78
66:20	68

Jeremiah

1:10	105
7:5–6	106
7:9	106
7:11	105
12:17	105
22:13	236
25:12	32
28:14	31
29:7 (LXX 36:7)	222
29:10	32
50:2—51:18	32

Ezekiel

22:6–31	114
34	104
34:1–22	114
34:2–3	104
34:4	104
34:8	104
34:10	104
34:11–22	104
34:16	104
34:17–19	104
34:25–30	105

Daniel

5:11 (LXX)	188
7	33
7:9	122
7:13–14	112, 122
7:23–27	33
12	112
12:1–3	107

Hosea

6:6	111, 115

Amos

5:10–12	114

Nahum

2:13	147

Habakkuk

3	80

Zechariah

1:18–21	32
3:1–2	50
9:9	120, 121

Malachi

3:5	236

NEW TESTAMENT

Matthew

1:1—4:16	101
1:1–17	109
1:1	109
1:17	109
1:18–25	110
1:21–23	105, 109
1:21	103, 110
1:23	110
2	102, 110
2:2	109, 121
2:4–6	102, 103
2:6	104

Matthew (cont.)

2:7–9	102
2:8	102
2:12	102
2:15	109
2:16	102
3:7–12	141
3:13–17	109
4:1–11	109
4:1	106
4:3	106
4:8	106, 110
4:15–16	109
4:17—11:1	101
4:17	109, 110, 113
4:18–22	110, 113, 114
4:23–25	103, 110
5–7	263
5:3–12	110, 111
5:3	115
5:5	115
5:7	115
5:9	114
5:16	114
5:17–48	111, 115
5:38–48	113
5:38–42	98
5:39	113
5:41	113
5:42	115
5:44	115
5:45–48	115
5:45	114
6:1–18	115
6:2–4	115
6:2	115
6:9–13	111
6:9	114
6:11	115
6:16–18	115
6:19–34	115
6:19–20	235
6:24	114
6:33–34	114
6:34	111, 115
7:12	115
8–9	103
8:5–13	263
8:23–27	110
8:28–36	110
9:1–8	105
9:4	106
9:9	114
9:13	111, 115
9:36	103
10:7–8	115
11:1—16:20	101
11:25	110
11:28–30	104
12:1–14	105
12:7	111, 115
12:14	103
12:22–45	105
12:25	110
12:34	106
13:19–22	114
13:38–39	106
14:13–21	111
15:1–20	105
15:5	105
15:13	105
15:31–39	111
16:1–4	106
16:21—20:34	101
16:27–28	112
17:14	102
17:24–27	114
18:20	110
19–20	114
19:4	109
19:16–30	114
19:21	114
19:23–24	114
19:28	112
20:1–16	233
20:12	114
20:25–26	111
20:25	8, 114, 125

Matthew (cont.)

20:26–28	114
21:1—27:66	102
21:5–9	121
21:12–17	105
21:12–13	105
21:14	105
21:15	103
21:23	103
21:28—22:14	106
21:41	106
21:45–46	103
21:45	103
22:7	106
22:15–22	103, 114
22:23–33	103
22:34–46	103
22:34–39	111
22:37–39	115
22:39	115
23	103, 106
23:9	114
23:10	114
23:11–12	114
23:23	106, 115
24:13	115
24:15–21	250
24:27–31	112
24:28	112
24:29	112
24:35	112
25:31–46	115
25:34	121
25:40	121
26:3–5	103
26:4	103
26:14	103
26:29	123
26:47	103
26:52	113
26:57–68	103
26:63–64	122
27:1–2	103, 106
27:3	107
27:11–26	106
27:11	106
27:11a	122
27:11b	122
27:15–19	107
27:17	123
27:20–21	107
27:22	107, 123
27:23–24	107
27:24–26	107
27:37	123
27:50	160
27:51–54	149
28:1–20	102
28:6–9	107
28:11–15	103, 107
28:18–20	113
28:18	107, 110
28:20	110

Mark

1:1	109
1:9–15	109
1:15	110
1:16–20	110, 113
1:21–34	110
2:1–12	105
2:23–28	105
3:6	103
3:20–27	105
4:19	114
4:35–41	110
5:1–20	106, 110
6:34	103
7:9–13	105
10	114
10:17–23	114
10:42–45	111, 114
10:42	8, 125
10:45	154
11:9–10	121
11:15–19	105
12:1–12	106
12:13–17	114, 141

Ancient Sources

Mark (cont.)

12:28–34	111
12:38–40	103
13:13	115
14:61	122
14:62	122
14:62b	122
15:1–15	106
15:2a	122
15:2b	122
15:9	123
15:12	123
15:15–20	146
15:18	123
15:24	153
15:26	123
15:34	157
15:37	160
15:38–39	149
16:1–7	107

Luke

2	219
2:8–12	219
2:51	187
3:12–14	141
3:14	263
4:14–19	6, 85
10:42	125
10:43	125
11:43	236
14:7–11	236
19:38	121
22:24–26	131
22:25	8, 125, 130, 131, 141
22:26	125
22:67–70	122
23:2	141
23:3a	122
23:3b	122
23:38	123
23:44–45	149
23:46	160

John

1:49	121
2:19–22	145
3	142
3:3	142
3:5	142
3:12	142
3:14–15	159, 161
6:15	121
8:28	159
10:18	159
12:12–19	159
12:13	121
12:15	121
12:31–33	159, 161
13:1–3	161
16:28	161
16:33	140, 159
18:1–9	161
18:29–31	156
18:33	122
18:36–37	161
18:36	142
18:38–39	156
18:39	123
19	153–55
19:1–3	146
19:3	123
19:4–6	156
19:10–11	161
19:11	159
19:12	123, 156
19:14–15	156
19:15	123
19:16–37	140, 143, 150, 151, 154, 162
19:16–18	152, 161
19:19–22	152, 156, 161
19:21	152
19:23–25	155
19:23–24	152, 153, 155, 161
19:24	153–56
19:25–27	152, 156, 158, 159, 161

John (cont.)

19:26–30	158
19:28–30	152, 156, 161
19:28	154, 156–59
19:30	158, 160
19:31–37	153, 162
19:36	156
19:36–37	154, 156
20:30–31	143

Acts

3:1–26	131
4:1–22	130
4:8b–10	131
9:5	200
9:17	200
10	263
10:1–33	131
10:36–38	131
10:38	136
13:46–48	85
16	263
16:12	208
16:20	208
16:21	208
16:36–40	208
17:7	123
22:4–5	135
22:8	200
22:16	200
26:11–18	8, 136
26:15	200

Romans

1:1	182
1:3	178
1:4	182
1:16	184
3:2	178
6:23	263
9:5	179
9:33	197
11:9	197
12:14	179

12:17	179
12:18–19	179
13	11, 16, 184–86, 269, 278
13:1–7	11, 12, 184–86
13:1	186, 188
13:3	189
13:6	187

1 Corinthians

1:12–13	190
1:22–24	148
1:23	197
5:1	190
6:1	190
6:12–16	190
7	12, 190
7:1–5	190
8:1	190
7:10	179, 191
7:12	191
7:25	191
9:5	179
9:21	224
11:20–21	190
11:23–25	179
12:1	190
15	154
15:1–3	154
15:3	154
15:4	179
15:5–7	179

2 Corinthians

1:2	175
2:14–15	218
2:14	205
4:1	190
5:20	8, 132, 190
8	12, 191
8:8	191
8:9	191
8:11	192

Galatians

1:19	179
2:20	200
3:13–14	200
3:13	147, 200–202, 210
4:4	179
4:5	200
5:11	148, 197
5:22–26	200
5:24	200
6:2	224
6:12	200, 203
6:14	200
6:17	202

Ephesians

1:20—2:22	203
1:20–23	203
2:1–22	203
2:15–16	211
4	204, 207, 210
4:8–16	13
4:8–10	203
4:8	204, 211, 218
4:8b	204
6:10–17	263
6:12	13, 214
6:18–20	8, 132

Philippians

1:2	13, 208
1:7	207
1:13	207
1:29–30	208
2	13, 207
2:3	188
2:8	179, 211
2:6–11	13, 209, 210, 212
2:9–11	210
3:8	188
3:20	13, 208, 220
4:7	188, 209
4:9	209

Colossians

1:15–20	13, 212
1:15–18a	212
1:18b-20	212
1:17	213
1:19–20	213
2:14–15	13, 212, 213
2:15	205, 217, 225

1 Thessalonians

1:9	215
2:2	217
2:12	215
2:14	215
2:15–16	179
4	217
4–5	219
4:13–18	13, 215
4:15	215
4:16–17	215
4:17	216
5:2–3a	217
5:3	13, 215, 217, 219

2 Thessalonians

1	219
1:5	215

1 Timothy

1:17	221
2:1–2	222
2:2	187
2:3–6	222
2:5	191
6:12	222
6:13	179
6:15–16	222
6:15	221
6:16	221

2 Timothy

2:2	268
2:3	222, 263

2 Timothy (cont.)

2:8	179
2:9	223
2:12	222
2:21	222
3:6	263

Titus

1:3	220
1:4	220
2:9	222
3:1	269
3:4–7	221

Philemon

8–10	8, 132
9–10	223
9	223
13	223
21	223

Hebrews

2:7	187
2:15	248
3:7–19	248
4:11—10:25	249
4:16	248
5:11—6:6	248
6:7–12	248
10:19–22	250
10:22–39	248
10:26–39	248
10:32—12:2	249
11	248, 250
11:36–38	251
12:1–29	250
12:1–11	249
12:4	248, 251
12:28	250
13:13–16	250
13:13–14	250

James

1:9–11	236
1:10–11	234, 236
2:1–7	236
2:2–4	233
2:2	233, 235
2:5	232, 236
2:6	232–35
2:15	233
4:7	187
4:13–17	232, 234, 237
4:13	234
4:14	236
5:1–7	232
5:1–6	234, 235, 237
5:2–3	235
5:4	233
5:4–5	235
5:6	233, 236

1 Peter

1:1—2:10	240
2:3	247
2:4–5	240
2:9	240
2:13–17	240
2:13–14	269
2:14	241
2:18–25	239, 241
2:18	222
2:20–25	85
2:21	242
2:22–25	242
3:1–7	239
3:1–6	242
3:6	242
3:8—4:19	239
5:5	187

2 Peter

2:1–10	247
2:1	246
2:10	246
2:13	246

Ancient Sources

2 Peter (cont.)

2:14–15	247
2:14	246
2:17–18	246
3:1–14	247

1 John

2:15–17	247
2:22–23	246
2:23	246
4:2–3	246
4:5	245
5:10	246
5:21	246

2 John

7	245
7–9	246

3 John

9–10	247

Jude

4	246
5–7	246
8	246
14–16	247

Revelation

2–3	253
2:8–9	253
2:9	252
2:9b–10	253
2:10	252
2:13	252, 253
2:14a	253
2:14b	253
2:20–23	253
2:20b	253
3:9	252
3:10	252
3:17–18	253
6:9–11	252
6:9–10	254
12:9–17	254
13:2b	254
13:4	254
13:5–6	274
13:6	254
13:12b–14	254
13:18	254
16:6	252, 254
17:6	252, 254
17:9	254
17:14	124
18	254
18:2	254
18:4–5	255
18:7b	254
18:24	252, 254
19	85
19:6	124
20:4	252
22:10–16	255

OLD TESTAMENT APOCRYPHA

2 Maccabees

4:2	129
6–7	107
7	112

3 Maccabees

3:19	129
6:24	129

4 Maccabees

18:6–8	238

Sirach

13:2–7	114
13:17–19	114
26:10	238
33:7	188
42:9–12	238

Wisdom of Solomon

13	246
14:12	246
16:11	130
16:24	130
19:14	129

OLD TESTAMENT PSEUDEPIGRAPHA

Apocalypse of Sedrach

14:1	135

2 Baruch

29	111
73	111

Letter of Aristeas

275	133

Sibylline Oracles

5	253

DEAD SEA SCROLLS

Pesher Nahum (4Q169)

3–4 II	147

Temple Scroll (11QT)

7–13 LXIV	147

NEW TESTAMENT PSEUDEPIGRAPHA

Acts of Pilate

9:2	130

APOSTOLIC FATHERS

1 Clement

59:3	130

Diognetus

7:4	124

Ignatius

To the Philadelphians

10:1	134

Martyrdom of Polycarp

9:3	124
17:3	124
21:1	124

Polycarp

To the Philippians

13:1	135

Shepherd of Hermas

3:9	124
17:8	124

OTHER ANCIENT WRITERS

Cicero

Rab. Post.

5.16	146

Demosthenes

Corona

43	126

Dio Chrysostom

2 De regno

26	126

Diodorus Siculus

Discourses

3.56.5	126
17.24.1	126
17.69.9	126, 127
17.94.3	127

Ancient Sources

Diogenes Laertius
6.78 — 187

Epictetus
1.4.19 — 187

Euripides
Heracleidae
1252 — 126

Eusebius
Historia ecclesiastica
6.14.7 — 142

Isocrates
4.95 — 188

Josephus
Antiquities
14.9 — 122
15.9 — 122
15.373 — 122
15.387 — 102
15.409 — 122
16.311 — 102
16.335 — 134
16.161 — 134
18.1 — 93
18.6 — 105
20.249–251 — 103

Jewish War
1.166 — 135
1.282 — 122
1.388 — 122
2.293 — 105
2.330–332 — 103
2.353 — 107
2.358–394 — 107
2.410–418 — 103
2.433 — 187
3.8 — 93
3.29 — 93
4.175 — 187
5.520 — 93
7.41–62 — 93
7.43 — 93
7.58–59 — 93
7.96 — 93
7.103 — 93
7.106-111 — 93

Pausanias
6.3.16 — 187

Philo
De specialibus legibus
1.272 — 129

Legatio ad Gaium
22 — 129
301–302 — 134

Polybius
289.4.9 — 187

Pseudo Callisthenes
1.22.4 — 187

Quintilian
Decl.
274 — 147

Thucydides
Historia
2.45.2 — 238

Virgil
Aen.
1.279 — 247

EPIGRAPHICAL CITATIONS

Att. Mich.

13 [1888] 61	171

Calendrical Inscription of 9 BC

I.4–5	127
I.17	127
II.34	127
II.46	127
IV.4–5	169
IV.6–8	169
IV.9–10	169
IV.10–14	169
IV.15	169
IV.30	171
VI.4	171
VI.33–34	169
VI.35–38	170
VI.40–41	170
VI.45–46	170
VII.80	171

CIA

3.30	172
3.34	172
3.428	127
3.444	173
3.444a	173
3.63	172
4.428	171

CIG

1810	172
2629	172

IBM

4.894	170
4.906	166

IG

II/III2 3274	173
II/III2 3278	173
VII 1835	171
VII 1836	127, 172
VIII 1835	127
XII 2.35b	171
XII 2.165b	171
XII 2.168	172
XII 3.469	172
XII 3.1104	172
XII 5	127
XII 5.556	127, 171
XII 5.557	171

IGR

1.901	127
1.1294	127
1.10007	172
3.137	172
3.159	173
3.426	127, 172
3.546	172
3.575	127
3.576	127
3.719	172
3.721	173
3.921	172
3.932	172
3.973	172
3.994	172
4.33	171
4.38	172
4.39	172
4.42	172
4.57	171
4.59	172
4.60	172
4.63	172
4.64	172
4.67	173
4.68	172
4.95	172
4.114	172

IGR (cont.)	
4.201	127, 172
4.303	172
4.304	171
4.305	172
4.306	172
4.307	171
4.309	172
4.311	127, 172
4.312	127
4.314	172
4.315	172
4.317	172
4.318	172
4.320	173
4.584	173
4.929	171
4.975	173
4.977	173
4.1094	173
4.1173	173
4.1302	173
4.1304	173
4.1444	173
9.57	127
9.303	127
9.305	127

Inschriften von Olympia	
53	172
365	171
366	172

Inschriften von Pergamon	
381	173

IM	
157b	173

MAMA	
6.250	173

OGIS	
90	166
458	127, 167
533	172, 173
583	173
666.2–7	128
668.5	128
814.22–23	128

Sardis	
7.1 no. 8	172

SB	
8897.1	127

SEG	
11.922	173
36 [1986] 1092	128

SIG3	
760	172
778	172
814	173

Syll3	
810	173